DIMENSIONS OF THE NEW ECONOMIC POLICY

VOLUME ONE
ECONOMIC SECTOR

DIMENSIONS OF THE NEW ECONOMIC POLICY

Volume One	:	Economic Sector
Volume Two	:	Social Sector

About the Authors

Dr. V.K. Agnihotri, an IAS Officer of the 1968 batch, belongs to Andhra Pradesh cadre of the service. Born on 25th August 1945, he obtained his Masters degree in English Literature and Political Science from the University of Allahabad, Allahabad. He has done his Ph. D. in Public Policy Analysis and Design from Indian Institute of Technology, Delhi. Before joining the IAS, he served on the Faculty of the Department of English Studies, University of Allahabad. He was the recipient of several awards and honours during his distinguished academic career, and has been a Visiting Fellow at the Queen Elizabeth House, University of Oxford, in 1991-92. Among several responsible positions with the State and Central Governments, Dr. Agnihotri, has held the posts of Collector, Visakhapatnam (Andhra Pradesh) and Development Commissioner for Handloom in the Ministry of Textiles, Government of India. He is presently Joint Director and Co-ordinator Public Administration Faculty at Lal Bahadur Shastri National Academy of Administration, Mussoorie. He is also the Chaiman of the Core Groups of the Centre for Micro-Planning and Regional Studies, SOFTRAIN and Village Study Unit at the Academy. His areas of specialisation are Public Policy, Rural Industries, Economic Reforms, Education and Panciayati Raj. He has several publications to his credit including books entitled *Environment and Development* (Concept), *Skills for Effective Administrators* (Vikas) and *Public Policy Analysis and Design* (Concept).

Dr. H. Ramachandran (bom on 15th September, 1947) is Professor and Faculty Co-ordinator in the Centre for Micro-Planning & Regional Studies, Lal Bahadur Shastri National Academy of Administration, Mussoorie. Prior to his joining the Academy he has been on the faculty of Department of Geography, Delhi School of Economics, Delhi University, and on the faculty of Institute of Social and Economic Change, Bangalore. His Publications include among others: Village Clusters and Rural Development (Concept, 1980), Behaviour in Space-Rural Marketing in an Underdeveloped Economy, (Concept, 1982), Schooling and Rural Transformation (Co-author), Environmental Issues in Agricultural Development (Concept, 1990) and Integrated Rural Development in Asia (Concept, 1991).

DIMENSIONS OF THE NEW ECONOMIC POLICY

VOLUME ONE

ECONOMIC SECTOR

Editors

Vivek K. Agnihotri, *I.A.S.*
Joint Director
Lal Bahadur Shastri National
Academy of Administration
Mussoorie

H. Ramachandran
Professor & Faculty Coordinator
Centre for Micro-Planning & Regional Studies
L.B.S. National Academy of Administration
Mussoorie

Published for

United Nations Development Programme
&
L.B.S. National Academy of Administration

by

CONCEPT PUBLISHING COMPANY PVT. LTD.
NEW DELHI-110059

ISBN: 978-81-7022-603-1 (Set)
ISBN: 978-81-7022-601-7 (Vol. 1)
ISBN: 978-81-7022-602-4 (Vol. 2)

Edition 2025

Published and Printed by

Since 1974

Concept Publishing Company Pvt. Ltd.
A/15-16, Commercial Block, Mohan Garden,
New Delhi-110059 (India)
T : 91-11-41101460
E : publishing@conceptpub.com, *W*: www.conceptpub.com

FOREWORD

Since 1992 we have organised a number of in-service courses with a focus on the New Economic Policy at the Lal Bahadur Shastri National Academy of Administration, Mussoorie. The interest of the Academy in the New Economic Policy relates to the ways in which liberalisation affects State administration. In the last one or two decades the bureaucracy has expanded at a very fast rate and government seems to be functioning to a significant extent for government servants. No wonder that of the plan and non-plan budget of some states about 90 percent is spent on government servants.

It is necessary to make administration more responsive. There is a need, and an urgent one, to simplify procedures and perhaps delete a large number of laws and regulations which have outlived their use. I have had an occasion to study in depth some villages of western Uttar Pradesh where I found that although we have liberalised and can set up industries worth billions without much of a licensing hurdle we still require a large number of licenses when a farmer wants to set-up a rice shelling plant or a wheat flour mill or a brick kiln unit or a cold storage. If we can make administration responsive and if we can encourage local entreprenureship it would be easier and politically feasible to think of ushering in rapid changes required to face the challenge of globalization.

However, it is not only the speed - the slow speed - that is of concern but some times the direction which we are taking itself needs to be analysed. Some time last year in a workshop at the Academy on the status of Dalits in India many participants criticised some of the policies which are being advocated in the name of liberalisation, as these could affect the interest of the poor and increase disparities at various levels. Two suggestions which are often made are that why don't we do away with land ceilings or why don't we give forest land to industries. There is a lot more work that needs to be undertaken on these issues since apparently such suggestions are anti-poor and anti-equity.

Considerable literature has accumulated in the last two years contributing significantly to the debate on the New Economic Policy. However, it is to be noted that a number of steps taken in the early 90's are irreversible and, therefore, the interface between economic policy and civil as well as development administration is of particular interest. It is with this view that a workshop followed by two modular programmes on the New Economic Policy - in fact on the management of the change - was organised by the Academy. The programme was financially supported by UNDP and sponsored by the Department of Personnel and Training, Government of India. My colleagues Dr.V K Agnihotri and Prof. H Ramachandran coordinated and edited the volumes based on the proceedings of the workshop and the two modular programmes on managing change in the context of the New Economic Policy.

N C Saxena
Director

December 1995

Lal Bahadur Shastri National Academy of Administration
Mussoorie

CONTENTS

LIST OF TABLES

LIST OF CONTRIBUTORS

Agnihotri, (Dr.) V.K., Joint Director, Lal Bahadur Shastri National Academy of Administration, Mussoorie.

Bajaj, J. L., Agricultural Production Commissioner, Government of Uttar Pradesh, Council House, Lucknow

Basu, (Dr.) Kaushik, Executive Director, Centre for Development Economics, Delhi School of Economics, Delhi

Joshi, S., Deputy Secretary, Ministry of Home Affairs, Government of India, North Block, New Delhi

Kumar, Sudhir, Director, Department of Economic Affairs, Ministry of Finance, New Delhi

Panchamukhi, (Dr.) V. R., Research & Information System for the Non-Aligned and Other Developing Countries, New Delhi

Pandit, (Prof.) V., Professor of Economics, Delhi School of Economics, University of Delhi, Delhi

Ramachandran, (Dr.) H., Professor and Faculty Coordinator, Centre for Micro Planning and Regional Studies, Lal Bahadur Shastri National Academy of Administration, Mussoorie

Rao, (Prof.) M. Govinda, National Institute of Public Finance and Policy, New Delhi

Reddy, (Dr.) Y. Venugopal, Additional Secretary, Ministry of Commerce, New Delhi

Saxena, (Dr.) N.C., Director, Lal Bahadur Shastri National Academy of Administration, Mussoorie

Sengupta, Nitish, Director General, International Management Institute, B10, 30 & 31, Qutab Institutional Area, Tara Crescent, NEW Delhi

Sen, (Dr.) Tapas Kumar, Professor, National Institute of Public Finance and Policy, New Delhi

Vyasulu, (Dr.) Vinod, Director, Institute of Public Enterprise, Osmania University Campus, Hyderabad

ABBREVIATIONS

ADB	Asian Development Bank
AL	(Receiving) Adjustment Loans
AP	Andhra Pradesh
BDO	Block Development Officer
BE	Budget Estimates
BHEL	Bharat Heavy Electricals Limited
BIFR	Board For Industrial and Financial Reconstruction
BLT	Build, Lease, Transfer
BOO	Build, Own and Operate
BOP	Balance of Payment
BOT	Buy, Own and Transfer
BOOT	Build, Own, Operate, Transfer
BOOST	Build, Own, Operate, Subsidise, Transfer
BPE	Bureau of Public Enterprises
BROT	Build, Rent, Operate, Transfer
BRT	Build, Rent, Transfer
BTRO	Build, Transfer, Rent, Operate
BTO	Build, Transfer, Operate
CACP	Commission on Agricultural Costs and Prices
CCI	Controller of Capital Issues
CCFI	Cabinet Committee on Foreign Investments
CIDA	Canadian International Development Agency
CPE	Central Public Enterprises
CPI	Consumer Price Index
CPWD	Central Public Works Department
CST	Central Sales Tax
DBO	Develop, Build, Operate
DFO	Division Forest Officer
DGS & D	Directorate General of Supply and Disposal
DGTD	Directorate General of Technical Development
DIC	District Industry Centre
DOPT	Department of Personnel & Training

ECU	Economic Coordination Unit
EPZs	Export Processing Zones
EOUs	Export Oriented Units
FAO	Food and Agriculture Organisation
FCNR	Foreign Currency Non-Resident
FD	Forest Department
FDI	Forest Direct Investment
FDC	Forest Development Corporation
FERA	Foreign Exchange Regulation Act
FII	Foreign Institutional Investors
FIPB	Foreign Investment Promotion Board
FM	Finance Minister
GATT	General Agreement on Trade and Tariff
GCC	Girijan Cooperative Corporation
GDCF	Gross Domestic Capital Formation
GDP	Gross Domestic Product
GDR	General Drawing Rights
GNP	Gross National Product
GOI	Government of India
GISFC	General Insurance and Finance Companies
HMT	Hindustan Machine Tools
IBM	International Business Machines
IFFCO	Indian Farmer's & Fertilisers Corporation
IMF	International Monetary Fund
ILPIC	Industrial Licensing Policy Inquiry Committee
IRDP	Integrated Rural Development Programme
IISC	Indian Institute of Science
IISCO	Indian Iron and Steel Company
ISRO	Indian Space Research Organisation
JRY	Jawahar Rojgar Yojana
KSCST	Karnataka State Council for Science and Technology
LDC	Least (Less) Developed Countries
LDO	Lease, Develop, Operate
LIC	Life Insurance Corporation
MEA	Ministry of External Affairs
MNC	Multi-National Corporations
MP	Madhya Pradesh
MRTPA	Monopolies and Restrictive Trade Practices Act
MOU	Memorandum of Understanding

NAL	Not (Receiving) Adjustment Loans / National Aeronautical Ltd.
NAIRU	Non-Accelerating Inflation Rates of Unemployment
NALCO	National Aluminium Corporation
NEP	New Economic Policy
NEM	New Economic Mechanism
NCAER	National Council for Applied Economic Research
NCE	Neo Classical Economics
NDC	No Due Certificate
NDE	Non-Departmental Enterprises
NDNF	Non-Departmental Non-Financial
NDP	Net Domestic Product
NGEF	New General Electric Factory
NGO	Non-Governmental Organisation
NHB	National Housing Board
NTFP	Nationalisation of Non-Timber Forest Products
NOC	No Objection Certificate
NOIDA	New Okhla Industrial Development Authority
NRI	Non-Resident Indian
NRU	Natural Rate of Unemployment
NTPC	National Thermal Power Corporation
OECD	Organisation for Economic Cooperation and Development
ORG	Operations Research Group
PDS	Public Distribution System
PE	Public Enterprises
PEP	Principle of Efficient Pricing
POC	Principle of Contract
PM	Prime Minister
PSE	Public Sector Enterprise
PSU	Public Sector Undertaking
PW	Wholesale Price Index
PWD	Public Works Department
R&D	Research and Development
RBI	Reserve Bank of India
RE	Revised (Budget) Estimates
REH	Rational Expectations Hypothesis
ROT	Refurbish, Operate, Transfer
RTC	Road Transport Corporation
SAL	Structural Adjustment Loan
SAIL	Steel Authority of India Limited

SAP	Structural Adjustment Programme
SAARC	South Asian Association for Regional Corporation
SBI	State Bank of India
SD	Standard Deviation
SDO	Sub-Divisional Officer
SEBI	Stock Exchange Bureau of India
SECAL	Sectoral Adjustment Loan
SFC	State Finance Corporation
SIA	Secretariat for Industrial Approvals
SIC	Small Industries Corporation
SIDA	Swedish International Development Agency
SINP	Standard Ideal Normative Paradigm
SLR	Statutory Liquidity Ratio
SSI	Small Scale Industry
TISCO	Tata Iron & Steel Company
UED	Union Excise Duties
UNCTAD	United Nations Conference on Trade and Development
UNDP	United Nations Development Programme
USSR	Union of Soviet Socialist Republic
UK	United Kingdom
UP	Uttar Pradesh
UPSIDC	Uttar Pradesh Small Industries Development Corporation
USA	United States of America
UT	Union Territory
UTI	Unit Trust of India

INTRODUCTION

V.K. AGNIHOTRI and H. RAMACHANDRAN

It is somewhat ironical that in many parts of the world there has been an unprecedented growth after Second World War accompanied by greater intervention, but now, for the same reasons of economic growth, a reduction in State intervention is advocated. Perceptible change in the economic policy of India was ushered in during the 1980s, albeit hesitantly, with a small degree of deregulation and decontrol. The cost of regulations, on the one hand, had become abnormally high and, on the other, resulted neither in bringing about equity nor promoted indigenous development in technology and competitiveness. As a result, performance was at a discount. Where performance was good it was not rewarded and failure did not invite punitive action. In fact, often failure attracted rewards and performance attracted penalty. The changes were introduced cautiously with a hope that the rate of economic growth would increase. Instead, they led to a balance of payment crisis in 1990 that reduced the choices that we had in the eighties and hastened the introduction of a crisis-driven package of structural adjustments and stabilisation programme.

However, India is not the first country to have faced such a crisis nor are the basic ingredients of the response to the crisis unusual. We have the experience of other countries before us. Unfortunately, these experiences vary considerably. Thus, the debate on the nature of economic reforms and their impact is continuing since 1990 in India, and will continue. It is also apparent that some of the changes brought about are not reversible unless the circumstances become abnormal. The change in economic policy is also not a one shot strategy and needs to be supported by policy changes in various sectors of the economy as well as administration.

It is necessary to emphasise that reforms in many sectors, particularly in terms of improving efficiency, cost reduction, cut in administrative delays, etc., need to be tackled irrespective of changes in the economic policy. At the cutting edge -- the states and lower levels -- there is an urgent need for reforms. Such reforms are not necessarily restricted to the economic sectors and economic policies but essentially include change in the administrative ethos and responsiveness.

It is against the back drop of these observations that an agenda of workshops, training courses and lectures was developed by the National Academy of Administration during 1993 and 1994. A number of issues relating to the reforms in various sectors, their sequencing and pacing, the problems of implementation and action agenda that could be implemented to activate change at the cutting edge level were discussed in these programmes. The deliberations included both economic and social sectors. As a part of this agenda, a Workshop on the New Economic Policy was organised by the National Academy of Administration in April 1994 The Workshop and two modular training programmes on Managing Change for serving officers from the higher civil services were funded by the UNDP and sponsored by the Department of Personnel and Training, Government of India. The material generated during these programmes is being brought out in two volumes.

We begin this volume with a review of cross-country experiences with reforms. Panchamukhi compares some of the experiences with the reforms process in a few countries. He starts with the proposition that 'reform' presupposes that something is distorted in the economy and, therefore, a process of reforms is required to correct such distortions. Except for this underlying condition he finds little in common in international experience of reforms. The reform process cannot be fully subsumed by the framework resource allocation through markets or through planning. Most reforms involve: (a) redefining the role of the State in the economic sphere, (b) some elements of integration of the country's economy with the rest of the world, and (c) an element of privatisation. However, an important and relevant set of questions relates to speed and sequencing of the reforms which is often influenced by prevailing domestic political considerations.

Panchamukhi classifies the countries that have initiated reform programmes as those that are either conscience-driven or crisis-driven. In the case of India, the reforms have been prompted by the crisis in the external sector of the economy which is clearly not the best way to go about reforming the economy. He cites the case of China as a reasonably successful one which is an example of conscience--driven reforms.

Panchamukhi's agenda for the reform process in India includes: (a) clear identification of the goals of reform, and (b) ensuring high levels of investment-to-GDP ratio. In addition, he argues that privatisation is not a necessary ingredient of the reforms process and stabilisation of the economy need not go hand-in-hand with structural adjustment but needs to be pursued separately.

While Panchamukhi takes a macro view, Kaushik Basu focuses on some micro economic aspects of the reform process. In a way, he provides a few rules of thumb that may be used to guide the reform process in India. These according to him are the prerequisites for successful reforms. He argues that there is a qualitative difference in our reforms to the extent that we continue to have the same objectives before and after the reforms. In India, the question is not one of markets versus Government because there were large parts of the economy over which the Government had little or no control even before the reforms process was initiated.

Basu recounts two principles which according to him must be kept in mind by the policy makers. These are the Principle of Contract and the Principle of Efficient Pricing. Using examples such as FERA, Industrial Disputes Act and Delhi Rent Control Act, he illustrates how laws and regulations in India repeatedly ignore these fundamental principles of economics to the detriment of the welfare of the citizen. If reforms are to have any real content in India, they must be guided, in large part, by the essence of such simple principles as the freedom to enter into contracts which do not harm any third parties and the need to minimise dead-weight losses.

The argument that stabilisation and structural adjustment need not go hand-in-hand is looked at from a different angle by V. Pandit. He observes that the objectives of structural adjustments and economic stabilisation are in confrontation with each other. Structural adjustment are slated to cause de-stabilisation in society, at least in the short run. Even inflation may follow, which affects the poor most. In a way, the NEP is a gamble; and there ought to be strategies, therefore, to recommend prescriptions for safeguarding the interests of the most vulnerable sections of the population.

Pandit argues that 'inflation has come to stay' and draws our attention to the inflation which has shot up to double digits since 1990-91. Generally speaking, inflation has been linked to demand pull factors like increase in the supply of money etc. However, while the increased supply of money has been exerting its influence in raising prices in the Indian economy, actually, the cost-push factors have been stronger. Notable amongst the cost-push factors have been wages and salaries and their indexation with prices, devaluation of exchange rates, higher prices of crude oil, rise in procurement prices of foodgrains, etc.

Govinda Rao and Tapas Kumar Sen review the performance of public finance instruments in the development process, given that fiscal policy is one of the principal instruments of intervention and the fact that fiscal deficit is held responsible for the economic crisis. They believe that fiscal policy in India has contributed to the loss of both efficiency and equity in the economy. They also reflect on the differences in strategies of South East Asian countries and China and India. Rao and Sen argue that the question is not more or less State intervention, but quality of State intervention.

Vinod Vyasulu presents a brief summary of the historical background of the growth of public enterprises in India after independence and their role in the new environment of economic reforms. He notes that public enterprises in India were started as "new enterprises" because private units were either non-existent or not able to grow in those areas. Public Steel Plants and BHEL, for example, have not only filled these gaps but have shown high technological and human resource competence. At the same time, public enterprises also grew up in areas where they were not needed at all, like in making of bread at Delhi or making of compost in Karnataka. Unfortunately, the existence of public enterprises is being defended in political quarters now just to maintain and protect the jobs thus created. The overall picture, therefore, does call for urgent reforms.

The big reform required is in the relationship of the Government and the public enterprises. Vyasulu urges the Government to give the public enterprises freedom of operation and keep back the chain of instructions and memos sent so frequently to them. Further, labour laws with respect to public enterprises must also be clearly stated, especially in terms of exit policy. The real objective and nature of government holding the equity shares of these enterprises needs to be made transparent. He describes differing response requirements of various types of products of public enterprises. Self-reliance in certain areas may be required, certain areas may require the ability of management to respond to market changes, certain other areas may be where basic R&D effort and its transformation into commercial products may be significant and so on; and, therefore, the role of public enterprises with respect to each of these areas must be explicitly recognised.

A review of the public sector enterprises in the context of their dependence on Budgetary support is undertaken by Y. Venugopal Reddy and S. Joshi. Based on a study of about 200 public enterprises of various types, they argue that the Government as a lender of money and owner of equity must earn dividends and also get back interest and the principal amount; but in reality the Government has received little. They note that public enterprises have heavy inventories, too much of inter-enterprise lending and too low profitability. Inter-enterprise lending shows only fictitious "hopeful" income from these lendings. Even the little profitability that they have is mainly due to non-operational "other" income. The Government has often played with these enterprises by giving them unwanted cash and liquidity at times. Reforms are urgently needed so that the public knows the real rationale of these enterprises. They argue that the regulatory ministry should not be the owner of the enterprise being regulated by it. Productive efficiency, financial viability, economic profitability and market attractiveness of the shares of public enterprises should be their hallmark. At the moment, the public enterprises are a drain on tax payers' money on all accounts.

The globalization facet of the economic reforms includes the important component of Foreign Investment. Based on discussions with foreign direct investors, international lawyers and an analysis of recent literature, Sudhir Kumar finds that India is a good case for foreign direct and indirect investments, but much of such possible investments fail to materialise because, despite liberalization, the number of clearances required continues to be mind boggling.

Sudhir Kumar points out that while reforms in this area were long overdue, since the timing of the reform package could not be chosen, even very radical reforms have produced very little impact by way of actual inflow of foreign direct investments. He notes that the attractiveness of a country as a destination for foreign direct and indirect investments depends upon a whole lot of objective and subjective factors. These considerations and concerns can be divided into a number of categories, like macro-level/micro-level, regional/state level, general and specific national policy concerns, and concerns specific to India. Foreign investment promotion can be better achieved if the Central and State governments play a more pro-active role in project identification and development.

He cautions that the pitfalls of global protectionism have to be recognized and India should not follow the policy of blind pursuit of foreign investments since we do have our strengths and weaknesses, and must build upon the areas of likely strength. However, emphasis would have to be laid upon attracting NRI foreign direct investors, even while reducing the dependence upon their FCNR deposits.

The administration-economic reform interface is addressed by three scholars. N. C. Saxena highlights the ground realities pertaining to reforms at the State level, where liberalization is yet to make any substantial impact. He brings to sharp focus the cumbersome procedure for obtaining government sanction for the sale of private trees which led to the declining trend (during 1981-89) in the sale of seedlings to farmers from forest nurseries. He suggests abolition of committed supply of raw material, introduction of supply of raw material at competitive prices and encouragement to farm forestry. He also points out that by changing the forest policy with regard to non-timber forest products in India, the generation of employment may be substantially increased in the country.

Saxena makes out a case for urgent review and changes in Rules, Regulations and Acts as well as our perspective on subsidies. He calls for a careful scrutiny of demand from the industries for access to forest resources. He also observes that demands from the industries to develop their own forest may not necessarily stand the test of efficacy since it does not ensure any additionality. The demand is limited in itself which constricts any major and substantial impact on the overall scenario and it would not ensure any reduction on the biotic pressure. Saxena suggests that the sugarcane model – i.e. raw material being produced by the farmer and the processing being done by industry – may be a suitable option to be emulated in this regard.

J. L. Bajaj discusses some aspects of fiscal and industrial policies and alternative practices in State governments with special reference to Uttar Pradesh, having implications for the New Economic Policy. Analyzing the consolidated budgetary position of State government and resource transfers to the States and Union Territories, he makes the point that if the target of 5% fiscal deficit in the operations of Central and State governments is to be achieved, the States will have to devote considerable attention to controlling expenditure and augmenting both tax and non-tax revenues. In addition, they must also improve the performance of State enterprises. He also stresses the need for fiscal correction by reviewing the budgetary transaction of Uttar Pradesh. He concludes that the State governments have to design a set of delivery systems whose attributes should be:

(a) greater transparency;
(b) meaningful planning;
(c) rationalization of functions;
(d) improved personnel management; and

(e) need based efforts at various levels.

Bajaj believes that there is enough scope for State governments to exercise expenditure control, improved tax revenues through widening of the tax base and better collection, realistic user charges and cutting down the losses of public enterprises.

Nitish Sengupta gives a brief outline of the earlier role of bureaucracy and lists the major changes in economic policy, particularly in the industrial sector, MRTP Act, FERA, partial convertibility of rupee, removal of blanket ban on imports, etc. He wants India to look for new areas of export and lists the constraints on these. Sengupta also draws our attention to the fact that the attitude of control and regulation and procedural delays continue to deter economic reforms. He identifies some key areas for concentrated efforts:

(a) cost control;
(b) identification of redundant manpower, their retraining and redeployment;
(c) putting together a good compensation package as retirement benefits;
(d) withdrawal from chronically non-profitable activities; and
(e) identification of newer and promising areas.

Taken together, the chapter included in this volume address both the concerns of concepts and of implementation of a package of economic reforms that call for supportive and complimentary measures at sub-national levels and in non-economic sectors. While there are, obviously, variations in the points of view and tenor of arguments of various authors and participants, the message is clear. Firstly, there is a strong plea for cutting down costs of production and distribution through an overhauling of cumbersome administrative procedures and by cutting down delays. These need to be undertaken irrespective of the change in the economic policy. Secondly, the need to sharpen the reform policy at the cutting edge level cannot be overemphasised. Thirdly, there are a number of areas in which certain level of uncertainties remain with reference to policy response including those of public enterprises and exit policy. Finally, what also emerges is the fact that decision making in a globalised economy involves a large number of parameters and, therefore, difficult. Some of the parameters are beyond the control of national Governments.

V.K. AGNIHOTRI
H. RAMACHANDRAN

1

ECONOMIC REFORMS
International Experiences

V. R. PANCHAMUKHI

Introduction

The subject of Economic Reforms has been at the central place of discussions in the academic and policy circles for the last one decade or so. The term "economic reform" is, however, older than the current debate and during its journey across the countries and over the globe, both the conceptual and the practical aspects of the theme have gathered so much moss, gloss and dust that it has now become an auction commodity of market place. Hard core politicians, well-entrenched media men, self-styled social workers, articulate trade union leaders, and more than anybody else the profound-looking professional economists, have – together and also separately – found in this, a new anchor for keeping their professions flourishing and prosperous. The debate has now reached the stage of losing all canons of objectivity and analytical rigour. The purpose of this chapter is to present at one place, the diverse perceptions of the scope and content of economic reforms, collate the empirical evidence on international experiences and to draw some lessons for the process of policy reforms in India.

Meaning of Economic Reforms

The term "Reform" has implied in it two corollaries: Firstly, the assumption that the entity which needs to be reformed has deviated from a Standard Ideal Normative Paradigm (SINP) of behaviour and it needs to be restored to the SINP. Secondly, there does exist a paradigm or the paradigm, which may be regarded as the Standard Ideal Normative Paradigm (SINP) of behaviour for that entity. Reforming a criminal means changing his behaviour and life style from the path of crimes. Reforming an erring student means putting him to the discipline of regularity in studies. Reforming an officer means putting him on to the rigour of performing his duties sincerely and honestly. In these examples, the SINP is a universally accepted somewhat unique paradigm and also the deviation from it is quite transparent and explicit. Of course, there could be different interpretations regarding the extent of departure from SINP of an individual entity, the tolerance limit of departure at which a reverse process of reforming the entity becomes imperative and the method required for removing the distortion and restoring the entity to the SINP. Further, the problem becomes more complex if there is no universally accepted SINP and if there are multiple interpretations of SINP itself.

The analogy given above should clearly convey the predicament one faces in explaining the meaning of the term Economic Reform, particularly when one uses the term to refer to the economy-wide reform with the canvass of both the macro, and the micro aspects of economic behaviour.

First of all we should be very clear that the concept of reforms applies to the economic system and the changes in policies or what is loosely called as 'policy reform' is only an instrumentality ultimately aimed at reforming the economic system. Hence, the first task is to clearly understand what this economic system means and what is the SINP in relation to the system. There is a plethora of other questions that also need to be squarely addressed. What constitutes the deviation from the accepted SINP; what is the tolerance limit of these distortions; and what are the policy variables that are relevant to influence the behaviour of the system and finally what are the changes in these policy variables which would restore the system to the SINP? This in brief is the menu of any intellectual exercise in understanding the meaning of Economic Reforms.

It is useful to recognise that the term Economic Reforms assumed prominence, perhaps for the first time in the economic literature, with the reforms process launched in Hungary in 1968. The New Economic Mechanism (NEM), introduced in Hungary in 1968, essentially refers to the reform of the Hungarian economic system. The range of issues that were covered in the NEM brings out the comprehensiveness of the reforms package. Before considering the package of the policies, it is useful to clarify the meaning of the economic system which needs to be reformed. Janos Kornai (1986) in his insightful review of the Hungarian reforms process describes very elegantly the contours of an economic system. Kornai writes: "instead of an abstract definition, I give a summary list of the main components of an economic system; the organisations functioning in the economy, for example, administrative organs, non-profit institutions, firms, households, associations, the distribution of the various forms of ownership and property rights, the distribution of decision making power, the information structure, types of information flowing between organisations, incentives motivating the decision makers, the political organs and the governments engaged in economic affairs; laws and governmental resolutions that is the formal legal regulation of the economic operations; informal "rules of the game" routine behavioural patterns enforcing, hindering or complementing the formal legal regulation. The list is not exhaustive. The components are interdependent and they cannot be chosen arbitrarily".

The above said definition of an economic system is very useful in any discussion on the process of Economic Reforms. This clearly brings out that the reforms ultimately refer to the behavioural patterns in a given economic system and not just to the changes in economic policies called as Policy Reforms. It is the interaction between the policy reforms and the changes in the economic system that determines the success or failure of the reforms process. Hence, a clear understanding of the economic system, its responses to the policy changes, and the complexities of *inter se* interactions become relevant.

The Hungarian NEM covered the various aspects of Hungary's economic system *viz*, The System of Macroeconomic Decision Making; The Price System; The Foreign Trade and the Exchange System; The Wage System and the Labour Market Policies; The Fiscal System; The Banking System and the Capital Market; Agriculture.

The Hungarian reforms process also covered issues like bureaucratic coordination versus market coordination, the functioning of social sectors versus that of the non-state sectors, the abolition of the command economy system or in a way dilution of the approach of central planning. Reforms in the decision making processes concerned with the determination of output, determination of inputs, choice of technology, determination of prices, determination of wages and employment, credit policies, taxes and subsidies, investment decisions, size distribution and monopolies, macro and micro regulations, and agriculture, reform in the so called informal and formal private sectors, were also covered.

The SINP in the case of Hungarian economy or for that matter, for all

Socialist economies was clearly that of total market economy. It is interesting to note how Kornai defines the reforms.

He stated that "reforms mean diminishing the role of bureaucratic coordination and increasing the role of the market". He further stated as follows: "the modernisation of a highly bureaucratic regulation of the economy with the help of computers is not reform. Nor do the efforts aimed at tighter labour discipline qualify the term reform." These policy measures are indeed useful, but they do not imply the change in the system. Anything that does not imply diminishing the role of the bureaucracy and increasing the role of the market, did not pass the criteria of being called as the reforms process.

The case of Hungarian Economic Reforms signifies clarity in terms of the present economic system and its deviation from the idealised economic system or from what we called as SINP and hence the path of reform could also be considered as clear and transparent. However, in many situations, the reference is only to some select deviations from SINP and the reforms are addressed to these select symptoms of the departure from SINP. These deviations from SINP are supposed to be manifesting themselves in several forms such as slow growth of the economy, general weakness of the supply side of the economy, excessive budget deficits at the enterprise level and at the economy level, excess demand conditions, hidden unemployment, low labour productivity, substantial level of unproductive rent seeking activities, inappropriate relative prices not reflecting the true relative scarcities, lack of economies of scale, etc. In fact, many of these features were found in Thatcher's United Kingdom or Reagan's United States, and Thatcherian reforms and Reagonomics were specifically aimed at dealing with these symptoms of the distortions from SINP through what came to be known as supply side economics.

It is obvious that identification of SINP is very crucial for the identification of deviations from it and hence for the identification of the policy measures required to correct these distortions. The conception of SINP is obviously linked to the goals and objectives which the process of structural transformation sets for itself. It is here that there is need for immense clarity in vision and perceptions. The ultimate goal of the development process is to realise high growth with equitous distribution of the benefits of growth in a reasonable period of time. Establishment of a full market economy, privatisation, globalisation, liberalisation, etc., are only to be viewed as a certain package of instruments for achieving these objectives. The main objective of high growth and equity is converted into several sub-objectives in terms of targets for the policy instrument variables. Viewed in this way, policy reforms cannot be considered in isolation of the conception of SINP and the main objectives embedded in it. What is the conception of SINP in the different countries of the world economy situated at the different stages of development and with diverse socio-economic, cultural and philosophical backgrounds? Does the literature on reforms process spell out these dimensions of the reforms process in unequivocal terms?

Without going into the detailed formulation of the SINP, one could easily conclude that there is no single universally accepted conception of SINP and as such there is no single framework or package of the instruments of reforms. However, despite these assertions, the economic reforms universally advocated in recent years have some common features. They are summarised in different research studies in different ways. The reforms process advocated by the Brettonwoods institutions is characterised by 3-D's : Devaluation, Deregulation and Deflation. To this package is also added the policy instruments of decentralisation, privatisation, globalisation, etc.

Macro–economic stabilisation and structural adjustment are regarded as the twin strategic elements of the reforms process. Control of inflation, management of fiscal deficits, increase in competitive environment, privatisation, reduction in bureaucratic intervention are considered as the different components of the reforms process. Of course, the choice of proper-mix depends upon the conception of SINP and the goals embedded in it.

In India, we launched our development process in the framework of planning in a mixed economy paradigm. The state, the market and the planning were designed to co-exist in a suitable blend. Over-time, the insulation of the economy from the rest of the world and also the protection of the domestic industry became excessive to breed inefficiencies of various kinds. The expansion of bureaucracy implied excessive bureaucratic interventions, which in turn created a new class of vested interests. Planning, the market and the state showed signs of failures and this led to several deviations from the SINP, adopted and vigorously pursued in the fifties and the sixties.

In the late seventies and the early eighties, there was growing realisation that the Indian policy paradigm was not functioning effectively and this required some radical changes. Several committees went into the rationale of the policies and the institutional framework and made many far reaching recommendations for changes in the policy system. To name only a few, these were – Alexander Committee on Import-

Export Policies and Procedures (1978), Dagli Committee on Controls and Subsidies (1979), Tandon Committee on Exports (1981), Abid Hussain Committee on Trade Policies, etc. The recommendations of these committees were gradualist approaches with the accepted framework of SINP. The visioned idealised paradigm of mixed economy in a planned framework was not seriously questioned. But now in the nineties, we seem to be at cross roads. We seem to be changing our conception of SINP itself. But there is not enough clarity as to whether we would like to totally discard it or only tinker with it marginally. What is the alternative SINP which we want to achieve? Without any clarity in regard to the goals, the process of reforms could be self-defeating.

Issues in the Reforms Process

In order to place the international experiences in the right perspectives, it is useful to raise at this stage several issue-specific analytical questions. Firstly, what is the SINP which the reforms process aims at? Does the shift towards market economy necessarily imply weakening of the state and abandonment of planning? Should the reforms process aim at a total free market economy system or should it aim at what one may call as a simulated market economy system? In the former system, decisions are left completely to the market forces. In the latter, the state intervenes but with the objective of enforcing the relative prices, which would have prevailed in the presence of the Free Market Economy Paradigm. There is a third category called as, Governed Market Paradigm, in which the market is governed by the dictates of the State. The recent literature on the Korean economy brings out that the success of the Korean economy was more due to the efficient governance of the market by the State, rather than due to a totally free market or simulated market paradigm.

In regard to the issue of integration with the world economy, a distinction is made between "close" integration and "strategic" integration. It is now argued in the framework of the new theory of strategic trade policies, that the Japanese model of openness and protection was one of strategic State intervention in the national and international marketplace. The analysis of China's reforms process brings out that the Chinese are seeking "strategic" rather than "close" integration with the world economy. It is true of the Korean Miracle as well that integration with the World Economy was strategic and selective.

The advocacy of privatisation is based upon the assumption that public ownership of the means of production does not provide enough incentive for efficient management of the production activities. But the question that needs to be addressed is whether private ownership of land and capital would automatically imply increase in efficiency. China's reforms process is a case of marketisation without enforcing massive privatisation in the system. Even if privatisation is accepted as a goal in itself, what are the criteria for reducing the role of the public sector enterprises and increasing the role of the private sector? Mexico is heralded as a success story of privatisation in recent times. Privatisation has also been adopted as a strategy in South-East Asia, but these privatisation initiatives have met with both successes and failures and the successes are often attributed to the existence of many favourable initial conditions, like good capital markets, availability of managerial skills and entrepreneurship and also to the adoption of a package of supportive policies which make privatisation a success. Further, there are issues on the methods of privatisation. Should the profit-making public sector enterprises be privatised or loss-making ones? How should the assets be priced?

In regard to the choice and implementation of the strategies of reforms, there are three basic questions: viz. the speed of reforms, comprehensiveness of the reforms and the sequencing of reforms. The debate on the speed of reforms has distinguished two extreme alternatives: big bang approach or a gradual approach. The proponents of the former argue that for a heavily distorted economic system, shock treatment with discrete, sudden and large scale changes in economic policies would generate more favourable impacts than otherwise. However, the proponents of gradualism argue that the big bang approach imposes heavy burdens on large sections of the society and also brings about social tensions and upheavals leading to self-defeating results for the reforms process. The gradualist school on the other hand argues that the fixed cost of adjustment could be spread over a long period during which the economy could bring about institutional and attitudinal changes to respond optimally to the reforms process. The critiques of the gradualistic approach argue that gradual and peacemeal changes in policies would question the credibility of the reforms process and lead to unwarranted speculative and expectational responses.

The issue of comprehensiveness of reforms refers to the imperatives of reform of the components of the economic system listed above,– at one go since these components are interdependent and mutually supportive. For example, the legal system of the country should also be adjusted and reformed simultaneously alongwith the reforms of marketisation and privatisation. While interdependence of the different components of the reforms process needs to be well recognised, it is difficult to believe that the comprehensiveness of the reforms could be practicable. The proponents of comprehensiveness argue that the value of the "whole" would exceed "sum of the parts". If, however, prioritisation is necessary on the ground that a particular component of the reforms process is a prerequisite for the other components then the question becomes as to what should be the nature of this prioritisation? The approach of comprehensiveness and that of big bang stated above seems to be complementary to each other.

When the reforms process is gradual and not comprehensive then the question of sequencing and timing of the various components of the reforms process becomes relevant. Should one reform the domestic supply side before launching upon the foreign trade liberalisation and currency reforms or should one do vice-versa? Should currency convertibility on the current account precede that on the capital account or should they be done simultaneously? Should macro-economic stabilisation precede the launching of economic liberalisation and structural adjustment or should stabilisation, liberalisation and structural adjustment go together? There are many arguments and counter arguments advocating different forms of sequencing of the policies. Some argue that it is the internal consistency and credibility of the policy changes that yield maximum results, irrespective of the speed, comprehensiveness or the sequencing of reforms.

Some Empirical Evidences

For evaluating the impacts of the reforms process and for drawing lessons from the varied experiences of the different countries, it is useful to collate the empirical evidence available on these issues. As stated earlier, the term economic reforms has meant different things in different countries and in different situations. It is therefore very risky to proclaim that the reforms processes in the different countries are indeed comparable in any meaningful way. However, even though there cannot be any generalised inferences, evaluation of individual experiences in an objective manner would atleast avoid the pitfalls of drawing wrong inferences from these experiences.

It might be useful to understand the genesis of the reforms process in the different countries, so that the subsequent process could be understood in terms of the factors which promoted the process. It is possible to distinguish between two categories of genesis: One may consider the reforms process that has been necessitated due to a crisis situation – this, we may call as the Crisis-Driven-Reforms Process. As against this, there could be a process which is initiated out of basic realisation about the imperatives and the advantages of such a process. We may call such a process as the Conscience-Driven- Reforms Process. Of course, it might be difficult to categorically state whether the crisis perceptions led to the arousing of a new conscience or the gradual realisation of a conscience was put into practice as a result of the crisis situation. Logically, the conscience about the imperative of change could lead to an intellectual crisis in regard to the alternatives and the options open for the course of changes in the policies. A long drawn period of such intellectual crisis and inadequate initiatives on the ground for the implementation of any of the options in a concerted and consistent manner may ultimately lead to the real crisis of economic phenomena. Thus between the two extreme situations of Crisis-Driven-Reforms Process and Conscience-Driven-Reforms Process there are various shades of the combination of the two.

One may make a subtle distinction between the reforms process driven by the conscience of the domestic policy-makers and thinkers and that driven by the conscience of the foreign observers and thinkers. The former may be called domestic-conscience-driven reforms process and the latter, foreign-conscience-driven reforms process.

While the reforms process initiated in Hungary or in Poland could be categorised as Domestic-Conscience-Driven-Reforms process, those which have been initiated in Russia, in African states, in the Philippines, or for that matter the reforms process of the 90's initiated in India could be categorised as basically Crisis-Driven-Reforms Processes. Of course, if we analyse the history of the initiatives taken for introducing policy changes in India in the last one and half decades, it would be more appropriate to categorise the Indian reforms process into the last category of conscience - intellectual crisis - non-implementation - real crisis driven reforms process.

The conceptual categorisation given above is not meant for simple academic exercise. The genesis or the origination of the reforms process determines the nature of choices in regard to the various issues that were discussed in the previous section. For instance, it would be logical to expect that a Crisis-Driven–Reforms process would initially opt for a big bang approach in a comprehensive manner, rather than adopting the gradualist approach in a sequenced manner. The crisis-driven initiatives would like to adopt stabilisation, structural adjustment, and also the 3-

D's, namely, devaluation, deregulation, deflation, and privatisation – all the possible instruments of the reforms process at one go. Often, the real crisis situation also brings about a peculiar domestic intellectual crisis and intellectual dependency and some sort of intellectual bankruptcy. Perhaps, it is legitimate that an entity in the crisis situation should keep its own conscience and consciousness closed to seek the maximum advice and guidance from those who are willing to offer such advice and also from those who offer support for eliminating or reducing the crisis situation. Most of the countries which have adopted the reforms process – stabilisation and structural adjustment under the IMF-World Bank programmes of Structural Adjustment Loans (SAL) or Sectoral Adjustment Loans (SECAL) or in general, under the policy based lending programmes have fallen in this category of crisis-driven external-conscience-based reforms process. The dangers of such crisis-driven external-conscience-based reforms process are many. Since the external conscience is not a substitute for the national conscience for sharing the responsibilities of the impacts of the reforms process, the crisis-external-conscience-driven reforms process often fails to realise the desired results unless and until the crisis-external conscience lead to the situation of crisis-internal-conscience for the imperatives of change. In order that the reforms process becomes effective and enduring it should be essentially domestic-conscience-driven even in the absence of the real or perceived crisis. One may categorise the Chinese reforms process as belonging to this category of domestic-conscience-driven process.

Most countries had introduced stabilisation and structural adjustment policies under the compulsions of the policy reforms imposed as part of the conditionalities of the World Bank and IMF loans. In an interesting study on Evaluation of Ten Years of Experience of Adjustment Lending brought out by the World Bank, some empirical evidence is available about the comparative performance of select macro-economic variables in the countries which introduced the policy reforms and structural adjustments in comparison to those who did not undertake these reforms. It may be noted that the reforms perceived under the structural adjustment programme cover a wide canvass such as external adjustment, exchange rate changes, replacement of QRs by tariffs, import liberalisation, tax reforms, containment of fiscal deficit, reforms in the financial sector, public sector management, reforms in industrial policies, etc. Table 1.1 gives the values of select economic variables in the different adjustment lending countries and in those who did not receive the adjustment lending.

TABLE 1.1 : **Indicators of the Sustainability of Adjustment for 30 Adjustment Lending Countries**

(percentages)

Indicator	Time	Low-income	Middle-income	Sub-Saharan Africa	Highly indebted countries	Manufacturing exporters
Investment/GDP	Before	19.2	24.7	20.6	23.1	25.0
	After	18.1	19.2	17.1	17.9	22.2
Annual GDP growth	Before	3.0	2.3	2.7	1.2	2.9
	After	2.3	2.2	1.8	1.9	4.9
Budget deficit/ GDP	Before	–7.6	–6.0	–6.5	–4.2	–4.4
	After	–7.6	–5.7	–7.5	–7.0	–3.4
Current account/GDP	Before	–9.0	–7.2	–9.4	–6.9	–5.0
	After	–7.0	–4.5	–6.5	–3.7	–2.6
Debt service/exports	Before	20.6	27.6	17.5	34.6	29.0
	After	22.6	30.9	23.4	36.5	28.0
Private consumption per capita growth	Before	–0.8	2.1	–0.7	1.5	3.0
	After	–0.5	0.0	0.7	0.9	2.2

Notes: All figures are unweighted group averages. Deficits and decreases are shown with minus signs. Except in the case of private consumption per capita, the data cover 30 pre-1985 AL countries and "before" and "after" refer to the three years before and after the first AL. In the case of private consumption growth per capita the data cover 48 AL countries (involving 18 that did not receive AL until 1985 or later) for which "before" is 1978-81 and "after" is 1982-86.

Source: *Background work for the report.*

This study measures the performance of the countries that received adjustment loans by using nine indicators, namely, GDP growth, investment GDP ratio, export growth, real exchange rate, current account balance to GDP ratio, budgeted balance to GDP ratio, inflation rate, external debt to export ratio and debt service to exports ratio. The performance of the 30 countries, receiving adjustment loan was compared with that of other countries, not receiving adjustment loans. The conclusions of this study are revealing: the performance of the AL countries has been only marginally better than the NAL countries. The burden of adjustment fell heavily on investment, as indicated by the relative worsening of the investment to GDP ratio for nearly two-thirds of the AL countries.

Debt service to exports ratio has also worsened after the structural adjustment except for the manufacturing exporters. Annual GDP growth has also worsened except for the manufactured exports. The following concluding observations given in this study are revealing:

> "Several factors nevertheless bring the sustainability of adjustment programmes into question. Investment ratios have declined, and budget deficits are higher in the highly indebted and Sub-Saharan countries. Although current account deficits have been reduced, debt service ratios and especially debt-export ratios have increased. It is not possible to conclude, therefore, that the AL countries are growing out of debt. Even though principal payments may be refinanced, the external debt interest burden seriously limits both import capacity and the domestic savings to finance investments. Another matter of concern is the near stagnation in nutrition levels since 1980, especially in the low-income and Sub-Saharan groups, where per capita caloric intake remains below required levels."

The evidence given above raises some doubt as to whether the structural adjustment envisaged in the conditionalities would lead to favourable results as stipulated in them.

An insightful study of Ajit Singh (1993) on the process of economic reforms in China brings out that there cannot be any generalisations about the content of the reforms process and their impacts. Chinese experience of economic reforms shows that contrary to much mainstream economic thought, it is perfectly possible to introduce markets in a signally planned Stalinist economy in a gradual way. It also demonstrates that extensive marketisation can occur without privatisation or a change in the social ownership of the means of production. The following concluding observations made by Ajit Singh are very pertinent:

> "A central policy implication of the foregoing analysis is that the Chinese authorities should continue with their step by step approach to reform. They need to be wary even of the 'gradualist' wing of the mainstream scholarship for as noted earlier, these economists regard complete marketisation and privatisation to be the end objective of the reform. The end objective for an economy like Chinese is surely industrialisation and development, providing jobs for an expanding labour force and raising the standards of living of the people. There are strong analytical grounds as well as

empirical evidence for the view that such goals are best achieved by purposeful guidance of the market by the plan rather than by unfettered market forces. Not only the Chinese story under the reform, but also that of the highly successful East Asian economies of Japan, the Republic of Korea and Taiwan, Province of China, over the last four decades, point in the same direction.

There are a number of other policy implications of the Chinese experience, including importantly for Russia and for Eastern Europe. However, a discussion of these must be left for another occasion since they involve *inter alia* an examination of other significant analytical issues. The latter relates to the differences in the economic and political circumstances of China and those of the former Soviet Union and other East European countries at the beginning of the reform process. A proper examination of these questions requires a separate paper in its own right."

Reflections on the Reforms Process in India

As stated earlier, it is not easy to draw lessons from the experiences of other countries. However, it is still useful to put together some of the observations, which the empirical analysis of the reforms process has brought out. Below is given a summary of these perceptions:

(1) The process of policy reforms is only an instrumentality for realising a certain standard ideal normative paradigm of economic system. There should be clarity in regard to this cherishable goal, so that the policy instruments required to achieve this goal can be identified in a rational manner.

(2) The State, the market and planning will have to co-exist and an optimum blend for their co-existence will have to be worked out for each country separately, in a manner best suited to its initial conditions.

(3) Structural adjustment often leads to reduction in investment to GDP ratio, at least during the transition period and this may have the effect of perpetuating low growth and debt dependence syndrome.

(4) Privatisation of the means of production is not always a necessary precondition for improvement in the efficiency in resource use.

(5) Stabilisation and structural adjustment cannot be launched

> simultaneously. After realising reasonable success in stabilisation programmes, structural adjustment should be initiated. Integration with the world economy should be done on a selective and strategic manner, so that the national interests are served in the best possible manner.

The reforms process in India in the framework of big bang has been launched since 1991. It is domestic conscience-crisis-external conscience-intellectual crisis-driven paradigm. Stabilisation policies were initially launched but in the recent months, there has been some slowing down of these policies. Fiscal deficit has once again been on the increase and inflation is not fully under control. This year some initiatives are taken for inducing structural adjustment with emphasis on supply side economics rather than that on demand management. Excise duties are rationalised, import duties are extensively reduced, exchange rate stability is being maintained through the intervention of the Reserve Bank of India. Exports are showing some signs of recovery; imports are sluggish; investment rate is stagnant; domestic saving rate is also stagnant; foreign exchange reserves position has improved largely due to the influx of the dollars through the foreign institutional investors in the Indian stock market.

In the midst of these conflicting signals, no categorical inferences about the failure or the success of the reforms process can be drawn. Some of the issues that deserve immediate attention in our discussions on the reforms process are the following:

Do we want a total and outright replacement of the system of mixed economy in a planned framework by the paradigm of total market economy, with minimum or zero planning or State intervention? If the issue is not one of either/or kind then what is the optimum blend of the State, Market and Planning? Where should one draw a line in the process of marketisation or what one may call de-stratification.

Has the reforms process percolated to the grass-root level of the Indian decision-making system? One of the objectives of the reforms process is to reduce or to eliminate bureaucratic interventions in the decision-making process at various levels. Complete operationalisation of the reforms process in this regard is extremely crucial for its success. Mere tinkering with some macro-economic variables will not bring about the much needed structural transformation in the country. What should be done to monitor and also to ensure this kind of operationalisation of the reforms process? This issue should not be brushed aside as a mundane one or as an issue not having much economic substance in it. The success of policy changes is not decided by either theoretical economists or by prophetic bureaucrats. The actors in the real economic scene finally decide the success or the failure of a policy system. Our understanding of the response mechanisms in the economic system is rather inadequate, if not ill-founded. What steps are being taken to educate the masses and to operationalise the reforms programmes?

Privatisation of the public sectors should be pursued in a gradual manner. Unless the loss making public sectors are restructured and brought to health, sale of equities of the healthy public sector units, with a view to privatising them could not be a useful step in the long run. Level playing field for the domestic industry as against competition from the multinationals is an important issue. The argument that the special incentives are required to attract foreign investments can be stretched only upto a limit. The real test of the advisability of these special incentives lies in examining the relative costs and benefits if the same incentives were given to the domestic industries.

The export front is not still very satisfactory. The proclaimed growth rate of 19 per cent or so in the first 10 months of 1993-94, compared to the similar period of 1992-93 is only a reflection of the recovery of the export sector after two years of very sluggish performance. This kind of recovery after two or three years of sluggish performance has always been a normal feature, even in the past. Even in absolute terms, the export level in dollars reached in 1990-91, is yet to be reached. Unless, there is an additionality of export earnings in regard to manufactured goods, one cannot infer that the export situation is really comfortable. Further, the slow growth in imports cannot be interpreted to mean a structural shift in the import curve of the economy. It is only a reflection of the domestic recessionary conditions and the temporary sluggishness of the import demand.

Should rupee be allowed to be appreciated, as a result of the improvement in the reserve positions? In other words, should the Reserve Bank stop buying dollars to monitor a reasonable level for the rupee dollar rate? This issue requires more careful analysis. What is the level of the exchange rate at which the exporters find it attractive to sell abroad, as against selling in the domestic economy, and at the same time, which ensures that the cost of imports is not very high? While depreciation of rupee increases the earning of rupee per dollar of exports, it also increases the cost of imports and hence it has a dampening effect on the demand for imports. In fact, for increasing the demand for imports, some sort of appreciation of the rupee seems advisable. In the midst of the complexity of changes in the various macro-economic parameters – dollar price of exports, dollar price of imports, import content of production, tariff on imports, domestic contents – a clear picture about the optimum exchange rate is not emerging. There is need for undertaking some systematic studies on identifying the optimum level of exchange rates that strike a balance between export promotion and stable import management.

To sum up, it should be observed that the current debate on the process of economic reforms – in general and in particular in India - has generated many analytical and policy questions for which there are as yet no meaningful and categorical answers. It is therefore advisable that the reforms process in India settles down on the middle path with a reworked blend of State, Market and Planning, instead of creating an euphoria about the prophesied advantages of Market alone, a kind of paradigm.

Summary of Discussion

Opening the discussion on the paper, the moderator of the session pointed out that cross-country experiences of reforms presented by Prof. Panchamukhi should be cause for skepticism about the success of the Indian reform process. Secondly, the few success stories that are available, indicate that carrying out successful reforms is a very complicated task indeed and one which cannot be guided by simple minded principles. This complexity of the task needs to be acknowledged and addressed adequately in India.

Some major observations on the presentation were :

(a) Perhaps Chinese reforms did quite well because of better sequencing and an early start. The Chinese started by reforming the agricultural sector first and the process started as early as in 1978. Also, the problem was less daunting for China where the extent of poverty was less and was more regional than general in nature. The Chinese also went against many free market recommendations. To this day, they pursue a dual exchange rate policy. About the reforms in India, Prof. Pandit was of the opinion that it is very important to focus on the political economy of the reforms and to work out very explicitly who will bear the costs of transition during the reform process;

(b) The so called new economic policies are a bit of a misnomer as far as India is concerned. In his view, the new policies are really an extension of old policies and at best are in the nature of mid-course corrections applied from time to time to deal with specific anomalies. Thus, the new economic policies do not repudiate State intervention to bring about distributive justice. All that is being attempted is to provide some corrections where policies have led to unintended results. Thus, for example, there is an effort to tighten the food security regime by weeding out those who are unintended beneficiaries but the reforms in India do not include doing away with PDS. The reforms process in India should address itself only to such corrective measures and not to a fundamental change in the economic policies of the State;

(c) The term percolation of reforms to the grass roots level did not convey any special meaning. It could refer to the effects of the reforms or it could mean that all levels of economic activity should be reformed; and

(d) Instead of privatisation of public sector undertakings (PSUs), it is possible to bring about higher levels of efficiency in their performance.

In his rejoinder to the comments offered on his paper, Prof Panchamukhi admitted that the initial conditions in China were much different from those in India. He was of the considered opinion that reforms need to be more transparent at the grass roots level. This will automatically discipline the administration and provide for free flows of information. Also, the structural change, which envisages some decentralisation, concentrates almost entirely on decentralisation in a geographical sense rather than the more appropriate sense of being oriented to the level of the economic agent. Our present decentralization efforts are themselves top down initiatives. On the question of public sector efficiency, he agreed that promoting efficiency is a key issue but he was skeptical whether this can be achieved by disinvestment. Further, he agreed that public sector dis-investment should not be viewed as a means of raising revenues for the state exchequer.

2

WHERE THERE IS NO ECONOMIST
Some Institutional and Legal Prerequisites of Economic Reform in India

KAUSHIK BASU

Introduction

The issues confronting the Indian economic policy makers are legion. Should the fertilizer subsidy be scrapped? Do our rent control laws need to be amended? Does FERA need modification? Should cotton exports be restricted? Should import restrictions on consumer goods be removed? Is front-running in the stock market to be banned? The questions depend on the context. If it is a district magistrate trying to craft policy for a small rural economy, one set of questions may confront her/him. Very different bundle of issues is likely to be the bread and butter of a senior bureaucrat in the North Block. It is impossible to anticipate all the possible and potential questions that can arise in a complex, modern economy such as India. Fortunately, how we answer many of these questions and craft specific policy depends on relatively few basic principles.[1]

I propose to outline and recommend two such basic principles. The idea is that a person who masters these will be able to work out many of the answers to questions that arise when one gets "down to the task" and craft appropriate economic reform, without each time having to refer to an economist. The principles I outline are implicitly taken for granted by most economists—and perhaps all good economists. This is the reason why, contrary to folklore, economists do agree among themselves on a whole range of issues. The agreement is, of course, not total because these principles are not exhaustive, their interpretations are not free of ambiguity and because a prescription involves both positive analysis and value judgements and the latter can always be subjective.

The first principle to be discussed here will be called the principle of contract. I shall argue that this principle, often conflicts with the 'bureaucratic instinct' and, therefore, has been repeatedly bypassed in the drafting of economic policy in India, to India's detriment. If this principle was followed, the endless succession of complicated legislation, acts and bills could be vastly simplified, to India's advantage.

The second principle will be called the principle of efficient pricing. This is as important to the bureaucrat as to the manager in the private sector. I would have taken it to be a most natural principle, which is instinctively adhered to by all, if it was not for the fact that it is so widely flouted.

The Principle of Contract

The principle of contract says that two or more adults should have the right to freely enter into any contract, which does not hurt individuals uninvolved in the contract, and, further, that the contracting individuals should be able to get support from the State and its judiciary in the event of someone reneging on the contract.

To take an example, suppose persons A and B agree that they will both be better off if A supplies B 100 apples from his orchard now and B supplies A 200 oranges six months later; and so they sign a contract to that effect. If Government adheres to the principle of contract, it will allow A and B to sign such a contract and, moreover, if B refuses to give the 200 oranges six months later, A should be able to get the judiciary to enforce his claim or to seek retribution from B.

This principle can be the basis of welfare enhancement or, to use the economist's jargon, effect Pareto improvements, and is the motivation behind legislation like The Indian Contracts Act, 1872. If A and B voluntarily agree to a contract, it must be that they are better off by virtue of the contract. And since this principle recognizes only those contracts where uninvolved third parties are not adversely affected, if this contract falls within the purview of this principle, its implementation must make some people better off (A and B) and no one worse off, which is the definition of a Pareto improvement. An example of a Government that does not adhere to this principle is one which has a law which says, for instance, that no one is allowed to exchange apples for oranges or that the only exchanges that are permitted are 1 apple for 1 orange. It is easy to see that such a law may well thwart transaction between A and B. It is possible that A would not agree to such an exchange because, given his preference, it is not worthwhile giving up one apple for only one orange. Even if it were the case that they could secretly agree to exchanging 100 apples for 200 oranges, a different problem can arise. Note that, if B reneges at the end of six months (that is, when the time comes for him to deliver the oranges), A will not get any help from the Government because he will not be able to reveal the original contract, which is in contravention of the law. Since B knows this it is very possible that B will renege. Since A, in turn, knows this, A may refuse to get into this contract in the first place.

This example makes it clear that a Government's non-adherence to the principle of contract can diminish social welfare by dampening trade and economic activity. Indeed, a market economy cannot function unless people can get into contracts and expect these to be enforced. And for this we need the Government to provide legal institutions which are supportive of this principle.

This principle is not an unexceptionable one. There are some contracts which come under the purview of this principle but may have to be overruled–I discuss some such exceptions later; but what is astonishing is the extent to which this principle or rule is disregarded in India. Legislation after legislation override the Indian Contracts Act and tell us how we should behave, with scant respect for voluntary contract. This cannot but thwart economic progress and the result, to wit, the Indian economy, is fair testimony. The Hindu rate of growth owes much less allegiance to the scriptures than to this failure of our legal environment.

To illustrate an overt violation of the principle of contract, consider the Delhi Rent Control Act, 1958. It is replete with references to "standard rent", "fair rent' and "lawful increase" of rent. The following are quotes from Section 4:

(1) Except where rent is liable to periodical increase by virtue of an agreement entered into before the 1st day of January, 1939, no tenant shall, notwithstanding any agreement to the contrary, be liable to pay to his landlord for the occupation of any premises any amount in excess of the standard rent of the premises, unless such amount is a lawful increase of the standard rent in accordance with the provisions of this Act.

(2) Subject to provisions of sub-section (1) any agreement for the payment of rent in excess of the standard rent shall be construed as if it were an agreement for the payment of the standard rent only.

Observe that clause (2) above says that even if a landlord and a tenant voluntarily agree upon a rent above the standard rent, the state will not recognize the contract. For a large class of tenancies, the annual standard rent is calculated in a mechanical fashion. It is 10 per cent of the actual cost of construction and the market price of the land on the date of the commencement of the construction. It is baffling why this should be treated as sacrosanct.

On the rules for rent increase the law is as severe. I quote from Section 6:

> "Notwithstanding anything contained in this Act, the standard rent, or where no standard rent is fixed under the provisions of this Act in respect of any premises, the rent agreed upon between the landlord and the tenant may be increased by 10 per cent every three years".

Every time the Government sets up a commission to examine our rental laws, the members of the commission invariably spend a lot of time on such matters. "Is 10 per cent every three years fair?" They ask. Some say that in these days of inflation this is not enough.

Some argue that, since tenants are generally poorer than the landlords, there should be no provision for a rent increase.

The rent control act and debates of the above kind reveal fundamental flaws in our thinking on policy. The question is not whether 3.3 per cent per annum is sufficient increase but why the Government should be fixing such things in the first place. These are matters which the tenant and the landlord should be free to fix at the time of entering into a tenancy agreement. Suppose a tenant and a landlord agree (a) on a high initial rent but no further increases after that, or, (b) on a low initial rent and an annual increase by the same percentage as the increase in wholesale price index.

The existing rent control law will not recognize (a) or (b). The rationale behind such wanton violation of the principle of contract is not evident. And, I believe, there is little. It stems from a failure to appreciate the principle of contract and the instinctive meddlesomeness of human beings or what may, alternatively, be called the 'bureaucratic instinct'.

The harm of ignoring the principle of contract and, equivalently, of exogenously fixing the terms of a contract can be very large. In the above example, at times of inflation, given the terms of the rent control act, it may be better for landlords not to lease out their property but simply benefit from the appreciation of value. I believe that, if in the matter of rental the principle of contract were recognized, many more houses would be available to tenants on the market and the increased supply would probably result in diminished average market rents.

Most Indian laws begin by saying "Notwithstanding any prior contract among the involved parties...." or something to this effect. What we need, however, are contract-regarding laws. Such a law would begin by saying, "In the event of the involved parties not having agreed to a prior contract...".

Thus a contract-regarding rent-control law, that is, one which respects the principle of contract, would urge every landlord and tenant to sign a contract at the time of leasing. Then it would specify a slim set of rules for cases where no such initial contract is available.

Given that so much of our laws are designed with the sole aim of trampling over voluntarily agreed upon contracts, the code of law would shrink vastly if the law were made to respect the principle of contract. The main purpose of such a legal system would be to enforce the contracts people sign instead of telling people what should be the nature of their contracts.

Before moving on, here are some more examples of contract-overriding laws. Suppose two ordinary citizens, A and B, agree to a contract whereby A (who has recently earned dollars but needs Indian money) will give B 100 dollars, and A will in exchange get 3000 rupees from B (who has the rupees but needs the dollars.). This contract would unfortunately be considered null and void because section 8 of the Foreign Exchange Regulation Act, 1973, disallows such transactions among ordinary citizens.

Suppose an employer A, and a workman B, have decided on certain compensation to be paid to the workman in the event of a retrenchment. Again this will be considered null and void by our judiciary unless it happens to coincide exactly with the terms written down in section 25F of the Industrial Disputes Act, 1947 which requires that:

> "The workman has been paid at the time of retrenchment, compensation which shall be equivalent to fifteen days' average pay for every completed year of continuous service or any part thereof in excess of six months".

Once again a legal system which respects individual freedom of contract would say that, whatever the terms of contract signed between the worker and the employer, they must be adhered to. Exogenous contracts should be used only in the event of the employer and the worker having signed no contract.

This is the reason why I find much of the debate on exit policy misplaced. The debate presumes that there must exist exogenous rules for the dissolution of firms and industries. But a more efficient system is to encourage workers and employers to enter into contingent contracts about how workers are to be compensated and how the assets are to be split in the event of the company's closure. The main aim of the law should be to help the implementation of such contracts.

The defenders of *status quo* may argue that workers and tenants are generally in a weaker bargaining position; so to allow free contract would necessarily mean a worse deal for them. This argument is wrong. It can be shown that in many situations adherence to the principle of contract would not only enhance total welfare but actually make the worker better off and the tenant better off (Basu, 1993; Fields, 1993).

One simple fallacy in this argument is easy to see. In Calcutta's Salt Lake City plots of land were sold by the Government below the market price. The idea was to enable the middle and lower-middle classes to acquire property which they would, otherwise, be unable to buy. This is indeed a desirable objective. Something similar is true of the land given to Delhi's ubiquitous cooperative housing societies. Having given this land, Government was worried that soon the rich would buy up the land from the not-so-rich and would displace the latter from Salt Lake City. So what did it do. Through a variety of laws Government has made it virtually illegal to sell land acquired from the Government to other citizens.[2]

If we were really serious about helping the not-so-rich then, after selling them the land, far from putting restrictions on what they can do with the land, we would give them as much freedom as possible. After all, if a person wishes to sell his land it must be because he expects to be better off by doing so. Hence, his not being allowed to do so leaves him worse off. He may, for instance, want to sell it because he has a good and permanent job offer from Bombay. The existing law hinders mobility and hurts him.

The right to sell, without the Government placing hurdles, is a minimal right which can generate a lot of welfare with no resource cost. There are countries, such as Sweden, which from complicated restrictions on property sales, have rapidly moved to a system of nearly-free transactions. India should do the same.

Let me now try to explain how respecting the principle of contract in labour markets can help the labourers.[3] Let us consider a model where an employer and a labourer can freely choose a daily wage (piece rates being ruled out by assumption). After that, once the worker begins to work, he can choose to be "lax" or "hard-working". It seems reasonable to assume that, other things remaining the same, he prefers to be lax, though productivity is, of course, higher if he is hard-working. The law that we shall consider pertains to the employer's right to dismiss the worker from employment. Consider two alternative legal scenarios.

Law 1 The employer cannot dismiss the worker even if he is lax.
Law 2 The employer and the worker have to agree on (a) or (b) below; and then they must adhere to what they have agreed upon.
(a) The employer cannot dismiss the worker even if he is lax.
(b) The employer has the right to dismiss the worker if he is lax.
Law 2 is closer to the principle of contract since it gives the involved parties *some* freedom of contract whereas law 1 gives no freedom. At first sight it looks as though this is a freedom to the advantage of the employer. Clearly, if law 2 is effective the employer will insist on (b). And this must hurt the worker.

Every sentence in the above paragraph is true, excepting the last one. To see this consider the data given below, where all numbers are rupee equivalents.

	Worker: Lax	Worker: Hard-working
Cost of worker	4	6
Output produced	6	10

Hence, it is being assumed that if the worker works all day in a lax manner the cost of sweat to him is 4 rupees. Hard work is more onerous than laziness; hence a day spent on hard work costs the worker more, namely, 6 rupees. The chart also shows that a day of lax work produces 6 rupees worth of output and a day of hard work produces 10 rupees worth of output. Finally, I shall assume that a worker would prefer not to lose his job (as long as he gets positive benefit from the job).

Let us now see what will be the outcomes under different legal regimes. If law 1 is effective, the worker will certainly not work hard. Once his daily wage is fixed, given that he cannot be dismissed, he is best off being lax. Hence, at the day's end there will be 6 rupees worth of output and 4 rupees worth of sweat lost by the worker. The net benefit of the enterprise is 2. Let me, for simplicity, assume that the worker and the employer will bargain to ensure that the wage is such that the net benefit is split equally.[4] In that case the wage will be 5. Let us denote the wage in a regime of law 1 by w_1. Hence, $w_1 = 5$. Note that this gives the worker a net benefit of $w_1 - 4 = 1$ and the employer a net benefit of $6 - w_1 = 1$.

Now suppose it is law 2 that is effective. If the employer and the worker opt for (a) the outcome will be exactly as under law 1. What happens if they opt for (b)? Since the worker knows that he will be dismissed if he does not work hard, he will choose to work hard. The cost of labour will be 6 and output 10, thereby creating a net surplus of 4. Hence, following the same reasoning as before wage, w_2, (that is, the wage that prevails under law 2) will now be 8. This will give the worker a net benefit of $w_2 - 6 = 2$ and the employer a net benefit of $10 - w_2 = 2$. Hence, given a choice between (a) and (b), they will voluntary contract to abide by (b). If this contract is then enforced, they are both better off. What is surprising is that by relinquishing the right not to be dismissed the worker is actually better off.

A different way of viewing law 2 is this. Law 2 is like law 1 with the worker having the additional right to give up his right not to be dismissed. Hence, to make my criticism in this light we could say that the Indian law gives individuals many rights but it typically does not give him the right to give up any of these rights.[5]

If we are hesitant to go all the way to contract-regarding laws, an intermediate step would be to make some provision for the "right to give up rights". When I first came to Delhi in the late seventies, I needed to rent an apartment for a few years, but could not afford a large rent. If I could credibly assure the landlords I saw that I would leave their premises in three years, many would have happily leased their apartment to me at a low rent (the scope for taking in new tenants three years later, by when rents would have risen, being adequate compensation) but there was no way I could thus assure them. My right as a tenant – generously conferred on me by the Government – not to quit became for me an albatross that I could not shake off. There is hardly any provision in the law which gave me the right to give up my right. The right to give up rights is not however an unheard of concept in world legal systems. A student who gets admission into an American university has the right to demand to see the recommendation his professor has written for him. However, U.S. law also gives him the right to "waive this right" if he so wishes.

As mentioned earlier, I am not recommending the principle of contract as gospel. There may indeed be cases where we would want to violate it. One class of exceptions concerns very long-term contracts. Many societies consider it right to prevent workers from making contracts for life. Such contracts can lead to serfdom and bondage. It may seem to many that human beings are inherently short-sighted. Hence, they should be prevented from signing away all their rights for the rest of their lives. Thus we may agree—I do—that a voluntarily agreed upon contract which is the basis of life-long bondage should be disallowed by law. The Bonded Labour System (Abolition) Act, 1976, while notably poor in its drafting as a piece of legislation, is a law in the spirit of the above argument.

Likewise, even if a consumer voluntarily buys a watch, if it turns out that the watch breaks down in a day because it is made of unacceptably poor components, the seller may be held guilty of cheating. The sale of a product amounts to an implicit contract, which says that the product contains what it is expected to contain. Hence, even though no explicit contract is violated, the sale of a dud commodity may be treated as an unlawful act. This is the basis of consumer protection laws.

Finally, there are indeed situations where the weaker party in a contract could benefit if the terms of the contract were exogenously specified or at least restrained by Government instead of being left to be determined through free bargain, and equity may, therefore, demand such exogenous restraint. This must not, however, result in an open mandate to Government to fix the terms of other people's contracts because well-meaning (and not so well-meaning) interventions can actually hurt the poor and the weak unless these are executed with great care and selectively. There are indeed certain prices which should ideally be kept low to increase the access of the poor. But in implementing a price ceiling it must be kept in mind that a lower price also means a lower incentive for the producer to produce and supply the commodity in question. Hence, there can be a cut-back in supply when a maximum-price legislation is brought into effect. If this happens too sharply, then, in trying to ensure that the poor do not buy the product at a high price, we will end up simply ensuring that the poor do not buy the product.

The more serious problem with the principle of contract is not that it has exceptions but that its applicability may be too slender. After all individual acts often have complicated general equilibrium effects and "third parties" are seldom unaffected. While this is true, it must be understood that the presence of a third-party effect does not mean an automatic right of Government to overrule voluntary contracts. What the principle of contract suggests is a way of thinking. Instead of beginning by having exogenous or imposed contracts, I am recommending that we go about this the other way around. That is, we should in general allow free contracting, and stop this only when there is good reason to believe that there may be large and adverse general equilibrium effects or third party effects. To sum up, the basis of economic progress is a contract-regarding legal system. There may be cases where we want contract-overriding laws but these should be the exception rather than the rule.

A Digression on Price Control

The principle of contract allows us to view the effect of price control in a different light. It is often argued that the price of essential goods should be controlled to ensure that everyone is able to buy them. What is not appreciated is that the success or failure of such a scheme depends critically on how price is controlled. I shall consider two mechanisms here. First, price can be controlled by decree, that is, by making it illegal to sell a product above a certain price. Secondly, price can be controlled by giving a subsidy.

If price is kept low by decree, it is true that many more people would demand the product. What is forgotten, however, is that a lower price would typically cause a lower supply. Hence, a lower price may actually result in fewer people getting to buy the product. To understand this look at Figure 1 where D and S are, respectively, the demand curve and the supply curve. If price were not controlled, it would settle at p*, and x* units would be bought. Now suppose that the goods, being an essential goods, the Government fixes its price at p. It is true that more people will now be able to buy the goods and demand will now be greater, as x. However supply will drop to x. Hence, the number of units of the goods sold will be x**, which is less than x*. In Russia, for instance, basic medicine is very cheap but it is frequently unavailable.

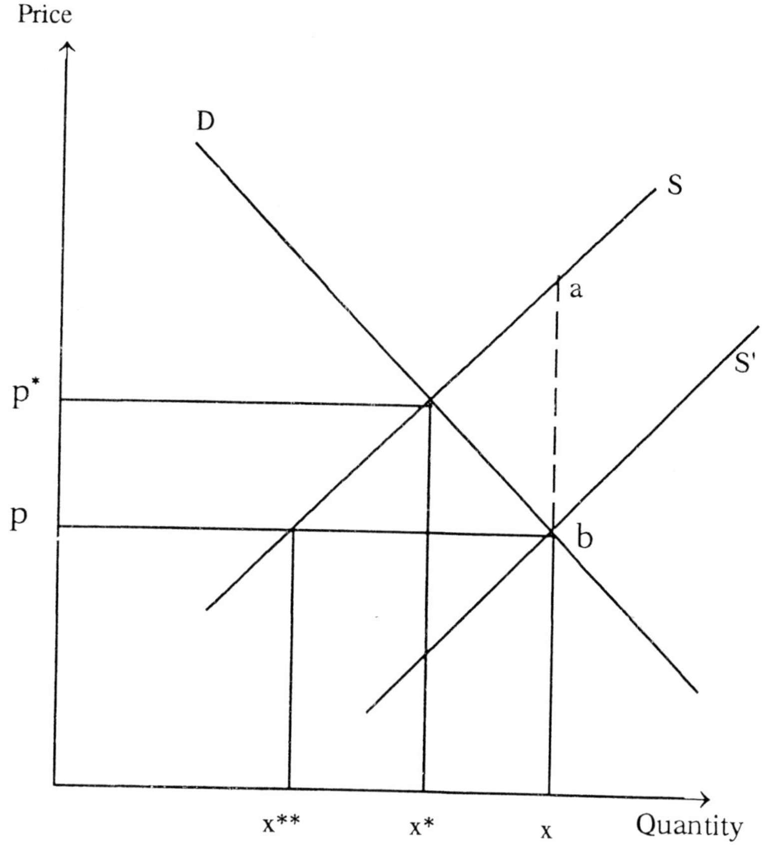

Figure 1

It is worth observing that a price control regime as just described violates the principle of contract, since there will exist individuals who would be willing to sell at a price above and there will exist individuals willing to buy at that higher price. But since such transactions are illegal, such transactions or contracts would be disallowed.

Note now that the same p can be achieved without violating the contract principle if it is attained through a subsidy. If, for instance, a specific subsidy of ab is given for each goods sold, the effective supply curve would be S' and equilibrium would occur at b. Hence, price would be p and the number of units sold would be x:

For this reason the Dunkel draft proposal to prevent price fixing for certain goods like drugs does not mean consumers will have to pay a higher price. If the Government suitably subsidizes the consumers purchasing this goods, the price to the consumer could continue to remain low. This is allowed under the Uruguay round GATT agreement. Hence, the popular view that the consumer price of these drugs will necessarily rise is erroneous. What is true is that once the GATT proposals are implemented, the Government will have to choose between allowing the prices of some drugs to rise and spending more money and keeping prices low by subsidizing the consumers.

To sum up, here are the pros and cons of the two methods of keeping consumer price down at p. If this is achieved through a subsidy, the Government will have to spend ab-multiplied-by-pb units of money on subsidy, thereby risking an enlarged fiscal deficit. Here the consumers will get to buy x*: units of the goods. If, on the other hand, price is fixed at p by decree, Government expenditure does not rise (except for the costs of enforcing the decree), but sales go down to only x** units.

The Principle of Efficient Pricing

The reason why everything that is valuable in life comes with a price tag is that otherwise demand would outstrip supply. If apples were free (that is, of zero price) then the demand for apples would increase manifold and supply would shrink rapidly. Why would anyone devote orchard space, fertilizer and labour to grow apples if he knows he will earn nothing from such activity. It is not even clear that anyone would grow apples for one's own consumption because if apples can be had for free one would be better off "buying" apples from the market and growing something else on one's own land.

While virtually all goods and services come with a price tag, it would be an error to think of the price of a goods as comprising only of a direct money payment. Villagers often spurn education even when it comes for "free", because there are hidden prices. Four hours spent in a school is after all four hours of foregone labour. This labour could have fetched him or her income. Hence, the price of education is not just the fees charged by the school but also the income foregone during the school hours.

Similarly we often decide not to try to buy tickets for a cricket match not because the ticket is too costly but because there are too many hidden costs. Either one has to spend long hours in queue or spend effort pretending to be a good friend of someone who is not a good friend but has easy access to tickets.

Likewise, a company may decide not to set up a new plant in a certain region not because wages are too high but because there are hidden costs. The labourers frequently go on strike, there are industrial disputes with costly litigation and there may be costly bureaucratic interference.

Hence, the true price of a product, service or a venture is what one gets by adding up all the above kinds of direct and indirect costs. While there are many different components to the true price, these can be broken up into two important categories: 'transfer price ' and 'deadweight price'. A transfer price is a price which the buyer pays and someone else acquires; so there is no social loss. When I pay my barber Rs. 10 for a haircut, I lose Rs. 10, true, but the barber earns it (as far as our local barber is concerned, this is money well earned). However, the half-hour that I have to wait for my turn at the barber shop, and which I notionally value at Rs. 20, is also a component of the price for a haircut, but this loss of Rs. 20 of mine, is no one's gain. I just waste my time, I do not give it to anyone. Hence, in my terminology Rs. 20 is deadweight price. If these were the only two components of the true price for a haircut, we would be able to say the following:

True price (30) = Trarsfer price (10) + Deadweight price (20).

The principle of efficient pricing (PEP) says that in organizing our markets we should try to keep deadweight price to a minimum.

As I said earlier, this should happen naturally. This is worth emphasizing because it does not. To see why it should happen naturally, return to the above barber example. Assume that each day the barber gets 25 customers. Hence his daily income is Rs. 250.

Now suppose the barber reorganizes his shop's management in such a way that customer waiting time goes to zero. This could be for instance, because he now gives haircuts only by prior appointment. Clearly he can now raise the haircut charge to Rs. 30 without losing any customer. This is because even after this reorganization the true price remains Rs. 30. This consists of a transfer price of Rs. 30 and deadweight price of zero. Hence by reducing deadweight price to zero the barber manages to raise his daily income to Rs. 750. Indeed, our local barber now has an appointments system and shorter queues and higher charges than he had earlier.

The moral is simple. It may not always be possible to reduce deadweight price to zero, but it always pays to reduce it to as low as possible. This is because every rupee shifted from the deadweight category to the transfer category is a rupee gained by someone since a transfer price is a price only to the buyer. Deadweight price, on the other hand, is a price to the buyer which goes to no one. Hence, a good businessman extricates what the customers are willing to pay as transfer price.

At times we hear people say "I'd rather not go to that shop because the shopkeeper is always so grumpy". Hence, one component of the true price of buying from that shop is the cost of putting up with the grumpiness of the shop-keeper. Given that non-grumpy behaviour is usually costless and a matter of habit, the shop-keeper would be better off if he abandoned his grumpiness and raised the (transfer) price of the product he sells by an equivalent amount.

While I would not go out of my way to recommend PEP to barbers or shopkeepers, since their profit-maximization is not a major concern of mine, Governments clearly ought to practice PEP and the Indian Government practices it too little. Until recently, making an industrial investment was unbelievably expensive in terms of deadweight cost.[6] To make an investment an entrepreneur first needed approval from the Ministry of Industry, which took the form of issuance of a Letter of Intent. If there were any capital goods import needed, the entrepreneur would have to use the Letter of Intent to acquire a capital goods import license from the Chief Controller of Imports and Exports, Ministry of Commerce. For raising funds from the capital market he would need permission from the Controller of Capital Issues, Ministry of Finance. Further permission would be needed for the import of raw material. For each of these things a non-availability certificate would be needed from the technical wing of the Ministry of Industry. After all this was cleared, he would have to apply for an industrial license.

I do not know what the true price of investment in India was but clearly a very large component of it was a deadweight bureaucratic cost, as the above paragraph amply demonstrates. The length of red tape is shorter now as a consequence of economic reforms since 1991 but it is still long enough. If this deadweight price is removed and replaced with an equivalent direct charge imposed on the entrepreneur, the increase in social benefit can be large because now the cost to the entrepreneur will be tapped by Government.

Similarly, when wooing foreign capital or when selling our products abroad, the aim should be to cut down deadweight charges to as little as possible and, as in the example of the barber, to extricate a part of the benefit, thereby imparted to the investor of capital or the purchaser of our goods, in the form of higher transfer price.

Likewise in the case of the labour market. It is very often said that Indian labour is one of the most expensive in the world. This is so not because wages are high but because other forms of cost—strikes, laxity at work, etc.—are high. Ideally we do want labour charges to be high. Labourers are typically poor; and the purpose of economic progress is to benefit the workers. However, labourers should be high-cost by virtue of wages being high and not by virtue of high deadweight cost. An indisciplined labour is costly for entrepreneurs. But since indiscipline is not something that the worker can directly consume to the enhancement of his utility or sell in street-corner shops and enhance his income, it is a price that entrepreneurs pay and no one collects. In brief, it is a deadweight price.

SUMMARY OF DISCUSSION

A large number of participants argued that the third party effects or 'externalities' necessitate intervention by government to regulate a large number of contracts. It was pointed out that a further complication to the application of POC is provided by general equilibrium effects of individual actions. Similarly, regarding PEP, it was felt that fewer deviations from the first best world does not necessarily constitute the second best solution in terms of welfare maximization. Further, there is a problem of recognition of the legitimate third party. In most situations, it can be argued that ultimately there is some burden on the consumer of the final product. Is the consumer then a legitimate third party when it comes to a wage settlement contract between the management and workers of a firm producing the consumer goods? Thus, however reasonable and logical POC may be, politically strong 'third parties' will always manage to force deviations from it in their own interests.

The pervasive presence of the 'third party', especially in the rural areas, makes it impossible to give the POC any practical shape. Social, as distinct from economic, pressures can also operate against the individual who may wish to enter into contracts in his own self interest. Thus, even in rural India, it may not be feasible for the individual to give up his right to minimum wages because of peer pressure. Such limitations to the Principle of Contract severely restrict its workable content in real situations.

It was also noted that the most essential prerequisite for successful economic reforms is the prior reform of the legal and judicial system. He observed that in terms of reforms, the phase of thinking of the executive and the judiciary do not necessarily coincide. Thus, there is a problem in that judicial review of executive actions can thwart any reform process. As for PEP, the political masters can always cash in on at least part of the deadweight loss involved in deviations from the principle. It is difficult to visualize a situation where they will voluntarily give this up.

Commenting on Prof Basu's recommendation of minimizing deadweight losses as a guiding principle of economic policy, one wondered why there is no endogenous move towards different contracts in cases where the deadweight losses are large. The other important matter which must be considered is the distribution of the deadweight loss among various groups in society. This could be either progressive or regressive.

It was noted that there are two obvious corollaries to the principles enunciated by Prof Basu. The principle of simplicity of contracts offered by government and the principle of prohibiting third parties from entering into the contracts in any way. If this cannot be ensured or followed, then there is little chance that the two principles enunciated by Prof Basu will be followed in any situation.

In India, the role of the State has expanded as a consequence of the realization that economic agents operate with very unequal powers. Therefore, the desirability of allowing contracting parties the freedom to contract in any manner they feel right is really no freedom but a way of perpetuating unequal power relations in society.

Prof Basu admitted that the Principle of Contract is a good principle only when there are no third parties. He was of the opinion that in India, there are numerous cases of laws and regulations which violate the principle even when there are no third parties. A case in point is that of the Delhi Rent Control Act which is discussed in his paper. On the question of adopting a general equilibrium approach, he was of the view that such an analysis is so complex that it does not yield any practical prescriptions. Also, it is perhaps best to begin with the primitive concept of individual self interest driving our actions rather than individual shortsightedness. He also agreed that there is a dire need to simplify the processes of administering justice. On a technical note, he pointed out that part of the deadweight loss is encashed as rents (corruption) which, being in the nature of a transfer payments, do not constitute a loss to society. Finally, he felt that the losses to society due to flouting these simple principles is enormous. Individual behaviour, which on the face of it seems irrational, can be seen to be rational if the deadweight losses are accounted for. For instance, in Bihar, the farmer does not go to the organized credit sector though the nominal interest rate is lower than the 18% or so charged in the informal sector because it is estimated that the true cost of credit, after taking into account the deadweight costs, is in the region of 200%!

NOTES

1. I call it the "basic principle" in Basu (1993).

2. Of course, Indians get around it. Through various powers of attorney and false declarations they do buy land and sell houses, but this entails considerable transactions costs and enriches lawyers and government officials in charge of enforcing the law. Indeed, some laws, such as the *Monopolies and Restrictive Trade Practices Act*, 1969, seem to exist only to be "got around" (Singh, 1993).

3. For a more detailed analysis the reader is referred to Basu (1993). For a discussion of the Indian law in the context of contracts in the labour market, see Chander (1993). I must emphasize that it is not being claimed that labourers invariably benefit from the principle of contract. What I wish to demonstrate is that the converse claim, that workers invariably lose out if the law gives them the freedom to enter into contracts, is false.

4. This is consistent with the Nash bargaining model. If, to capture the greater bargaining power of the employer, we assume that the employer gets a fraction, d, of the benefit and the worker the rest and d > 1/2, we could do so without affecting my claim. The assumption d = 1/2 is purely for simplicity.

5. I formalize the right to give up rights in a social choice theoretic framework in Basu (1984).

6. The description that follows is taken from Mohan (1992).

3

INFLATION
Experience and Emerging Scenario

V. PANDIT

Introduction

There are few subjects in economics which have received greater attention than inflation. The subject, has been as much of practical importance - touching the lives of people in all walks of life and all dispositions -as of analytical significance. Formal deliberations on the subject have stretched over nearly two centuries - though informal discussions on it are perhaps even older than economics as a discipline. Curiously, the more the subject is discussed and debated the less one appears to get into grips its mystique[1].

Strictly speaking, inflation is a state of "sustained increase" in prices. It is a continuing process than a one-short increase, belonging thus to the realm of dynamics rather than comparative statistics. Also, one is talking about endogenous rather than exogenous forces at work. However, in normal parlance and at a practical level these fine methodological nuances and matters of taxonomy are not of overriding importance. An exogenous shock like a drought or oil price hike could unleash a process of upward price movement which would then be sustained and propagated for a while by indigenous forces that get released in the process. More often than not it appears to be safer to talk about price movements reserving the notion of inflation to steady state equilibrium. All the same, we shall not adhere to this maxim and indulge in a certain measure of looseness in our terminology.

Inflation: Desirable and Undesirable

Inflation generally evokes a sense of panic sometimes justifiably but many times unnecessarily. The latter has been true in case of India. It would appear on both empirical as well as analytical grounds the inflation has asymmetric consequences around a critical threshold. The threshold itself would understandably depend on a number of factors rather than be rigidly defined for all economies and all situations. From the policy viewpoint it is obviously quite helpful to know what the threshold is in a given situation.

It can be argued that within this threshold inflation would promote growth by maintaining a regime of received incentives for future economic activities. With fixed or administered nominal interest rates it would also reduce the real cost of borrowing and thus promote investment. In this way, inflation tilts the balance in favour of investor and away from savers. Clearly, this is helpful only so long as it does not upset the perceptions of savers - which are predominantly households. By giving a boost to profits inflation would also cause an upswing in internal finance which in turn promotes capital formation. This is important for developing countries where external finance may be severely rationed - particularly in case of the small, unorganised household enterprises who account for a larger part of production and investment activity in such countries.

However, it is easy to see that all the phenomena mentioned above would not work monotonically. Once the rate of inflation crosses the critical threshold its adverse impact will outweigh the advantages. A basic reason for this is that at higher rates inflation becomes visible and generates expectations and perceptions which have undesirable consequences. In this context it is important to note that the expectation that inflation will continue at a high rate, turns into a self-fulfilling prophecy even though this may not be warranted on objective grounds. The reasoning is that inflationary expectations induce economic agents to shy away from holding money and assets whose rate of return is fixed in nominal terms. In turn, this makes the same stock of money to run faster - adding a further impetus to the existing inflation. The resulting dynamics may be stable to unstable. In the latter case the result is "hyper-inflation" or more popularly termed "run-away inflation". In the former case too the rate of inflation will eventually settle at a level, significantly higher than zero.

Continued inflation at high rates generates a lot of adverse consequences for the economy. First and foremost, it tilts the distribution of real income and even wealth against the lower echelons of the society whose incomes are not only low but also fixed in nominal terms. This has obvious welfare consequences[2]. Second, continued inflation would dampen the rate of saving because the households, which account for the lion's share of domestic saving have a tough time maintaining their levels of living with saving taking a back seat. Third, inflation also has an undesirable effect on the composition of savings[3]. Savers would not like to hold financial liabilities issues either by the private corporate sector or by the Government. They will prefer to undertake on their own investment which are likely to have lower levels of efficiency/productivity. Alternatively, they will tend to hoard goods with speculative motive, which will further fuel inflationary pressures. Moreover, there will, in general, be a tilt in the composition of investment in favour of inventories and against fixed investments. Fourth, in a growing economy, outlays for investment projects either by the private corporate sector or by the Government are usually fixed in nominal terms. Continued inflation obviously erodes the real value of such investments. Finally, inflation gives rise to considerable uncertainties and disruptions in the economy and the society. If a predominant proportion of economic agents, e.g., producers, investors and savers are risk-averse, as they are in developing countries, the level of economic activity gets dampened.

Inflation and Unemployment

The quantity theory of money together with the argument that the level of output is inflexibly fixed at the full employment or full capacity level provides the traditional framework for a theory of inflation. The critical assumption that the general price level equilibrates the money market implies that the rate of inflation is directly determined by the rate of increase in money supply less the rate of growth of real output. For a long time this simple rule of thumb provided the basis for policy initiatives relating to inflation particularly in developing countries. However, in industrialised countries price stabilisation came to be related to unemployment under the influence of Keynesianism during the post war years stretching over the fifties and the sixties. The theoretical and empirical basis for this policy-paradigm was provided by the "Phillips curve" originally discovered by Phillips (1958) and rationalised by Lipsey (1960). The influential paper by Samuelson and Slow (1960) explicitly introduced the notion of a policy trade-off between inflation and unemployment in industrialised countries. The "Phillips curve" which posited a stable inverse relationship between the rate of unemployment and the rate of change of the nominal wage implied that price stability would be consistent with a certain measure of unemployment - believed to be about 3 to 4 percent. Alternatively, if the society was willing to tolerate a higher rate of inflation unemployment could be reduced to a more acceptable lower level.

During the late sixties the trade-off paradigm was under attack in two stages. The first in 1968 came independently from Friedman (1968) and Phelps (1968) both of whom questioned the stability of the trade-off. It was argued that since workers would be interested in real wages they cannot overlook the prevailing inflation. Hence the Phillips curve would keep on shifting by a measure depending on the perceived rate of inflation. Assuming that expectations are generated by an adaptive model it would turn out that there would be a positive trade-off between inflation and unemployment in the short run but none in the long run. In other words, unemployment can be reduced to some extent in the short run by inflating the economy through monetary/fiscal policies but over long periods such policies will turn out to be ineffective.

This line of reasoning gave rise to what is now well known as the Natural Rate of Unemployment (NRU) or Non-accelerating Inflation Rate of unemployment (NAIRU). Friedman defines NRU as the rate of unemployment which would come out a (Walrasian) general equilibrium process in an economy characterised by market imperfections, which may be due to inadequate information, sluggish adjustments and such other things. The implication is that the economy has to live with this rate of unemployment and deal with its adverse welfare consequences independently.

The second and the more severe attack on the trade-off theory came in the early seventies in the wake of new classical economics (NCE) which itself rests on the rational expectations hypothesis (REH). REH asserts that economic agents will form expectations that are very much like efficient statistical the forecasts making an optimal use of all the available information. The term "Inflation", includes not only the policy rules that the Government, or broadly, the policy makers are likely to use but also the economic theoretic model regarding the variable in question.

REH also assumes that all expectations are unbiased about which expectations are being formed in the sense that economic agents do not make systematic errors. The REH together with assumptions of perfect markets which clear every period - constitute the NCE. The implication of REH and commodity markets clearing imply that the inflation-unemployment trade-off does not exist even in the short run. This difference is sometimes captured by labelling the neoclassical economics of Phelps and Friedman as Monetarism Mark-I and the new classical economics of Sergeant, Wallace and Lucas as Monetarism Mark-II[4].

Inflation and Economic Development

Whereas inflation is visualised as being tied up with employment (or unemployment) in developed industrial economies it is viewed as a companion of economic growth and development in the less developed countries. A very early articulation of this came from Rao (1953), Kalecki (1976) and some other eminent economists who were very intensely interested in the development of the third world in a steady and stable manner. That inflation should result from economic growth is due to several reasons. But, at the heart of this phenomenon lies the problem of inadequate resources, in one form or the other.

First of all, it has been argued that if growth has to be stimulated resources must be bid away from low productivity uses to high productivity uses. This would require creation of incentives through higher factor prices. Also, while such incentives may be warranted only in some segments of the economy, they will inevitably slip over to several other segments too. This process will lead to a spell of inflation lasting for a while till higher productivity and larger volume of production catches up. In principle, if a developing economy is characterised by surplus labour of all types then increasing demand for it as a result of industrialisation should not raise wages. But, in practice, this does happen partly because of increasing union power of labour, partly because of increased productivity and partly also because of progressive labour legislation setting minimum wages, limits on hours of work etc.

Another source of inflation would come from the spillover effects of wages in the faster growing sectors of the economy for example those relating to exportable. A similar spillover may be associated with wages set by the Government for its employees either in general administration or in the public sector enterprises. Also, in a mixed economy like that of India where Government produces and/or markets a number of essential intermediates as well as final goods and services escalation in their prices to cover inefficiency or to generate resource, would be yet another source of inflation.

However, the most widely held view of the inflation process in developing countries runs in terms of fiscal and monetary policy compulsions that are believed to prevail in these countries. Government may on the one hand try to step up the rate of economic growth by undertaking large investments in the public sector. But since the extent to which revenues can be raised through either taxation or borrowing from the public are limited, a good part of the required resources are generated through borrowing from the central bank. This means deficit financing or what is sometimes referred to as inflationary finance. This mode of resource mobilisation leads to a multifold increase in money supply which in turn causes inflation *a'la'* the quantity theory of money.

Rao (1953) argued that if Government's expenditures are allocated to productive uses they should result in augmented output after a lag. This should in turn reduce the excess demand in the economy and help in the eventual stabilisation of prices. The basis of this argument is not only the quantity theory of money but also the proposition that the economy operates at an inflexibly given and physically determined capacity level. Growth too is correspondingly related to the rate of capital formation with capital and foreign exchange being regarded a binding constraint in the economy.

One of the most widely known and provocative articulations of the monetarist approach to inflation is associated with the so called Polak model which has given rise to the well known IMF conditionalities. These have typically included a number of things - some related to inflation, others to growth. The former consist mainly of (a) reduction in budgetary deficit to less than, say, 5 per cent of GNP, (b) restraints on wage hikes - relating these to productivity, (c) lower growth of money supply and, (d) devaluation of currency so as to promote exports and discourage imports.

The Polak model serves as a framework for IMF policy advice to LDC even today. Though some modifications have been made it remains monetarist in its character and has been subjected to severe criticism by professional economists as well as many policy-makers. The earliest criticism which came from several Latin American economists lead by Raul Prebisch. This viewpoint has widely been known under the label 'Structuralism"[5]. A more recent articulation of the structuralist approach in terms of persuasive analytical and empirical methodology has been put forward by Taylor in a number of books and papers[6].

The basic thrust of structuralist argument has been two fold; both in sharp contrast to the IMF viewpoint. First, whether inflation control should be so high on the policy-makers' agenda that it should be undertaken at any cost. Second, how far can inflation be tackled with the monetarist prescriptions involving monetary and fiscal policy. In fairness structuralist have never argued that inflation was not bad. What was at stake was: (i) the policy-makers' priorities; (ii) available policy options;

and (iii) and the appropriate *modus operandi* of an anti-inflation programme.

The distinguishing feature of the structuralist proposition is the view that in developing countries inflation (and growth) are not purely economic phenomena in so far as they are both linked with a number of social and political realities pertaining to these countries. These relate to the highly skewed distributions of income and wealth, undemocratic and inefficient Governments, vested interests of foreign enterprises, organised labour unions, role of Government in promoting investment and social services, and finally the concern for the welfare of the poor. Under these circumstances, it is argued that inflation - so long as it is not at a rate that threatens the very viability of the economic system - need not enjoy a high priority; the primal concern in these economies being those of overall growth and distribution. The structuralist assumptions are empirically valid in varying degrees for most countries in Latin America but not equally so for India or even some other Asian economies.

Under the structuralist assumptions severe cuts in either money supply or in Government expenditure are believed to stagnate economic growth on the one hand and worsen the condition of the poor on the other. This is because of fiscal crunch is likely to fall on public investment, which may largely be on the provision of infrastructure, and social services like health and education. In so far as cut in Government expenditure would also reduce subsidies on exports or in the public distribution of essential commodities the adverse effects will again be on growth and poverty alleviation. It is important to note here that monetary and fiscal policies in most developing countries are not independent. More precisely, the former is, in fact, subservient to the latter. Independent monetary policy, may mainly be limited to administered interest rates and credit rationing.

The foregoing description of the macro-economic functioning of a developing economy implies that restrictive monetary and fiscal policies could upset fragile Governments, result in strikes and lockouts, push a lot of people below the subsistence level, and accentuate bottlenecks that already exist in these economies due to say, dependence on imported consumable, investment goods and raw-materials. With a lag this would bring back inflationary forces to work with a vengeance. The final outcome thus is likely to be stagflation.

More recent statements of the structuralist argument have been in terms of the severe constraints under which both policy-makers, and other economic agents have to work in LDCs - given their priorities and objective functions. One logical implication of the structuralist reasoning, both old and new is that no rational and efficient policy can be formulated unless the economies in question undergo structural changes not only in the economic but also in the social and political spheres. It is also imperative that the nature of relationship that these economies have with the international markets and the dominant economies undergo drastic changes.

India's Record of Inflation

There are three alternative measures of the general price level giving rise to the three corresponding measures of inflation. The three measures are: the wholesale price index (PW), the consumer cost of living index (PC) and the implicit GDP deflator (PX). Which of these one may use depends on the context in which inflation is being examined. It should be clear that PW includes all kinds of goods but no service. On the other hand, PC includes retail prices of all "goods and service" that normally enter household budgets. The implicit deflator PX includes all goods and all services - whether used for consumption or for investment. It is thus the most comprehensive price index, but for most purposes it is not the ideal one to measure inflation. In developed countries inflation usually refers to the rate of increase in the consumer price index (PC) in all policy discussions. In these countries PC is also calculated with much greater care and punctuality than in India. In what follows we shall keep to the tradition and refer to the increase in PW as inflation. In a sense this is not too bad because with some predictable lags and adjustments the movements in other prices closely follow those in the wholesale prices.

In India unlike most other developing countries both the general public as well as the policy-makers have been sensitive to inflation and, in my view, excessively so.[7] The economy also has shown remarkable resilience and a quick response to anti-inflation correctives from time to time. Consequently, the country's record of inflation has been impressively good - though sometimes, at the cost of growth. It appears that price stability has often been given a higher priority than growth. To what extent, this reflects the policy-maker's bias is a moot question. Table 3.1 gives the frequency distribution of inflation rates measured in terms of PW for the 42 year period, 1951-52 through 1991-92 subdivided into two equal sub-periods 1951-52 through 1971-72 and 1972-73 through 1991-92.

TABLE - 3.1 : **Frequency Distribution of Inflation Rate**

Rate of Inflation (Per cent)	Subperiod I 1951-52 to 1971-72	Subperiod II 1972-73 to 1991-92	Total Period 1951-52 to 1991-92
Less than	4	1	5
0-5	8	4	12
5-10	5	9	14
10-15	4	3	7
15-20	0	2	2
More than 20	0	2	2
Total	21	21	42
Average	3.84	9.19	6.51
S.D.	6.70	5.59	7.10

Figures in Table 3.1 show a number of interesting things. Most important, the distribution has undergone a visible shift. While the SD remains more or less the same for the two periods the average inflation rate for period II is more than twice as high compared to period I. Second, in period I negative inflation rates occurred four times, which is partly the reason why the average is lower, whereas in period II prices fell only once that too very marginally. Third, while inflation rates in excess of 15 never occurred in period I, these occurred four times in period II. For all the 42 years, however, inflation rate exceeded 20 only twice.

Also, for the entire period the economy never had to undergo a prolonged period of sustained inflation. In fact, annual inflation rates since 1951 given in Annexure 3 reveal only four episodes of significant inflation when price rise went into double digits. Three of these lasted two successive years. The fourth one chronologically the last is still going on and has already lasted three years. The four episodes in question are as follows:

A: 1966-67 and 1967-68
B: 1973-74 and 1974-75
C: 1979-80 and 1980-81
D: 1990-91, 1991-92,1992-94 and 1993-94

The latest trends firmly indicate that 1993-94 will also form a part of episode D. It is important to note that the causes of high inflation during

A, B and C can rightaway be identified with unusually poor monsoons with the consequent drought and famine conditions. In addition, there was a sizable currency devaluation in 1966, the first oil shock in 1974 and the second in 1979, and, hostility along our borders in 1965 and 1971 whose impact was felt with a lag.

It is not at all surprising that price behaviour in India should directly be linked with the fortunes in agriculture and with shocks from the external sector. Food continues to be the principal wage good in the economy. Agriculture, even after a significant decrease continues to account for about a third of the GDP and provides the bulk of raw materials to the country's industrial sector. Price increase in agricultural products directly induces increase in wages as well as other costs. It may also be noted that poor harvests tend to sag the demand for industrial goods, and hence cause recession, thus giving rise to stagflationary conditions. Finally, it is interesting to note all the three episodes A, B, and C coincide with regimes of political disturbance. That this factor would have given rise to inflationary expectations in a significant way cannot be ruled out.

The implicit explanations of inflation during episodes A, B and C fail to hold good with regard to episode D. As mentioned earlier this episode will span over a fourth year and possibly a fifth one, whereas all the others have lasted only two years or so. However, the annual rates of inflation have been nearer to 10 than to 20. Since 1988, the country has had normal or better than normal monsoons for six years consecutively. Thus, the agricultural sector performance can by no means be held responsible for the current inflation. We shall return to this question later.

Sources of Inflation

As we have discussed earlier there are two major sets of factors which are believed to cause inflation. These are associated with demand-pull and cost-push theories. In principle, there are no disputes as far as this classification and taxonomy go because the question of what does or does not enter the two sides of the market is still open-ended. But in practice, since the two do not operate in water tight compartments it is empirically nearly impossible to identify whether a particular inflation impulse may come from the demand side and then generate reactions that get entangled on to the supply side.

In India the emphasis in academic circles as well as in policy fora has been not only on demand-pull but more specifically also on the role of monetary expansion in a monetarist tradition. An early exception to this has been the work of Raj (1966) who analysed price behaviour in terms of Keynesian inflationary gap. Over the last two decades, however, the pure monetarist model has been questioned by academics on analytical as well as on empirical grounds. Policy-makers as well as casual empirical researchers and of course, some academics do continue to think in terms of a monetarist framework[8]. It is now believed that the assumption that the level of activity in the economy is always at its maximal capacity level, which is basic to the monetarist model, is no longer obviously valid - as it perhaps was during the fifties and the sixties. An implication of this empirical judgment is that inflation cannot be exclusively explained in terms of demand pull factors and much less be related to money supply growth by means of a rule of thumb[9].

Another point relevant in this context is that undoubtedly, the economy has grown quite complex since the late sixties and is now much more characterised by price rigidities than it was ever before. This is partly a natural consequence of the proliferation of modern large scale industry and partly the result of Government's price intervention in the economy, particularly in agriculture. In the earlier phase, such intervention was confined largely to the industrial sector only. Thus the flex-price segment of the economy has contracted and the fix-price segment expanded.

For effective policy formulation it is extremely important to have a proper understanding of the structure of the economy. The new policy regime aimed at structural adjustments and stabilisation on the one hand makes it necessary to be able to predict, howsoever accurately, what the levels of growth and inflation are going to be and on the other hand renders our past experience less relevant as a guide to future developments. All the same, the experiences of the eighties with some modifications should be meaningful for the ensuing years.

In the context of inflation our immediate concern is to identify whether prices are subject to cost-push or demand-pull factors. Needless to say that money supply growth, howsoever quantified; would form one and perhaps an important factor in the latter category. Policy evaluation is clearly and critically dependent on this basic judgment. It appears to us *prima facie* that over the last decade and a half the cost-push factors have played a far greater role than what is usually recognised by the policy makers. One cost-push factor which has traditionally been given much prominence and remains important in western industrialised economies is the wage cost, i.e., movements in the nominal wage rate relative to those in the productivity of labour. While this is important in case of India, as in most other developing countries, many other factors have assumed as much, if not greater in recent years. These include import prices - particularly of oil, Government determined procurement and issue prices of agricultural products, and administered prices of critical intermediates either produced or marketed by the Government. It should be noted that even if import costs do not rise much in dollar terms they would acquire a cutting edge in the face of devaluation - particularly if it is sharp and frequent.

It is by no means being argued here that the demand-pull factors have no role at all or, in particular, that monetary expansion has no effect on prices, it is our assessment, on the contrary, that:

(a) demand conditions during any given period would considerably influence the mark-up factors that producers may decide to use;
(b) the economy would sometimes be supply constrained and sometimes demand constrained; and
(c) certain specific sectors may be subject to demand-pull even when there is no excess demand present in the economy as a whole. It follows from this line of reasoning that inflation cannot be properly understood in isolation of how the level of activity (measured by real gross national product) in the economy is determined.

In recent years, a number of researchers have empirically examined questions relating to price behaviour and inflation using sophisticated econometric methods. The focus has mainly been on the role of money supply and cost factors in the determination of price behaviour. Balakrishnan (1991) comes to the sharp consolation that money supply growth is of limited relevance in explaining price movements in India during the seventies and the eighties. On the other hand, Ray and Kanagasabapathy (1992) and, Nag and Samanta (1994) examine the problem from a time series point of view emphasizing the need for a sophisticated time series analysis. In contrast to the conclusions drawn by Balakrishnan both these studies argue that monetary/credit policy has a definite though not an exclusive role in dealing with inflation.

An Empirical Model[10]

Strictly speaking, one cannot model price behaviour (or inflation) in isolation of how output adjustments (or growth) take place. However, since the objectives of this chapter are fairly modest, we may go ahead with half of the question. In doing so, we follow, in spirit, a model that I had used in the late seventies (Pandit, 1978), and outline a preliminary structural sub-model to explain price behaviour. We postulate that price dynamics is subject to demand-pull as well as cost-push factors. The former are captured by money supply relative to real GDP, real per capita consumption expenditure and the level of industrial activity. The cost-push factors are represented by price of raw material energy and imported inputs. In addition, we have Government's price intervention in the form of procurement prices for rice and wheat, exerting an upward pressure on food prices. We also treat energy price as being exogenous since these are largely administered by the Government[11].

The model basically explains three components of the wholesale price index (PW). These are the wholesale price index of food articles (PWF), the wholesale price index of non-food agricultural products (PWNF) and the wholesale price index of manufactures (PWMN). The first two together determine the wholesale price index of all agricultural products (PWAG), PWAG and PWMN together account for nearly 85 per cent of the total weight in the wholesale price include for all commodities. The remaining weight in the wholesale price index for all consumers. The remaining weight of nearly 15 per cent is assigned to PADMN - the wholesale price index of energy and mineral items namely, coal, power, light, lubricants, metals etc. Energy cost is clearly the dominant component of PADMN. The important aspect of this price index is that all its ingredient prices are administered by the Government. For this reason PADMN is taken to be exogenous in the model.

Both the prices relating to agricultural products must be viewed as reduced forms with inelastic supplies in the short run. It is also presumed that price adjustments are not instantaneous. Prices of manufactures are largely cost determined with mark-up rates influenced by the state of overall liquidity in the economy - measured by money supply to real GDP ratio.

The consumer price index (CPI) is determined by the prices of food and manufactures. The five components of the implicit GDP deflator (PX), namely, PXAG, PXMN, PXIN, PXSR and PXAD are linked to the appropriate components of the wholesale price index. Since we do not have an up-to-date series on wage rates it assumed that it moves in sympathy with the consumer price index (CPI), with a lag in some cases. With this general approach we estimate the following equations for the sample period, 1970-71 through 1990-91 so as to constitute a submodel for price behaviour.

The four basic behavioured equations relating to PWF, PWNF, PWMN and CPI are specified in linear form, whereas the five equations linking the sectoral implicit deflations to the corresponding wholesale price indexes are specified in log-linear form. These nine estimated equations together with six identities give us a 15-equation submodel for price behaviour as follows. Numbers in parentheses below each coefficient give the student's t-ratio. ARI indicates that errors in the equation are serially correlated and estimation procedure takes this into account. For all equations thus estimated we also give the serial correlation coefficient r. For the first-four equations values below the t-ratio (not in parentheses) are the mean elasticities.

1. $$PWF = \underset{(0.61)}{-25.3329} + \underset{\substack{(1.95)\\0.27}}{56.4087}\,\frac{[M3 + M3(-1)]/2}{GDP} \underset{\substack{(2.26)\\-1.00}}{-0.7704}\,[QFG + QFG(-1)$$

$$+ QFG(-2)]/3 + \underset{\substack{(3.67)\\0.86}}{0.924B}\ PPRW + \underset{\substack{(1.94)\\1.12}}{020772}\ CON/N$$

ARI = $\bar{R}^2 = 0.99$, DW = 2.11, r = 0.3912

2. $$PWNF = \underset{(0.08)}{13875} + \underset{\substack{(8.60)\\0.56}}{111.9261}\,\frac{[M3 + M3(-1)]/2}{GDP}$$

$$+ \underset{\substack{(1.84)\\0.44}}{0.2361}\ [XMN/QNF(-1).100]$$

OLS: $\bar{R}^2 = 0.98$, DW = 1.62

3. $$PWMN = \underset{\substack{(4.45)\\0.26}}{16.2231} + \underset{(3.48)}{49.9767}\,\frac{[M3 + M3(-1)]/2}{GDP}$$

$$+ \underset{\substack{(4.29)\\0.20}}{0.2364}\ PADMN + \underset{\substack{(4.46)\\0.17}}{0.1663}\ IMUV + \underset{\substack{(1.58)\\0.20}}{0.1860}\ PWAG$$

OLS: $\bar{R}^2 = 0.99$, DW = 1.54

4. $$CPI = -6.6560 + 0.6363\,PWF + 0.3794\,PWMN$$
$$\quad (1.54) \quad (8.13) \quad (4.20)$$
$$\quad 0.69 \quad 0.38$$

ARI: $\bar{R}^2 = 0.99$, DW = 2.22, r = 0.7312

5. $$PWAG = 0.633\,PWF + 0.367\,PWNF$$

6. $$PW = 0.2747\,PWAG + 0.5704\,PWMN + 0.1549\,PADMN$$

7. $$\text{Log } PXAG = -0.0206 + 1.0205\,\text{Log } PWAG$$
$$(0.14) \quad (31.33)$$

ARI $\bar{R}^2 = 0.99$, DW = 1.52, r = 0.4159

8 $$\text{Log } PXMN = 0.0505 + 1.0078\,\text{Log } PWMN$$
$$(0.68) \quad (61.40)$$

ARI: $\bar{R}^2 = 0.99$, DW = 1.65 r = 0.4086

9. $$\text{Log } PXIN = -0.6099 + 0.1485\,\text{Log } PADMN + 1.0491\,\text{Log } CPI$$
$$(4.61) \quad (1.74) \quad (11.40)$$

OLS: $\bar{R}^2 = 0.99$, DW = 1.59

10. $$\text{Log } PXSR = 2.7569 + 0.3462\,\text{Log } \frac{[M3+M3(-1)]/2}{GDP} + 0.4850\,\text{Log } CPI$$
$$(5.12) \quad (4.71) \quad (4.59)$$

ARI: $\bar{R}^2 = 0.99$, DW = 1.37, r = 0.5153

11. $$\text{Log } PXAD = 0.3878 + 0.9630\,\text{Log } CPI$$
$$(2.65) \quad (29.75)$$

ARI: $\bar{R}^2 = 0.99$, DW = 1.66, r = 0.3721

12. $$PX = [PXAG.XAG + PXMN.XMN + PXIN.XIN + PXSR.XSR + PXAD.XAD]/GDP$$

13. $$INFW = 100.[PW/PW(-1) - 1]$$

14. $$INFX = 100\,[PX/PX(-1) - 1]$$

15. $$INFC = 100[CPI/CPI(-1) - 1]$$

Some Implications and Interpretations[12]

The estimated relationships, *prima facie,* indicate that for all sectors of the economy money supply growth relative to that of output remains an important determinant of price movements. The coefficient as well as mean elasticities of the money-GDP ratio are statistically significant as well as large in magnitude for all the three basic price variables. However, it is no longer as dominant a factor as it was during the fifties and the sixties when compared to the results of earlier studies e.g., Krishnamurty (1984). Another noteworthy feature of the model is the increased role of cost factors which are partly policy induced and partly exogenous. While the former include procurement/support prices in the agricultural sector the latter are represented prominently by import prices.

The model has been simulated with a view to examine its accuracy and then to determine the relative importance of the money supply growth and increase in administrative and procurement prices are import costs. The simulation exercises show the model to be quite reliable. Predictions based on it are accurate not only for the sample period but also for the years beyond it. Counter factual simulations also confirm all the three sources of inflation to be important - though the actual relative contribution of each to inflation varies over different years. This is not surprising because the exogenous variables, notably output levels are not the same for all years.

Very briefly, it can safely be concluded that:

(a) Monetary growth remains a significant factor in determining the rate of inflation but neither the only nor the most important one. Its role has also decreased in recent decades.
(b) Price intervention in agriculture and industry by means of procurement/support prices of agriculture products and energy prices, is more important than before. This is likely to increase further.
(c) Unlike before, the impact of import prices on domestic industrial prices is now more visible than it used to be. This too is likely to go up further in the years to come.

The Emerging Scenario

The eighties almost began with a double-digit rate of inflation in two successive years. For the remaining years the rate moved into single digit but remained all along significantly above 5 per cent. The early years of the present decade witnessed a turmoil in the economy. For the three years for which we have the data, the inflation rates have been again in two digits 10.3 per cent in 1990-91, 13.7 per cent in 1991-92 and 10.1 per cent in 1992-93. During the last few months of 1992-93 and the first few months of 1993-94 there was a deceleration in inflation but this has again been followed by an opposite trend. It appears to us that the last year (1993-94) will have closed with an average wholesale price index close to 10 per cent above that for the preceding financial year[13].

Writing in June 1992[14], I have argued that the current spell of double digit inflation would continue for another two to three years. The same view was taken a few months later in early 1993 (Pandit, 1993), with the claim that Government's hopes of controlling inflation by cutting back on money supply growth via restrictions on monetised deficit was based on faulty grounds. As mentioned earlier work on modelling the Indian economy is progressing jointly at the Delhi School of Economics and the Institute of Economic Growth. A preliminary model dealing with outputs, prices, as well as other important indicators shows that inflation around 10 per cent will continue in 1994-95 also. This means that the present episode of a double digit inflation will last at least for five years. The track record of our forecasts of inflation, given as Annexure 2, lends reliability to this prognosis.

It appears thus, that what I foresaw in June 1992, may very well come true. Inflation will persist in double digits for another year or even longer. But, is this an alarming prospect? My considered response is 'No'. First the rate of inflation is not going to be far above 10 per cent. Second, all countries that undertook stabilisation-adjustment programmes have managed with much higher inflation rates. Third, attempts to control it at any cost will jeopardise growth. Fourth, Government can and should effectively counter the adverse welfare consequences of inflation. Our primary concern at this juncture should be with growth.

SUMMARY OF DISCUSSION

One was compelled to observe that "while inflation has been a problem in all the developing countries, growth prospects signal 'hope'; hence, what about the growth prospects for the Indian economy?", It was noted that despite normal and good rainfall successively for the past six years, and a very comfortable foodgrains position, inflation has been above two digits. It only shows that the demand pull factors are not so strong. There were others who did not agree in this observation. The demand pull factors have been exerting significant influence, as for example, of cotton', - in which case the global shortage had led to rise in prices. It was further observed that there are some prices which are more rigid whereas there are other items whose prices are more flexible. Somehow, we appear to concentrate more upon the flexible prices.

It was also pointed out that the procurement prices have been raised not necessarily on the basis of recommendations of the CACP, these have often been raised for political considerations. In regard to issue prices, moreover, there is a need to include coarse cereals if we wish to utilize the PDS for the benefit of the poor in India. Indeed, it was painful to note that consequent to rise in the issue prices, the off-takes of foodgrains had declined. The PDS system in India would stand to gain if it is decentralized, and taken over by the states.

There were also comments upon the linkage between the inflation rates in the domestic economy and the rest of the world and the need for periodic devaluation of exchange rates. The dilemma of a ten per cent rise in commodity taxes leading to a 15 per cent rise in prices, are also noted. Prof. Pandit stated that indeed, one should always hope, where growth prospects are concern! However, it appears that while the NEP marks an end of the old, the new is not in. India is not a lost case. Yet, it may be noticed that there is sagging investment and despite finance ministry's efforts to woo the investors through various tax concession in the last budget, the investments have not gone up. At the same time public sector investments have also increased. These could have been at least directed towards the infra-structure sector. A beginning in this direction would only provide a boost to the private sector investments since public sector investments crowd-out private sector investments. He further observed that the Indian economy is very resilient and it responds to policy initiatives if they are in the right direction. Prof. Pandit, however, observed that it is not a good thing to fall prey to the devaluation trap. He cited in this case the example of Ceylon, where devaluation every few months has been a big reason for abrupt rise in prices through imports. Rise in prices have become a nightmare for the people, and caused social discontent and militancy. It is better, therefore, to go for a policy of price stability and a stable exchange rate. Prof. Pandit argued that it has much to do with the cascading effect, and the attempt of the trading community to manipulate taxes to its advantage.

ANNEXURE I

NOTATION

CON	Real private consumption expenditure in domestic markets
CPI	Consumers price index
DUM90	Dummy variable equal to 1 for 1989-90, 0 for all other years
GDP	Real gross domestic product
INFC	Rate of inflation measured by consumer price index
INFW	Rate of inflation measured by wholesale price index
INFX	Rate of inflation measured by GDP implicit deflator
M3	Money supply (broad) with the public
N	Population - mid year
PADMN	Index of the prices of minerals, fuel, power, light and lubricants
PPRW	Index of the procurement prices of rice and wheat
PW	Wholesale price index - all commodities
PWAG	Wholesale price index - agriculture products
PWFG	Wholesale price index - foodgrains
PWMN	Wholesale price index - non-agricultural products
PWNA	Wholesale price index - non-food agricultural products
PX	Implicit GDP deflator
PXAD	Implicit GDP deflator - Public administration and defence
PXAG	Implicit GDP deflator - agricultural sector
PXIN	Implicit GDP deflator - infrastructural sector
PXMN	Implicit GDP deflator - manufacturing
PXSR	Implicit GDP deflator - services
QFG	Index of foodgrains output
QNF	Index of non-foodgrains agricultural output
XAG	Real value-added in agriculture and allied activities
XMN	Real value-added in manufacturing
XIN	Real value-added infrastructure
XSR	Real value-added in public administration and defence

Note: All implicit price deflators have base 1980-81, while wholesale price indices are with base 1981-82. The base for CPI is 1982.

ANNEXURE 2

TRACK RECORD FOR FORECASTING THE RATE OF INFLATION

Forecast for the financial Year	Date of the Year	Publication Forecast*	Forecast Rate	Actual Rate
1986-87	August 1987	–	6.0	5.8
1987-88	August 1987	–	8.0	8.2
1988-89	November 1988	–	7.5	7.5
1989-90	November 1988	–	8.5	7.5
	August 1989	–	7.5	7.4
1990-91	16 March 1990	Financial Express	8..0	10.3
	18 March 1990	Financial Express	9.0+	
1991-92	17 March 1991	Financial Express	10.0+	13.7
	29 Sept. 1991	Financial Express	14.0	
1992-93	11 March 1992	Financial Express	12.0	10.1
	14 Sept. 1992	Economic Times	10.0	
1993-94	22 March 1993	Economic Times	9.0	
	21 Oct. 1993	Financial Express	8.0	9.5 (expected)

*All forecasts were actually made more than a month prior to their publication.

ANNEXURE 3

INFLATION AND GROWTH IN THE INDIAN ECONOMY

Year	Inflation Rate(%)	Growth Rate(%)	Year	Inflation Rate(%)	Growth Rate(%)
1951-52	5.7	2.5	1972-73	9.9	–0.3
1952-53	–15.3	2.9	1973-74	22.8	4.9
1953-54	1.3	6.1	1974-75	23.0	1.6
1954-55	4.0	4.1	1975-76	–1.1	9.2
1955-56	–4.9	2.8	1976-77	2.1	1.3
1956-57	13.9	5.6	1977-78	5.2	7.5
1957-58	3.0	–1.3	1978-79	0.1	5.6
1958-59	4.2	7.5	1979-80	17.1	–4.9
1959-60	3.7	2.0	1981-82	9.3	5.8
1961-62	0.2	2.9	1982-83	4.9	2.6
1962-63	6.2	5.1	1983-84	7.5	7.9
1963-64	3.8	2.0	1984-85	6.5	3.8
1964-65	11.0	7.4	1985-86	4.4	4.1
1965-66	7.6	–3.8	1986-87	5.8	4.0
1966-67	13.9	1.1	1987-88	8.2	4.1
1967-68	11.6	8.0	1988-89	7.5	10.5
1968-69	–1.1	2.7	1989-90	7.4	5.6
1969-70	3.8	6.5	1990-91	10.3	5.2
1970-71	5.5	5.7	1991-92	13.7	1.4
1971-72	4.0	0.9	1992-93	10.1	4.0

NOTES

1 The literature on inflation has been subjected to several surveys in the recent decades, see, e.g., Laidder and Parkin (1975) and Frisch (1983) to name only two.

2. See Jain and Tendulkar (1992) and Radhakrishna and Sarma (1976).

3 See Pandit (1985).

4. See Tobin (1980) for this labelling. More detailed discussion of NCE is to be found in any standard textbook. See, for example, Cuthbertson and Taylor (1987).

5. For an early discussion of the various underlying issues, see Baer Karstenetzky (1964).

6. See, for example, Tylor (1988a, 1989).

7. In a way Taylor (1988b) corroborates this view.

8. The recent literature is surveyed by Bhattacharya and Lodh (1990). For a review and earlier works, see Krishnamurty and Pandit (1985).

9. See e.g., Balakrishnan (1991) and Pandit (1993).

10. This section draws heavily from a recent paper presented to a seminar on "The Indian Economy During the Eighties" at M.S. University of Baroda. See Krishnamurty, Pandit and Palanivel (1994).

11. Strictly speaking this is not entirely correct because government more or less keeps on adjusting this price in response to domestic inflationary pressures as well as the unit value index of POL products.

12. The submodel for price behaviour outlined in the preceding section forms a part of a larger model for the Indian economy being developed at the Institute of Economic Growth as a project jointly with the Delhi School of Economics. The main collaborators on the project besides me are professors K. Krishnamurty of IEG and K.L. Krishna of DSE.

13. For the week ending March 19, 1994 PW was 9.9 per cent above that 52 weeks earlier.

14 See Pandit (1992).

4

PUBLIC FINANCE AND ECONOMIC DEVELOPMENT
Lessons from India

M. GOVINDA RAO and TAPAS KUMAR SEN

Introduction

Although the quest for rapid economic growth in India began with the introduction of development planning in 1951, it was only in the formulation of the Second Five Year Plan (1956) that the logic of the development strategy was fully articulated. This Nehru-Mahalanobis strategy of development emphasised "rapid industrialisation with particular emphasis on the development of basic and heavy industries". The fear of foreign domination arising from the colonial past and the feeling of export pessimism naturally led to the adoption of import substituting strategy and this social engineering could not be achieved without the public sector being assigned "commanding heights" in the economic activities of the country. This, in short, was a unique experiment of democratic centralised planning in the framework of a mixed economy.

The developmental strategy chosen at the time was influenced by both the philosophy of the times as well as the ground realities and constraint. The success of the Keynesian type of policies in fighting the Great Depression and more importantly, the achievements of Soviet industrialisation signified the importance of social engineering and centralised planning in allocating investments. The dominant opinion of development economists was that the problem of 'vicious circle of poverty' constrained the poorer countries in achieving transfer of surplus labour from the less productive agricultural sector to the more productive manufacturing sector (Nurkse, 1953). To achieve speedy industrialisation, large investments in social overhead capital to create generalised externalities were necessary and this could be undertaken only by the State (Rosenstein-Rodan, 1943).

The development strategy was also partly influenced by the structural constraints faced by the economy. The low levels of saving and investment, weak industrial base, lack of infrastructure, obsolete technology, scarcity of skilled manpower and virtual non-existence of a modern entrepreneurial class necessitated the State to take up the role of a catalyst to as well as an active participant in industrial progress.

In this public sector dominated, heavy industry based industrialisation strategy, fiscal policy had to be designed to fulfil three important objectives namely, (i) raising the level of saving and capital formation; (ii) allocating the available resources in accordance with plan priorities; and (iii) achieving the desired state of redistribution.

The achievements of four decades of planning have been significant in a number of respects, but in many others falls much short of the potential. Indeed, in contrast to the virtual stagnation in the preceding fifty years, the economy recorded the growth rate of 3.6 per cent in real terms during the First Plan (1951-56) and almost 4 per cent during the Second (1956-61). But this momentum could not be maintained and the long-term annual GDP growth rate hovered around just 3.5 per cent to be characterised as 'Hindu' rate of growth until the beginning of 1980s. Of course, the economy got into a higher growth path in the 1980s (5.3 per cent), yet, the performance was far below what was seen in many other countries. A comparison of GDP growth rates for India and other countries presented in Table 4.1 shows that during 1965-80, Indian growth performance was close to the bottom, better than only Bangladesh and Chile, and in the next decade (1980-90), its performance was in the middle range (Ahluwalia, 1993). Countries like China, Korea, Malaysia and Thailand with per capita income levels as much as or below India in the 1950s reached the income levels far higher by 1990.

The efficacy of the State-dominated, heavy industry-based strategy of import substituting industrialization came into serious questioning when the country slipped into the worst economic crisis following the sharp rise in oil prices consequent to the U.S.-Iraq conflict in August, 1990. It may be noted that the economic crisis of such a magnitude occurred after a buoyant growth performance of the economy for about a decade. The diagnoses unambiguously point towards large and persisting fiscal imbalances as the principal cause of macro-economic and foreign trade account imbalance driving the economy to the crisis situation. This led to serious reconsideration of the role of the State vis-a-vis the market and to the questioning of the efficacy of a State dominated, import substituting development strategy. Given that fiscal policy is one of the principal instruments of intervention and as the persistent fiscal deficit was held to be the major cause of economic crisis, the emphasis naturally focused on the efficacy of public finance instruments in the developmental process. It is felt that instead of correcting the market failure, fiscal policy interventions in India have contributed to serious loss of efficiency and equity in the economy. In this background, it is important to review the performance of the application of public finance instruments in the developmental process of the economy so that the lessons drawn from the past experience can be used to beneficially reorient these policies. This chapter attempts such an evaluation keeping in view the three developmental objectives of fiscal policy mentioned earlier namely, (i) raising the level of savings and investments, (ii) allocation of resources according to plan priorities and, (iii) achieving the desired state of income. In the final section, we summarise the lessons drawn from the Indian experience.

TABLE 4.1 : **Growth Rates of Real GDP in Selected Countries**

(per cent per annum)

Country	1965 - 1980			1980 - 1990		
	Total Agriculture Industry			Total Agriculture Industry		
	1	2	3	4	5	6
Bangladesh	1.7	0.6	1.5	4.3	2.6	4.9
India	3.6	2.5	4.2	5.3	3.1	6.1
China	6.8	2.8	10.0	9.5	6.1	12.5
Pakistan	5.2	3.3	6.4	6.3	4.3	7.3
Sri Lanka	4.0	2.7	4.7	4.0	2.3	4.6
Indonesia	7.0	4.3	11.9	5.5	3.2	9.0
Thailand	7.3	4.6	9.5	7.6	4.1	9.0
Turkey	6.2	3.2	7.2	5.1	3.0	6.2
Chile	1.9	1.6	0.8	3.2	4.2	3.4
Mexico	6.5	3.2	7.6	1.0	0.4	1.0
Brazil	9.0	3.6	10.1	2.7	2.8	2.1
Korea	9.9	3.0	16.4	9.7	2.8	12.2

Source : Ahluwalia (1993).

TABLE - 4.2 : **Saving-Investment Gap in Indian Economy**

(as percentage of GDP at current market prices)

Household Sector			Private Corpo-rate Sector			Public Sector		Total			% of Public Savings in Total Savings		
	S	I	S-I	S	I	S-I	S	I	S-I	S	IS-I		
1954-55	6.9	5.6	1.3	1.0	1.4	–0.4	1.7	3.1	–1.4	9.6	10.1	–0.5	17.7
1960-61 to 1964-65	8.1	5.1	2.9	1.7	3.6	–1.9	3.0	7.5	–4.4	12.9	16.2	–3.42	3.6
1965-66 to 1969-70	10.4	7.6	2.8	1.3	2.2	–0.8	2.4	6.8	–4.4	14.1	16.5	–3.4	17.3
1975-76	13.4	8.5	4.9	1.3	2.7	–1.4	4.2	9.6	–5.4	19.0	20.9	–2.4	22.4
1978-79	17.0	10.6	6.4	1.5	2.2	–0.6	4.6	9.5	–4.9	23.4	22.3	–0.9	9.8
1980-81	16.1	9.7	6.3	1.7	2.8	–1.1	3.4	10.3	–6.9	21.2	22.8	–1.7	16.2
1985-86	1 5.2	8.1	7.1	2.1	5.6	–3.5	3.2	11.8	–8.5	20.4	25.4	–5.0	15.8
1989-90	17.8	8.9	8.9	2.7	4.3	–1.6	1.6	10.3	–8.7	22.2	23.5	–1.3	7.0
1990-91	18.4	9.8	8.6	2.6	4.5	–1.9	0.9	9.7	–8.8	21.9	24.0	–2.1	4.0

Source : National Accounts Statistics, Ministry of Planning, Government of India.

Public Finance and Saving and Investment

One of the significant achievements of the Indian economy has been to raise the levels of private saving and total investment within a relatively short period of time (Table 4.2). From just about 10 per cent of GDP in the early fifties, the investment levels increased steadily to form over 25 per cent of GDP in 1985-86 and thereafter, declined marginally to stabilise at around 23-24 per cent of GDP. It is notable that this increase in investment was financed not by foreign savings but by increasing domestic savings. The gross domestic savings increased from less than 10 per cent of GDP. Thus, despite high levels of investment the resource gap did not exceed 2 per cent of GDP throughout the Sixties and the Seventies, though during the first seven years of the Eighties, it averaged around 4 per cent.

While the increase in the level of savings and investments is really a notable achievement, it is necessary to know whether this can be attributed to the efficacy of the Government's fiscal policy. In fact, public finance policies can enhance the level of savings either by generating savings in the public sector or by encouraging private sector savings. Let us examine the efficacy of public finance instruments in enhancing the level of savings in either of the two ways.

A. *Trends in Public Sector Savings*

The most disturbing aspect of the Indian economy is the failure of the public sector in generating the level of savings required for its investments. The savings-investment gap in the public sector has shown a steady increase over the years (Table 4.2) and the withdrawl from the household sector to finance public sector investments increased steadily from 1.4 per cent of GDP in the 1950s to 8.8 per cent of GDP in 1990-91. The public sector savings constituted almost a quarter of gross domestic savings in the economy in the early sixties, but over the years it declined sharply to form an abysmal 4 per cent in 1990-91. As a proportion of GDP, public sector savings increased from 1.7 per cent of GDP in 1950s to 4.6 per cent in 1978-79, but thereafter declined to form less than one per cent of GDP in 1990-91 (Tables 4.1 and 4.3).

TABLE 4.3 : **Structure of Public Sector Savings**

(As a Percentage of GDP)

	1970-71	1975-76	1980-81	1985-86	1989-90	1990-91
1. Government Administration	1.4	2.8	1.9	–0.2	–2.5	–3.0
2. Public Sector Enterprises	1.7	1.7	1.5	3.4	4.1	3.9
(a) Departmental	0.7	0.5	0.2	0.5	0.6	0.7
(b) Non Depart-mental	1.0	1.2	1.4	2.9	3.5	3.2
3. Total Gross Savings (1+2)	3.1	4.5	3.4	3.2	1.6	0.9

Source: National Accounts Statistic (various issues), Central Statistical Organisation, Ministry of Planning, Government of India.

(i) *Budgetary Dissavings:* The analysis of the composition of public sector savings (Table 4.3) brings out that the principal reason for the decline has to be found in the very high and increasing volume of budgetary dissavings. The budgetary dissavings emerged first in 1982-83, and thereafter steadily increased to form 3 per cent of GDP in 1990-91. The saving performance of public enterprises too leaves much to be desired. The level of savings remained virtually stagnant at a little over 1.5 per cent of GDP throughout the 1970's and thereafter, increased to 3.5 to 4 per cent of GDP, but considering the volume of investment made in the public sector the saving levels were abysmally low and if capital consumption (depreciation) is taken account of, the savings became negligible (0.06 per cent)[1].

A basic reason for the emergence of governmental dissavings is the outpacing of the rate of growth of resources by the expenditure growth. The Government revenues in the 1980's grew at an average rate of 15.1 per cent per year and the growth of tax revenues was slightly higher at 15.6 per cent (Table 4.4)[2]. Yet, as the current expenditure of the Governments increased at over 18.3 per cent per year, the emergence of significant levels of dissavings was unavoidable. Consequently, rather than generating surpluses for investment in the revenue account as was the case until 1982-83, the situation deteriorated to a level wherein household savings amounting to almost 3 per cent of GDP had to be drawn merely to meet public consumption needs.

TABLE - 4.4 : **Growth of Revenues and Expenditures**

(per cent per annum)

		1970-71 to 1980-81	1980-81 to 1990-91	1970-71 to 1990-91
1.	Direct Taxes	12.4	12.5	12.5
2.	Indirect Taxes	16.1	16.2	16.2
3.	Total Tax Revenue	15.4	15.6	15.5
4.	Non-Tax Revenue	14.2	13.0	13.6
5.	Total Revenue Receipts	15.2	15.1	15.2
6.	Capital Receipts	18.0	20.6	19.3
7.	Total Receipts	15.8	16.5	16.1
8.	Revenue Expenditure	15.0	18.3	16.7
9.	Capital Expenditure	18.3	11.8	15.0
10.	Total Expenditure	15.9	16.6	16.3

Note: Growth rates have been estimated using the kinked exponential regression models. See, Boyce (1986).

Source: Indian Economic Statistics, Ministry of Finance, Government of India.

The emergence of fiscal imbalance has to be attributed to the high and accelerating growth of current expenditures (Table 4.5). The growth rate of per capita total current expenditures excluding interest payments increased from 4.4 per cent during 1974-75 to 1981-82 to 8.9 per cent during 1981-82 to 1986-87 and continued to grow at 7 per cent thereafter even as the growth of per capita aggregate expenditures decelerated to 3.4 per cent during the latter half of the eighties (Table 4.5). Interest payments in per capita terms (at constant prices) increased at over 13 per cent per year during the eighties and other items which recorded very high and accelerating growth rates were wages and salaries, and subsidies and transfer payments. In contrast, both per capita gross fixed capital formation of the Government and capital transfers showed a sharp decline even in absolute terms. Our analysis shows that the decline was particularly severe in the infrastructural sectors like irrigation, energy and transport and communication. These trends have had adverse effects on both the growth potential of India as well as equity (Rao and Sen, 1993 and Mundle and Rao, 1992).

TABLE - 4.5 : **Growth of Per Capita Government Expenditure in India**

(1981-82 Prices) (Per cent)

	1974-75 to 1981-82	1981-82 to 1986-87	1986-87 to 1990-91	1974-75 to 1990-91
1. *Consumption Expenditure*				
(a) Compensation to Employees	2.27	8.25 *	6.39	5.28
(b) Net Government Maintenance	4.30	8.09	2.60*	5.69
Total	3.03	8.20 *	4.91 *	5.43
2. *Transfers*				
(a) Subsidies	11.78	10.90	10.38	11.23
(b) Transfer to Local Bodies	2.24	4.96	12.39	4.58
(c) Other Transfers	5.39	10.37*	9.03	7.93
Total	6.96	9.96	10.00	8.60
3. Total Current (1+2)	4.39	8.93	7.01	6.62
4. Gross Fixed Capital Formation	1.99	12.57 *	-7.05 *	5.15
5. Financial Outlay	3.42	7.97 *	-9.78 *	3.62
6. Total Capital Transfers and Advances				
(a) Local Bodies	5.26	5.93	-1.19 *	4.74
(b) Others	2.51	1.12	-2.65	1.28
(3) Total	2.81	1.77	-2.35	1.73
7 Total Capital Expenditure (4+5+6)	2.64	5.56	-5.05 *	2.91
8. Total Expenditure (3+7)	3.72	7.04 *	-3.37 *	5.41

Note : Growth rates have been estimated by using kinked exponential regressive model. See, Boyce (1986).

* Significantly different from the previous period.

Source : Central Statistical Organisation.

As already mentioned, tax revenues have been reasonably buoyant during the entire period. Therefore, increasing governmental dissavings cannot be attributed to the lower revenue productivity of the tax system[3]. However, the growth rate of non-tax revenues have not only been relatively stagnant but have shown a decelerating trend. The non-tax revenues grew at an annual average rate of just about 13 per cent per year in nominal terms and this was even lower than the growth recorded during the Seventies. The principal reason for this relative stagnancy was the low and declining cost recoveries on social and economic services provided by both Central and State Government (Table 4.6). The recovery rates (cost recoveries as a ratio of cost of providing public service) in the case of economic services declined from 55 per cent in 1977-78 to 41 per cent in 1987-88 and in the case of social services, the declined was from 6.3 per cent to 3.6 per cent. In fact, in higher education, the recovery rate was just about 2 per cent. The implicit subsidies arising from uneconomic pricing of public services as a proportion of GDP increased from 8.2 per cent of GDP to 15 per cent during the decade. Even in commercial sectors like power, irrigation, transport and communication, the volume of subsidy was significant. Inability to raise non-tax revenues by collecting users charges at the appropriate rate has been one of the major factors causing erosion of Governmental savings.

TABLE 4.6 : **Subsidies in Social and Economic Services: States and Centre**

	Recovery rate (Per cent)		Subsidies (Rs million)		Subsidy as percentage of total subsidy	
	1977-78	1987-88	1977-78	1987-88	1977-78	1987-88
Economic Services						
1. Agriculture and Allied Services	35.93	20.49	12590	71170	15.97	16.02
2. Irrigation and Flood Control	25.77	20.27	9730	48150	12.34	10.84
3. Poverty and Energy	45.77	32.29	3720	36190	4.72	8.15
4. Industry	39.11	16.81	6360	57350	8.07	12.91
5. Transport	69.55	74.30	11010	33610	13.96	7.57
6. Communication	114.85	68.58	900	11310	1.14	2.55
7. Other Economic Services	64.94	31.43	2350	17800	2.98	4.01
8. *Total Economic Services*	54.69	40.74	44870	275570	56.90	62.03
Social Services						
1 Education	2.75	1.30	20540	95850	26.04	21.58
2. Health	5.33	3.07	6840	29370	8.67	6.61
3. Water Supply, Sanitation and Housing	14.39	5.82	3690	24300	4.68	5.47
4. Other Social Services	18.93	12.15	2920	19160	3.70	4.31
Total Social Services	6.26	3.62	33990	168680	43.10	37.97

Note : Includes data for fourteen major states and centre.

Source: Mundle and Rao (1992).

(ii) *Declining Savings of Public Enterprises :* One of the reasons for the proliferation of subsidies is the poor financial performance of central and State level public enterprises and large budgetary support given to cover their losses year after year. At the central level in 1989-90, 244 public enterprises with Rs 844 billion capital employed made a net profit of Rs 38 billion. However, oil sector alone generated a profit of Rs 29 billion and the remaining enterprises together made a profit of just Rs 9 billion. A detailed analysis of the working of these enterprises further reveals that quite a good proportion of the losses have accrued not in the core-sector enterprises. The non-core sector industries of fertilizers, consumer goods, agro-based industries, textiles and construction services together made a net loss of Rs 8.5 billion. Although this partly reflects the Government's taking over loss-making units in the private sector to protect the interests of labour, the fact that they have continued to function year after year without any form of restructuring has only contributed to inefficiency and decline in productivity. Nor can the problem be attributed entirely to such "loss swapping". The enterprises started by the Government to produce consumer goods and services have also made losses in a number of cases[4]. Even the units making profits have done so in spite of poor physical performance, mainly due to the monopoly status in the market and charging administered prices. As many of these are in the nature of basic raw materials, intermediate and capital goods, this cost increase arising from their inefficient operation has contributed to the non-competitiveness of downstream industries. The situation is equally worrisome at the State level. The State Electricity Boards in 1990-91, made a net loss of 14.4 per cent of the capital employed and the losses in road transport corporations were over 12 per cent. Among the departmental commercial concerns, the losses on account of irrigation in 1987-88 worked out to Rs 52 billion. There were also several "promotional" corporations draining the exchequer to the tune of Rs 5 billion.

The above discussion brings to the fore a major weakness of the Nehru- Mahalanobis development strategy of not having a proper financial plan to correspond to the material balances exercise for major commodity sectors (physical plan). The implicit assumption was that, "what was physically possible and desirable could also be rendered financially viable" (Chakravarty, 1987, p.23). The inability to generate reasonable returns from the investment in public enterprises and effect cost recoveries from various 'quasi-public' and private goods directly provided by the Government has turned out to be a major constraint in generating savings for reinvestment.

The large and persistent fiscal imbalances and governmental savings have been held primarily responsible for the economic crisis of 1990. The expanding expenditures created an excess demand situation, a part of which spilled over into imports. At the same time, declining public investments created infrastructural bottlenecks. Increasing resort to fiscal deficits to finance public consumption and investment needs led to higher interest rates (including administered interest rates) and crowding out of private investment. The excess demand created by current public expenditure, and declining public and private investments together tended to create a stagflationary situation. The situation also warranted larger dependence on foreign savings and as noted earlier, during the period from 1981-82 to 1986-87,on an average, dependence on foreign savings was over 4 per cent of GDP in contrast to just about 1.5 per cent in the previous period. Further, as the household saving was pre-empted by the Government at low interest rates by prescribing Statutory Liquidity Ratio (SLR) and as positive real rate of interest had to be given to the savers, the commercial banks indulged in serious irregularities in the securities market and these have resulted in further irregularities down the line, the discovery of which has affected the capital market significantly.

b. Fiscal Incentives and Some Private Savings

The second method of influencing the saving behaviour in the economy is through various fiscal incentives. Both personal and corporate income taxes were used to encourage household and corporate savings. The research on the subject, however, shows that while these have altered the after-tax rates of return in unintended ways and have thereby changed the choice of saving instruments, it is doubtful whether they have been effective in enhancing the level of total savings in the economy (Das-Gupta, 1989, Rakshit, 1987). At the same time, the various forms of tax incentives for savings have in fact contributed to the complications in the tax structure. The myriad tax incentives have in fact been used as loopholes to avoid taxes; subsequent attempts to close these have further complicated tax laws.

Fiscal Policy, Resource Mobilisation and Resource Transfers

An important objective of planning is to ensure that the available resources in the economy are utilised in accordance with plan priorities. In a mixed economy, this has to be achieved by transferring resources to make investment in the public sector and by influencing the allocative decision of the private sector through various policy instruments, to correspond to the plan size and composition. In this section, we will examine to what extent the Government has been effective in achieving these tasks and what have been the overall consequences of these measures on the economy.

The inability of the public sector to generate the savings required for investments necessitated the large scale transfer of resources from private to public sector. The mobilisation of resources and their transfer to the desired activities are crucial to successful plan implementation. But with major pressure groups influencing the pattern of resources mobilisation, achieving it in a cost-effective and non-inflationary manner has been difficult.

Resource Mobilisation through Taxes

Quantitatively, it must be stated that the tax system in India has largely fulfilled the role of mobilizing financial resources. The tax revenues over the years have grown steadily and as a ratio of GDP, increased from less than 7 per cent in 1950-51 to almost 17 per cent in 1991-92. However, difficulties in raising revenues through direct taxes on income and wealth have caused the spreading of the burden of development among the masses mainly through indirect taxes. In fact, the share of direct taxes declined from 37 per cent in 1950-51 to less than 16 per cent in 1991-92 (Table 4.7). At both central and State levels, revenue from indirect taxes presently constitute more than 80 per cent of tax revenue. Even within indirect taxes, the emphasis has been on easy and non-transparent means of tax collections. This has resulted in collecting taxes at the entry points by the Centre, the States and by the local bodies. In the case of the Centre, apart from the above reasons, the constitutional requirement that personal income tax and excise duty should be shared with the States has led them to concentrate on import duties as a revenue instrument. At the State level, the 'free-riding' behaviour of the States has resulted in rising inter-State tax exportation and this is aided by the constitutions permitting the levy of taxes on inter-State sales. At the local level too, it is easy to collect taxes on the entry of goods into urban areas by erecting barriers. The consequence of these has been to divide the country into several tariff zones with unintended effects on resource allocation and impediments to free movement of goods.

TABLE 4.7 : **Composition of Tax Revenue**

(1950-51 to 1991-92) (Percentages)

	1950-51	1960-61	1970-71	1980-81	1985-86	1990-91 (RE)	1991-92
1. Direct Taxes	36.8	29.8	21.21	16.5	14.4	14.0	15.8
1.1 Corporation Tax	6.3	8.1	7.8	6.6	6.6	6.1	7.1
1.2 Personal Income Tax	21.4	12.5	9.9	7.6	5.6	6.1	6.6
1.3 Other Taxes	9.1	9.2	3.5	2.3	2.0	1.8	2.1
2. Indirect Taxes	63.2	70.2	78.8	83.5	85.6	86.0	84.2
2.1 Customs	25.1	12.6	11.0	17.2	22.0	23.5	22.4
2.2 Union Excise Duties	10.8	30.8	37.0	32.7	30.0	27.9	27.0
2.3 State Excise Duty	8.0	4.1	4.3	4.5	5.1	5.7	5.5
2.4 Sales Taxes	9.3	12.1	16.6	20.2	20.2	20.8	21.3
2.6 Others	5.6	7.1	7.1	6.7	6.3	5.7	5.5
3. Total Taxes	100.0	100.0	100.0	100.0	100.0	100.0	100.0
4. Total tax as Percentage of GDP	6.7	8.3	11.0	14.6	16.5	16.5	16.8

Source: Indian Economic Statistics, Ministry of Finance, Government of India.

The practice of levying taxes in an easy and concealed manner ignoring the resource distortions, it can cause, is seen even in the levy of internal indirect taxes. In fact, there is a parallel regime of commodity taxes at all the three levels of Government – manufacturing excises at the centre, sales taxes at the State level and octroi levied by the urban local bodies[5]. This has created an overlapping system of taxes and as a significant portion of revenues is derived from taxing inputs and capital goods at all the three levels, a highly distortionary tax system has evolved over the years rendering Indian manufactures non-competitive.

At the State level, there have been other types of distortions. In their eagerness to raise more revenues in the way least painful to their residents, the States have indulged in acute inter-State tax competition to attract trade and industry into their jurisdictions. We have already referred to the 'free-rider' behaviour of the States and the resulting tax exportation. The consequence of these has been to make minute differentiation in the sales tax rates not based on economic rationality but simply to 'free-ride' on other States. This has complicated the structure of taxes, opened up several avenues of tax avoidance and evasion and distorted the relative prices.

Borrowing and Fiscal Deficits : Another method by which the Government has been financing consumption and investment expenditures has been through borrowing. As a proportion of GDP, the fiscal deficit steadily increased from 4.6 per cent in 1975-76, to reach almost 11 per cent in 1986-87 and thereafter, stabilised around 10-11 per cent until the programme of stabilisation was initiated in 1991-92 (Table 4.8). In addition to the steady increase in fiscal deficit-GDP ratio, two important features in the trends in deficit must be noted (Table 4.8). First, an increasing proportion of fiscal deficit was incurred to meet growing revenue deficits or governmental dissavings. The revenue deficits, which emerged for the first time in 1982-83, increased steadily to form 4.5 per cent of GDP in 1990-91. Second, an increasing proportion of the fiscal deficit has been monetised over the years. The monetised budget deficits increased from less than one per cent of GDP in the early 1960's to almost 4.7 per cent in 1986-87 and thereafter stabilised around 3.5 to 4 per cent until 1991-92. As a consequence of these trends, the ratio of outstanding public debt to GDP increased from 32 per cent in 1950-51 to about 65 per cent in 1991-92. With an increasing proportion of borrowing being used to meet consumption requirements and with the public investments not

TABLE 4.8 : **Deficits as a Percentage of GDP**

Year	Revenue Deficit (–)/ Surpluses	Budget Deficit (–)	Fiscal Deficit (–)
1971-72	–0.20	–1.72	–5.32
1975-76	+2.34	–0.46	–4.59
1981-82	+0.64	–1.58	–6.74
1985-86	–1.92	–1.31	–9.33
1986-87	–2.66	–3.13	–10.91
1987-88	–3.05	–1.65	–9.60
1988-89	3.11	–1.29	–9.06
1989-90	–3.40	–2.34	–9.48
1990-91	–4.46	–2.16	–10.04
1991-92	–3.67	–1.46	–8.03
1992-93 (RE)	–2.70	–1.02	–6.83

Note : RE indicates Revised Estimates.

Source: Indian Economic Statistics, Ministry of Finance, Government of India.

yielding commensurate economic returns, the vicious circle of growing deficits, rising debt, increasing interest costs and higher deficits was unavoidable. This self-propelling character has led governmental indebtedness to grow to unsustainable proportions (Chelliah, 1993, Buiter and Patel, 1992, Rangarajan, Basu and Jadhav, 1990). Further, pre-emption of funds from the nationalised banking sector for Government consumption and investment has led to distortions in the capital and financial markets.

Fiscal Policy and Redistribution

Economic activities in a mixed economy necessarily bring in inequalities in income and wealth[6]. The expansion of the public sector was intended, *inter alia,* to contain the concentration of wealth and incomes in the hands of a few persons and regions. But, in spite of the expansion of public sector investment, private sector's contribution of income generation was 75 to 80 per cent to achieve the desired state of distribution of incomes, a number of other fiscal and non-fiscal measures were adopted. In the sphere of inter-personal incomes, the important redistributive fiscal measures were, levying of progressive taxes, encouraging small scale industries as they are presumed to be employment intensive and adopting long-term and short-term poverty alleviation programmes by reorienting expenditure policies. To achieve balanced regional growth, the measures adopted consisted of equitable federal transfers and locating Central public enterprises in backward regions.

Fiscal Policy and Inter-personal Redistribution

For a long time, in bringing about vertical equity, the emphasis of fiscal policy in India was to reduce the incomes of the rich rather than on increasing the incomes of the poor. Until recently, apart from the highly progressive income tax with the highest marginal tax rates of 95 per cent, wealth tax was levied with the marginal rate going upto 8 per cent and the combined effect of the two on high income earners was confiscatory. Even after the marginal income tax rates of 95 per cent in the seventies to 54 per cent in the eighties, the combined incidence of the two taxes for the persons falling into the highest income bracket was nearly 70 per cent. Of course, since 1991-92, there has been a substantial rationalisation of the tax structure on the lines recommended by the Tax Reforms Committee (Government of India, 1992). With over 80 per cent of the revenue derived from indirect taxes, progressivity to the tax structure could be imparted only by making minute rate differentiation among commodities based on the judgments about their income elasticity of demand. Of course, the incidence studies done in a partial equilibrium framework show that the distribution of tax burden is moderately progressive (Ahmed and Stren, 1983; Jha and Srinivasan, 1988).

However, in a general equilibrium sense, it is doubtful whether the distribution of tax burden has been progressive, for various reasons. First, the highly progressive tax system created serious disincentives for income-earning activities and risk taking, and the consequent adverse effects on growth must have decelerated the growth of employment in the organised sector. The major consequence of the progressive taxes was widespread evasion and avoidance of income taxes. According to the best known study, the tax evaded income in 1985-86 constituted about 20 per cent of the reported GDP (Acharya, *et al.* 1985). It is also seen that the number of income tax assessees in 1989-90 formed just about 0.05 per cent of population, which meant that all attempts at having a progressive distribution of the tax burden was confined to a miniscule proportion of population. The minute rate bracketing in the case of income tax to obtain a continuously progressive distribution of the tax burden, and excessive rate differentiation in the case of excises and sales taxes enormously complicated the structure of these taxes. Thus, while the efficacy of the tax structure to redistribute incomes is doubtful, it has certainly led to complications in the tax structure, caused allocative distortions by altering relative prices in unintended ways and of course, led to the expansion of the illegal informal sector. These issues have been adequately addressed to in the report of the Tax Reform Committee. In particular, the Report has emphasised the need to expand the tax base to cover the income of the unorganised sector and hard-to-tax groups, though the progress in implementing these recommended measures has been limited.

A more important way in which redistribution is accomplished is by enhancing the incomes of the poor and that can be achieved by directing Government expenditures to programmes which would directly benefit the poor or endow them with capital in the medium or long term. Enhancing economic growth, and ensuring that its benefits trickle down to the poor, can complement the direct attack on poverty in a sustainable fashion. Indeed, there has been considerable expansion of direct poverty alleviation programmes in rural areas particularly since 1979-80 and despite the inefficiencies and leakages in these anti-poverty programmes, they have contributed to the reduction in the incidence of poverty over the years (Minhas, Jain and Tendulkar, 1991). However, the amount of money spent on these short-term relief measures in 1987-88 in per capita terms worked out to a mere Rs. 25 in 1981-82 prices. Adding to this the money spent on primary educations and health, the total redistributive package works out to a mere Rs. 97 per capita which is less than 10 per cent of total expenditures. This is even lower than the per capita amount spent on interest payments (Rs. 150), defence (Rs. 100) and other general administrative services (Rs. 148).

Fiscal Policy and Balanced Regional Growth

An important goal of planning in India was to bring about balanced regional development and reduce inter-regional disparities in the levels of living. To achieve this, fiscal policies can be employed in two ways: first, by allocating centre's own investments in the public sector on the desired lines, and second, through a well-designed policy on federal transfers to the States so that each State, howsoever deficient, is enabled to have given normative levels of social and economic infrastructure at a standard tax-price (effective tax rate). Our analysis shows that the spread of Central Government's own investments in public enterprises have not adequately taken account of inter-regional disparities (Table 4.9). Over 24 per cent of the gross block of capital in Central public enterprises was located in high income States as on 31st March, 1990 though these States had the population of only 18.8 per cent of the total. In contrast, in the low income States with 43.3 per cent of total population, the capital stock of central public enterprises was just 34.1 per cent and the direct employment generated in these enterprises was only 42 per cent of the total employment generated by the central public enterprises[7]. Nor were the federal transfers designed to offset the fiscal disabilities of the poorer States. Although the Finance Commission's transfers were progressively distributed, this was not adequate to offset their inherent disabilities and consequently, the plan expenditure during the seventh plan (like the earlier plans) had a regressive distribution (Table 4.10). The average per capita plan outlay in the high income States was 66 per cent higher than the all-State average and that of low income States lower by 12 per cent. In the event, it is not surprising that the States with higher infant mortality and low life expectancy at birth had lower per capita spending on health services, States with lower literacy rates had lower expenditure per child (5 years to 11 years) on elementary education and

States with low per capita income from the industrial sector had low per capita allocation on economic infrastructure like energy, irrigation, transport and communication. It is, therefore, not surprising that the regional disparities have continued to persist in India.

TABLE 4.9 : **Statewise Distribution of Capital Stock (Gross Block) and Employment in Public Sector Enterprises as on 31.3.1990**

(in Percentage)

	Population*	Gross Block	Employment
High Income States	18.77	24.1	13.39
Punjab	2.38	0.74	1.01
Haryana	1.96	0.79	0.79
Maharashtra	9.02	17.58	9.81
Gujarat	4.91	4.99	2.32
Middle Income States	31.34	25.31	32.38
Karnataka	5.42	2.28	5.24
West Bengal	7.88	6.25	17.51
Andhra Pradesh	7.68	10.07	4.34
Tamil Nadu	6.76	5.21	3.38
Kerala	3.60	1.50	1.46
Low Income States	43.33	34.13	42.31
Rajasthan	5.30	1.51	1.72
Madhya Pradesh	7.67	11.10	12.48
Uttar Pradesh	16.28	7.76	6.17
Orissa	3.76	5.26	3.27
Bihar	10.32	8.50	18.67
Special Category States	5.23	7.47	3.61
Union Territories	1.33	8.99	7.77
Others and Unallocated	–	4.92	1.56

* Mid-Year estimates.

Sources:

1. Public Enterprises Survey, 1989-90 (Vol. 1), Ministry of Programme Implementation, Government of India.
2. Office of the Registrar General, Government of India.

Table 4.10 : **Per Capita Federal Fiscal Transfers and Plan Outlay in the States**

States	Per Capita SDP Avg. (1982-83) (Rs.)	Index Taxable Capacity 1984-85	States Own resources for the Plan Before Statutory Transfers	Statutory Transfers, Shared Taxes & FC Grants	(Rupees) At Constant (1981-82) Prices: Non-Plan Loans	States own Loans for the Plan After Statutory Transfers	Central Plan Assistance Including Centrally Sponsored Schemes	Plan Outlay
(1)	(2)	(3)	(4) (7–6–5)	(5)	(6) (9–8)	(7)	(8)	(9)
High Income States	3340	146.30	–134.24	321.24	534.83	722.02	533.18	1255.20
Punjab	4013	169.18	–459.28	280.45	318.05	139.23	1131.83	1271.06
Maharashtra	3384	142.75	229.72	316.24	509.77	1055.73	233.52	1289.25
Haryana	3043	151.11	–175.07	344.39	570.99	740.31	463.18	1203.49
Gujarat	2919	122.16	–132.35	344.62	740.53	952.79	304.20	1256.99
Middle Income States	2206	112.82	–271.46	439.65	255.78	423.96	227.88	651.84

Karnataka	2461	117.68	–49.98	389.70	112.06	451.76	213.36	655.12
West Bengal	2230	76.09	–421.11	483.04	278.40	340.34	140.56	480.90
Kerala	2144	117.66	–521.60	440.26	380.98	299.65	308.19	607.84
Tamil Nadu	2142	138.64	–186.56	439.21	316.60	569.25	229.51	798.59
A.P.	2053	114.04	–178.07	446.02	190.87	458.82	247.77	706.59
Low Income States	1689	50.06	–265.69	472.19	171.11	377.60	287.94	665.55
M.P.	1860	58.14	–139.69	422.13	227.32	509.75	200.00	709.79
Rajasthan	1820	67.46	–380.23	389.99	291.74	301.50	421.77	709.76
Orissa	1728	37.72	–250.75	582.07	126.74	301.50	421.77	23.27
U.P.	1713	54.14	–256.19	440.86	143.54	328.21	272.18	00.39
Bihar	1323	32.85	–301.61	525.89	66.20	290.49	235.21	25.70
14 States' Average	2345	99.97	–211.92	428.94	261.35	478.36	276.90	755.27

Source: Column 1 and 2 : Second Report of the Ninth Finance Commission. (Ministry of Finance, Government of India, 1990. Other columns: Finance/Planning Department of the State Governments.

Fiscal Policy for Development : Lessons from Indian Experience

The broad review of public finances and Indian Economic Development attempted above has brought to the fore many interesting lessons on development policy. In comparison with the socio-economic environment that prevailed before independence, the achievements after independence are certainly notable. Surely, the adoption of planned strategy has hastened the developmental process in the economy and the public finance instruments have played a crucial role in this task. Yet, one cannot help the feeling that the rigidities imposed by the development strategy have constrained the economy from reaching its full potential and the Indian performance compares poorly with the experiences of the countries of the South East Asian region and China. The major difference in the strategies must be found in the role of the State. The review of successful developmental experiences of these countries shows that the State in these countries undertook to (i) monitor the competition in markets by enforcing property rights through an effective system of regulation; (ii) assisted and encouraged entrepreneurial competition to produce and to export; and (iii) provided adequate social and economic infrastructural facilities. In contrast, controlling the allocation of resources by the State acting as a direct participant in the production-distribution network and directing the private sector allocation through various policy instruments has curbed entrepreneurial competition in India and this has not served the cause of either growth or equity. Governmental intervention in India has been to a large extent negative in nature, preventing various activities rather than encouraging them. Such negative intervention should have been reserved only for activities causing harm to the society, but were indiscriminately used through widespread controls.

The problem with the Indian developmental strategy is not the lack of internal inconsistency of the plan models. Of course, many of the assumptions made in the plans were not fulfilled in practice and there were serious problems of implementation. The most important problem, however, was the basic assumption that the State is a benevolent entity and relentlessly works towards maximizing the welfare of its citizens. In a democratic polity which is relatively stable, electoral competition leads to the emergence of coalitions or special interest groups. The individuals with a common agenda having organisational abilities disproportionate to their numerical strength form interest groups for collective action and they work to influence policies to enhance their share of benefits from public services while trying to minimise their share of payments to the services to the Government (contractors or government employees) and their successful action results in enhancing the cost of public service provision. The interest group may also attempt to influence policies and their implementation to direct the benefits in their favour and this is typically done by enhancing allocation to quasi-public goods, subsidies and transfers benefiting indentifiable groups. In the Indian context, low and declining cost recoveries, declining importance of direct taxes, increasing resort to inflation tax and passing on the burden to the unenfranchised sections by taking recourse to heavy borrowing can be easily explained by the above phenomenon. The low and declining efficiency of public enterprises too can be traced to this phenomenon. On the expenditure side too, sharp increases in wages and salaries, subsidies and transfers and declining expenditures on infrastructural facilities can be attributed to this phenomenon. These trends come out sharply during periods of hard budget constraint (Rao and Sen, 1993).

The above observation leads to the conclusion that the issue is not whether there should be more or less or State intervention but the quality of intervention. Unhampered interest group action can lead to over expansion of the activities beneficial to them, but this may be achieved by displacing socially productive expenditures or social and economic infrastructure having a strong complementarily with the private sector. The success of the South East Asian economies must be attributed to the positive role the State has taken in encorcing the property rights and complementing the market by providing goods and services with high degree of externalities including spending on human resource development.

Indeed, even within the given constraints it is possible to bring about certain improvements to improve efficiency and growth in the Indian economy. For example, making the tax system simple and transparent will help in directing the burden on the targeted sections; higher cost-recoveries on public services and targeting the subsidies and transfers to the intended groups can also improve efficiency and accountability. Detailed studies on equity and efficiency implications done in the general equilibrium framework, and public debates on the results of such studies can help in choosing the right set of policies. This can help reorienting the Government expenditure benefits to more encompassing groups. More importantly, the multilateral lending institutions can play a crucial role in prescribing the right set of policies (not 'omnibus' policies) suiting the objective conditions prevailing in the country.

An important aspect of fiscal policy relevant to any developing country like India, but often ignored in economic analyses, is the implementation and administration of the set of policies decided upon. Tax administration is hampered by a substantial non-monetised sector, and low levels of literacy causing lack of proper account keeping and lower tax compliance. Under development manifests itself in the administrative machinery also; there is only a limited use of modern technology and modern management practices. Vestiges of feudalism and years of subjugation have made sections of the population completely passive; they do not fight for what is rightfully theirs. These make designs succeed because of almost insurmountable hijack benefits meant for the poor; their designs succeed because of almost insurmountable difficulties in adopting selection procedures like means testing. The only sure way to target benefits under these circumstances is to build in as much self selection as possible. The institutional set-up also comes in the way of efficient administration. For example, tax disputes often take twenty years to be decided, as the courts are overloaded. Under these circumstances, simplicity is not only a virtue, it is necessity. For the same reasons, a certain degree of stability in the tax regime is also required. But neither of these qualities mark Indian public finance. The federal structure further complicates the fiscal scenario, because different levels of Government, and different units of Government at the same level do not necessarily work with a unity of purpose. These problems are, however, not unique to India, and can probably be tackled through a judicious mixture of perseverance, ingenuity, and advice from those who have successfully dealt with similar problems.

NOTES

1. The capital formation in the public sector in 1991-92 formed about 45 per cent of gross domestic capital formation. During the 1970s it was even higher, close to 50 per cent. The share of public sector enterprises in this was approximately 75 to 80 per cent.
2. The terms 'current' expenditure and revenue' expenditure are used interchangeably.
3. This is not to imply that there is no scope for tax reform, even with the specific objective of raising resources. Corporate income tax receipts, for example, show little increase in real terms when only the private sector is considered.
4. For a more detailed analysis of public enterprises, see, Ahluwalia (1993).
5. Octroi is a tax on the entry of goods into a local area for consumption, use or sale.
6. In terms of Myrdal (1957), the 'backwash effects' necessarily outweigh 'spread effects' in less developed economics in the context of regional development.
7. Typically, in poorer states, a sizable part of the employment generated does not benefit the residents of that state due to the lack of necessary skills among locally available workers.

5

PUBLIC ENTERPRISE IN A RESTRUCTURING ECONOMY

VINOD VYASULU

I

The 90s promises to be a decade of continuing change. Internationally, the end of the 80s saw sweeping changes across the world. The Second World, that champion of the public sector, suddenly collapsed and ceased to exist. A super power like the erstwhile USSR, after tentative experiments with perestroika, simply disintegrated[1]. There were changes in the relative power balances among the industrialized nations, with Japan and Germany claiming a larger share of influence in world affairs. US fortunes declined, especially after the Vietnam War. The delinking of the dollar from gold in 1971, an essential ingredient of the Bretton Woods accords, is dramatic acknowledgment of the beginning of this decline. The post war political equations, perpetuated in the Bretton Woods Institutions, are rapidly changing: witness the new role of the GATT in the Uruguay Round and the dramatic loss of influences of UNCTAD. The role of the United Nations is also changing, as the Iraq war tragically showed. This process of modification of international relations will accelerate in the 90s.

While all this was happening abroad, the Indian economy in the 80s, and particularly in the late 80s, experienced relatively rapid growth in what may then have seemed an unchanging environment. It is only in this decade that this country exceeded a growth rate of 5 per cent per year (Nagaraj, 1990a; 1991a). This was the result of many factors including some gradual changes in the system of economic management (Rangarajan, 1991; Ahluwalia, 1991). But the end of the 80s saw Government finances in crisis (Vyasulu & Chokkalingam, 1989 and Vyasulu *et al.*, 1991). Much of the blame for the resources crunch was laid on the public sector and its supposed inefficiency (Ahluwalia, 1991). Adhoc and emergency measures, such as pledging gold to the Bank of England as security for loans, were resorted to till the elections of 1991, which resulted in a new Government being formed. And from July 1991, India too began to experience rapid change especially in terms of deregulation, liberalization, privatization and globalization. India had fallen in line with the rest of the world. To borrow a phrase from the Managing Director of the IMF, "the tigerization of India" had begun.

Interestingly, the most rapid changes in our society and economy have come from a minority Government. The Rajiv Gandhi Government, with its bulldozer majority in Parliament, did not attempt anything this radical. These changes involve the abandonment of the goal of self-reliance set before the country during the freedom struggle in favour of efficiency in the market as measured by profits. It involves facilitating private enterprise, particularly by the shrinking of Government activity whenever possible. These reforms bring India in line with a host of less developed countries which have decided to globalize using the World Bank-IMF strategy of stabilization and structural adjustment (Krishna Kumar, 1993; Gulati, 1993). These changes involve a reduction in Government deficits largely by reducing the role of Government in society: quite in contrast to what prevailed in the 70s and 80s when Government could do no wrong. Quite clearly, we live in a time of change; and the coming years will belong to those who can adapt to this change in a purposeful way. Public enterprise in particular, faces major challenges in the emerging scenario.

This chapter attempts to examine the role that public enterprise may be expected to play in this changing world. First, I look at the context of change; this is followed by a brief overview of the content of change. Then dimensions such as the sequencing and pace of change are addressed. In this background, issues of the management of change are identified. The chapter concludes with an indicative and tentative agenda of research.

II

It is important to understand the context of change clearly if we are to develop a strategy to cope successfully with the emerging challenges. The post-independence inheritance saw, in what now seems to be a rather simple minded way, the merits of Government intervention in the economy. Interestingly enough, the private industrialists of India had a stake in building up a large public sector. One needs only refer to the experience of Mysore under Visveswaraiah and later to the Bombay Plan of 1944, drafted by India's major industrialists, to realize this[2]. At the same time, another stream, drawing inspiration from the experience of the Soviet Union after 1917, developed an abiding belief that planning could do what the market could not. The socialist tradition or the Marxist tradition, which gives heavy weightage to equity in human affairs, saw the abolition of private property as a necessary precondition for the establishment of a just social order (Patnaik, 1990). In the minds of many, the public sector did just that. In India, therefore, we had a confluence of interests among various groups on the need to establish a vibrant public sector that held the "commanding heights of the economy"[3].

The major groups in Indian society after 1947, each for its own reasons, wanted a strong and growing public sector. Nehru clarified through the Industrial Policy Resolution of 1948 that this growing public sector would be established *de novo* and not through the nationalization of existing enterprises. This was meant to reassure foreign capital. And it succeeded in doing so.

For the private industrialist, interested in quick profits and without the means and ability to undertake large investments, the public sector represented technological and manufacturing expertise on the foundation of which he or she could build his or her private business empire: in post-Independence India, the level of private investment has depended on public investment (Nayyar, 1993). What was attractive to him or her was that he or she would get the benefits of a strong industrial base that would be paid for by the general public[4].

For the socialist, this policy was seen as an ideological victory. He was against private property. The opposite of private property was Government ownership, as Soviet experience taught. And through Government ownership, he saw a role for a rational system of planning that would take the country in the desired direction: a socialistic pattern of society[5]. The Planning Unit of the Indian Statistical Institute in Delhi brought together the best minds in this tradition to work on problems of Indian development – Bettleheim, Baran Kelecki and many others. And hence the strategy of the Second Five Year Plan, technically called the Mahalanobis model[6].

For the bureaucrat and the educated Indian, the commitment to a strong public sector meant an opportunity for secure employment and an increasing influence in the affairs of the State, as evidenced by the ballooning of the Government's salary payments. The share of Public

Administration grew from Rs. 3179 crores in 1970 to Rs.9713 crores in 1989, at 1980-81 prices (Table 5.1).

TABLE 5.1 : **NDP by Industry Origin and Growth Rates**

	(in Rs. crores)			Percent Growth		
	1970-71	80-81 (At 1980-81 Prices)	88-89	1970-71 to 79-80	80-81 to 88-89	70-71 to 88-89
Agriculture	34545	40056	54477	1.80	2.80	2.60
Forestry	3547	3229	3026	–0.60	–1.30	–1.40
Fishing	619	806	1138	2.80	4.80	3.20
Mining	1027	1474	2077	3.20	3.20	3.90
Manufacturing (Regtd.)	6946	10050	19466	5.00	8.10	5.90
Manufacturing (Unregtd.)	5817	8648	13540	4.50	5.40	4.40
Electricity	567	912	1838	6.00	8.50	6.10
Construction	4271	5771	7509	3.10	3.30	3.40
Trade	9556	14322	23248	4.70	5.80	5.00
Transport	1946	3724	6545	7.00	7.20	6.70
Banking	1783	3344	8366	7.50	11.60	8.30
Real Estate	4313	5920	8047	3.20	3.90	3.40
Public Administration	3179	5370	9392	4.70	7.50	5.90
Others	5056	6777	9713	2.80	4.30	3.60
Total	83712	110340	168382	3.20	4.90	3.90

Source: Mohanty Deepak (1992): Growth and Productivity in the Indian Economy. *RBI Occasional Papers*, Vol. 13, No. 2, 1992.

Thus, what was built up was a system of Government ownership, and centralized regulation through the bureaucracy, which, it must be admitted, did, in the early years, strengthen the economic base of the country. Production capabilities were built up across a wide range of major industries (Bhagavan, 1985). However, with the failure of land reforms and continuance of exploitative relations in agriculture, a foreign exchange crisis, and so on, the vast rural and agricultural sector acted as a break, and the economy ran into a crisis when there were major famines by the end of the 60s. One has only to refer to the debates on the 1966 devaluation, on PL480 loans, etc., to see this. Reports of the Industrial Licensing Policy Inquiry Committee and the Planning Commission's studies on licensing (ILPIC, 1969, Hazari 1985) made recommendations that were not mutually consistent to regulate monopoly and to reform licensing. The need for a two-year Plan Holiday after the Third Five Year Plan becomes clear.

Of course, this crisis of the 1960s was complicated by wars with China (1962) and Paksitan (1965, 1972). But they were additional factors in precipitating the crisis: they resulted in defence expenditure increasing at the cost of development and thus aggravating the situation.

At that point of time (after the 3rd Plan) the way out was through the green revolution technology in agriculture which through the 70s supported a modest rate of the growth of the economy. During this time, the growth of the public sector was not by the establishment of new enterprises but by the acquisition of sick units in the private sector as in textiles and through measures like the nationalization of banks and coal mines. The purpose was no longer creation of new production capacity but employment protection based on union pressure and political populism. By the end of the 70s, the system had run out of steam (Shetty 1978) and once again the bureaucratic regulatory system came under fire. The Emergency of the mid-70s, had shown up the limitations of "baburaj". The late 70s were, to use a felicitous phrase from Isher Ahluwalia (1991) "Years of reflection in economic policy making".

All this can be illustrated by readily available data . Table 6.1, which looks at growth rates of net domestic product by sector, for the 70s and 80s, shows a 1 percentage point increase in the average growth rate in agriculture in the 80s (from 1.8 per cent in seventies to 2.8 per cent in eighties); a 3.1 percentage point higher rate in registered manufacturing; a 2.5 percentage point increase in electricity; and over 4 percentage points in banking. What is clear is that the growth rates for 1970-71 to 1988-89 are, in general, well above the growth rate for 1970-71 to 1979-80 – clearly, the 80s were good for growth.

The picture is similar for growth rates of Net domestic capital stock, as Table 5.2 shows – except in agriculture, where the evidence suggests that investment has been falling (Shetty, 1990; Mallick, 1993).

TABLE 5.2 : **Net Domestic Capital Stock by Industry Use**

	(Rs. Crores)			Percent Growth		
	1970-71 (At 1980-81 Prices)	1980-81	1988-89	1970-71 to 1979-80	1980-81 to 1988-89	1970-71 to 88-89
Agriculture	49539	66563	78857	2.70	2.10	2.70
Forestry	728	923	1559	1.90	6.70	4.60
Fishing	433	558	936	2.20	6.70	4.20
Mining	3108	6921	19263	8.20	12.90	11.20
Manufactu -ring (Regtd.)	27268	51248	82465	6.20	5.70	6.20
Manufactu-ring (Unregtd.)	6765	16612	27299	9.40	6.00	7.60
Electricity	14341	25672	49282	5.50	8.10	6.80
Construction	1828	3300	6084	5.10	6.60	7.70
Trade	5719	20144	42058	13.60	8.60	11.60
Transport	1485	28714	40632	3.20	4.40	3.40
Banking	800	1254	4259	4.50	4.80	8.30
Real Estate	68291	77955	91864	1.30	2.00	1.70
Public administration	20542	31768	47146	4.60	5.00	4.60
Others	4844	646	9610	2.70	4.90	3.80
Total	225691	338093	501314	4.00	4.80	4.50

Source : Mohanty Deepak (1992): Growth and Productivity in the Indian Economy *RBI Occasional Papers*, Vol. 13, No. 2, 1992.

But, disturbingly, total factor productivity did not increase significantly. Brahmananda (1982) pointed this out a decade ago. Over the economy, Mohanty (1992) shows that it was Minus 0.0035 in the seventies and minus 0.0039 in the eighties (Table 5.3). It was negative in registered manufacturing in both decades. Thus, the quality of growth was not satisfactory. And this at a time when employment did not follow growth. Ajit (1992) shows that the growth rate differential between employment and net value added in Industry was –6.4 in 1981-88 compared to –2.3 between 1971-80 (Table 5.4). Growth rates of employment in most sectors and in the economy as a whole, slowed down in the eighties (Table 5.5). This is a serious problem in India which has a fast growing labour force on a large population base.

TABLE 5.3 : **Growth Rates of NDP, Domestic Capital Stock and TEP**

	Net Domestic Product			Net Domestic Capital Stock			T. Factor Productivity (TEP)		
	1970-71 to 1979-80	1980-81 to 1988-89	1970-71 to 1988-89	1970-71 to 1979-80	1980-81 to 1988-89	1970-71 to 1988-89	1970-71 to 1979-80	1980-81 to 1988-89	1970-71 to 1988-89
Agriculture	1.8	2.8	2.6	2.7	2.1	2.7	0.0030	0.0020	0.0240
Forestry	–0.6	–1.3	–1.4	1.9	6.7	4.6	0.0001	–0.0200	0.0130
Fishing	2.8	4.8	3.2	2.2	6.7	4.2	–0.0001	0.0042	0.0620
Mining	3.2	3.2	3.9	8.2	12.9	11.2	0.0015	0.0004	0.0120
Manufacturing (Regtd.)	5.0	8.1	5.9	6.2	5.7	6.2	–0.0030	–0.0065	0.0092
Manufacturing (Unregtd.)	4.5	5.4	4.4	9.4	6.0	7.6	–0.0006	0.0003	0.0850
Electricity	6.0	8.5	6.1	5.5	8.1	6.8	0.0008	–0.0003	0.0180
Construction	3.1	3.3	3.4	5.1	6.6	7.7	0.1800	0.0003	0.0750
Trade	4.7	5.8	5.0	13.6	8.6	11.6	0.0008	0.0007	0.0490
Transport	7.0	7.2	6.7	3.2	4.0	3.4	0.0002	0.0015	0.0190
Banking	7.5	11.6	8.3	4.5	14.8	8.3	–0.0030	0.0010	0.0040
Real Estate	3.2	3.9	3.4	1.3	2.0	1.7	0.0060	0.0005	0.0004
Public adminis-tration	4.7	7.5	5.9	4.6	5.0	4.6	0.0020	0.0026	–0.0090
Others	2.8	4.3	3.6	2.7	4.9	3.8	–0.0010	–0.0007	0.0036
Total	3.2	4.9	3.9	4.0	4.8	4.5	–0.0035	–0.0039	–0.0001

Source : Mohanty Deepak (1992); Growth and Productivity in the Indian Economy *RBI Occasional Papers*, Vol.13, No. 2, 1992.

TABLE 5.4 : **Rate of Growth of Industrial Output and Employment**

(percent per annum)

Period	Employment	NVA	GRD Real
1960/70	3.7	5.3	–1.6
1971/80	4.3	6.6	–2.3
1974/80	4.7	8.3	–3.6
1981/88	–0.4	6.0	–6.4
1974/88	1.9	5.9	–4.0
1960/88	3.1	5.6	–2.5

Note : GRD - Growth Rate Differential

Source: Ajit, D(1992): "*Industrial Growth and Employment: An Analysis of Labour Absorption in Manufacturing Section in India*" RBI Staff Studies, Dec. 1992, DEAP, RBI.

TABLE 5. 5 : **Labour Units by Industry**

	(in Rs. Thousands)			Percent Growth		
	1970-71	80-81	88-89	70-71 to 79-80	80-81 to 88-89	70-71 to 88-89
Agriculture	127569	154307	166102	1.90	0.90	1.50
Forestry	147	232	250	4.60	0.90	3.00
Fishing	583	958	1031	5.00	0.90	3.30
Mining	915	1446	2306	4.60	5.80	5.10
Manufacturing (Regtd.)	5045	5672	5850	1.20	0.40	0.80
Manufacturing (Unregtd.)	11789	19350	24370	5.00	2.90	4.00
Electricity	514	1017	1486	6.80	4.70	5.90
Construction	2444	4172	9321	5.20	10.00	7.40
Trade	894	12584	13768	3.40	1.10	2.50
Transport	430	6181	8797	3.60	4.40	3.90
Banking	539	1067	1536	6.80	4.50	5.90
Real Estate	294	491	707	5.10	4.50	4.90
Public administration	874	5854	7011	1.80	2.30	2.00
Others	0301	12621	14764	2.00	2.00	2.00
Total	78251	225952	257298	2.40	1.60	2.00

Source: Mohanty Deepak (1992); Growth and Productivity in the Indian Economy *RBI Occasional Papers*, Vol. 13, No. 2, 1992.

The private sector has enjoyed growth piggy-backing on the investment in the public sector. At the same time, there was an enormous growth in the bureaucracy, in Government and government related departments and undertakings[7]. This was also the time when, in a burst of socialistic fervour, in the midst of an economic crisis, laws like the MRTPA (1969) and FERA (1973)[8] were passed and the ambit of controls increased. What Anne Krueger calls the rent-seeking system[9] was gradually getting into place replacing the idealism of the earlier generation that was part of the freedom movement. The pricing of services provided by public enterprise was manipulated to provide subsidies to various groups, without thought to cost or efficiency considerations (Mundle and Rao, 1991, for an estimate of the size of subsidies; Vyasulu and Gadgil, 1992, for reflections on consequences).

Quite clearly these bureaucratic regulations, which became synonymous with Planning, had begun to act as a fetter to the growth process. The crisis emerging at the end of the 70s was averted by recourse to foreign capital, at first concessional, and later commercial, then to internal borrowings and then again to foreign loans. India took its first large loan from the IMF in 1981 when there was no emergency or crisis, a fact that seems to have been forgotten today. This pattern is clearly seen in the increasing deficits in the Government budget in the 1980s (Table 5.6). The revenue deficit, as a per cent of GDP at market prices was 1.1 per cent in the 6th Plan but 2.6 per cent in the 7th Plan. The gross fiscal deficit was, 6.3 per cent and 8.2 per cent in the 6th and 7th Plans respectively. The growth rate of the 80s was financed at least in large part on a liquidity overhang through government deficits and through external borrowings which eventually led to the balance of payments crisis at the end of the 80s (Table 5.7) and of course, to inflationary pressures that aggravated the situation all around. This borrowing abroad has burdened the country with a heavy repayment schedule (Tabel 5.8) which could only have gotten worse since 1991.

TABLE 5. 6 : **Deficit of the Central Government**

(as % of GDP at Current Market Prices)

	Budget Deficit	Revenue Deficit	Monitored Deficit	Gross Fiscal Deficit
1975-76	0.5	1.1	0.3	4.1
1980-81	1.9	1.5	2.6	6.2
1981-82	0.9	0.2	2.0	5.4
1982-83	0.9	0.7	1.9	6.0
1983-84	0.7	1.2	1.9	6.3
1984-85	1.6	1.8	2.6	7.5
Average Sixth Plan	1.2	1.1	2.2	6.3
1985-86	2.0	2.2	2.4	8.3
1986-87	2.8	2.7	2.4	9.0
1987-88	1.7	2.7	2.0	8.1
1988-89	1.4	2.7	1.6	7.8
1989-90	2.4	2.6	3.1	7.9
Average Seventh Plan	2.1	2.6	2.3	8.2
1990-92 (RE)	2.0	3.3	2.8	8.2
1990-91 (Provisional Act)	2.1	3.5	2.8	8.4
1991-92 (BE)	1.3	2.3	1.3	6.2

Source: Economic Survey, Ministry of Finance, 1991-92, p.3.

TABLE 5.7 : **India's Overall BOP-Deficit: 1970-1990**

Period	Current Account (In Rs. Crores)	Capital Account	Total
1970/71	–445.4	502.3	–21.7
1980/81	–1656.6	916.4	–358.0
1985/86	–5927.3	4893.7	–1286.6
1986/87	–5830.0	5899.4	–602.9
1987/88	–6292.6	7493.1	–8.5
1988/89	–10410.0	10304.6	–1652.7
1989/90	–9823.8	10771.0	–512.4

Source: RBI (1991) : Report on Currency and Finance 1990/91.

It has often been argued that the growing fiscal crisis is due to the inefficiency in public sector enterprises and Government. This has been suggested time and again. But this may not be fully true, at least in the case of public sector enterprises. [The story of Government finances is something else]. A disaggregated analysis of public sector performance in eighties is available. Even if we disagree with his methodology and recognise all the qualifications, it is worth of quoting Nagaraj (1991b) in some detail.

TABLE 5.8 : **Projected Debt Service payments on the Basis of Debt Outstanding As on March 31,1991.**

	Actuals			Projected				
Items	1988-89	1989-90	1990-91	1991-92	1992-93	1993-94	1994-95	1995-96
External Assistance								
Principal				1831	2056	2096	2255	2356
Interest				1476	1688	2009	1998	1964
External Commercial Borrowing								
Principal				1116	1386	1624	1814	1996
Interest				1050	997	918	804	676
IMF								
Repurchases				483*	340	187	919	907
Charges				225*	175	148	136	71
NRI Deposits FCNR								
Principal				3362	1592	1258	626	-
Interest				505	328	178	59	-
NRI Deposits NRER								
Principal				210	929	322	400	357
Interest				375	354	261	229	189
Total	6069	6226	6616	10633	9845	8951	9240	8516
Principal	3159	2944	3206	7002	6303	5437	6016	5616
Interest	2917	3282	3610	8631	3542	3514	3226	2990

*Actuals

Note : Principal repayments and purchases are projected based on repayment or repurchase Schedule. Interest payment on external assistance and commercial borrowings (those at fixed interest rate) are estimated based on the interest indicated in loan agreements. Interest on commercial borrowings (those at floating rates), FCNR/ NR (E) A deposits and charges payable to IMF are estimated on the basis of the latest rates. Principal repayments under NRI deposits are based on a quick survey of selected banks.

Source : Reproduced from EPW Research Foundation, EPW, June 5, 1993.

"... India's economic performance in terms of real (measured) GDP has shown a distinctly higher trend growth rate since 1980-81 and the decade ended with a growth rate of 5.3 per cent per annum. There is little evidence to suggest a decline in the trend growth rate of GDP originating in public sector since 1980-81; nor of a statistically unambiguous increase in that of private sector ..."

"... An improvement in some aspects of public sector performance in the 80s could be, among other factors, an important explanation for the higher trend growth rate of manufacturing industries ..."

"... As a result of shift in public investment, infrastructure industries have shown a distinct improvement in this output growth in 80s ..."

"... Contribution of gross savings of public sector declined steadily since 1976-77. But among different constituents of public sector, the contribution of non-departmental enterprises has in fact steadily increased especially so since 1980-81 – although from an extremely low base. Correspondingly, the share of savings of administrative departments declined sharply since 1981-82 turning negative since 1984-85 ..."

"... Gross savings of Non Departmental Enterprises (NDE) has steadily increased from around 1 per cent in 1966-67 to over 5 per cent of GDP savings in 1986-87. The relatively sharper increase, since 1980-81, in the rate of savings is unambiguously more pronounced with respect to Non-Departmental Non-Financial (NDNF) enterprises. Saving of NDNF enterprises increased not only as a proportion of gross domestic saving but also as a proportion of gross domestic capital formation in that sector, thus suggesting that an increasing share of internal resources in financing public investment and a corresponding decline in the share of borrowed funds ..."

"... The share of internal resources in financing Gross Domestic Capital Formation (GDCF) of NDNFs declined during the period 1969-70 and 1980-81 from around 25 per cent of GDCF to about 15 per cent, shows an unambiguous increase thereafter attaining a level of 43 per cent in 1988-89. Profitability of Central Government PSEs defined as profit as a proportion of total capital employed, increase sharply from around 8 per cent in 1980-81 to about 13 per cent in the following year and remained roughly at that level, with perhaps a marginal decline towards the end of the decade ..."

"... But the profitability of PSEs, excluding petroleum industry – ignoring the sharp dip in 1983-84 for which we have no explanation

– shows a steady increase since 1977-78, reaching a figure of about 9 per cent in 1989-90 . . .".

Nagaraj's analysis clearly vindicates the PSEs from the blanket criticism of inefficiency that has been levelled at them. It is the Administrative departments whose expenditures are rising which have contributed most to the fiscal crisis – a point made in a different context by Vyasulu, *et al.*, (1991). The data do not support the popular view of public sector inefficiency.

Thus, the changes that are needed today after the short term balance of payments crisis is averted are a focus on productivity and employment and it is this that the changes initiated in July 1991, are meant to usher in (Panchamukhi, 1992).

The changing economic thinking in the Government circles, especially towards Planning and the role of public sector can be captured in the words of C. Rangarajan, Governor, RBI, who spoke at IPE on 8th March 1993[10]. To quote:

> ". . . The changing role of Government is fully reflected in the Eighth Five-Year Plan, which mentions that planning in India will be increasingly `indicative'. In fact, planning in our country in a large measure has been indicative. An outstanding example of indicative planning in this country is planning for agriculture. Agriculture is a sector where millions of farmers take their independent decisions. However, when self-sufficiency in food was set as a goal, Government went about creating conditions in which the farmers would take such decisions in their own interest which would help in achieving the targets. This is a successful example of policy influencing private behaviour to achieve public goals. The area of indicative planning will further enlarge in future. The 'prescriptive' component will come down as the `indicative' component rises.

In order to give some concreteness to the changing role of public sector, the Eighth Plan has identified the principles governing public sector investments. These are:

(a) The public sector should make investment only in those areas where investment is of main infrastructural in nature and where private sector participants are not likely to come forth to an adequate extent within a reasonable time perspective;

(b) The public sector must withdraw from the areas where no public purpose is served by its presence; and

(c) The principle of market economy should be accepted as the main operative principle by all public sector enterprises unless the commodities and services produced and distributed are specifically for protecting the poorest in the society".

The fiscal crisis is real; but the contribution of PSEs to this crisis has been overstated. And their role in coming out of it needs greater discussion and clarity. It is encouraging that the debate has at last begun.

III

Just as there was an overall agreeement about the need for a national strategy of development after Independence, which had built into it an important role for the public sector, there was similarly a widespread feeling at the end of the 80s that the centralized system which had been built up over the years and which had resulted in the BOP crisis had to change. Some called this system Planning[11]. It is important to remember that this agreement, if it can be called that, was on the negative proposition: that is, the existing system had to change. There were differences among scholars and policy makers about the kind of change that was needed.

There was also a certain amount of despair and despondency in the beginning of 1990 about the magnitude of the problem and our ability to cope with it. This sense of despair was compounded by irrational (sectional) demands in society and irresponsible decisions on them by the Government. One cannot ask for a more striking example of irresponsibility than the loan waivers granted by the Government in 1990 to farmers. At the time of severe financial crisis, several thousand crores of rupees were given away. At one stroke it nearly destroyed the entire banking system (SSM Unit, ISEC 1991). It contributed greatly to the loss of confidence abroad in India's ability to service its debt and loans became so much harder to get as India's credit rating was downgraded. It was in this background that elections were held and a new Government came into office with a mandate to bring about the changes needed in consultation with international financial agencies to rescue the country from the chaos that seemed to be looming before it.

Quite clearly one has to examine the decisions of the Government in such a situation with more than a single dose of sympathy. It was courageous indeed to try and convert a crisis into an opportunity. The response to this crisis has been at two levels. One, the short term, refers to the stabilization programme: essentially an exercise to put Government finances in order. Quite clearly this is a necessary but by no means sufficient step in steering the economy in the right direction. Stabilization can be achieved through a (drastic) pruning of Government expenditure, tight credit control, compressed imports, increased tax revenues and a drive to boost exports aided by a depreciation of the exchange rate of the rupee. These measures had to be undertaken.

But it is necessary in the medium term to build on the foundation set by the stabilization policies and this is what is called the Structural Adjustment Programme, which the Finance Minister hopes to implement over a three-year span (Singh, 1991; Raghuram, 1992; Panchamukhi, 1992). The aim of the SAP is to place the economy on a self-sustaining growth path over the long term.

In this Structural Adjustment Programme, efforts are being made to encourage the productive sectors by liberalizing the administrative and legal framework to facilitate production[12]. Competition has been increased through market friendly changes in rules and regulations, thus putting pressure on firms to cut cost and increase efficiency. Imports have been liberalized and consumer movements encouraged to put pressures of quality and price on producers. Laws have been amended to encourage the inflow of foreign capital as equity so that not only is the BOP deficit reduced but future outflows will be based on increasing productive capability resulting from such investment. The import of technology has been made free to facilitate the modernization that is necessary to face global competition. To complement all this, basic reforms are planned in the sphere of labour via an exit policy cushioned by a safety net through the National Renewal Fund[13]. Financial sector reforms are proposed, for example, the freeing of interest rates from administrative controls and the reduction of priority sector lending as well as the reduction of SLR requirements[14]. Reforms are promised in the public sector so that the return on capital increases and further growth is based on internal mobilization of resources rather than budgetary support.

All this is fine. There is more than one way in which each of these measures can be implemented. The Government has chosen a particular path arguing that it has no alternative. It is true that there is no alternative to drastically changing the old system: but there are many ways of doing so; and not only the one the Government has chosen in consultation with international agencies. What the Government has chosen is a path that puts the burden of adjustment on the poor[15]. Thus, the reference to reforms in the SAP, is to the revealed preference of the government: not to the many possibilities available but to the choice actually made. For example, infructuous Government expenditure has hardly been cut but social services are being reduced – health and education[16] for example. Since the reform measures have been introduced, the revenue deficit of the Government of India has actually been increasing[17].

If the fiscal deficit has been brought down, it is by cutting public investment. While cutting public investment will reduce the deficit in the immediate short run, it also reduces the ability of the economy to increase production in the medium and long run. To the extent public investment stimulates private investment, this measure may also dampen private investment. Thus, the stabilization measures chosen by the Government appear to work at cross purposes with its stated long term objectives. While it is necessary to improve the performance of public enterprise, this cannot be done by starving it suddenly of resources. That will be like curing a headache by cutting off the head.

This can be further substantiated by noting that an area like defence expenditure, which yields no returns, has not been subjected to any drastic cuts inspite of suggestions from the World Bank and IMF. Defence expenditure, in a world where tensions are coming down, could have been cut drastically so as to give the Government the freedom to maintain investment in the social service sectors of education and health. What is relevant is not how much is spent on defence, but how much security we get for each rupee spent on defence. The Comptroller and Auditor General's reports have shown that there is much waste in the expenditure of various defence departments[18]. This could be cut down, on the contrary, it is still growing. In making the choices it has made, the Government has once again taken the soft option in doing so, it has chosen a path that hurts the interests of the vulnerable and weaker sections[19]

Another example of such short sighted stabilization measures is the disinvestment in the public sector[20]. The money earned by the Government by selling the shares of the public sector companies helps to reduce the fiscal deficit[21]. Instead, it could have been used to retire debt as suggested by Raja Chellaiah, now fiscal adviser to the Finance Ministry. There is no guarantee that such disinvestment will automatically lead, *ipso facto*, to an improvement in the performance of public enterprises. And that is the crucial issue.

In the same way, encouraging the entry of foreign capital and liberal import of technology may in some sectors (like consumer durables) help the process of modernization. The other side of the coin is the negative impact on domestic R&D and self- reliance, especially in the core or basic industries. Competition from goods produced abroad will adversely affect the demand for goods domestically produced, if domestic firms are not given a chance, they will go under; and by this type of globalization of the economy, the result may well be the de-industrialization of the Indian economy (Chandrasekhar & Chatterjee 1993; Vyasulu 1993).

Public enterprise is often in a strong position if it has the required support. BHEL has built its strength, over the years even in collaboration with MNCs, and has been successful in winning global tenders. NTPC has a hard-earned reputation for technical competence and professionalism. ISRO has built up a capability that has scared the United States, so much so that the US has, with brazen disregard for international law, forced the Russians to back out of a contract for cryogenic engine technology transfer to India. C-DAC, NAL, and IISc have developed parallel processing computers that can compete with the Cray Super Computer in world markets. In fact, many MNCs have chosen public enterprise partners as their domestic collaborators in preference to private companies. For example, Pechiney Ugine Khulman of France chose to work with NALCO in India – a fact now apparently forgotten.

Thus, while structural adjustments are necessary, it is far from clear that the (few) measures that have been undertaken have been thought and will produce the desired results over the medium and long term. Rather the fear is that they are myopic reactions to the immediate crisis, not a policy package or programme for the long term being implemented systematically. They could make things worse, instead of better.

IV

If reforms are to be successful over the long term, the sequencing of such changes is of crucial importance. The measures that have been undertaken so far do not give the impression that the sequencing issue has been adequately considered. Economists have agreed that a sustained process of growth can only take place on a foundation provided by a vibrant agriculture [22]. Agricultural production in the 80s seems to have peaked. The Green Revolution technology seems to have reached its limits. Yields have not been increasing over a wide range of crops[23]. There is increasing evidence that critical inputs like water and fertilizers are not being used in an optimal manner in Indian agriculture (Vyasulu & Gadgil, 1992; Vaidyanathan, 1993). Part of the reason lies in the fact that in India land reforms have failed[24]. The successful cases of economic growth to which we refer today, such as South Korea or Taiwan, have based their rapid industrialisation on a successful land reform. In India, such land reform would appear to be a necessary condition for a sustained growth process. But it is not in the political agenda. In ignoring land reforms the structural adjustment strategy starts on a weak foundation; a strong agricultural base is essential for the success of the SAP.

Secondly, when it comes to reforms in the public sector, more has been said than done. There are a large number of reports starting from the Economic Administrative Reforms Commission (Chairman: L.K. Jha) and going on to the Sengupta Committee on what ails the public sector and what has to be done. There has been experience with the experiments on memoranda of understanding. But after all this, there have not been substantial reforms other than the disinvestment which has essentially been undertaken for fiscal reasons.

The danger comes from the fact that Indian industry, which has been thriving in a protected market, and which has forgotten the customer, is suddenly being exposed to international competition. The argument is that it must learn to cut costs by modernising and survive by increasing its efficiency. While the argument is valid, how is this to be achieved? If Indian industry is flabby, it must exercise and shed excess fat before it can take part in the Olympics. Thus, it must be gradually exposed to competition. The license raj of bureaucratic controls must go domestically first. Units already in production within the country must learn to compete: entry and exit must be realistic options. Investment in R&D and diffusion of technologies is a must. On some of these issues, Indian industry, especially private industry, does not have a glorious record. To that extent, it is necessary to bring pressures to bear on it: but the level of pressure has to be carefully judged. There will be differences among sectors. There are no clear answers here.

Once some restructuring on this basis has taken place, then, and only then, should tariff protection be reduced on a large scale, and Indian firms asked to compete with MNCs on global terms in a level playing field. Thus, a domestic liberalisation is a pre-requisite to globalisation. Protection must not be for ever. It may have a clear time frame of three to five years, depending on the specific circumstances of each sector. Globalisation without this will not serve the cause of self-reliance[25]. Particularly so, when the world is entering an era of managed trade, with free trade a myth, even in the U.S.[26]. In this system, Government are expected to act in favour of domestic firms; an example being the Super

301 and Special 301 Sections of the US Trade Act of 1988. India has already been targeted for retaliation under these provisions of US (not international) law.

Related to this is the question of the pace of change. One view – the big bang theory – is that it is the best to do everything at once, or in a short span of a year or so. Many of these changes will be painful, and there will be political pressure and resistance. Rather than give time for pressures to build up, let the economy go "cold turkey" and in a few years it will emerge stronger.

Perhaps, but there is no guarantee that the economy will not collapse, let alone emerge stronger. The collapse of the USSR suggests that such an outcome is not impossible. In such a strategy, the poor, who are most vulnerable, will be hit the hardest. If the investment made in Indian industry since Independence is to yield results, then it must be restructured so as to be productive: not subjected all at once to unfamiliar competition that will kill it in the name of a "level playing field", which it does not have. Inefficiency in working has to be gradually reduced – a gradual loss of fat is what is required. This is not to say there are no faults with Indian Industry. There are many. But for these faults, a death sentence is not the answer.

Thus, long-run concerns of survival, as well as welfare considerations, suggest a gradual pace of change beginning with internal reforms. This does not mean that the pace must not accelerate once the process is underway. But caution is necessary and the changes introduced must be in tune with the circumstances. Industry must focus on productivity and modernisation. It must invest in R&D and nurture markets on a long term basis. It must move out of uncompetitive areas, and grow where it has competitive advantage following the Porter diamond[27]. Thus, the costs of adjustment can be kept at a minimum, the pain of reform shared, and synergies developed as changes take place. And self-reliance need not be given up.

V

Along with issues of sequencing and pace of change, are others, closely interlinked, related to the management of change and the instruments for implementing the chosen strategy. In the past, public enterprise has been an important instrument of policy. A public enterprise has been understood as an organisation, often registered as a company under the

Companies Act, that is wholly owned by the Government of India. It was so set up to keep it free from the rules/work culture of Government departments. While talking of public enterprises, the examples that come to mind are HMT, BHEL, SAIL, and the like. (There are also departmental undertakings like the Railways or the Posts and Telegraphs which were set up before Independence.) In recent years State level public enterprises have also come to be recognised as an important part of public enterprises. This is an important matter because public enterprises have been understood in the restricted sense of Government owned and Government controlled organisations with business goals, modified by "social" considerations in various ways. This was the spirit of the times.

The only important distinction in this understanding has been the differentiation between the Union Government which owns Central Public Undertakings and the various States/Provincial Governments which own and control the State level public enterprises. Often the State level public enterprises have been set up in the image of the Central public enterprises especially in the promotional field. This has meant that debate about change has been confined to procedural matters, of modifications in the relationship between the Government (meaning the concerned Ministry) and the public sector company concerned: whether they should come "under" this administrative ministry or that; whether there should be Government officials sitting on the Boards of the companies or not and if yes, what their functions should be; what the terms of a Memorandum of Understanding should be and so on. Thus, the question of public sector reform has been understood somewhat narrowly.

In recent years there has been experience of disinvestment of Government's holding of shares in selected public sector companies. But these shares have been sold to mutual funds which are themselves owned by the Government. While this does change the ownership structure, it is a moot point as to whether this is a genuine privatisation. What has been our experience of this limited type of ownership change?

It is important also to learn from past experience. There has been considerable experience in privatisation and deregulation. In the 80s, tentative efforts were made to privatise management, when successful private sector managers were asked to head public sector companies: the well known case being the induction of Rahul Bajaj as Chairman of Indian Airlines. What has been learnt from such experiments? Without a deeper understanding of the successes, failures and limitations of such experiments, it will not be possible actually to privatise on any large scale.

It might be worth noting, in passing, that private management does not necessarily mean an enterprise is in the private sector logically. The Tata Iron and Steel Company is under the management control of the Tatas who own around 5 per cent of the shares. Public financial institutions like LIC own over 40 per cent. These issues were items of debate a decade ago when Swaraj Paul tried to take over Escorts. India has a large number of privately managed public companies of this type. The genuine private sector – of the sort typified by Cargill Seeds Inc – is minuscule in size in India. Thus, much that is attributed to the so-called private sector may have to be re-examined in the current context from a logical and empirical point of view.

There are also other cases of privatisation such as the experience of the Andhra Pradesh Government in privatising Hyderabad Allwyn Limited or of the Karnataka experience of selling off shares in Keonics Yokagawa. There are proposals afoot to privatise the Indian Iron and Steel Company in Burnpur. And there are many experiences in other countries of privatisation across a host of industrial sectors. Has post-privatisaiton experience always lead to commercial success? How have privatised companies fared, after, say 10 years? Or can privatisation be the reverse of nationalisation – when textile mills were taken over for the wrong reason and companies are now sold off only for revenue considerations? There are many such questions for which answers are urgently needed. Such studies are essential if public enterprise reform is to be taken a step further successfully.

It is also important to go deeper into the question of Government ownership. It is increasingly being realised that there are atleast four levels of Government – Union Government, State Governments, the District Level Local Governments such as the Jilla Parishads and Mandal Panchayats on the one hand and Nagar Palikas for cities on the other. With the recent Constitutional amendments, these will become a reality very soon all over the country. There are Constitutional divisions of responsibilities across these levels of Government. These divisions require that each of these Governments become responsible for activities coming within its Constitutional mandate. Publiç enterprise reform in this context can no longer be seen in the narrow sense in which it has been dealt with till now.

It will have to be seen in terms of how the new policies of decentralisation of powers, devolution of finances, accountability to appropriate local level elected bodies etc., begin to influence the managerial functions of various agencies that are meant to perform specific tasks. Thus, it may be, that for certain functions, the appropriate – for example, an Electricity Board. For others, the appropriate form may be a National level enterprise, for example, the Space Commission whose responsibility can only be limited in national terms. Others may have a regional responsibility such as the Hyderabad-Karnataka Development Board. There may be other situations that require cooperation between the Union and the States, or between States–Andhra and Orissa have cooperated successfully in the area of power generation.

There will be some enterprises that function only at Nagar Palika or Jilla Parishad levels, for example, City Water Supply Systems or district roads. All of these activities must be considered under the broad category of public enterprise.

The question of public enterprise reform cannot be divorced from the changing political reality and therefore the discussion must now go much deeper into the relationship between the function and level of Government, and the relation between different stake holders in its work. For example, labour in public enterprises is a critical factor of production and a major stake-holder. Scholars such as V.M. Dandekar and D.M. Nanjundappa have long been advocating worker ownership of enterprises[28]. In countries like Sweden, Unions are important share holders in many enterprises. The debate on public enterprise reform must include the question of employee ownership of shares; the role of workers and union as stake holders; of incentives like stock options for top officials in the interests of efficient management and many other such issues.

What has been the experience of worker cooperatives that have taken up sick units – like Kamani Tubes in Bombay? What is the role of a trade union, which is clearly a stake holder in any enterprise say in reviving a sick unit in the process of restructuring of the economy? And so on.

If an enterprise is seen as a nexus of contracts, as modern industrial organisation theory teaches us, there is no reason why public enterprises could not be reorganised taking these principles into account. Such reform would be fundamental even if it does not privatise ownership in the traditional and ideological sense. For example, apart from workers, the Railways, Coal mines or City Corporations could hold shares in SAIL. This would by itself lead to changes in how it functions. Much can be learned of strategic management in this kind of context. The challenges before researchers is fantastic.

All this can be seen in the following matrix:

A Taxonomy of Public Enterprise

	Types of Agencies						
Level of Govt. Ownership/ Control	Company	Statutory	Commi-ssion	Cooperative	Society	Volag	Other
Local				Milk Coop Credit Coop	NGO Link	NGO	Water Supply
District				Coop Bank			
State	RTC/ NGEF		Finance	Apex Coop	KSCST		Electricity Board
Nation	HMT/ BHEL	LIC/ UTI	ISRO	IFFCO			
RBI etc.	NHB						
Public Share Holding	TISCO						
Different Combinations of the above						Literacy Mission	
(a)	SBI						
(b)	SFCs						
(c)	GIFC						
Others				Kamani Tubes			

This taxonomy only begins the process of clarifying the position regarding the nature of public enterprise. It may not be complete enough to include all the types that exist. But the point that each cell–each Aij to use matrix terminology – must be analysed in depth in its own context comes throughout clearly. Apart from the sector of operation, which will be critical for any enterprise, and which should be treated as another dimension, ownership, purpose and control are important variables in understanding a public enterprise. And such an understanding is a pre-requisite for designing suitable management systems.

Some thought could also be devoted to the question of whether it is only companies that should be considered as public enterprises as is the habit today. Given the interpretations of the Indian Courts on Article 12 of the Constitution, which deals with the State, it is necessary to go deeper into what the terms 'public' and 'State' mean. It is my impression that in much of the relevant literature, the term public has been used synonymously with both the terms 'Government' and 'State'. Thus, public sector companies mean Government owned companies; but Government is only one arm of the State, as the judicial interpretations of Article 12 have clearly brought out. Other arms of the State are, for example, the Civil Service, the Armed Forces, the Legislature, as well as public sector companies like HMT or even universities so far as the writ jurisdiction of the courts under Article 226 is concerned. Thus, the term 'public' is very much broader than the narrow meaning of Government enterprise or somewhat wider meaning of an arm of the State. Also, it is necessary to include Government/State as financier in some form for an organisation to be "public". Does not publicness of purpose give an enterprise a public character even if the Government is not involved? Many legal issues are involved here that need to be studied.

Thus, when we speak of public enterprise, there is no reason to restrict attention to (Union or State) Government owned enterprises alone. The term could include, for example, cooperative efforts where people voluntarily come together for a common purpose. Board with cooperatives in the fields of milk, edible oils, etc., makes it very clear that there is a large and growing role that cooperative forms of enterprise can play in fostering economic development. These are not private enterprises. They are not Government enterprises. They often work in fields that are consistent with those entrusted to the State in the Directive Principles of the Constitution[29]. They involve the efforts of large numbers of people who voluntarily come together for a public purpose. They involve initiative and enterprise.

I would argue that public enterprise should include cooperative and/or any voluntary association of persons coming together for a public purpose in the economist's language, in internalizing an externality or in providing merit good in cases of jointness of production or consumption. The publicness of an enterprise would then depend, not on ownership issues alone, but also on the purpose for which it is set up, and how it is managed or controlled. Instead of black or white, we get a range of grey. This would broaden the field of public enterprise tremendously. It throws up a challenge to researchers.

Perhaps to keep a limit on what is being done, administrative functions of Government can be kept out of the purview of this taxonomy by restricting it to "enterprise", that is activity carried out along business lines for meeting specified ends, and not routine administrative or regulatory functions which should be the responsibility of Public Administration. Some of the many issues that merit study can now be mentioned, even if only in passing

The nature of the business would impose its own restrictions and pose its own specific challenges. Enterprise may be private or not. It may be large or, to use a recent term, micro. The creation of an environment that facilitates the growth of micro-enterprise is an issue of public concern that cannot be ignored in any research effort dealing with public enterprise.

There are also certain other issues which cannot be neglected in this debate. First and foremost is the question of whether public enterprise should be self-sustaining or merits continual subsidies. Today the Government's emphasis is on eliminating subsidies. The reasons are well known. Subsidies distort cost hide inefficiencies and lead to sub-optimal solutions. And since this is a valid argument it is necessary to try and reduce/eliminate subsidies in public enterprises. But, given history, this task is difficult to implement.

First, in a society like India that has a large number of poor people, welfare considerations demand that the constitutional guarantee of right to life and liberty be implemented by providing certain essential social services to the poorest people of the country, even if they cannot afford it. This was reinforced by the Supreme Court in its well known judgment against Ratlam Municipality in Madhya Pradesh.[30] This would particularly include social services such as education, access to health facilities, a minimum of housing and the like, even if such a policy requires a subsidy. It is interesting indeed to find that the World Bank now recommends such a course in terms of Government taking a direct lead in the provision of social services. Thus, some system of redistribution is essential for the success of the SAP and it will have to be worked out at a macro level and implemented across regions and classes at meso and micro levels.

Subsidies provided in hidden fashion by not recovering the full cost of service through tariffs, would of course need to be eliminated. They are very large in India (Mundle and Rao, 1991). Examples that spring to mind are subsidies in power and water rates. But even in such situations there may be categories of users, such as marginal farmers, who in existing conditions merit a subsidy on welfare grounds. Primary education is another good example of such a merit good. It would be my argument that such a subsidy should be openly given from budgetary sources and not in a hidden manner through manipulation of prices and costs in the public sector (Vyasulu and Gadgil, 1992). Thus issues of utility costing, subsidy free pricing, equity in the provision of social services, investment in decreasing cost industries etc., are major areas requiring research.

If self-reliance continues to be an important national goal it will be necessary for the country to maintain a lead in selected sectors through technological excellence (Vyasulu, 1993). Companies like BHEL, NTPC and SAIL are valuable reservoirs of technology. But without clear support from the Government they will not be able to hold their own against MNCs in the short run. This will require investment in R&D on a larger scale. Till now in India, it has been funded from Government sources and I think it will continue to be the case. But such funds need to be better targeted, the sectors more carefully chosen and the entire process better managed. It is a task eminently suited for public enterprise[31]. In fact, India has a success story in the Indian Space Research Organization (ISRO) which is a public enterprise. (Now, to commercialise its activities, it has set up the Antrix Corporation).

It is not my argument that India should be technologically self-sufficient in all industrial areas. The world is a large place and we can trade with others to mutual benefit. But in order to trade, we must have something to sell. There must be some areas where we have expertise ourselves and it is towards this question that we must focus our attention. Thus, the selection of areas for public enterprise as well as the issue of managing technology and R&D in the selected area must receive immediate attention.

The sequencing of reforms is critical and must be seen from a self reliance point of view. Globaliaztion of the economy must follow, not precede, this. Only in this situation will exports grow over the long term.

The question of pollution control and environmentally benign production, energy conservation, etc., touch on issues of long run sustainability that are not well captured by financial ratios or the popular cost benefit analyses on which investment decisions are often based. This is an area of ignorance in technology, management, planning, etc. It is also an area where the public has an interest, as it cannot deny the rights of unborn generations. Public enterprise may not have a good environmental record–witness the problems of the former USSR. But in the post Rio world, it will be necessary to integrate environmental concerns into the functioning of public enterprise in a meaningful manner.

The issue of public enterprise reform is inextricably tied up with what is being called the exit policy. Given the fact that India experienced "jobless growth" in the 1980s; and given also the fact that total factor productivity has shown little improvement in Indian industry, the need to create productive and remunerative employment assumes urgency. The rigidities, that have developed in the economy, do not promote productivity growth. They do not permit the kind of adjustment that needs to take place. And they are promoting a casualization of labour that will undoubtedly aggravate tensions in society. While there have been many laws and regulations, India has not had clear labour policy. The many factors that go into this productivity growth, skills enhancement retirement policy and so on have all to be tackled in a manner that will facilitate the creation of productive jobs rather than each by itself in isolation resulting in monstrous and unmanageable system. The need for institutional innovations is clear. Unfortunately, this is an under-researched area; and it is an area where managers, union workers and administrators must interact if we are to have any hope of success. Given the antagonistic relations that exist across these groups, it is not an easy task.

In sum, it would appear that the term public enterprise covers a broad spectrum of organisations and activities whose proper functioning is critical to the success of structural adjustment and reform. The popular view in the newspapers that the public sector has outlived its utility and needs only to be shut down misses the essentials of what the reforms are all about. True, private initiative and entrepreneurship are seen differently now. But so also public enterprise : and the interaction between the two can now be studied more rationally and with less of preconceived bias.

The reforms require, not less, but more, and qualitatively better State intervention. They will succeed only if we get State Intervention Right. And in this public enterprise in the broad sense has a vital role. That realisation is a step forward.

NOTES

1. This has led many to assert that Marxism has failed. That may be premature. See my "Class and Surplus Value: A Re-examination of Concepts", ISEC, Unpublished, 1992.
2. See Vinod Vyasulu "Nehru and the Visveswaraiah Legacy" in Ray, Amal *et al.* (eds) (1991).

3. The Industrial Policy Resolution of 1956; The Science Policy Resolution of 1958. The Second Five Year Plan 1957-62; and the resolutions passed in the Avadi Session of the Congress. It may be useful to remember that Industrial Development and Regulation Act which empowered the Government to regulate industrial growth on a wide-ranging basis was passed by Parliament in 1951 – before the First Five Year Plan was launched.
4. See the Bombay Plan of 1944.
5. Perhaps the best example being Nehru himself. See Ray, Amal *et al.* (eds) (1991).
6. See J.N. Bhagwati and S. Chakravarty, (1969). Also the biography of P.C. Mahalanobis by A. Mahalanobis (1982).
7. Those working in the Government Department gave themselves hefty pay increases of over 20 per cent in real terms in the Fourth Pay Commission in 1986, adding to the fiscal deficit.
8. On this, see the enlightening discussion in Nasir Tyabji (1990).
9. Written after reading the Santhanam Committee Report it must be noted, as Arun Ghosh (1993) does, that rent-seeking activities can take place even when controls are eliminated.
10. These ideas, in the context of disinvestment, have been further elaborated upon in the Rangarajan Committee Report recently submitted to the Government.
11. Like Isher Ahluwalia, in her two books on Indian Industrial Growth. Thus, the recommendation: give up Planning and welcome market forces which bring in competitive pressures.
12. For a lucid definition of the various terms used, see Jayati Ghosh, (1993).
13. See the ILO (1991) and the special issue of the *Indian Journal of Labour Economics*; 1993 (January), especially the paper by Veerashekerappa.
14. See Report of the Committee on Financial Reforms (Chairman: M. Narasimham) submitted to GOI in November, 1992). Some of these recommendations have been implemented.
15. See for example, the 1993 Conference issues of the *Indian Journal of Labour Economics;* and a number of papers in the Economic and Political Weekly in 1991 and later by a host of scholars.
16. See C. Upendranath (1993).
17. In the budget presented in February 1993, it is over Rs. 14,000.00 crores; the final estimate is even higher. On the implications, see I.S. Gulati (1993).
18. CAG, 1992.
19. On the logic of defence expenditures, see Baran and Sweezy, (1967).
20. An area in which Institute of Public Enterprise, led by Professor R.K. Mishra, has been in the forefront of technical research efforts.
21. The procedure followed has also received a reprimand from the Comptroller and Auditor General recently, according to newspaper reports.
22. See the Reports of the Economic Advisory Council to the Prime Minister (Chairman: S. Chakravarty) in 1990 and 1991.
23. In case of Karnataka, B.P. Vani and Vinod Vyasulu (1993): 'A Disaggregated Analysis of Agriculture Production in Karnataka' – ongoing study at ISEC. The Karnataka Government has set up an Expert Committee to study the problem of agricultural stagnation in the 1980s.
24. The term usually refers to tenancy reform. And even this has had only limited success.
25. A point made by I.G. Patel in his Kingsly Martin Lecture some years ago. See his paper in S.N. Chary and Vinod Vyasulu (eds), (1992).

26. See Biswajit Dhar (1992).
27. Michael Porter (1990) for a detailed study across several countries.
28. In their respective Presidential Addresses to the Indian Society of Labour Economics annual conference. There is also a vast literature on self-management by labour. See Vanek (1971).
29. Discussed in the Research Perspectives of the RBI Endowment Unit at ISEC, Bangalore (1993).
30. The National Law School of India University, set up by the Bar Council of India in Bangalore, has many innovative programmes of research.
31. An area where IPE has done some work. See Mani (1991).

Note : The summary of discussion on this paper is combined with that of the paper by Y.V. Reddy & S.Joshi on the same theme.

6

PUBLIC ENTERPRISES AND BUDGET LINKAGE

Y. VENUGOPAL REDDY and S. JOSHI

Introduction

There are a number of reasons why the budget and the public enterprises[1] linkages require to be examined carefully at the current juncture of changes in policy frame-work. Firstly, as part of fiscal discipline, decisions have been taken to minimise the budgetary support to public enterprises and hence the need to look at the form and the nature of support of the Government, alongwith the justification. Correspondingly, the Government is entitled to dividends on equity, interest and repayment of loans as appropriate, on schedule. These are required by Government as the owner of the Enterprises and a lender of funds, apart from other receipts as a sovereign, such as tax receipts or cesses (to Central or Provincial Government).

Secondly, a decision has been taken that the assistance from multilateral agencies and other external flows should be received directly by the public enterprises without routing through the Government budget. However, many of these agencies may require Governmental clearance or even guarantees. With the disintermediation of the Government in the flow of external assistance, the nature of budgetary relationship also changes.

Thirdly, increasing attention is being paid to provide access for public enterprises to capital markets as an important source of funds. In granting access to capital markets through bonds, there may be allocative mechanisms on the part of Government; whereas with regard to debentures, there may be no such mechanism but these would be subject to capital regulations. Where tax exemptions are given for bonds, there is certainly an element of revenue foregone. Though strictly not related directly to the budget, these have a bearing on budget in terms of contingent liability or alternative source of funds to enterprise, or use of funds by Government, or revenues foregone by Government.

Fourthly, having opened up a number of activities for private sector, public enterprises are no longer mere instruments of policies of the Government without reference to commercial considerations in a competitive environment. Hence, the public enterprises, as well as the Government, would have to evaluate costs and benefits of financial and non-financial support from the Government and non-Governmental sources.

Fifthly, since some disinvestment has already been made in a number of public enterprises, there is an element of diversified ownership. Hence, each public enterprise will have to consider appropriate dividend policies and the earlier practice of Government generally foregoing dividends, to provide resource support to the enterprise, may no longer be valid. Similarly, with regard to the decisions relating to purchases and sales, the private shareholders may insist (if need be through recourse to judiciary) that the majority shareholders should not utilise the company for its benefit against the basic interests of the Company. Also, Government has decided to corporate certain entities, refer some of the enterprises to BIFR and consider mergers and financial restructuring in some others. All these measures require a full assessment of the assets and liabilities in the relationship between Government and the enterprises. In fact, to assess the costs and benefits involved in any restructuring, a clear identification of the relative financial claims is essential.

In addition to the above reasons, there are certain transitional costs which have to be borne by the public enterprises. These include enhanced debt liabilities, consequent upon devaluation, where the public enterprise was used merely as an instrument for providing the balance of payment support. A conscious view has to be taken in such cases whether any relief would be provided.

In the light of the report of the Joint Parliamentary Committee on the recent stock exchange problems, the dangers of excess liquidity in public enterprises has come to force. In fact, many public enterprises were provided either direct Government budgetary support, or indirect support through access to bonds, though the funds were not required at that point of time by the enterprises. In some cases, profits were allowed to be retained by enterprises, though they were not strictly necessary to meet their cash requirements. At the same time Government, which made these resources available to enterprises, irrespective of their needs, has been borrowing in the financial markets to finance its budget. In other words, the inadequate cash management practices of the Government, and excess liquidity with the enterprises, may have partly benefited the enterprises in terms of other income but has led to excess liquidity in the money markets and fiscal burden on the Government. The future relationship should take into account the lessons of this experience.

In general, greater transparency in the relationship would be warranted, and accountability for most of the public enterprises would now be to both the private shareholders and the Government as a shareholder, in addition to the public enterprises' accountability to the Government as a lender. The relationship between the public enterprises and the Government as a sovereign would perhaps be no different from that between the Government as a sovereign and all enterprises (public or private).

The objectives of this chapter therefore are to:

(a) narrate the importance of study of linkages between public enterprises and Government budget;
(b) provide a conceptual account of such linkages with reference to various instruments;
(c) identify other aspects, such as accounting and business practices of public enterprises, which may have a bearing on the budget;
(d) illustrate the status and the magnitude, with an account of Central Government budgets and selected Central Public Enterprises; and
(e) list some areas requiring attention on part of both the Government and the enterprises.

Linkages with Budget

There are different levels at which public enterprises are affected due to changes in policy of the Government. Without going into details about the changed relationship, the following general observations, relevant to linkages with budget, may be made about the new policies with regard to the public enterprises.

(a) There is no presumption that investments in public enterprises necessarily generate benefits for the people commensurate with the costs incurred by the Government in providing such support.
(b) The instrumentalist view towards public enterprises, rather than

an ideological view, seems to be in order and thus public ownership is only one of the options of Government intervention towards defining and achieving social or economic objectives. It is, therefore, necessary and desirable to constantly identify ways of achieving the desired objectives and view, public ownership as one of such ways, among other ways; another way is regulation.

(c) Further, there is no reasons to presume that public enterprise would continue to be publicly owned. Today's public enterprise may be tomorrow's private enterprise, and vice-versa.

(d) Public ownership need not necessarily mean a 100 per cent ownership by the Government or other public sector bodies. It is possible that there are different mixes of public and private ownership.

(e) Market structures appear to be important now as maintaining competition between public enterprises or between public and private enterprises is an important objective. In such a situation, it is possible that separate regulatory bodies are required. Further, in the matter of consumer protection, there may be no special treatment for public enterprises.

(f) With the diverse price-driven market structures in which public enterprises are to operate, and diversified ownership of public enterprises, there is an increasing need for disaggregated and unit-focussed approaches by the owner/lender, i.e. Government.

At the conceptual level various mechanisms of financial outflows from the Government areas are as follows:

(a) Equity (providing ownership to Government at a cost, and in practice, at least till recently, virtually cost-free resources to public enterprises); (b) Loan (essentially for commercial purposes and reflecting a cost to both the Government and the enterprise); (c) Specific purpose plan grants (to fund activities of a non-commercial but developmental nature), and (d) Non-plan grants usually to cover cash losses (euphemistically called working capital needs).

In addition to the transparent flows from the budget to enterprises, there are certain others which are required to be noted as being relevant but seldom linked to a broader economic or social purpose. These are :

(a) write-off of loans or interest dues from the enterprises;
(b) rescheduling of loans, including conversion into equity or into zero coupon bonds, etc.;
(c) providing a guarantee without a fee;
(d) dividends due, but foregone;
(e) special tax concessions;
(f) provision of land free of cost (especially by State Governments);

In regard to inflows into the budget (other than those under sovereign powers of taxation), these are as under :

(a) dividends;
(b) payment of interest;
(c) repayment of principal;
(d) guarantees and other fees payable;
(e) cess and other dues from enterprises; when they operate as agents of the Government;
(f) receipts due to disinvestment; and
(g) payment of loans due.

An important aspect of inflows to Government from public enterprises are the tax receipts – both direct (Corporate Tax) and indirect (Excise and Customs). There is reason to believe that these are paid more readily and willingly by the Public Enterprises, compared to the Non-Public Enterprises. However, it is not easy to compute or assess such contribution.

Linkages with a Bearing on Budget

The financial health of an enterprise has an important bearing on the budget because of the size of the Public Sector Enterprises and the reality that the Government has unlimited liability by being a sovereign owner, though technically a Company may have limited liability. Important areas, specially relevant to public enterprises in this regard, are:

(a) accounting practices;
(b) the level of inventories;
(c) sundry debtors and sundry creditors;

(d) other income, i.e. income other than operating income; and
(e) interpublic enterprise, financial transactions and settlement of mutual claims.

There are also other relationships between the enterprises and the Government, where transactions may have an effect of either a tax or a subsidy, without appearing to be so. These relate to the impact of mandated business, (such as canalisation), directed business, (where the enterprises are directed to undertake a business including cross subsidisation) and price preference (whenever it is accorded).

Scope and Coverage of Budget and CPEs

We attempt to illustrate the status and the magnitude of budgetary relationship by:

(a) a study of budgets from 1990-91 to 1994-95;
(b) a detailed account of 45 Central Public Enterprises.

Budgets of 1990-91 to 1994-95 have been selected, merely for convenience of illustrating the accounting of relationships and the broad orders of magnitude of such relationships. Similarly, there is no scientific basis for selecting enterprises, but maximum weight has been given to the level of assets in selecting the enterprises. Thus, the forty-five enterprises account for a gross block of Rs. 85,92,179 crores and net sales of Rs. 85,54,870 crores out of the gross block of Rs. 1,18,54,215 crores and Net Sales of Rs. 1,23,88,701 crores of all the Central Public Enterprises covered by BPE in 1991-92 (all definitions are as per BPE and data has been obtained from the Annual Reports of the Undertakings). The narration is intended to focus on areas of concern rather than prove or disprove any particular hypothesis.

Budget Documents

The inflows from public enterprises are available in receipts budget - both under non-tax-revenue and under capital receipts. The picture, from 1990-91 to 1994-95, is given in Table 6.1 :

TABLE 6.1 : **Inflows of Budget**

(In Rs. Crores)

		1990-91 Actual	1991-92 Actual	1992-93 Actual	1993-94 R.E.	1994-95 B.E.
1.	Total Int. Receipts of which on Loans to	8730	10933	12487	14538	15978
(a)	States, U.T., Railways and Telecommunications	6332	7892	9589	11257	12762
(b)	Other Int. Receipts, Includes PSUs, Port Trusts, Other Statutory Body Cooperatives Government/Servants, Departmental/Commercial Undertakings	2398	3041	2899	3251	3180
2.	Dividends & Profits/of which on Account of	774	1058	2493	2737	2793
(a)	RBD. Banks, Insurance. IDBI & Other Financial Institutions & Others	451	628	1836	1761	1766
(b)	Dividends from Public Sector Enterprises mainly by Government Companies	323	404	632	976	1027
3.	Recoveries of Loans of which	5712	6021	6356	6655	6700
a.	States, U.T.s, Foreign Govt., etc.	4395	4492	4444	4343	4276
b.	Others encompassing Industrial & Commercial Enterprises, Railways, Fin. Institutions in Public Sector, Municipalities, Port Trust, Private Sector Companies, Institutions, etc.	1216	1416	1785	2310	2422
4.	Disinvestment of PE's	–3088	1961	2500	4000	

Source : Finance Accounts & Receipts Budget for 1994-95.

The statement of assets (i.e. Capital investments and loans by the Central Government) gives the following picture (Table 6.2):

TABLE 6.2 : **Capital Investments and Loans by the Central Government**

	1990-91 Actual	1991-92 Actual	1992-93 Actual	1993-94 R.E.	1994-95 B.E.
1. Capital Outlay of which	122015	135075	155291	177419	194036
Economic Services	87243	99301	113200	127714	136359
2. Loans (Inc. State, U.T. & Foreign Governments)	114724	126402	135671	14943	61499
of which Public sector enterprises including Banks & Financial Instt. but excluding net Loans to P & T & Railways).	37587	40254	42518	45917	48145

Source : Finance Accounts and Budget Documents of 1994-95.

From the information available in the budget documents, it is difficult to correlate the inflows to the budget attributable to the enterprises covered by Bureau of Public Enterprises (BPE) since, firstly, interest receipts include those of Port Trusts, Cooperatives, Governmental Servants, Other Statutory Bodies and Departmental/Commercial Undertakings. Secondly, dividends from Public Sector Enterprises are indicated to be "mainly from", and thirdly, recoveries of loans cover financial institutions and railways, in addition to the above.

However, in order to analyse for illustrative purposes, though crudely, the following assumptions are made:

(a) The proportion of interest receipts to total loans outstanding in the budget documents for all categories covered in Table 6.2 is treated as applicable to the subset of Public Enterprises covered by BPE.

(b) All the dividends indicated in the Table above are attributed to Government companies alone, thus perhaps overestimating the dividends.

(c) The loan repayments cover railways, while the outstanding loans exclude loans to Railways, and by calculating the ratio of repayment of total loan, a net receipt from Railways is implicitly assumed. Further the proportion, which is arrived at for a larger set is assumed to be valid for the subset of public enterprises covered by BPE.

Hence, it would be necessary to use data on paid up capital, equity (paid-up capital + reserves) and loans outstanding to Government in respect of the CPEs (as per BPE sources). Table 6.3 indicates the paid-up capital, equity and loans outstanding of Public Enterprises as per BPE survey:

TABLE 6.3 : **Paid-up Capital, Equity and Loans Outstanding of Public Enterprises**

	1990-91	1991-92	1992-93
Paid-Up Capital	43245	45696	51867
Equity	75725	82689	95650
Loans Outstanding (Consolidated Balance Sheet Item)	70651	89747	95103

Source : Public Enterprise Survey, BPE.

The interest received as percentage of loans outstanding, dividend as a percentage of paid-up capital, as well as equity, and proportion of loans repaid to total loans outstanding for the years 1990-91 to 1992-93, (the latest for which information from BPE is available) subject to the assumptions listed in para 17, is tabulated (Table 6.4).

TABLE 6.4 : **Interest Received as Percentage of Loans Outstanding**

(in percentage)

	1990-91	1991-92	1992-93
Interest Payment on Loans from Central Govt.	6.37	7.55	6.81
Dividend Received on Paid-up Capital Equity	0.74	0.88	1.21
Proportion of Loans Actually Repaid (Incl. Railways)	3.23	3.51	4.19

Outflows

The outflows of CPEs are, undoubtedly constrained in the last few years.

The Budget Documents do capture "direct" outflows. These are summarised in Table 6.5. This does not include VRS which was Rs. 700 crores. in 1994-95.

TABLE 6.5 : **The Direct Outflows**

(in percentage)

	1990-91 Actual	1991-92 Actual	1992-93 Actual	1993-94 R.E.	1994-95 B.E.
(a) Non-Plan Subsidies	349	323	113	112	112
(b) Non Plan Loans	1069	758	600	779	637
(c) Plan Loans	2477	2735	2403	4071	3537
(d) Equity	5118	4185	4173	3379	3663

On the basis of the above data, the following inferences can be drawn :

(a) Interest receipts on loans as a percentage of loans outstanding ranged between 6.37 and 7.55 while the cost of borrowings to Government has been well over 10 per cent and, from all accounts, the lending rates generally increased from 10.5 in 1974 to 17 per cent in 1993. This gives rise to a distinct possibility of interest-waivers, capitalisation of interest, etc.

(b) Dividend received on paid-up capital ranged between 0.74 and 1.21 per cent. Dividend as a percentage of equity works out to be even less, being in the range of 0.42 to 0.66 per cent. This should be viewed in the light of consistent general practice of foregoing dividends in the past and cost of capital of Government at over 10 per cent.

(c) The proportion of loans actually repaid ranged between 3.23 per cent and 4.19 per cent. In general, for commercial purposes, repayment period should be ten years and thus repayment, purely on a proportionate basis, 10 per cent per year. With such a low level of repayment, the effective repayment period would be in the range of twenty five years indicating a possible mismatch between maturity of loans taken by the Government and repayment receipts.

(d) It is necessary to clearly identify the sources of difference between loans displayed in the Budget at Rs. 42,518 crores in 1992-93, which includes Banks and Financial Institutions, and as shown by BPE at Rs. 95,103 crores. It appears that PEs have borrowed from other sources more than what they have borrowed from the Government. Also the consolidated Balance Sheet of PSUs, drawn up by BPE, shows loans assets of Rs. 44,863 crores, which may contain inter-corporate loans. It is quite possible that the quality of some of the loan assets is quite suspect.

(e) While dividends from Public Sector Enterprises have gone up steadily over the last few years, this inflow has been more than matched by an increase in the quantum of loans.

(f) The resource flows to CPEs have also contributed in terms of increase in paid-up capital as well as retained earnings.

(g) While Non-Plan Loans, Subsidies and Equity contributions by Government appear to be decreasing, the paid-up capital plus reserves, have gone up by 25 per cent since 1990-91. There is, therefore, a net outflow of resources from the Government of the CPEs.

Study of Select CPEs

We now move on to an analysis of companies for the last three years viz. 1990-91, 1991-92 and 1992-93. However, in certain cases, the annual accounts for 1992-93 had not yet been prepared. In such cases, data for the year 1989-90, 1990-91 and 1991-92 only, are used. PSUs have been contributing to inflows of the Government in the form of dividends and repayments of loans. Full details of such contributions are not available in respect of a large number of undertakings from Government records. Hence, these are not covered in this study. Certain PSUs owe to the Government sums collected by them in the form of cess or other revenues, but retain or appropriate these for themselves, thus technically depriving the Government of inflows. It is necessary to quantify such dues, but such information is not readily available.

A large source of PSU funding comes from inter-PSU transactions, including, in some cases, overdues from one PSU to the other. Such transactions could be in the nature of parent companies extending loans to subsidiaries, or in the form of inter-corporate loans between PSUs. To ensure that values shown in the Balance Sheet are correctly matched, and to avoid any potential development on the Government, it is necessary to assess the magnitude of these transactions. Since most PSUs do not detail inter-corporate loans in their Annual Accounts, it has not been possible to gather this data.

Efficiency can be assessed, in one form, by the capacity utilisation of each company. For the years under study, such data has been collected but not used in this study since it has no direct bearing on the subject of the chapter. On the basis of available record, and the analysis of forty-five companies, it is seen that few guarantees have been issued by the Government of India and hence the cost of waiver of guarantee fee by Government has not been attempted.

Most Public Sector Undertakings have reported profits before tax which include other income as well as Contingent Liabilities not provided for. The return on investments on basis of such profits before tax, reported by various PSUs, is detailed in Table 6.6. There are a large number of undertakings, in each of the three years studied, which have either negative returns or returns less than six per cent.

Many companies have significantly high other income, and if this other income is deducted from the profits displayed in the Annual Reports, then the profitability of most PSUs falls sharply. For each company, this information has been displayed on the basis of PBT, Return on Equity and Net Worth as displayed by the company, and the similar calculations made without taking into account other income and Contingent Liabilities. A summary of this information, for all the companies, is at Table 6.7.

Similarly, Tables 6.7A and 6.7B reflect the situation in the years 1991-92 and 1992-93 respectively. The tables also display the net worth of each company, as indicated by it, and the net worth as it would be if Contingent Liabilities are taken into account. It may be observed that the return on equity declines significantly in many cases if other income is not taken into account. If Contingent Liabilities are taken into account, every company shows a distinct decline in profits and the net worth of many PSUs fall sharply. While, it is not correct to add all Contingent Liabilities without further detail, it nevertheless gives some indication of the future liabilities of an Enterprise.

Analytically, it would also be helpful to take into account certain indirect forms of support provided by the Government of PSUs. This has normally taken the form of directed business, price preference on purchases and loans at interest rates much below market rates. In view of the difficulty in gathering this data accurately, it has not been included in this study. However, an analysis of rates of interest on which Government extends loans to PSUs for various purposes, has been made and compared to term-lending rates. The details in Table 6.8, however, indicate that the differential between lending rates of the Government and the term-lending rates is not very significant.

TABLE 6.6 : **Return on Paid-up Capital on Basis of P.B.T. Reported by PSU (in Rs. Crs)**

Name of PSU	Paid-up Capital in			P.B.T. in			Return on Paid-up Capital (%) in		
	1990-91	1991-92	19 92-93	1990-91	1991-92	1992-93	1990-91	1991-92	19 92-93
1	2	3	4	5	6	7	8	9	10
1 Bharat Petroleum Corpn. Ltd.	50.00	50.00	50.00	215.55	255.46	292.07	437.10	510.92	584.14
2. Bongaigaon Ref. & Pet. Ltd.	199.82	199.82	199.82	48.50	65.18	50.17	24.27	32.62	25.11
3. Cochin Refineries Ltd.	68.93	68.93	68.93	96.84	98.04	153.62	140.49	142.23	222.86
4. Gas Authority of India Ltd.	845.32	845.32	845.32	22.72	93.55	210.58	2.69	11.07	24.91
5. Hindustan Petroleum Corpn.	63.84	63.84	63.84	201.29	205.74	383.75	315.30	322.27	601.12
6. Indian Oil Corpn. Ltd.	123.27	123.27	123.27	907.04	1084.78	934.99	735.82	880.00	758.49
7. IBP Ltd.	7.36	7.36	7.36	9.32	14.26	18.67	126.63	193.75	253.67
8. Oil & Natural Gas Commission	342.85	342.85	342.85	1048.30	408.32	788.20	305.76	119.10	229.90
9. Madras Refineries Ltd.	114.13	114.13	114.13	90.95	75.37	91.62	79.69	66.04	80.28
10 National Hydro Elec. P. Ltd.	2045.33	2322.53	2632.48	52.76	49.30	41.49	2.58	2.12	1.58
11. N.T.P.C.	6355.11	7021.81	7549.84	700.95	1007.06	886.86	11.03	14.34	11.75
12. Rural Electrification Corpn.	322.60	362.60	402.60	83.48	104.74	125.31	25.88	28.89	31.13
13. Indian Iron & Steel Co. Ltd.	386.28	387.67	387.67	(133.55)	(22.29)	(58.96)	(34.57)	(5.75)	(15.21)
14 Rashtriya Ispat Nigam Ltd.	3505.85	3505.85	6170.57	(477.55)	(986.93)	(568.29)	(13.62)	(28.15)	(9.21)
15. Steel Authority of India	3985.89	3985.89	3985.89	248.26	367.30	423.40	6.13	9.22	10.62
16. Andrew Yule & Co. Ltd.	11.08	10.91	10.74	11.00	8.15	4.45	99.28	74.70	41.43
17. B.H.E.L	244.76	244.76	244.76	201.46	186.66	309.00	82.31	76.26	126.25
18. H.M.T. Ltd.	78.56	87.73	87.73	15.58	38.15	(12.53)	19.83	43.49	(14.28)
19. H.P.C. Ltd.	479.35	479.35	479.35	(61.37)	(69.91)	(51.34)	(12.80)	(14.58)	(10.71)
20. Maruti Udyog Ltd.	110.24	110.24	132.29	48.12	35.79	36.61	43.65	32.47	27.67
21. Air India	79.24	79.24	79.47	81.23	145.89	333.14	102.51	184.11	419.20
22. Indian Airlines	54.92	55.03	55.16	(64.59)	(198.85)	(195.11)	(117.61)	(136.28)	(353.72)

23. Vayudoot	27.95	36.17	NA	(29.83)	(31.63)	N.A.	(106.73)	(87.45)	N.A.
24. Coal India Ltd.	5713.31	6000.76	6097.84	(27.87)	(22.62)	(41.40)	(0.49)	(0.38)	(0.68)
25. Neyveli Lignite Corpn. Ltd	1435.82	1565.82	1699.37	95.24	101.69	80.69	6.63	6.49	4.75
26. Bharat Aluminium Co. Ltd.	488.85	488.85	488.85	0.34	0.93	1.86	0.07	0.19	2.17
27 Hindustan Copper Ltd.	304.20	304.20	304.20	45.10	54.90	26.40	14.83	18.05	8.68
28. Hindustan Zinc Ltd	403.73	404.53	412.53	84.05	93.36	62.86	20.82	23.08	15.24
29 National Almmium Co.	1288.62	1288.62	1288.62	71.94	59.14	134.88	5.58	4.59	10.47
30. Fertiliser Corpn of India Ltd.	616.39	616.39	623.39	(168.35)	(225.41)	(225.98)	(27.32)	(36.57)	(36.25)
31. Fertilizers & Chemicals (Travancore) Ltd.	342.77	342.77	342.77	23.61	29.00	2.85	6.89	8.46	0.83
32. Hindustan Fertilizers Corpn.	669.22	670.02	686.02	(231.45)	(330.53)	(349.45)	(34.59)	(49.33)	(50.94)
33. Madras Fertilizers	44.74	58.73	98.33	6.38	16.36	12.13	14.26	27.86	12.34
34. National Fertilizers Ltd.	490.58	490.58	490.58	29.74	83.61	111.47	6.06	17.04	22.72
35. Rashtriya Chem. & Fert. Ltd.	551.69	551.69	551.69	40.76	18.78	18.42	7.39	3.40	3.34
36. State Trading Corp. Of India Ltd.	30.00	30.00	30.00	34.59	36.30	(26.93)	115.30	121.30	(89.77)
37. Minerals & Metals Trading Corp. of India Ltd.	50.00	50.00	50.00	143.39	199.17	101.15	286.78	398.34	202.30
38. India Drugs & Pharmaceuticals Ltd.	111.91	113.08	114.25	(88.26)	(110.40)	(83.44)	(78.87)	(86.47)	(133.75)
39. Bharat Electronics Ltd.	80.00	80.00	N.A.	53.97	67.50	N.A.	(67.46)	84.38	N.A.
40. India Petro Chem. Corp.	186.00	186.00	195.46	46.53	51.78	131.06	25.02	27.84	67.05
41. Cochin Shipyard Ltd.	74.36	77.29	79.79	(20.97)	(14.92)	(7.95)	(28.20)	(19.30)	(10.22)
42. Hindustan Shipyard Ltd.	67.43	69.88	70.18	(78.56)	(104.12)	(113.95)	(116.51)	(149.00)	(162.37)
43. Shipping Corpn. of India Ltd	282.30	282.30	282.30	54.46	107.54	134.68	19.29	38.09	47.71
44. Delhi Transport Corpn.	–	–	–	(197.48)	(203.82)	(245.28)	–	–	–
45. National Textiles Corpn.	437.85	437.85	N.A.	(4.10)	4.50	N.A.	0.94	1.03	N.A

Note : Operating Income is net profit less other income and indicates income arising from the main operations of a PSU

Source : Annual Reports of PSUs

TABLE 6.7 : **Return on Equity of Selected Companies 1990-91**

Names of PSU	Equity	PBT			Return on Equity (in % age)			Net Worth	
		As per Company	If O.I. is taken into a/c.	If Cont. Liab. taken into a/c	As per Company	If O.I. is not taken into a/c	If Cont Liab. are taken into a/c	As per Company	If Cont. Liability are taken into a/c
1	2	3	4	5	6	7	8	9	10
1. BPCL	50	215.55	183.13	117.30	437.10%	366.26%	234.60%	664.01	565.76
2. BRPL	199.82	48.50	42.07	41.30	24.27%	21.05%	20.67%	336.02	328.82
3. CRL	68.93	96.84	88.25	85.00	140.49	128.03	123.31	251.82	247.36
4. GAIL	845.32	22.72	11.47	(1053.06)	2.69	1.36	(124.58)	766.99	(308.79)
5. HPCL	63.84	201.29	164.35	45.75	315.30	257.44	71.66	781.62	626.08
6. IOCL	123.27	907.04	39.57	368.85	735.82	32.10	299.22	3576.68	3035.24
7. IBPCL	7.36	9.32	(0.30)	4.41	126.63	(4.08)	59.92	71.88	52.09
8. ONGC	342.85	1048.30	335.89	(79.89)	305.76	97.97	(23.30)	11201.18	10046.19
9. MRL	114.13	90.95	80.54	43.81	79.69	70.57	38.39	261.13	186.01
10. NHPC	2045.33	52.76	29.22	(406.17)	2.58	1.43	(19.86)	2287.21	1822.63
11. NTPC	6355.11	700.95	685.77	(2008.63)	11.03	10.79	(31.61)	8793.01	4784.59
12. REC	322.60	83.48	91.91	104.61	25.88	28.49	32.43	726.06	525.13
13. IISCO	386.28	(133.55)	(142.47)	(214.03)	(34.57)	(36.88)	(55.41)	(358.89)	(439.37)
14. RINL	3505.85	(477.55)	(482.34)	(602.13)	13.62	(13.76)	(17.18)	3003.60	2879.02
15. SAIL	3985.89	248.26	31.91	241.83	6.23	0.80	6.07	4675.60	4669.17
16. AYULE	11.08	11.00	8.12	(43.99)	(99.28)	73.29	(397.02)	42.47	14.27
17. BHARL	244.76	201.46	(22.30)	(390.80)	82.31	(9.11)	(159.67)	836.81	186.21
18. HMT	78.56	15.58	(14.88)	(64.15)	19.83	(18.94)	(81.66)	226.39	146.66
19. HPCL	479.35	(61.37)	(68.43)	(132.07)	(12.80)	(14.28)	(27.55)	153.31	76.08

TABLE 6.7 (*Contd.*)

20. MUL	110.24	48.12	(19.48)	104.63	43.65	(17.67)	(94.91)	232.77	79.53
21. AI	79.24	81.23	32.96	(43.25)	102.51	41.60	(54.58)	611.83	342.18
22. I.A.	54.92	(64.59)	(109.48)	(100.61)	(177.61)	(199.34)	(182.50)	469.67	306.35
23. Vayudoot	27.95	(29.83)	(30.62)	N.A.	(106.73)	(109.55)	N.A.	(47.67)	N.A.
24. CIL	5713.31	(27.87)	(65.14)	(31.10)	(0.49)	(1.14)	(0.54)	5543.83	5540.60
25. Neyveli	1435.82	95.24	74.65	(2.54)	1.63	5.20	(0.18)	1980.18	1730.51
26. BALCO	488.85	0.34	(4.78)	(16.63)	1.07	(0.98)	(3.40)	499.84	473.17
27. HCL	304.20	45.10	39.96	35.60	14.83	13.14	11.70	311.02	295.39
28. HZL	403.73	84.05	75.29	41.40	10.82	18.65	10.25	614.33	571.03
29. NALCO	1288.62	71.94	3.61	(23.52)	5.58	0.28	(1.83)	1415.67	1320.21
30. FCI	616.39	(168.35)	(187.23)	(213.05)	(27.32)	(30.38)	(34.56)	(769.46)	(865.22)
31. FACT	342.77	23.61	17.74	(0.78)	1.89	5.18	(0.23)	389.80	364.37
32. HFC	669.22	(231.45)	(242.06)	(658.25)	(34.59)	(36.17)	(98.36)	(522.68)	(950.85)
33. MFL	44.74	6.38	3.25	(7.52)	14.26	7.26	(16.81)	52.49	38.59
34. NFL	490.58	29.74	12.24	(66.90)	6.06	2.50	13.64	709.22	611.65
35. RCF	551.69	40.76	29.15	7.9	7.39	5.28	0.14	878.59	844.70
36. STC	30.00	34.59	(63.28)	(188.26)	115.30	(210.93)	(627.43)	328.84	136.16
37. MMTC	50.00	143.39	(7.6)	(518.72)	186.78	(15.2)	(1037.44)	350.07	(312.04)
38. IDPL	111.91	(88.26)	(96.77)	(149.68)	(71.72)	(86.47)	(73.03)	(322.45)	(455.79)
39. BEL	80.00	53.97	2.79	(9.97)	(67.46)	3.49	(12.46)	255.62	187.88
40. IPCL	186.00	46.53	13.37	13.37	15.02	7.19	7.19	692.48	607.97
41. CSL	74.36	(20.97)	(22.84)	(164.45)	(28.20)	(30.72)	(221.15)	(91.75)	(235.23)
42. HSL	67.43	(78.56)	(80.29)	(136.24)	(116.51)	(119.07)	(350.35)	(280.85)	(438.53)
43. SCI	282.30	54.46	26.23	26.47	19.29	9.29	9.38	529.23	483.64
44. DTC	–	(197.48)	(201.43)	(208.81)	–	–	–	(644.84)	(656.17)
45. NTC	437.85	4.10	(38.53)	(328.06)	0.94	(8.80)	(74.93)	434.61	102.15

O.I stands for Other Income and figures in brackets denote negative amounts.

Source: Annual Report.

TABLE 6.7 *(Contd.)*

Names of PSU	Equity	PBT			Return on Equity (in % age)			Net Worth	
		As per Company	If O.I. is taken into a/c.	If Cont. Liab. taken into a/c	As per Company	If O.I. is not taken into a/c	If Cont Liab. are taken into a/c	As per Company	If Cont. Liability are taken into a/c
CIL	6097.84	(41.40)	(42.56)	(61.33)	(0.68)	(0.70)	(1.01)	5888.28	5865.03
NEYVELI	1699.37	80.69	34.73	(145.36)	4.75	2.04	(8.55)	2361.04	1692.81
BALCO	488.85	1.86	(10.60)	(29.68)	2.17	(2.17)	(6.07)	502.58	461.37
HCL	304.20	26.40	8.26	4.78	8.68	2.72	1.57	392.17	355.11
HZL	412.53	62.86	51.71	8.05	15.24	12.53	1.95	712.76	629.34
NALCO	1288.62	134.88	77.76	(49.95)	10.47	6.03	(3.88)	1569.95	1442.25
FCI	623.39	(225.98)	(258.19)	(299.34)	(36.25)	(41.89)	(48.02)	(1214.51)	(1484.71)
FACT	342.77	2.85	(6.53)	(66.26)	0.83	(1.91)	(19.33)	422.79	352.20
HFC	686.02	(349.45)	(368.94)	(1519.96)	(50.94)	(53.78)	(221.56)	(1185.84)	(2357.72)
MFL	98.33	12.13	8.94	(2.20)	12.34	9.09	(2.24)	(118.92)	104.59
NFL490.58	111.47	92.90	(98.14)	22.72	18.94	20.00	859.20	647.67	
RCF551.69	18.42	3.33	24.45	3.34	0.60	4.43	809.75	765.87	
STC	30.00	26.93	(33.65)	(168.24)	89.77	(112.17)	(560.80)	369.36	(353.35)
MMTC	50.00	101.15	(17.53)	(339.85)	202.30	(35.06)	(679.70)	504.04	63.04
IDPL	114.25	(83.44)	(89.69)	(242.02)	(133.75)	(78.49)	(211.83)	(513.66)	(801.11)
BELN.A.	N.A.	N.A.	NA	NA	NA	NA	NA	NA	
IPCL	195.46	131.06	73.50	75.70	67.05	37.60	38.73	942.40	611.55
CSL	79.79	(7.95)	(17.21)	(251.30)	(10.22)	(21.57)	(323.05)	(109.18)	(352.53)
HSL70.18	(113.95)	(119.91)	(230.31)	(162.37)	(170.86)	(328.28)	(499.01)	(615.45)	
SCIL	282.30	134.68	57.09	98.19	47.71	20.22	34.78	719.60	668.85
DTC	–	(245.28)	(256.23)	(266.62)	–	–	–	(1093.94)	(1115.95)
NTC	NA	NA	NA	NA	NA	NA	NA	NA	NA

O.I. stands for other Income.

Figures in Brackets denote negative amounts. *Source* : Annual Reports

TABLE 6.7 A : **Return on Equity of Selected Companies 1992-93**

Names of PSU	Equity	PBT			Return on Equity (in % age)			Net Worth	
		As per Company	If O.I. is taken into a/c.	If Cont. Liab. taken into a/c	As per Company	If O.I. is not taken into a/c	If Cont Liab. are taken into a/c	As per Company	If Cont. Liability are taken into a/c
1	2	3	4	5	6	7	8	9	10
BPCL	50	255.46	214.34	117.34	510.92	428.68	234.68	797.47	659.35
BRPL	199.82	65.18	52.83	54.28	32.62	26.44	27.16	362.13	351.23
CRL	68.93	98.04	79.23	73.44	142.23	114.94	106.54	293.38	351.23
GAIL	845.32	93.55	35.44	(1520.44)	11.07	4.19	(179.87)	860.62	(753.37)
HPCL	63.84	205.74	154.94	24.55	322.27	242.70	38.46	901.37	712.07
IOCL	123.37	1084.78	212.12	473.59	880.00	172.08	384.19	4322.79	3708.04
IBPL	7.36	14.26	(5.71)	(2.57)	193.75	(77.58)	(34.92)	84.37	52.65
ONGC	342.85	408.32	(330.78)	(1591.57)	119.10	(96.48)	(465.97)	9579.59	7552.50
MRL	114.13	75.37	64.86	17.53	66.04	56.83	15.36	283.12	190.31
NHPC	2332.53	49.30	23.53	(437.48)	2.12	1.01	(18.84)	2613.75	2126.97
NTPC	7021.81	1007.06	905.66	(1908.89)	14.34	12.90	(27.19)	10470.49	5611.09
RECL	362.60	104.74	112.40	117.54	28.89	31.00	32.42	845.43	63.26
IISCO	387.67	(22.29)	(31.43)	(132.98)	(5.75)	(8.11)	(34.30)	(378.68)	(480.23)
RINL	3505.85	(986.93)	(999.38)	(1128.62)	(28.15)	(28.51)	(32.19)	1993.85	1852.16
SAIL	3985.89	367.30	159.87	361.39	9.22	4.01	9.07	4942.69	4936.78
AY[illegible]LE	10.91	8.15	4.84	(74.14)	74.70	44.36	(679.56)	44.13	41.10
[illegible]EL	244.76	186.66	(115.91)	(631.42)	76.26	(47.36)	(257.98)	729.29	(194.20)
HMT	87.73	38.15	21.50	(40.17)	43.49	24.51	(45.79)	251.64	173.32
HPCL	479.35	(69.91)	(83.54)	(143.31)	(14.58)	(17.43)	(29.90)	84.91	5.63
MUL	110.24	35.79	(40.52)	(114.97)	32.47	(36.76)	(104.29)	254.48	103.20
AIR INDIA	79.24	145.89	55.54	(3.56)	184.11	70.09	(4.49)	767.66	467.84

(Contd)

TABLE 6.7 A (*Contd.*)

Names of PSU	Equity	PBT			Return on Equity (in % age)			Net Worth	
		As per Company	If O.I. is taken into a/c.	If Cont. Liab. taken into a/c	As per Company	If O.I. is not taken into a/c	If Cont Liab. are taken into a/c	As per Company	If Cont. Liability are taken into a/c
1. I.A.	55.04	(198.85)	(249.92)	(273.57)	(361.28)	(454.15)	(497.04)	332.48	68.53 ES
2. Vayudoot	36.17	(31.63)	(32.08)	N.A.	(87.45)	(88.69)	N.A	(115.88)	NA
3. CIL	6000.76	(22.62)	(50.03)	(33.04)	(0.38)	(0.83)	(0.55)	5520.55	5509.13
4. Neyveli	1565.82	101.69	67.51	(0.69)	6.49	4.31	(0.04)	2175.00	1780.43
5. BALCO	488.85	0.93	(8.95)	(26.34)	0.19	(1.83)	(5.39)	(500.73)	463.78
6. HCL	304.20	54.90	47.95	44.85	18.05	15.76	14.74	365.72	349.80
7. HZL	404.53	93.36	80.07	67.44	23.08	19.79	16.67	668.62	642.05
8. NALCO	1288.62	59.14	(26.78)	(86.06)	4.59	(2.08)	(6.68)	1446.13	1300.93
9. FCI	616.39	(225.41)	248.88)	(296.65)	(36.57)	(40.38)	(48.13)	(994.09)	(1295.39)
10. FACT	342.77	29.00	24.63	(6.15)	8.46	7.19	(1.79)	419.16	382.95
11. HFC	670.02	(320.53)	(357.52)	(695.68)	(49.33)	(53.36)	(103.83)	(852.24)	1218.76
12. MFL	58.73	16.36	14.39	3.59	27.86	24.50	6.11	75.87	63.10
13. NFL	490.58	83.61	66.08	(26.26)	17.04	13.47	5.45	772.04	659.97
14. RCF	551.69	18.78	1.83	50.81	3.40	0.33	9.21	795.49	724.88
15. STC	30.00	36.30	(205.89)	(361.58)	121.00	(686.30)	(1205.27)	359.82	(195.26)
16. MMTC	50.00	199.17	100.79	(738.07)	398.34	201.58	(1476.14	426.75	(510.49)
17. IDPL	113.06	(110.40)	(118.57)	(248.32)	(86.47)	(104.85)	(78.49)	(431.454)	(666.22)
18. BEL	80.00	67.50	11.01	(28.91)	(84.38)	13.76	(36.14)	(279.68)	179.28
19. IPCL	186.00	51.78	17.39	52.67	27.84	9.35	28.32	719.40	593.04
20. CSL	77.29	(14.92)	(18.34)	(214.31)	(19.30)	(23.73)	(277.28)	(103.73)	(303.12)
21. HSL	69.88	(104.12)	(107.11)	(242.27)	(149.00)	(153.28)	(346.69)	(385.81)	(523.96)
22. SCIL	282.30	107.54	68.69	54.70	38.09	24.33	19.38	615.35	546.56
23. DTC	–	(203.82)	(211.84)	(216.50)	–	–	–	(848.66)	(861.34)
24. NTC	437.85	4.50	(42.70)	(384.80)	1.03	(9.75)	(87.88)	438.17	48.12

TABLE 6.7 B : **Return on Equity of Selected Companies 1992-93**

Names of PSU	Equity	PBT			Return on Equity (in % age)			Net Worth	
		As per Company	If O.I. is taken into a/c.	If Cont. Liab. taken into a/c	As per Company	If O.I. is not taken into a/c	If Cont Liab. are taken into a/c	As per Company	If Cont. Liability are taken into a/c
1. BPCL	50	292.07	234.42	162.89	584.14	468.84	325.78	951.04	821.86
2. BRPL	199.82	50.17	28.72	4.87	25.11	14.37	2.44	381.19	335.89
3. CRL	68.93	153.62	143.10	119.43	222.86	207.60	207.60	363.96	338.26
4. GAIL	845.32	210.58	157.16	(1449.48)	24.91	18.59	(171.47)	1051.08	(608.98)
5. HPCL	63.84	383.75	338.30	108.24	601.12	529.92	169.55	1102.97	818.75
6. IOCL	123.27	934.99	435.20	292.15	758.49	353.04	237.00	4950.48	4303.78
7. IBPL	7.36	18.67	(2.21)	9.03	253.67	(30.03)	122.69	95.24	68.91
8. ONGC	342.85	788.20	(195.29)	(1104.42)	229.90	(56.96)	(322.13)	10155.53	8232.64
9. MRL	114.13	91.62	79.14	20.02	80.28	69.34	17.54	324.93	218.87
10. NHPC	2632.48	41.49	36.17	(674.56)	1.58	1.37	(25.62)	2962.06	2246.01
11. NTPC	7549.84	886.86	815.53	(3012.07)	11.75	10.80	(39.90)	11885.87	5614.42
12. REC	402.60	125.31	(107.80)	(102.45)	31.13	(26.78)	(25.45)	791.68	548.60
13. IISCO	387.67	(58.96)	(68.12)	(90.73)	(15.21)	(17.57)	(23.40)	(436.41)	(459.02)
14. RINL	6170.57	(568.29)	(683.80)	(754.92)	(9.21)	(11.08)	(12.23)	4097.27	3910.64
15. SAIL	3985.89	423.40	175.72	216.73	10.62	4.41	5.44	5272.19	5065.52
16. AYULE	10.74	4.45	0.14	(83.88)	41.43	1.30	(781.01)	42.27	48.42
17. BHEL	244.76	309.00	105.48	(720.43)	126.25	43.10	(294.34)	871.57	(263.22)
18. HMT	87.73	(12.53)	(37.08)	(110.01)	(14.28)	(42.27)	(125.40)	245.53	148.05
19. HPCL	479.35	(51.34)	(64.45)	(163.88)	(10.71)	(13.45)	(34.19)	35.29	(83.78)
20. MUL	132.29	36.61	(36.23)	(361.79)	27.67	(27.39)	(273.48)	342.96	(54.88)
21. AIR INDIA	79.47	333.14	204.62	218.81	419.20	257.48	275.34	1121.06	856.35
22. IA	55.16	(195.11)	(260.82)	(310.48)	(353.72)	(472.84)	(562.87)	239.38	(117.10)
23. Vayudoot	N.A.	N.A.	N.A.	N.A.	N.A.	N.A.	N.A.	N.A.	N.A.

Table 6.9 details the returns on paid-up capital in most PSUs on the basis of dividend paid by the companies. As may be seen, nearly half the companies paid no dividend at all in 1990-91, although the situation improved slightly in 1992-93 and the return on paid-up capital equity, at its highest, was only 1.41 per cent. To the extent reserves are essentially dividends foregone, any analysis of return on equity should be conducted on the basis of return on paid-up capital plus reserves. Table 6.10, therefore, details the return on Equity (i.e. paid-up capitals+reserves). It may be seen that on this criteria, the return declines sharply and there only four companies which have a return of more than 5 per cent in 1992-93. All are in the Petro-chemical Sector. The total return on this basis ranges from a low of 0.49 per cent in 1991 to a high of only 0.82 per cent in 1992 showing a marginal decline to 0.81 per cent in 1992-93.

Table 6.11 details the return on equity (i.e. paid-up capital+reserves) made in PSUs on the basis of operating income (net profit less other income) and indicating income arising from the primary operations of the company. The highest return was earned in 1992-93 and was 0.74 per cent, whereas the lowest was in 1991-92 at (–) 1.16 per cent.

Table 6.12 details the return on turnover on the basis of Operating Income. Most PSUs have a return on turnover which is negative, and only five companies in 1990-91, three in 1991-92, and two in 1992-93, have a return exceeding 12.5 per cent. On the basis of return on turnover, as calculated on Operating Income basis, only two companies earn a return exceeding 15 per cent in 1992-93.

Table 6.13 details the ratio of total inventory to value of production, measured in number of days which perhaps indicate the idling of resources and also to an extent, efficiency of operations. Except for five companies, this ratio exceeds 35 days in all cases. In 19 companies, this ratio exceeded 100 days, whereas in eight companies it exceeds 200 days.

Table 6.14 details the Pending Claims made by Government of India against companies but not accepted by the Companies and Table 6.14A details the Claims made by the companies against the Government but not accepted by the Government of India. The net figures displayed in Table 6.14B, therefore, indicate the total additional liability which may devolve on the Government of India, in cases all these claims are not accepted by the PSUs. Such a liability would be in the range of Rs.143 crores in 1992-93.

Table 6.15 details Pending Claims made by the State governments against companies but not accepted by companies and Table 6.15A details the claims made by companies against State governments but accepted by the State governments. The net figures displayed in Table 6.15B, therefore, indicate the total additional liability of the various State governments towards these PSUs in case all these Claims are not accepted by them and devolve on the State governments. Such a liability would be in the range of Rs. 1555 crores in 1992-93.

Table 6.16 indicates the position of Sundry Debtors on the basis of number of days of cross sales. In 12 companies, this figure exceeds 100 days in 1991-92. In most cases, the figure exceeds 50 days.

ISSUES

Major areas needing attention, when analysing budget relationship with PEs are:

(a) Reconciling the figures of budgetary inflows and outflows as depicted by PEs in their accounts, and as presented in the budget, and reconciling the figures of loans outstanding from PEs in the budget;

(b) Ensuring disaggregated unit-wise analysis of financial relationships.

(c) Focussing on identifying and obtaining the dues from PEs to Government and not be content merely with reducing further support, in fact, it may be possible to provide budget support to deserving PEs if receipts are ensured.

(d) Reconciling the genuine needs of PEs with budgetary constraints including cash management to avoid the spectacle of huge 'other income' of PEs and burgeoning fiscal deficits;

(e) Setting expeditiously mutual claims between Governments (Central and State) and CPEs after ascertaining their veracity.

(f) Assessing financial health of the enterprises in terms of high inventories, sundry debtors/creditors, inter-enterprise claims, streamlining of accounting practices, etc.

(g) Making transparent, operations such as debt rescheduling, write-offs, tax concessions, etc. so that costs and benefits are assessed.

(h) Equipping Financial Advisors in Government and Finance Directors in Public Enterprises, through training and seminars, to handle financial transactions in an environment that is capital market oriented for financial resources, and competitive for market access.

TABLE 6.8 : **Statement Showing Interest Rates Chargeable on G.O.I Loans Lent to:**

(All Amounts in %)

	1993	92	91	90	89	88	87	86	85	84	83	82	81	80	79	78	77	76	75	74
1.LOANS GIVEN -TO INDUSTRIAL & COMMERCIAL UNDERTAKING IN THE PUBLIC SECTOR & COOPERATIVES HAVING EQUITY CAPITAL EXCEEDING Rs.1Cr.																				
INVESTMENT LOAN	17	17	16	15	15	15	15	14.5	14	13.5	13	12.5	12	11	11	11	11	10.5	10.5	10.5
-W.C LOAN & LOANS	19.5	19.5	18	17	17	17	17	17.5	17	17	15.5	15.5	15	15	–	–	–	–	–	–
TO MEET CASE LOSSES																				
2.FINANCIAL INSTITUTIONS IN THE PUBLIC SECTOR, PORT TRUSTS, KVIC, MCD, DESU, COMMODITY BOARDS, SOCIAL SERVICES INSTITUTIONS ETC.																				

TABLE 6.8 (*Contd.*)

A. RURAL ELECTRIFICATION CORPN.																				
(i) MIN. NEEDS PROG. & LOANS TO SEBs, & DESU, DVC FOR RENOVATION & MOD. OF T. POWER PLANTS	12	11.75	10.75	10.25	9.75	9.75	9.25	11	11.5	11	10.5	10	9.5	9	9	9	9	9	9	8
(ii) Min. Needs Prog	12	11.75	10.75	10.25	10	10	10	11	9	8.5	8	8	8	7.5	7.5	7.5	7.5	7.5	7.5	–
B. NABARD	12	11.75	10.75	10.25	10	10	10	11	9.5	9	8.5	8.5	8.5	8	8	8	8	8	–	
C. OTHERS	13	12.50	11.50	11	10.5	0.5	10.5	11	11	10.5	10.5	0	9.5	9	9	9	9	9	9	
3. TERM LENDING RATES :																				
NORMAL L. RATE	15.5 TO 18%	17.5 TO 19%	14	14	14	14	14	14	14	14	14	14	–	–	–	–	–	–	–	

Notes

1. Rates of interest before 1987 varied with the periodicity of the loan. The spread of interest between loans sanctioned for a period of one year, and those sanctioned for a period exceeding 15 years, normally being 1.75%. Higher interest was paid for loans with longer repayment periods. In the years before 1987, such higher figures are, therefore, displayed.
2. Normally loans are not given to the Private Sector except under exceptional circumstances under Category 1 (a) and the interest rate then is 1/2% higher.
3. In August 1991 Term Lending Rates were freed and ranged from 18.5% to 20% with no concessional rates.
4. Term lending rates are inclusive of 0.5% investment tax.

TABLE 6.9 : **Return on Paid-up Capital in PSUS**

(*in Rs. Crs.*)

	Name of PSU	Paid-Up Capital in			Dividend Paid in			Return on Paid-up Capitl (%) in		
		1990-91	91-92	92-93	90-91	91-92	92-93	90-91	91-92	92-93
1.	Bharat Petroleum Corpn. Ltd.	50.00	50.00	50.00	10.00	15.00	16.50	20.00	30.00	33.00
2.	Bongaigaon Ref. & Pet. Ltd.	199.82	199.82	199.82	9.99	9.99	9.99	5.00	5.00	5.00
3.	Cochin Refineries Ltd.	68.93	68.93	68.93	14.47	14.48	16.54	21.00	21.00	24.00
4.	Gas Authority of India Ltd.	845.32	845.32	845.32	–	–	20.00	–	–	2.37
5.	Hindustan Petroleum Corpn.	63.84	63.84	63.84	12.77	19.15	25.54	20.00	30.00	40.00
6.	Indian Oil Corpn. Ltd.	123.27	123.27	123.27	27.12	40.68	49.31	22.00	33.00	40.00
7.	IBP Ltd.	7.36	7.36	7.36	1.62	1.77	1.99	22.00	24.00	27.00
8.	Oil & Natural Gas Corpn. Ltd.	342.85	342.85	342.85	61.71	61.71	61.71	18.00	18.00	18.00
9.	Madras Refineries Ltd.	114.13	114.13	114.13	23.97	3.97	28.53	21.00	21.00	25.00
10.	National Hydro Elec. P. Corpn.	2045.33	2322.53	2632.48	–	–	–	–	–	–
11.	National Thermal Power Corpn.	6355.11	7021.81	7549.84	–	–	–	–	–	–
12.	Rural Electrification Corpn.	322.60	262.60	402.60	6.64	7.04	–	2.06	1.94	–
13.	Indian Iron & Steel Co. Ltd.	386.28	387.67	387.67	–	–	–	–	–	–

TABLE 6.9 (*Contd.*)

14.	Rashtriya Ispat Nigam Ltd.	3505.85	3505.85	6170.57	–	–	–	–	–	–
15.	Steel Authority of India	3985.89	3985.89	3985.89	–	79.63	79.72	–	2.00	2.00
16.	Andrew Yule & Co. Ltd.	11.08	10.91	10.74	1.61	2.40	1.90	14.53	22.00	17.69
17.	Bharat Heavy Electricals Ltd.	244.76	244.76	244.76	24.48	36.71	36.71	10.00	15.00	15.00
18.	Hindustan Machine Tools Ltd.	78.56	87.73	87.73	2.29	5.21	–	2.83	5.94	–
19.	Hindustan Paper Corpn. Ltd.	479.3	5479.35	479.35	–	–	–	–	–	–
20.	Maruti Udyog Ltd.	110.24	110.24	132.29	8.82	6.61	7.65	8.00	6.00	5.78
21	Air India	79.24	79.24	79.47	–	–	–	–	–	–
22.	Indian Airlines	54.92	55.03	55.15	–	–	–	–	–	–
23.	Vayudoot	27.75	36.17	N.A.	–	–	–	–	–	N.A.
24.	Coal India Ltd.	5713.31	6000.76	6097.84	–	–	–	–	–	–
25.	Neyveli Lignite Corpn. Ltd.	1435.82	1565.82	1699.37	–	–	–	–	–	–
26.	Bharat Aluminium Co. Ltd.	488.85	488.85	488.85	–	–	–	–	–	–
27.	Hindustan Copper	304.20	304.20	304.20	–	–	–	–	–	–
28.	Hindustan Zinc Ltd.	403.73	404.53	422.53	–	41.16	26.47	–	10.17	6.26
29.	National Aluminium Co.	1288.62	1288.62	1288.62	–	–	15.46	–	–	1.20
30.	Fertilisers Corpn. of India	616.39	616.39	623.39	–	–	–	–	–	–

(*Contd.*)

TABLE 6.9 *(Contd.)*

Name of PSU	Paid-Up Capital in			Dividend Paid in			Return on Paid-up Capital (%) in		
	1990-91	91-92	92-93	90-91	91-92	92-93	90-91	91-92	92-93
31. Fertilisers & Chemicals (Travancore) Ltd.	342.77	342.77	342.77	–	–	–	–	–	–
32 Hindustan Fertilisers Corpn.	669.22	670.02	686.02	–	–	–	–	–	–
33. Madras Fertilisers Ltd.	44.74	58.73	98.34	6.37	6.99	8.67	14.24	11.90	8.82
34. National Fertilisers Ltd.	490.58	490.58	490.58	–	21.56	24.52	–	4.39	5.00
35. Rashtriya Chem. & Fert. Ltd	551.69	551.69	551.69	11.03	11.03	11.03	2.00	2.00	2.00
36 State Trading Corpn.of India Ltd.	30.00	30.00	30.00	6.00	9.00	9.00	20.00	30.00	30.00
37. Minerals & Metals Trading Corpn.	50.00	50.00	50.00	10.00	15.00	15.00	20.00	30.00	30.00
38 Indian Drugs & Pharmaceutical Ltd	111.91	113.08	114.25	–	–	–	–	–	–
39. Bharat Electronics Ltd.	80.00	80.00	N.A	9.60	12.80	N.A	12.00	16.00	N.A.
40. Indian Petro Chemicals Ltd.	186.00	186.00	195.46	11.16	27.90	37.52	6.00	15.00	19.20
41. Cochin Shipyard Ltd.	74.36	77.29	79.79	–	–	–	–	–	–
42. Hindustan Shipyard Ltd.	67.43	69.88	70.18	–	–	–	–	–	–
43. Shipping Corpn. of India	282.30	282.30	282.30	13.06	16.94	28.23	4.63	6.00	10.00
44. Delhi Transport Corpn.	–	–	–	–	–	–	–	–	–
45. National Textiles Corpn.	437.85	437.85	N.A.	–	–	N.A.	–	–	N.A.
TOTAL	33172.45	34614.66	37940.24	272.65	486.73	531.	990.82	1.41	1.40

Source: Annual Reports .

TABLE 6.10 : **Return on Equity in PSUS**

(in Rs. Crs.)

	NAME OF PSU	Equity # in			Dividend Paid in			Return on Equity in		
		1990-91	91-92	92-93	90-91	91-92	92-93	90-91	91-92	92-93
1	2	3	4	5	6	7	8	9	10	11
1.	Bharat Petroleum Cropn. Ltd	664.01	797.47	951.03	10.00	15.00	16.50	1.51	1.88	1.73
2.	Bongaigaon Ref & Pet. Ltd.	252.27	252.27	252.27	9.99	9.99	9.99	3.96	3.96	3.96
3.	Cochin Refineries Ltd	134.48	140.09	149.24	4.47	14.48	16.54	10.75	10.34	11.08
4.	Gas Authority of India Ltd.	845.32	860.62	1051.15	–	–	20.00	–	–	1.90
5.	Hindustan Petroleum Corpn	300.82	318.91	346.63	12.77	19.15	25.54	4.25	6.00	7.37
6.	Indian Oil Corpn. Ltd	3514.01	4259.82	4887.20	27.12	40.68	49.31	0.77	0.95	10.08
7.	IBP Ltd.	57.00	69.60	78.74	1.62	1.77	1.99	0.03	2.54	2.53
8.	Oil & Natural Gas Corpn Ltd.	11520.28	11866.88	12593.37	61.71	61.71	61.71	0.53	0.52	0.49
9.	Madras Refineries Ltd.	158.38	163.38	23.97	23.97	28.53	15.13	15.13	17.46	158.38
10.	National Hydro Elec. P. Corpn.	2068.78	2555.98	2865.93	–	–	–	–	–	–
11.	National Thermal Power Corpn.	8369.11	9835.81	11145.53	–	–	–	–	–	–
12.	Rural Electrification Corpn.	525.29	611.02	651.02	6.64	7.04	–	1.26	1.15	–
13.	Indian Iron & Steel Co. Ltd.	410.71	419.73	428.13	–	–	–	–	–	–
14.	Rashtriya Ispat Nigam Ltd.	3509.12	3510.31	6175.80	–	–	–	–	–	–
15.	Steel Authority of India	4484.69	4491.37	4145.64	–	79.63	79.72	–	1.77	1.92
16.	Andrew Yule & Co. Ltd.	39.99	41.78	40.44	1.61	2.40	1.90	4.03	5.74	4.70
17.	Bharat Heavy Electricals Ltd.	781.47	844.88	941.33	24.48	36.71	36.71	3.13	4.34	3.90
18.	Hindustan Machine Tools Ltd.	235.59	259.16	255.74	2.23	5.21	–	0.95	2.01	0
19.	Hindustan Paper Corpn. Ltd.	479.35	479.35	479.35	–	–	–	–	–	–

(Contd.)

TABLE 6.10 (*Contd.*)

1	2	3	4	5	6	7	8	9	10	11
20.	Maruti Udyog Ltd.	148.82	148.33	208.20	8.82	6.61	7.65	5.93	4.46	3.67
21.	Air India	518.31	674.10	1020.13	–	–	–	–	–	–
22.	Indian Airlines	381.72	189.81	186.33	–	–	–	–	–	–
23.	Vayudoot	32.81	40.15	N.A.	–	–	N.A.	–	–	NA.
24.	Coal India Ltd.	5716.76	6004.21	6101.29	–	–	–	–	–	–
25.	Neyveli Lignite Corpn. Ltd.	1435.82	1565.82	1599.37	–	–	–	–	–	–
26	Bharat Aluminium Co. Ltd.	488.85	488.85	488.85	–	–	–	–	–	–
27.	Hindustan Copper	334.20	334.14	335.09	–	–	–	–	–	–
28.	Hindustan Zinc Ltd.	444.59	665.39	683.39	–	41.16	26.47	–	6.19	3.87
29.	National Aluminium Co.	1288.62	1288.62	1288.62	–	–	15.46	–	–	1.20
30.	Fertilisers Corpn. of India	617.47	617.47	624.48	–	–	–	–	–	–
31.	FACT	363.27	363.27	363.27	–	–	–	–	–	–
32.	Hindustan Fertilisers Corpn.	670.59	671.49	687.39	–	–	–	–	–	–
33.	Madras Fertilisers Ltd.	48.71	63.40	104.15	6.37	6.99	8.67	13.07	11.02	8.32
34.	National Fertilisers Ltd.	708.29	770.34	857.28	–	21.56	24.52	–	2.80	2.86
35.	Rashtriya Chem. & Fert. Ltd.	877.52	885.27	847.66	11.03	11.03	11.03	1.26	1.25	1.30
36.	State Trading Corpn. of India Ltd.	324.42	354.58	364.73	6.00	9.00	9.00	1.85	2.54	2.47
37.	Minerals & Metals Tr. Corpn.	350.08	426.75	504.05	10.00	15.00	15.00	2.86	3.51	2.98
38.	Indian Drugs & Pharmaceutical Ltd.	111.91	113.06	114.25	–	–	–	–	–	–
39.	Bharat Electronics Ltd.	254.06	276.62	N.A.	9.60	12.80	N.A.	3.78	4.63	N.A.
40.	Indian Petro Chemicals Ltd.	365.26	365.26	387.72	11.16	27.90	37.52	3.06	7.64	9.68
41.	Cochin Shipyard Ltd.	74.36	77.29	79.29	–	–	–	–	–	–
42.	Hindustan Shipyard Ltd.	74.91	77.23	77.17	–	–	–	–	–	–
43.	Shipping Corpn. of India	488.74	578.87	688.98	13.06	16.94	28.23	2.67	2.93	4.10
44.	Delhi Transport Corpn.	–	–	–	–	–	–	–	–	–
45.	National Textiles Corpn.	438.68	440.45	N.A.	–	–	N.A.	–	–	N.A.
	TOTAL	54909.44	59254.24	65313.61	272.65	486.73	531.99	0.49	0.82	0.81

Equity includes Reserves.

Source: Annual Reports.

TABLE 6.11 : **Return Equity on Operating Income Basis**

(in Rs. Crs.)

	Name of PSU	Equity # in			Operating Income in			Return on Operating in IIncome (%) in		
		1990-91	91-92	92-93	90-91	91-92	92-93	90-91	91-92	92-93
1	Bharat Petroleum Cropn. Ltd.	664.01	797.47	951.03	183.11	214.34	234.42	27.58	26.88	24.65
2.	Bongaigaon Ref. & Pet. Ltd	252.27	252.57	252.57	42.07	52.83	28.72	16.68	20.94	11.38
3.	Cochin Refineries Ltd.	134.48	140.09	149.24	88.25	79.23	143.10	65.62	56.56	95.89
4.	Gas Authority of India Ltd.	845.32	860.62	1051.51	11.47	35.44	157.16	1.36	4.12	14.95
5.	Hindustan Petroleum Corpn.	300.82	318.91	346.63	164.35	154.94	338.30	54.63	48.58	97.60
6.	Indian Oil Corpn. Ltd.	3514.01	4259.82	4887.20	39.57	212.12	435.20	1.13	4.98	8.90
7.	IBP Ltd.	57.00	69.60	78.74	(0.30)	(5.71)	(2.21)	(0.53)	(8.20)	(2.81)
8.	Oil & Natural Gas Corpn.	11520.28	1866.88	12593.37	335.89	(330.78)	(195.29)	2.92	(2.79)	(1.55)
9.	Madras Refineries Ltd.	158.	158.38	163.38	80.54	64.86	79.14	50.85	40.95	48.44
10.	National Hydro Elec. P. Corpn.	2068.78	2555.98	2865.93	29.22	23.53	36.17	1.41	0.92	1.26
11.	National Thermal Power Corpn.	8369.11	9835.81	11145.53	685.77	905.66	815.53	8.19	9.21	7.32
12.	Rural Electrification Corpn.	525.29	611.02	651.02	91.91	112.40	(107.80)	17.50	18.40	(16.56)
13.	Indian Iron & Steel Co. Ltd.	410.71	419.73	428.13	(142.47)	(31.43)	(68.12)	(34.61)	(7.49)	(15.91)
14.	Rashtriya Ispat Nigam Ltd.	3509.12	3510.31	6175.80	(482.34)	(999.38)	(683.80)	(13.75)	(28.47)	11.07
15.	Steel Authority of India	4484.69	4491.37	4145.64	31.91	159.87	175.72	0.71	3.56	4.24
16.	Andrew Yule & Co. Ltd.	39.99	41.78	40.44	8.12	4.84	0.14	20.31	11.58	0.35
17.	Bharat Heavy Elect. Ltd.	781.47	844.88	941.33	(22.30)	(115.91)	105.48	(2.85)	(13.72)	11.21
18.	Hindustan Machine Tool Ltd.	235.59	259.16	255.74	(14.88)	21.50	(37.08)	(6.32)	8.30	(14.50)
19.	Hindustan Paper Corpn. Ltd.	479.35	479.35	479.35	(68.45)	(83.54)	(64.45)	(14.28)	(17.63)	13.45
20.	Maruti Udyog Ltd.	148.82	148.33	208.20	(19.48)	(40.52)	(36.23)	(13.09)	(27.32)	17.40

(Contd.)

TABLE 6.11 (*Contd.*)

21.	Air India	518.31	674.10	1020.13	32.96	55.54	204.62	6.36	8.24	20.06
22.	Indian Airlines	381.72	189.81	186.33	(109.48)	(249.92)	(260.82)	(28.68)	131.67	139.98
23.	Vayudoot	32.81	40.15	N.A.	(30.62)	(32.08)	N.A.	(93.33)	79.90	N.A.
24.	Coal India Ltd.	5716.76	6004.21	6101.29	(65.14)	(50.03)	(42.56)	(1.14)	(0.83)	0.70
25.	Neyveli Lignite Corpn. Ltd.	1435.82	1565.85	1699.37	74.65	67.51	34.73	5.20	4.31	2.04
26.	Bharat Aluminium Co. Ltd.	488.85	488.85	488.85	(4.78)	(8.95)	(10.60)	(0.98)	(1.83)	(2.17)
27.	Hindustan Copper	34.20	334.14	335.09	39.96	47.95	8.26	11.96	14.35	2.47
28.	Hindustan Zinc Ltd.	444.59	665.39	683.39	75.29	80.07	51.71	16.93	12.02	7.57
29.	National Aluminium Co.	1288.62	1288.62	1288.62	3.61	(26.78)	77.26	0.28	(2.08)	6.00
30.	Fertilizers Corpn. of India	617.47	617.48	624.48	(187.23)	(248.88)	(258.19)	(30.32)	(40.31)	41.34
31.	FACT	363.27	363.27	363.27	17.74	24.63	(6.53)	4.88	6.78	(1.80)
32.	Hidustan Fertilisers Corpn.	670.59	671.49	687.39	(242.06)	(357.52)	(368.94)	(36.10)	(53.24)	53.67
33.	Madras Fertilisers Ltd	48.71	63.40	104.15	3.25	14.39	8.94	6.67	22.70	8.58
34.	National Fertilisers Ltd.	708.29	770.34	857.28	2.24	66.08	92.90	1.73	8.58	10.84
35.	Rashtriya Chem. & Fert. Ltd.	877.52	885.27	847.66	29.15	1.83	3.33	3.32	0.21	0.39
36.	State Trading Corpn. of India	324.42	354.58	364.73	(63.28)	(205.89)	(33.65)	(19.51)	(58.07)	(9.23)
37.	Minerals & Metals Tr. Corpn.	350.08	426.75	504.05	(7.60)	100.79	(17.53)	(2.17)	23.62	(3.48)
38.	Indian Drugs & Pharmaceutical	111.91	113.06	114.25	(96.77)	(118.57)	(89.67)	(86.47)	104.87	78.49
39.	Bharat Electronics Ltd.	254.06	276.62	N.A.	2.79	11.01	N.A.	1.20	3.98	N.A.
40.	Indian Pertro Chemicals Ltd.	365.26	365.26	387.72	13.37	17.39	73.50	3.66	4.76	18.96
41.	Cochin Shipyard Ltd.	74.36	77.29	79.29	(22.84)	(18.34)	(17.21)	(30.72)	23.73	21.71
42.	Hindustan Shipyard Ltd.	–	–	(80.29)	(107.11)	(119.91)	–	–	–	–
43.	Shipping Corpn. of India	488.74	578.87	688.98	26.23	68.69	57.09	5.37	11.87	8.29
44.	Delhi Transport Corpn.	–	–	–	(204.43)	(212.84)	(256.23)	–	–	–
45.	National Textiles Corpn.	438.68	440	NA	(38.53)	(42.70)	NA	(8.78)	(9.69)	NA
	TOTAL	54909.44	59254.24	65313.61	267.85	(688.44)	485.10	0.48	(1.16)	0.74

Note: Operating Income is net profit less other income and Indicates income arising from the main operations of a PSU.

Equity Includes Equity and Reserves

Sources: Annual Reports.

TABLE 6.12 : **Return on Turnover on the Basis of Operating Income**

(In Rs. Crs.)

	Name of PSU	Turnover in			Operating Income in			Return on Turnover in		
		1990-91	91-92	92-93	90-91	91-92	92-93	90-91	91-92	91-92
1.	Bharat Petroleum Cropn. Ltd.	5283.06	5698.44	5994.42	183.11	214.34	234.42	3.46	3.76	3.91
2.	Bongaigaon Ref. & Pet. Ltd.	414.62	466.68	480.67	42.07	52.83	28.72	10.74	11.32	5.97
3.	Cochin Refineries Ltd.	1488.78	1486.34	1811.76	88.25	79.23	143.10	5.92	5.33	7.89
4.	Gas Authority of India Ltd.	799.18	1096.65	2884.70	11.47	35.44	157.16	1.43	3.23	5.44
5.	Hindustan Petroleum Corpn.	6283.25	6863.05	7806.05	164.35	154.94	338.30	2.61	2.25	4.33
6.	Indian Oil Corpn. Ltd.	19553.94	20745.72	24319.88	39.57	212.12	435.20	0.20	1.02	1.78
7.	IBP Ltd.	903.83	1034.12	1173.77	(0.30)	(5.71)	(2.21)	(0.03)	(0.55)	(0.18)
8.	Oil & Natural Gas Corpn. Ltd.	9594.38	8128.05	8729.54	335.89	(330.78)	(195.29)	3.50	(4.06)	(2.23)
9.	Madras Refineries Ltd.	1647.96	1612.98	1627.48	80.54	64.86	79.14	4.88	4.02	4.86
10.	National Hydro Elec. P. Corpn.	223.95	243.94	78.90	29.22	23.53	36.17	13.04	9.64	20.21
11.	National Thermal Power Corpn.	2400.59	3854.43	485.37	685.77	905.66	815.53	28.56	23.49	18.18
12.	Rural Electrification Corpn.	426.47	491.00	316.18	91.91	112.40	(107.80)	21.55	22.89	(34.09)
13.	Indian Iron & Steel Co. Ltd.	493.92	708.75	814.74	(142.47)	(31.43)	(68.12)	(28.84)	(4.43)	(8.36)
14.	Rashtriya Ispat Nigam Ltd.	275.85	782.19	1293.04	482.34	999.38	683.80	174.85	127.76	52.88
15.	Steel Authority of Ltd.	8359.19	9545.42	10174.87	31.91	159.87	175.72	0.38	1.67	1.72
16.	Andrew Yule & Co. Ltd.	173.59	205.15	211.51	8.12	4.84	0.14	4.67	2.35	0.06
17.	Bharat Heavy Electricals Ltd.	3237.16	3330.83	3508.30	(22.30)	(115.91)	105.48	(0.68)	(3.47)	3.00
18.	Hindustan Machine Tools Ltd.	767.71	869.80	760.27	(14.88)	21.50	(37.08)	(1.93)	2.47	(4.87)
19.	Hindustan Paper Corpn. Ltd.	206.731	83.90	254.88	(68.45)	(83.54)	(64.45)	(33.11)	45.42	25.28
20.	Maruti Udyog Ltd.	1497.61	1931.43	2150.05	(19.48)	(40.52)	(36.23)	(1.30)	(2.09)	(1.68)
21.	Air India	1626.88	1965.19	2435.86	32.96	55.54	204.62	2.02	2.82	8.40
22.	Indian Airlines	1123.73	1436.25	1513.12	109.48	249.92	260.82	(9.74)	17.40	17.23

(Contd.)

TABLE 6.12 *(Contd.)*

Name of PSU	Turnover in			Operating Income in			Return on Turnover in		
	1990-91	91-92	ꞁ2-93	90-91	91-92	92-93	90-91	91-92	91-92
23. Vayudoot Ltd.	27.39	24.56	N.A.	(30.62)	(30.08)	N.A.	(111.79)	103.61	N.A.
24. Coal India Ltd.	134.30	153.80	100.27	(65.14)	(50.03)	(42.56)	(48.50)	32.52	52.41
25. Neyveli Lignite Corpn. Ltd.	470.86	528.43	666.68	74.65	67.51	34.73	15.85	12.77	5.20
26. Bharat Aluminium Co. Ltd.	467.15	518.60	513.18	(4.78)	(8.95)	(10.60)	(1.02)	(1.72)	(2.06)
27. Hindustan Copper	639.00	663.67	685.18	39.96	47.95	8.26	6.25	7.22	1.20
28. Hindustan Zinc Ltd.	457.06	667.60	758.31	75.29	80.07	51.71	16.47	11.99	6.81
29. National Aluminium Co	905.00	993.62	1169.11	3.61	26.78	77.76	0.3	9 2.6	9 6.65
30. Fertilisers Corpnn of India	304.45	344.43	354.39	(187.23)	(248.88)	(258.19)	(61.29)	72.25	72.85
31. FACT	462.15	810.98	752.79	17.74	24.63	(6.53)	3.83	3.03	(0.86)
32. Hindustan Fertilisers Corpn	213.53	253.08	320.33	242.06	357.52	368.94	113.36	141.26	115.17
33. Madras Fertilisers Ltd.	393.16	456.50	430.90	3.25	14.39	8.94	0.82	3.15	2.07
34. National Fertilisers Ltd.	1121.28	1147.28	1214.29	12.24	66.08	92.90	1.09	5.75	7.65
35. Rashtriya Chem. & Fert. Ltd.	922.66	1031.94	1068.14	29.15	1.83	3.33	3.15	0.17	0.31
36. State Trading Corpn. of India Ltd.	1819.97	1518.31	1012.51	(63.28)	(205.89)	33.65	(3.47)	(13.16)	3.32
37. Minerals & Metals Tr. Corpn.	5622.98	8115.78	5122.44	(7.6)	(100.79)	(17.53)	(0.13)	(1.24)	(0.34)
38. Indian Drugs & Phar. Ltd.	183.15	163.64	163.90	(96.77)	(118.57)	89.67 5	2.83	72.45	(54.71)
39. Bharat Electronics Ltd.	722.02	714.80	N.A.	2.79	11.01	N.A.	0.38	1.54	N.A.
40. Indian Petro Chemicals Ltd.	1329.85	1935.18	2246.68	13.37	17.39	73.50	1.00	0.89	3.27
41. Cochin Shipyard Ltd.	76.98	48.90	70.05	(22.84)	(18.34)	(17.21)	(29.67)	37.50	24.56
42. Hindustan Shipyard Ltd.	95.42	81.88	101.26	(80.29)	107.11	119.91	84.14	130.81	118.41
43. Shipping Corpn. of India	1119.07	1326.63	1405.67	26.23	68.69	57.09	2.34	4.30	4.06
44. Delhi Transport Corpn.	120.05	139.30	178.85	(201.43)	211.84	256.231	67.78	152.07	43.26
45. National Textiles	17.94	22.56	N.A.	(38.53)	(42.70)	N.A.	(214.77)	189.27	N.A.
TOTAL	84407.80	94341.78	101260.32	267.85	688.44	485.10	0.31	(0.72)	0.004

Note : Operating Income is net profit less other income and indicates income arising from the main operations of a PSU.

TABLE 6.13 : **Total Inventory : Value of Production**

(in No. of Days)

	NAME OF PSU	1989-90	90-91	91-92	92-93
1.	Bharat Petroleum Cropn. Ltd.	28.90	37.73	33.39	–
2.	Bongaigaon Ref. & Pet. Ltd.	103.90	105.58	103.45	–
3.	Cochin Refineries Ltd.	26.18	32.77	33.06	–
4.	Gas Authority of India Ltd.	31.46	20.52	23.72	–
5.	Hindustan Petroleum Cropn.	29.12	44.20	44.58	–
6.	Indian Oil Corpn. Ltd.	41.94	46.40	49.05	–
7.	IBP Ltd.	8.26	17.13	18.53	–
8.	Oil & Natural Gas Corpn. Ltd.	81.61	70.47	94.68	–
9.	Madras Refineries Ltd.	83.01	96.51	73.65	–
10.	National Hydro Elec. P. Corpn.	28.11	196.67	201.77	–
11.	National Thermal Power Corpn.	66.36	83.90	70.25	–
12.	Rural Electrification Corpn.	0.00	0.00	0.00	–
13.	Indian Iron & Steel Co. Ltd.	128.34	113.60	95.72	–
14.	Rashtriya Ispat Nigam Ltd	0.00	487.53	258.50	–
15.	Steel Authority of India	140.32	138.44	153.03	–
16.	Andrew Yule & Co. Ltd.	83.06	85.98	81.94	–
17.	Bharat Heavy Electricals Ltd.	152.93	153.55	158.16	–
18.	Hindustan Machine Tools Ltd.	176.52	171.76	166.17	–
19.	Hindustan Paper Corpn Ltd.	124.16	124.71	225.69	–
20.	Maruti Udyog Ltd.	62.46	80.06	72.87	–
21.	Air India	70.72	64.22	51.69	–
22.	Indian Airlines	49.63	44.51	37.46	–
23.	Vayudoot	120.20	120.20	82.06	–
24.	Coal India Ltd.	104.64	91.72	72.07	–
25.	Neyveli Lignite Corpn. Ltd.	241.28	280.63	274.62	–
26.	Bharat Aluminium Co. Ltd.	135.81	139.88	157.64	–
27.	Hindustan Copper	237.44	179.76	187.03	–
28.	Hindustan Zinc Ltd.	144.65	200.77	181.66	–
29.	National Aluminium Co.	81.18	97.32	115.79	–
30.	Fertilisers Corpn. of India	161.46	200.44	159.14	–
31.	FACT	86.84	116.38	78.22	–
32.	Hindustan Fertilisers Corpn.	379.68	359.04	259.37	–
33.	Madras Fertilisers Ltd.	94.66	84.60	69.28	–
34.	National Fertilisers Ltd.	196.96	123.07	97.54	–
35.	Rashtriya Chem. & Fert. Ltd.	94.10	126.22	122.45	–
36.	State Trading Corpn. of India Ltd.	56.34	48.35	49.87	–
37.	Minerals & Metals Tr. Corpn.	28.95	34.48	18.67	–
38.	Indian Drugs & Pharmaceutical	192.92	183.05	144.41	–
39.	Bharat Electronics Ltd.	266.06	241.27	238.44	–
40.	Indian Petro Chemicals Ltd.	73.93	87.87	83.41	–
41.	Cochin Shipyard Ltd.	296.32	224.49	237.54	–
42.	Hindustan Shipyard Ltd.	161.89	182.88	237.69	–
43.	Shipping Corpn. of India	7.97	9.92	8.39	–
44.	Delhi Transport Corpn.	34.31	35.21	41.61	–
45.	National Textiles Corpn.	72.75	90.94	87.00	–

Source: BPE.

TABLE 6.14 : **Pending Claims Made by the Government of India against the Company but not Accepted by the Company**

	Name of PSU	1990-91	1991-92	1992-93
1.	Bharat Petroleum Cropn. Ltd.	11.46	21.60	4.15
2.	Bongaigaon Ref. & Pet. Ltd.	0.63	2.12	3.59
3.	Cochin Refineries Ltd.	–	–	–
4.	Gas Authority of India Ltd.	–	–	–
5.	Hindustan Petroleum Cropn.	1.57	16.41	6.70
6	Indian Oil Corpn. Ltd.	317.86	330.61	228.23
7.	IBP Ltd.	0.20	0.29	0.99
8.	Oil & Natural Gas Corpn. Ltd.	387.38	458.19	404.75
9.	Madras Refineries Ltd.	–	–	–
10.	National Hydro Elec. P. Corpn.	5.81	–	–
11.	National Thermal Power Corpn.	70.02	0.96	–
12.	Rural Electrification Corpn.	–	–	–
13.	Indian Iron & Steel Co. Ltd.	20.93	22.22	25.00
14.	Rashtriya Ispat Nigam Ltd.	8.03	7.96	5.78
15.	Steel Authority of India	–	–	–
16.	Andrew Yule & Co. Ltd.	4.03	3.78	–
17.	Bharat Heavy Electricals Ltd.	0.83	3.44	4.13
18.	Hindustan Machine Tools Ltd.	–	–	0.24
19.	Hindustan Paper Corpn. Ltd.	–	–	–
20.	Maruti Udyog Ltd.	19.33	62.73	128.77
21.	Air India	–	–	–
22.	Indian Airlines	32.53	69.62	95.75
23.	Vayudoot	N.A.	N.A.	N.A.
24.	Coal India Ltd.	–	–	–
25.	Neyveli Lignite Corpn. Ltd.	10.88	11.66	12.48
26.	Bharat Aluminium Co. Ltd.	2.51	2.57	2.58
27.	Hindustan Copper	1.65	1.65	3.03
28.	Hindustan Zinc Ltd..	–	–	–
29.	National Aluminium Co.	5.39	29.78	36.85
30.	Fertilisers Corpn. of India	7.67	33.98	36.47
31.	FACT	1.81	2.34	2.95
32.	Hindustan Fertilisers Corpn.	14.99	48.33	33.34
33.	Madras Fertilisers Ltd.	5.84	5.84	5.84
34.	National Fertilisers Ltd.	0.08	1.57	3.73
35.	Rashtriya Chem. & Fert. Ltd.	9.10	10.02	10.62
36.	State Trading Corpn. of India Ltd.	0.47	0.47	–
37.	Minerals & Metals Tr. Corpn.	–	–	–
38.	Indian Drugs & Pharmaceutical	4.73	3.36	6.82
39.	Bharat Electronics Ltd.	–	–	–
40.	Indian Petro Chemicals Ltd.	50.61	56.24	36.24
41.	Cochin Shipyard Ltd.	–	–	–

(Contd.)

TABLE 6.14 *(Contd.)*

	Name of PSU	1990-91	1991-92	1992-93
42.	Hindustan Shipyard Ltd.	0.15	0.15	–
43.	Shipping Corpn. of India	–	–	–
44.	Delhi Transport Corpn.	–	–	–
45.	National Textiles Corpn.	0.14	0.01	0.01
	Total additional Claims of towards the Govt. of India	1328.15	1207.90	1099.04

Source: Annual Reports.

TABLE - 6.14A : **Claims made by the Company against the Government but not Accepted by the Government of India**

	Name of PSU	1990-91	1991-92	1992-93
1.	Bharat Petroleum Cropn. Ltd.	0.18	0.18	–
2	Bongaigaon Ref. & Pet. Ltd.	–	–	–
3.	Cochin Refineries Ltd.	–	–	–
4.	Gas Authority of India Ltd.	–	–	–
5.	Hindustan Petroleum Cropn.	–	–	–
6.	Indian Oil Corpn. Ltd.	–	–	–
7.	IBP Ltd.	–	–	–
8.	Oil & Natural Gas Corpn. Ltd.	–	–	–
9.	Madras Refineries Ltd.	–	–	–
10.	National Hydro Elec. P. Corpn.	–	–	–
11.	National Thermal Power Corpn.	5.92	5.92	–
12.	Rural Electrification Corpn.	–	–	–
13.	Indian Iron & Steel Co. Ltd.	–	–	–
14.	Rashtriya Ispat Nigam Ltd.	–	–	–
15.	Steel Authority of India	–	–	–
16.	Andrew Yule & Co. Ltd.	–	–	–
17.	Bharat Heavy Electricals Ltd	–	–	–
18.	Hindustan Machine Tools Ltd.	–	–	–
19.	Hindustan Paper Corpn. Ltd.	–	–	–
20.	Maruti Udyog Ltd	0.58	0.06	2.97
21.	Air India	–	–	–
22.	Indian Airlines	0.06	–	–
23.	Vayudoot	N.A.	N.A.	N.A.
24.	Coal India Ltd.	–	–	–
25.	Neyveli Lignite Corpn. Ltd.	–	–	–
26.	Bharat Aluminium Co. Ltd.	–	–	–

(Contd.)

TABLE 6.14A *(Contd.)*

Name of PSU	1990-91	1991-92	1992-93
27. Hindustan Copper	–	–	–
28. Hindustan Zinc Ltd.	–	–	–
29. National Aluminium Co.	1.53	–	–
30. Fertilisers Corpn. of India	22.44	21.19	12.34
31. FACT	2.76	6.14	21.47
32. Hindustan Fertilisers Corpn.	30.75	2.80	1.56
33. Madras Fertilisers Ltd.	6.56	15.05	14.16
34. National Fertilisers Ltd.	–	–	–
35. Rashtriya Chem. & Fert. Ltd.	7.60	33.55	90.81
36. State Trading Corpn. of India Ltd.	–	–	–
37. Minerals & Metals Tr. Corpn.	–	–	–
38. Indian Drugs & Pharmaceutical	0.31	0.13	–
39. Bharat Electronics Ltd.	–	–	–
40. Indian Petro Chemicals Ltd.	–	–	–
41. Cochin Shipyard Ltd.	–	–	–
42. Hindustan Shipyard Ltd.	–	–	–
43. Shipping Corpn. of India	–	–	–
44. Delhi Transport Corpn.	–	–	–
45. National Textiles Corpn.	–	–	–
Total Additional Claims of the PSU Against the Govt. of India	78.69	85.02	143.31

Source: Annual Reports.

TABLE 6.14B : **Net Amounts of Pending Claims made by the Government of India against the Company but not Accepted by the Company and Claims made by the Company Against the Government but not Accepted by the Government of India**

Name of PSU	1990-91	1991-92	1992-93
1. Bharat Petroleum Cropn. Ltd.	11.64	21.78	4.15
2. Bongaigaon Ref. & Pet. Ltd.	0.63	2.12	3.59
3. Cochin Refineries Ltd.	–	–	–
4. Gas Authority of India Ltd.	–	–	–
5. Hindustan Petroleum Cropn.	1.57	16.41	6.70
6. Indian Oil Corpn. Ltd.	317.86	330.61	228.23
7. IBP Ltd.	0.20	0.29	0.99
8. Oil & Natural Gas Corpn. Ltd.	387.38	458.19	404.75

(Contd.)

TABLE 6.14 B *(Contd.)*

	Name of PSU	1990-91	1991-92	1992-93
9.	Madras Refineries Ltd.	–	–	–
10.	National Hydro Elec. P. Corpn.	5.81	–	–
11.	National Thermal Power Corpn.	75.94	6.88	–
12.	Rural Electrification Corpn.	–	–	–
13.	Indian Iron & Steel Co. Ltd.	20.93	22.22	25.00
14.	Rashtriya Ispat Nigam Ltd.	8.03	7.96	5.78
15.	Steel Authority of India	–	–	–
16.	Andrew Yule & Co. Ltd.	4.03	3.78	–
17.	Bharat Heavy Electricals Ltd.	0.83	3.44	4.13
18.	Hindustan Machine Tools Ltd.	–	–	0.24
19.	Hindustan Papern Corpn. Ltd.	–	–	–
20.	Maruti Udyog Ltd.	19.91	62.79	131.74
21.	Air India	–	–	–
22.	Indian Airlines	32.59	69.62	95.75
23.	Vayudoot	N.A.	N.A.	N.A.
24.	Coal India Ltd..	–	–	–
25.	Neyveli Lignite Corpn. Ltd.	10.88	11.66	12.48
26.	Bharat Aluminium Co. Ltd.	2.51	2.57	2.58
27.	Hindustan Copper	1.65	1.65	3.03
28.	Hindustan Zinc Ltd.	–	–	–
29.	National Aluminium Co.	6.92	29.78	36.85
30.	Fertilisers Corpn. of India	30.11	55.17	48.81
31.	FACT	4.57	8.48	24.42
32.	Hindustan Fertilisers Corpn.	45.74	51.13	34.90
33.	Madras Fertilisers Ltd.	12.40	20.89	20.00
34.	National Fertilisers Ltd.	0.08	1.57	3.73
35.	Rashtriya Chem. & Fert. Ltd.	16.70	43.57	101.43
36.	State Trading Corpn. of India Ltd.	0.47	0.47	–
37.	Minerals & Metals Tr. Corpn.	–	–	–
38.	Indian Drugs & Pharmaceutical	5.04	3.49	6.82
39.	Bharat Electronics Ltd.	–	–	–
40.	Indian Petro Chemicals Ltd	50.61	56.24	36.24
41.	Cochin Shipyard Ltd.	–	–	–
42.	Hindustan Shipyard Ltd.	0.15	0.15	–
43.	Shipping Corpn. of India	–	–	–
44.	Delhi Transport Corpn.	–	–	–
45.	National Textiles Corpn.	0.14	0.01	0.01
	Total Additional Claims of the PSU against the Govt. of India	1075.32	1292.92	1242.35

Source: Annual Reports.

TABLE 6.15 : **Pending Claims made by the State Governments against the Company but not Accepted by the Company**

	Name of PSU	1990-91	1991-92	1992-93
1.	Bharat Petroleum Cropn. Ltd.	–	–	–
2.	Bongaigaon Ref. & Pet. Ltd.	–	–	–
3.	Cochin Refineries Ltd.	–	–	–
4.	Gas Authority of India Ltd.	–	–	–
5.	Hindustan Petroleum Cropn.	44.45	45.94	58.36
6.	Indian Oil Corpn. Ltd.	25.17	42.60	66.72
7.	IBP Ltd.	–	–	–
8.	Oil & Natural Gas Corpn. Ltd.	302.63	513.19	691.60
9.	Madras Refineries Ltd.	46.21	46.67	46.67
10.	National Hydro Elec. P. Corpn.	–	–	–
11.	National Thermal Power Corpn.	67.40	90.54	116.18
12.	Rural Electrification Corpn.	–	0.01	0.02
13.	Indian Iron & Steel Co. Ltd.	1.03	0.40	0.48
14.	Rashtriya Ispat Nigam Ltd.	22.17	31.19	31.77
15.	Steel Authority of India	–	–	–
16.	Andrew Yule & Co. Ltd.	1.18	2.57	8.33
17.	Bharat Heavy Electricals Ltd.	163.30	183.04	199.88
18.	Hindustan Machine Tools Ltd.	13.97	15.42	18.52
19.	Hindustan Paper Corpn Ltd.	1.75	2.23	30.19
20.	Maruti Udyog Ltd.	4.42	5.02	7.03
21.	Air India	–	–	–
22.	Indian Airlines	–	–	–
23.	Vayudoot	N.A.	N.A.	N.A.
24.	Coal India Ltd.	0.27	–	–
25.	Neyveli Lignite Corpn. Ltd.	5.96	7.02	8.66
26.	Bharat Aluminium Co. Ltd.	4.97	15.91	12.15
27.	Hindustan Copper	3.16	4.03	2.09
28.	Hindustan Zinc Ltd.	–	1.00	0.61
29.	National Aluminium Co.	44.25	51.70	47.05
30.	Fertilisers Corpn. of India	2.47	2.09	1.90
31.	FACT	20.02	20.84	22.14
32.	Hindustan Fertilisers Corpn.	–	–	–
33.	Madras Fertilisers Ltd.	–	–	–
34.	National Fertilisers Ltd.	6.34	18.66	46.36
35.	Rashtriya Chem. & Fert. Ltd.	–	–	–
36.	State Trading Corpn. of India Ltd.	54.91	29.44	30.94
37.	Minerals & Metals Tr. Corpn.	49.59	59.45	92.26
38.	Indian Drugs & Pharmaceutical	14.34	15.16	15.16
39.	Bharat Electronics Ltd.	–	–	–
40.	Indian Petro Chemicals Ltd.	–	–	–
41.	Cochin Shipyard Ltd.	11.84	11.84	0.11

(Contd.)

TABLE 6.15 *(Contd.)*

Name of PSU	1990-91	1991-92	1992-93
42. Hindustan Shipyard Ltd.	38.81	0.06	0.11
43. Shipping Corpn. of India	–	–	–
44. Delhi Transport Corpn.	–	–	–
45. National Textiles Corpn.	–	0.05	0.05
Total Additional Claims of the State Government	950.61	1216.07	1555.39

Source: Annual Reports of PSUS.

TABLE 6.15A : **Claims made by the Company against State Governments but not Accepted by the State Governments**

Name of PSU	1990-91	1991-92	1992-93
1. Bharat Petroleum Cropn. Ltd.	–	–	–
2. Bongaigaon Ref. & Pet. Ltd.	–	–	–
3. Cochin Refineries Ltd.	–	–	–
4. Gas Authority of India Ltd.	–	–	–
5. Hindustan Petroleum Cropn.	–	–	–
6. Indian Oil Corpn. Ltd.	115.04	136.07	199.04
7. IBP Ltd.	–	–	–
8. Oil & Natural Gas Corpn. Ltd.	–	–	–
9. Madras Refineries Ltd.	–	–	–
10. National Hydro Elec. P. Corpn.	–	–	–
11. National Thermal Power Corpn.	566.00	840.00	1028.00
12. Rural Electrification Corpn.	–	–	–
13. Indian Iron & Steel Co. Ltd.	–	–	–
14. Rashtriya Ispat Nigam Ltd.	–	–	–
15. Steel Authority of India	–	–	–
16. Andrew Yule & Co. Ltd.	–	–	–
17. Bharat Heavy Electricals Ltd.	–	–	–
18. Hindustan Machine Tools Ltd.	–	–	–
19. Hindustan Paper Corpn. Ltd.	–	–	–
20. Maruti Udyog Ltd.	–	–	–
21. Air India	–	–	–
22. Indian Airlines	–	–	–
23. Vayudoot	N.A.	N.A.	N.A
24. Coal India Ltd.	–	–	–
25. Neyveli Lignite Corpn. Ltd.	–	–	–
26. Bharat Aluminium Co. Ltd.	-	-	-
27. Hindustan Copper	-	-	-

(Contd.)

TABLE 6.15 A *(Contd.)*

	Name of PSU	1990-91	1991-92	1992-93
28.	Hindustan Zinc Ltd.	–	–	–
29.	National Aluminium Co.	65.02	67.64	67.58
30.	Fertilisers Corpn. of India	0.08	–	–
31.	FACT	0.28	0.25	0.26
32.	Hindustan Fertilisers Corpn.	–	–	–
33.	Madras Fertilisers Ltd.	–	–	1.66
34.	National Fertilisers Ltd.	–	–	–
35.	Rashtriya Chem. & Fert. Ltd.	–	–	–
36.	State Trading Corpn. of India Ltd.	–	–	–
37.	Minerals & Metals Tr. Corpn.	–	–	–
38.	Indian Drugs & Pharmaceutical	–	–	–
39.	Bharat Electronics Ltd.	–	–	–
40.	Indian Petro Chemicals Ltd.	0.25	–	–
41.	Cochin Shipyard Ltd.	–	–	–
42.	Hindustan Shipyard Ltd.	–	–	–
43.	Shipping Corpn. of India	–	–	–
44.	Delhi Transport Corpn.	–	–	–
45.	National Textiles Corpn.	–	–	–
	Total Additional Claims of the PSUs against the State Governments	746.67	1043.96	1296.54

TABLE 6.15B : **Net Pending Claims made by State Governments against the Company but not Accepted by the Company and Claims made by the Company against State Governments but not Accepted by the State Governments**

	Name of PSU	1990-91	1991-92	1992-93
1.	Bharat Petroleum Cropn. Ltd.	–	–	–
2.	Bongaigaon Ref. & Pet. Ltd.	–	–	–
3.	Cochin Refineries Ltd.	–	–	–
4.	Gas Authority of India Ltd.	–	–	–
5.	Hindustan Petroleum Corpn.	44.45	45.94	58.36
6.	Indian Oil Corpn. Ltd.	140.21	178.67	265.76
7.	IBP Ltd.	–	–	–
8.	Oil & Natural Gas Corpn. Ltd.	302.63	513.19	691.60
9.	Madras Refineries Ltd.	46.21	46.67	46.67
10.	National Hydro Elec. P. Corpn.	–	–	–
11.	National Thermal Power Corpn.	633.40	930.54	1144.18
12.	Rural Electrification Corpn.	–	0.01	0.02
13.	Indian Iron & Steel Co. Ltd.	1.03	0.40	0.48

(Contd.)

TABLE 6.15 B *(Contd.)*

	Name of PSU	1990-91	1991-92	1992-93
14.	Rashtriya Ispat Nigam Ltd.	22.17	31.19	31.77
15.	Steel Authority of India	–	–	–
16.	Andrew Yule & Co. Ltd.	1.18	2.57	8.33
17.	Bharat Heavy Electricals Ltd.	163.30	183.04	199.88
18.	Hindustan Machine Tools Ltd.	13.97	15.42	18.52
19.	Hindustan Paper Corpn. Ltd.	1.75	2.23	30.19
20.	Maruti Udyog Ltd.	4.47	4.02	7.03
21.	Air India	–	–	–
22.	Indian Airlines	–	–	–
23.	Vayudoot	N.A.	N.A.	N.A.
24.	Coal India Ltd.	0.27	–	–
25.	Neyveli Lignite Corpn. Ltd.	5.96	7.02	8.66
26.	Bharat Aluminium Co. Ltd.	4.97	15.91	12.15
27.	Hindustan Copper	3.16	4.03	2.09
28.	Hindustan Zinc Ltd.	–	1.00	0.61
29.	National Aluminium Co.	109.27	119.34	104.63
30.	Fertilisers Corpn. of India	2.55	2.09	1.90
31.	FACT	2.30	21.09	22.45
32.	Hindustan Fertilisers Corpn.	–	–	–
33.	Madras Fertilisers Ltd.	–	–	1.66
34.	National Fertilisers Ltd.	6.34	18.66	46.36
35.	Rashtriya Chem. & Fert. Ltd.	–	–	–
36.	State Trading Corpn. of India Ltd.	154.91	29.44	30.94
37.	Minerals & Metals Tr. Corpn.	49.59	59.45	92.26
38.	Indian Drugs & Pharmaceutical	14.34	15.16	15.16
39.	Bharat Electronics Ltd.	–	–	–
40.	Indian Petro Chemicals Ltd.	0.25	–	–
41.	Cochin Shipyard Ltd.	11.84	11.84	0.11
42.	Hindustan Shipyard Ltd.	38.81	0.06	0.11
43.	Shipping Corpn. of India	–	–	–
44.	Delhi Transport Corpn.	–	–	–
45.	National Textiles Corpn.	0.05	0.05	0.05
	Total Additional Liability Towards the State Governments	1779.38	2259.03	2841.88

TABLE - 6.16: S **Debtors (No. of Days of Gross Sales)**

	Name of PSU	1989-90	1990-91	1991-92	1992-93
1.	Bharat Petroleum Corpn. Ltd.	19.94	5.37	6.57	N.A.
2.	Bongaigaon Ref. & Pet. Ltd.	18.45	19.96	43.15	N.A.
3.	Cochin Refineries Ltd.	45.80	19.06	11.55	N.A.
4.	Gas Authority of India Ltd	13.27	16.57	51.56	N.A.

(Contd.)

TABLE 6.16 *(Contd.)*

	Name of PSU	1989-90	1990-91	1991-92	1992-93
5.	Hindustan Petroleum Corpn.	3.01	3.44	4.14	N.A.
6.	Indian Oil Corpn. Ltd.	10.33	9.72	16.10	N.A.
7.	IBP Ltd.	7.43	7.56	7.34	N.A.
8.	Oil & Natural Gas Corpn. Ltd.	76.12	148.15	154.38	N.A.
9.	Madras Refineries Ltd.	3.02	2.68	3.87	N.A.
10.	National Hydro Elec. P. Corpn.	362.34	240.89	297.25	N.A.
11.	National Thermal Power Corpn	207.23	229.63	152.32	N.A.
12.	Rural Electrification Corpn.	–	–	–	N.A.
13.	Indian Iron & Steel Co. Ltd.	39.48	39.66	128.71	N.A.
14.	Rashtriya Ispat Nigam Ltd.	N.A.	5.66	2.47	N.A.
15.	Steel Authority of India	22.67	24.84	18.06	N.A.
16.	Andrew Yule & Co. Ltd.	121.23	129.69	131.36	N.A.
17.	Bharat Heavy Electricals Ltd.	180.84	210.14	235.33	N.A.
18.	Hindustan Machine Tools Ltd.	52.27	47.73	57.40	N.A.
19.	Hindustan Paper Corpn. Ltd.	31.65	43.01	50.06	N.A.
20.	Maruti Udyog Ltd.	7.03	4.13	16.44	N.A.
21.	Air India	63.94	67.47	62.54	N.A.
22.	Indian Airlines	74.12	66.31	52.29	N.A.
23.	Vayudoot	41.98	41.98	52.31	N.A.
24.	Coal India Ltd.	10.77	13.40	21.45	N.A.
25.	Neyveli Lignite Corpn. Ltd.	92.10	99.70	116.04	N.A.
26.	Bharat Aluminium Co. Ltd.	27.34	18.01	49.22	N.A.
27.	Hindustan Copper	20.75	21.35	12.92	N.A.
28.	Hindustan Zinc Ltd.	15.01	24.68	67.62	N.A.
29.	National Aluminium Co.	42.30	42.24	80.38	N.A.
30.	Fertilisers Corpn. of India	129.41	146.59	129.72	N.A.
31.	Fertilisers & Chemicals (Travancore Ltd.)	33.54	40.64	27.36	N.A.
32.	Hindustan Fertilisers Corpn.	58.32	79.54	76.34	N.A.
33.	Madras Fertilisers Ltd.	1.14	4.92	0.98	N.A.
34.	National Fertilisers Ltd.	92.37	88.92	91.80	N.A.
35.	Rashtriya Chem. & Fert. Ltd.	85.07	123.68	140.81	N.A.
36.	State Trading Corpn. of India Ltd.	10.80	10.62	6.72	N.A.
37.	Minerals & Metals Tr. Corpn.	22.36	45.35	75.32	N.A.
38.	Indian Drugs & Pharmaceutical	79.02	79.72	35.11	N.A.
39.	Bharat Electronics Ltd.	88.15	82.07	104.80	N.A.
40.	Indian Petro Chemicals Ltd.	16.70	14.55	17.72	N.A.
41.	Cochin Shipyard Ltd.	106.17	76.86	106.37	N.A.
42.	Hindustan Shipyard Ltd.	126.46	110.43	233.36	N.A.
43.	Shipping Corpn. of India	42.35	61.01	66.19	N.A.
44.	Delhi Transport Corpn.	2.96	2.83	2.99	N.A.
45.	National Textiles Corpn.	25.78	37.23	34.46	N.A.

(i) Considering the advantages of bringing all PEs under administrative control of a separate Agency representing only exercise of ownership rights. Under the new policy, a distinct regulatory framework has to be administered by the administrative Ministry and conflict of interest as regulator and owner has to be avoided.

Further, the Administrative Ministry would tend to perpetuate and plead for its PEs interests. Moreover, the importance of fiscal diversions and past record, interface with PEs by Government as a professionally equipped owner or principal, has to be avoided.

(j) Paying urgent attention to the fiscal impact of, and justification for, an effective annual financial subsidy on account of inadequate dividends and interest payments compared to cost of capital at about 10%, apart from possible mis-match in maturity of repayment of principal. These magnitudes are in addition to the possible adverse consequences of levels of inventories, Sundry Debtors, Creditors, other income, quality of non-Government borrowings and intercorporate lending and other loans.

(k) Government and Public Enterprises are no longer part of one big joint family where transactions are neither at arms length nor transparent (indeed are secretive). Not only is the happy big joint family being broken up but the rest of the world is rightly demanding transparency.

Summary of Discussion

The discussion that followed supported and reinforced most of the points raised by the authors of the two papers but also gave some new rationale for certain enterprises. The points brought out were that public enterprises would always exist in some areas not only on ideological grounds but on the basis of their inherent competence. The criterion of their existence should always be economic efficiency, technological necessity and special interest of growth and development. But most of the participants agreed that a big majority of the public enterprises need to be dispensed with by selling off completely their equity rather than a simple tinkering of 10 to 20 per cent here and there. Even where, rationale of ownership does exist, it does not follow that government must have majority of shares as most big business houses control the enterprises by holding 20 to 30 per cent of the shares only. The touch-stone of ownership is economic efficiency. In any case, budgetary support to an enterprise is uncalled for once it is established. It was pointed that, if general public owned a significant chunk of equity, then the pressure to earn profits would be in-built into the system.

Case of Germany, Japan and other countries were cited where public enterprises, actively supported by the government, did play a crucial role in development. Cases were also cited where even when the managing directors and Secretaries of the concerned Ministry had proposed to close or liquidate some of the units in mid 80s, the Government had not agreed to it. But now in the new environment of urgent economic reforms it should be possible. Some of the speakers had doubts about the Government being serious in closing down even the perennially losing enterprises.

Another important point of discussion was that in the case of disinvestment by the Government, who would really claim the money– the government, the tax payers or the labour? The difficult case of IISCO was mentioned. In Bharat Electronics employees have already staked their claims. It was suggested that if workers of a public enterprise are prepared to take over that unit in its entirety, it should be welcome but half-way ownership should not be allowed. On equity, the important point to consider was efficiency. Public enterprises should not be allowed to squander the taxpayers' money. Again, public sector enterprises of high technological efficiency should not be handed over to the competitors, especially the international competitors, who might stifle our indigenous R&D in order to protect their parent organizations.

It was noted that bureaucratic convenience and political convenience had created some of the enterprises and over the time deficits of the public enterprises have become the deficits of the Government budget. In a way it is these deficits that have brought forth into the open the question of reforms. On the question of workers it was difficult to decide by taking into consideration only efficiency. It was a complicated social and political question. Multiplicity of corporations in the same field and the growth of public enterprises just to suit some bureaucrats are also encountered. The general consensus in conclusion was a hope that rationality would return in the ownership and management of public enterprises and in addition to efficiency other multifarious dimensions would be taken into account in the final revamping of the public sector.

7

FOREIGN DIRECT AND INDIRECT INVESTMENTS

SUDHIR KUMAR

Background

Reversal of Government of India's approach towards foreign direct and indirect investments has been the most marked economic reform introduced in the New Economic Policy. These economic reform measures were initiated more out of necessity, initially, than out of a sudden change of political or economic convictions/compulsions. For the first time in India's history, the foreign exchange reserves in June-July 1991 had dropped below \$1.2 billion, and were sufficient just for meeting two to three weeks' imports requirements of the country (0.63 months' requirements at 1990-91 level of imports). The severe compression in imports at that time, which continued more or less upto March 1992 (i.e. till the introduction of the new Import-Export Policy on 31.3.1992) was already having a telling effect on the domestic industrial production (and export capabilities), and there was no way for India to have continued with its isolated-island-type of economy protected by stiff tariff barriers, and perpetuating low-technology-low-quality domestic production. Reforms had been long overdue, and the conditionalities of International Monetary Fund only provided the necessary impetus (and, to some extent, protection from political criticism within the ruling party for the brick-by-brick demolition of the Nehruvian Model economy.

And, there could have been no better signal of this reform than permitting majority equity holding to direct foreign investors, and, later (in February 1992 budget) announcing permission for foreign indirect investments in Indian Companies through Offshore Funds, Global Depository Receipts mechanism (Euro-Equity Issues), and through direct portfolio investments in Indian Capital Markets by reputed Foreign Institutional Investors. The edifice of majority equity holding by Indians under all circumstances, which was built into the Foreign Exchange Regulation Act passed in 1973, even more zealously pursued and coercively implemented in 1977 (with the unceremonious ouster of IBM and Coca Cola) and protected upto illogical limits in 1982, even against efficient NRI outfits trying to dislodge inefficient and pestiferous family-based managements who were sucking their companies dry, was demolished in one single stroke on 24th of July 1991.

The Timing of India's Economic Reforms

Even though reforms in Indian economic scenario were long overdue, and were started with a complete turnaround in India's policy towards foreign investments, unfortunately the timing of India's economic reforms has been most inopportune, since in July 1991 there was no time left for the country to wait, survive, and choose its own opportune time. The developed countries are experiencing one of the worst recessions in recent history, and there is a perceptible lack of economic activity and insufficient capital in the world market, which has adversely affected the possible inflow of capital from the developed countries. Another negative factor has been the emergence of a number of newly competing countries, which are all unfolding equally (if not more) revolutionary and radical reforms for attracting foreign (direct and indirect) investments. The emergence of East European and Central Asian countries (with the dismantling of the U.S.S.R.), and serious reforms undertaken by China and Vietnam, in particular, have provided investors with a wider choice than ever before, and foreign investment decisions are now based upon even more pragmatic and practical considerations than in the past. Agonizing delays in the conclusion of Uruguay Round of GATT negotiations also helped delay economic recovery in the developed nations. With Germany not yet being able to cope up with the burden of East Germany's economic woes, and USA, UK, Japan and France still grappling with their domestic recession, there are not many foreign investors hunting for a place to invest their excess capital as foreign direct investments.

But domestic recession in these developed countries has freed a lot of floating capital available with their institutional investors undertaking portfolio investments, who are always on the lookout for equity markets with greater potential for growth in the shortest possible term. There is however, a limit in every country's Capital Markets to absorb such capital, beyond which such portfolio capital investments start yielding only sub-optimal returns for the foreign institutional investors, and at which limit that market turns unattractive enough for any further inflow of such floating capital, forcing these foreign indirect investors to start looking for some other greener pastures where they can make a bigger killing, in a shorter time. This optimal/sub-optimal returns limit can be reached very early in the case of markets with low capitalisation (or lower quantity of floating stocks), and can be reached very late, after absorbing substantial inflows, in the case of larger markets (with greater quantity of floating stocks).

The Determinants of Foreign Investments

Attractiveness of a country as a destination for direct foreign investments depends upon any number of objective and subjective factors. But the following broad or macro considerations go towards compelling foreign investors to start looking towards a country as a possible contender, before they go into the finer details/micro considerations

(1) *Geography* : Size, population, distribution of human and natural resources.
(2) *Politics* : Governmental system and its operation, Party Politics/ democratic setup, and Stability of the Political Process. (irrespective of the set up being democratic or autocratic).
(3) *Economy:* Its health, and certainties/uncertainties, planned or unplanned economy, process of economic planning, general perceptions about past, performance of the economy, performance of the main economic indicators, and general economic perspective.
(4) *Industrialisation* : Composition of present industries, prospects for industries sectors, emerging strategic industries-sectors, and emerging export strengths.
(5) *Industrial Relations:* Labour regulations, organisation/ unionisation/ qualified human resources availability, workers' participation in management, codetermination/consensus, wage levels, linkage of productivity to wage levels, work output quality, system of rewards for better productivity/quality, work ethics, availability of specialised workforce for capital intensive

industries, quality of managerial personnel, and their levels of motivation, and managerial remunerations/restrictions.

(6) *Educational System :* Formal and non-formal systems of education available, and its quality technical education, and its standard, Universities and Business Schools, suitability/adaptability of the systems of education for expatriates, and availability of advanced/highly specialised fields of education

(7) *General Infrastructure*

(a) *Transportation :* Roads, Railways, Airports, Ports, and Multipurpose Terminal Facilities.

(b) *Communications :* Sophisticated matrix of communications, on demand availability reliability, penetration of the communications network business networks (including flexible office networking and Private Leased Circuits), International Operations, Hubbing or relay facilities, Fibre Optics, Satellites, Local Mobile Telephones, and Paging Operations.

(c) *Power :* Availability, Shortages/breakdowns/ interruptions, Stable supply, Voltage fluctuations, quality of supply, Energy rates, and Transmission and Distribution bottlenecks.

(d) *Industrial Estates :* Land prices, Transportation links, Planned and fully serviced sites, Convenient amenities, Pleasant environment, Good supply of manpower, Banks and other financial services, Quick processing of applications, Equal treatment for local and foreign companies, and Industrial housing.

(8) *Banking and Financial Services Infrastructure :* Banking Services, Stock Markets and their regulation, Framework for foreign investment in Securities Markets, and Legal Structures.

(9) *Macro-Economic Indicators :* Inflation, Interest rates, Currency trends, Total GNP, GNP growth, GNP Per capita, Stock Market Growth per cent, Exports, Imports, Trade Balance, Main Exports, Main Imports, Budget Deficit or Surplus, International Reserves, Foreign Debt, Debt/Reserve Ratio, Debt Servicing Ratio, Unemployment, Money Supply, Corporate Earnings, P.E. Ratios over the last few years, Corporate Earnings Growth, Price Rise to Cash Flow, Tax Rate on Dividends, Tax rate on Capital Gains, Repatriation of Capital (Disinvestment Restrictions), Repatriation of Profits, Exchange Controls, Exchange

Rates, Total Market Capitalisation, Daily Volume of Capital Market transactions, Population and Population growth, Literacy Rate, People per telephone tourism facilities and tourist arrivals, Leisure activities, Major international trade fairs and exhibitions, Investment incentives, and Investment promotion organisations.

Another set of micro-level considerations which determine the pattern of flow of foreign investments, and the preference for one country as compared to the other, mainly relate to the Project Financing patterns permissible, Risk Management issues, and the legal or structural framework, available within the country concerned for attracting/regulating foreign investments. These factors can be categorised as follows:

(1) Financing Patterns and Structures : (a) Sources of financing prescribed/allowed, and (b) Investment structures scribed/allowed.

(2) Project Elements.

(3) Legal Issues Relating to : (a) Land, (b) Laws affecting use of leased/owned structures, (c) Partnership structures, (d)Bankruptcy and (e) Contractual Jurisdiction, and (f) Creation and perfection of lenders' lien/security interests.

(4) Opportunities for a fair allocation of risks between foreign and domestic investors in the case of Joint Ventures : (a) Market related risks, (b) Financial risks, (c) Project Development Risks, and (d) Project Operation risks.

Within the chosen country for making direct foreign investments, the ultimate choice of a particular State or region as the destination for investment depends upon further detailed/micro considerations. Factors which really determine the competitiveness of one State/region over the other appear at a very local, narrow level, and not at the level of the nation as a whole. Real leverage for competitiveness thus occurs not at the national level, but at the State/regional or local level.

Policy Concerns of Foreign Investors

Even when a foreign investor has been convinced about the attractiveness of a country (or a State/region within the country) as a destination for foreign direct or indirect investments after considering all the major and minor considerations, certain policy parameters remain as the possible concerns of the foreign investors. These concerns can be the same, different, or overlapping for the direct investors and the indirect investors. Also, there can be any number of ways, permutations and combinations to categorise the same concerns, as follows.

Broad National Policy Concerns

Concerns specific to India relate to :

(a) Absence of any declared guidelines or criteria for scrutiny (and approval/ rejection) of applications for the foreign investment proposals by FIPB.
(b) Its unapproachability for the common foreign investors because of its being housed in the Prime Minister's Office.
(c) A top heavy approval mechanism with about 10 Secretaries of Government of India attending FIPB meetings.
(d) Even after FIPB approval is accorded, the foreign investment cases are again put up for approval by the Cabinet Committee on Foreign Investments, or its Empowered Sub-Committee chaired by the Finance Minister, before a final approval is issued to the foreign investor by the Secretariat for Industrial Approvals (SIA) in the Department of Industry.
(e) This FIPB mechanism therefore functions more as a Foreign Investment Approval Recommendation Board, with the "Promotion" aspect being totally absent.
(f) The only high level delegation to tour abroad so far for promoting foreign investments in Power Sector was led by the then Cabinet Secretary, and not by the Chairman of the FIPB, thus giving a confused signal to the foreign investors about the role of the FIPB.
(g) There is no minimum cut off limit for the foreign investment cases to be considered by FIPB (if they do not qualify for automatic approval by RBI), and the majority of the cases approved by FIPB are for very small amounts of foreign investments, the lowest so far being Rs.1 lakh equivalent.

Besides these there is a lack of a promotional body (like the Singapore's Economic Development Board) to specifically promote foreign investments in India. High level visits abroad cannot perform the function of investment promotion, and have very little impact. A useful organisation like the Indian Investment Centre has been relegated to the background, and has been made disfunctional without a full time head, and without its foreign offices. As a result, there is a total lack of reliable information in respect of GOI's foreign investment policies amongst foreign investors.

The problem regarding lack of information on GOI's foreign investment policies afflicts even the State Governments, and no efforts have been made by GOI, FIPB, or the Ministries of Industry and Finance to undertake a publicity drive for educating the State Governments (including both State level Ministers and Civil servants) about the changes that have taken place in our perception of foreign investments (as a major driving force of the domestic economic growth), and the manner in which the State Governments should deal with the foreign investors, and their investment proposals even more helpfully.

The establishment of an Economic Coordination Unit within the Ministry of External Affairs at New Delhi has also not met with the desired level of success in propagating the changes brought about in the investment climate in India, because of lack of both infrastructure and first hand (up-to-date) information with the ECU and the Missions abroad. While the ECU of MEA has published a limited number of attractive brochures (about doing business in India), these brochures were six months obsolete on the date of their publication itself, and have now become totally obsolete after the changes in taxation rates brought about by the Budget of February 1994, and also the progress made towards near complete convertibility of the rupee for current account transactions in the Budget of 1994 (accompanied by the new Exchange Control Manual released by RBI in February 1994 and its further amendments after the Budget).

Lack of clarity of perception/information among foreign investors regarding Central Government's relations with the State Governments, the Constitutional separation of roles and responsibilities (and jurisdictions) of GOI and State Governments. This has led to a persistent demand from the foreign investors of many countries for a "single window" approval for all the requirements of foreign investment projects (including land, water and power etc.) at the FIPB level at New Delhi. Even the ECU brochures printed by the Ministry of External Affairs explain only the policies and procedures at GOI level, and almost wish the State Governments away, making only passing references to the State level approvals, incentives and problems.

Besides these, no information on restrictions on movements of goods and agricultural produce even within the country (placed in some cases by GOI, and in some cases by the State Governments concerned), thus hindering the purchase of raw materials and inputs at the lowest prices even within the country, and/or increasing the cost of such purchases on account of taxes and levies on such movements (like Octroi, and Entry of Goods Tax etc.) which are State Government's' subjects are easily available to the potential investors.

Specific laws aimed at promoting and protecting foreign investments have been passed by a number of developing countries (and a few developed countries as well), which provide (among other things) protection to foreign investors in respect of their right to repatriation of proceeds of their disinvestments, or incomes from such investments in the currency of original investment, their right of guarantees against expropriation etc. without payment of compensation repatriable in the currency of original investments, and their right of access to international arbitration etc. in the case of a dispute. India also needs to codify such rights of foreign investors into a single piece of legislation, laying down (explaining) the already existing policy and procedures relating to dividend repatriation, disinvestment, non-discrimination (subject to conditions that may be specified), employment of foreign nationals, non-expropriation, sanction and servicing of external commercial borrowings, permitting new instruments and structures for private commercial debt and equity flows (including BOO, BOOT etc.) and the applicability of all the concerned local and international laws, agreements and treaties etc., and the relaxations and exemptions provided to the foreign investors under various laws, regulations, and rules.

At present, India has bilateral arrangements for protection of investments with USA (entered into in 1957, and amplified in 1959) and with FR Germany (entered into in 1964) which are now considered inadequate and imperfect, since they were not proper treaties or agreements, and were the result of mere exchange of letters, even though they possess many features of a bilateral investment protection treaty/agreement, and both these countries have requested for fresh treaties/agreements.

A Bilateral Investment Protection Agreement has just been signed with UK in March 1994, which is a proper and detailed agreement, though it does not have the status of an international treaty (under International law), but would perhaps require ratification by the Parliament in UK even though it does not require ratification by the Indian Parliament. Even the recent agreement with UK has bypassed the problem regarding NRIs (Non Resident Indians living in UK with

British Nationality/passports), who already enjoy a special status under the Indian Income Tax and Foreign Exchange laws, and therefore, should not have been allowed to seek protection as UK nationals under this agreement over and above their already existing privileges and concessions.

About 40 more countries have already requested Government of India for similar agreements/treaties, and since GOI has almost ruled out the passing of a domestic law for protection and promotion of foreign investments, the agreements/treaties with the other major investing countries should be hastened, in order to boost the confidence of foreign investors from those countries.

Significantly, Japan does not consider such a bilateral agreement/treaty to be sufficient safeguard against expropriation and other risks associated with foreign investments, and considers a domestic law passed by the Parliament of India, which would be more difficult to repeal, (and more permanent than the 10-year agreement with UK), to be a better option/protection, and, as a result, atleast till very recently, Japan has not requested for entering into such a bilateral agreement/treaty for protection of foreign investments;

A similar, but multilateral, agreement or treaty would be advisable under the SAARC umbrella also, so that the real economic power and clout of the six nations constituting SAARC is unleashed, utilising the complimentarity of their economies, and to assert their significance as the world's single biggest (and most populous) market, with very high, but latent, purchasing power.

Even though nearly complete convertibility for current account transactions has already been allowed in the Budget for 1994-95 Exchange Control regulations are still perceived to be cumbersome. All capital transactions, including those involving remittances on account of dividends/royalty/lump-sum knowhow fees etc. still require prior approval of RBI.

Company taxation, withholding taxation and Direct/Indirect taxation by State Governments are still considered to be higher than the international levels, or the rates prevailing in other countries which are competing with India as the destination of foreign investments. Levels of taxation applicable to the Foreign Institutional Investors (registered with SEBI for making portfolio investments in Indian Capital Markets) are considered to be higher than the international levels;

Individual foreign investors are still not permitted to make portfolio investments in Indian Capital Markets (except NRIs);

Besides these we have a large black economy and foreign investors coming into India have a very tough time in understanding, grappling with, and by-passing the "black market" economy, specially in the case of purchase/renting out/leasing out of property/real estate for their bona fide personal use, or for office/industrial purposes.

Among other constraints we may also note :

(a) Government has so far failed to evolve a proper reporting mechanism for monitoring the actual inflow of foreign investments, and has therefore been unable to project the correct picture of the foreign investment scenario in India for attracting further foreign investments,

(b) We do not have an exit policy, a network of international banks.

(c) Improvement and stabilisation of call-money market,

(d) GOI rules still do not permit remittance of insurance premia in foreign exchange for any insurance against such public liabilities being taken abroad by the foreign investors for their comfort,

(e) Branch offices of foreign companies are not permitted to undertake manufacturing activities in India under FERA and Exchange Control regulations;

(f) Immigration and customs clearance procedures are cumbersome.

Overcoming these Constraints

Foreign investment promotion can perhaps be achieved better if the Central and State Governments play a more proactive role in project development, atleast in the case of major and medium industrial projects. This project development role should at least include: (a) Project Definition — with the size and other parameters of the potential industrial projects (fit, suitable or viable enough for attracting foreign investments) being outlined, and the site locations, fuel supply linkages, and power supply needs and linkages being identified; and (b) Project Feasibility — with the feasibility of the project having been examined by reliable experts and/or consultants, and a site specific "fatal flaw analysis" having been carried out to determine and establish the feasibility of the project at the proposed site.

If this much of project development role has been performed, and feasible projects identified for the foreign investors, the following aspects of project development can be left for the investors themselves:

The task of attracting foreign investments becomes comparatively very easy if a shelf of such identified feasible projects is ready with the investment promotion agencies of the country. China, in particular, follows this method very effectively and efficiently, and even utilises its various Joint Commission meetings and Bilateral Trade Conferences for the purpose of attracting foreign investments. It may be worth noting here that after a gap of nearly 15 years, in April 1994, China is staging its largest ever investment promotion exercise in USA at a Washington Conference on US-China Bilateral Trade, at which about 800 industrial and agricultural projects are being offered to US investors. About 60 of these would be hydraulic and thermal power stations, and another 100 projects are related to the construction of roads, railways, airports and wharfs. About 500 other projects concern machinery, electronics, petro-chemical, metallurgical, animal husbandry and forestry sectors.

One wonders if the flow of foreign investments into India would not show a quantum jump, if the Central Government and the State Governments could put their acts together, and could save the foreign investor the need for grappling with the first and foremost teething problems of any industrial project like - (a) defining opportunity; (b) assessing fuel supply; (c) determining the need for the end products; (d) screening the leads to the raw material resources; (e) assessing purchase rates for raw materials etc.; (f) determining the competitiveness of the proposed industry; (g) determining the time frame of implementation; (h) evaluating the project site; and (i) defining the project scope.

The International Scenario

However, improved conditions for foreign investments cannot be achieved by a reforms package laying emphasis only on deregulation, and it is necessary to lay even more emphasis on making the economy efficient, and pursuing development policies aimed at sustainable development. With the OECD countries themselves following renewed protectionism in investment (1991 Review Report of OECD for the period 1984-1991), for poorer developing countries like India it is all the more necessary to protect the interests of our poor and low income groups even while further pursuing the economic reforms and deregulation package presently being unfolded. Poor and low-wage earning groups are affected maximum in any structural adjustments, as the IMF and World Bank studies themselves indicate (Development Committee Report Number 13 – "Protecting the Poor during Periods of Adjustment" – Joint Ministerial Committee of the Board of Governors of the World Bank and the IMF on the Transfer of Real Resources to Developing Countries – August 1987).

We must also recognise that it is not always in the national interest of the developing countries to bend over backwards and change every rule of the book to please foreign investors, who would still continue to prefer making investments in their home countries, unless they are either driven out on environmental considerations by their own countries to countries less vigilant environmentally, or they can shift older technology investments to the developing countries and undertake higher technology investments in their home countries, or the cost of production in their own country becomes so high that they are forced to shift their production to cheaper labour areas of developing countries, or the profit margins in developing countries become so high as compared to the profit margins in their home countries that profit considerations alone are sufficient for their shifting their capital, or the size of the market offered in the developing country concerned is so large (and so much more profitable) that it becomes essential to make investments locally for capturing the whole of the local market. Whether it is Motorola, IBM, Coca-Cola and Pepsi now, or Cadbury's, Lever, Bata, Colgate and Philips earlier, all the foreign investment decisions even in India's case were based upon similar considerations only. The fact that the Industrial Nations deliberately follow policies which not only protect their own investments (against each other, as mentioned in the OECD report cited above, or against the developing countries also), but also adversely affect (or even damage) the industrial policies of the developing countries, has been accepted even by the World Bank and IMF (Development Committee Report Number 20 –"The Impact of the Industrial Policies of Developed Countries on Developing Countries" – March 1989).

The multilateral GATT negotiations at Uruguay Round were our only hope of reducing the adverse impact of industrial countries' industrial policies on India and other developing countries, but in the war of protectionism which was fought in December 1993 among the developed countries themselves, the developing countries including India were reduced merely to the status of bystanders, waiting for the leftover of the growth in international trade to fall in their laps. All the developing countries put together cannot claim to have influenced even five to ten per cent of the decisions which were taken during the Uruguay Round of GATT negotiations. But, we didn't have a choice in December 1993, and nor do we have it now.

The future prospects of foreign investments have, therefore, to be viewed in the international context. We must examine as to how and where we are well-placed as compared to other countries, and how and where we have to reformulate our strategy. This becomes even more difficult to decipher and comprehend, since all competing nations are pursuing basically the same economic strategy. Every country wants to depend upon or aim towards value-added, knowledge based, export-led economies. But the crucial or deciding factors in this competition could be the following :

(1) Industrial productivity and productivity per worker;
(2) Leadership, excellence and productivity in services sectors;
(3) Gradual elimination of inferior jobs, and creation of more and more valuable and high value addition jobs;
(4) Restructuring of Corporate entities; and
(5) Medium sized companies becoming the engines of growth, jobs creation, and sustained levels of exports;

Prospects of Foreign Investment Inflows into India in the Short and Long Term

Before concluding this chapter, it is necessary to comment upon the need for and/or desirability of continuing to give the same level of importance to foreign investments as was necessary nearly three years back, when the present economic reforms were started in July 1991, as also the prospects of foreign (direct and indirect) inflows into India in the short and the long term, with or without any further economic reforms.

Well, June-July 1991 was a bad time for India, as bad as it can ever be. We were closest even to losing our national pride, and defaulting on our loan repayments. We were reduced to the pitiable stage of having to mortgage plane-loads of gold reserves of the country to further borrow in order to be able to repay our loans on the due dates. We have come a very long way since then, and we are now sitting on foreign exchange reserves of $15 billion, which is more than sufficient to cover over six months' import needs (as compared to the reserves of around $1.2 billion, enough for only 0.63 month's requirements in July 1991). The current account deficit in our balance of payments during 1993-94 will be less than half a per cent of GDP, compared to over 3 per cent in 1990-91 and 2 per cent in 1992-93. The trade balance during 1993-94 is likely to be adverse by as little as $500 million. We have even ventured to pre-pay a huge sum of over $1 billion to IMF during 1994-95, which was not falling due immediately. We have deliberately brought down our FCNR burden, and now provide only three year maturities, thus eliminating most of the arbitrage money kept in such accounts. And, Foreign direct and indirect investment in India during 1993-94 is likely to be over $5 billion, as compared to only $150 million during 1991-92.

However, only around $500 million (or 10 per cent) out of this $5 billion inflow during 1993-94 has been on account of direct foreign investments, which would remain within India for atleast 3 years' initial lock-in period. The remaining $4.5 billion (or 90 per cent) has only gone to buy the cheap Indian shares, thus lifting the Sensex from 1600 points to the high of 4000 points and more. $1.5 billion was brought in by the SEBI registered Foreign Institutional Investors investing under the FII guidelines dated 14.9.1992 (and enjoying concessional rates of taxation under section 115 AD of the Income Tax Act). $2.5 billion was mopped up through the Euro-Equity and Foreign Currency Convertible Bonds issues of Indian companies under the Global Depository Receipt mechanism (scheme notified by GOI on 12.11.1993, and enjoying concessional rates of taxation under Section 115AC of the Income Tax Act). And the rest around $500 million has come in through the portfolio investments of the Offshore Funds floated abroad, dedicated for investments in Indian Stock Markets alone (which enjoy concessional rates of taxation under section 115AB of the Income Tax Act, and for which no separate scheme has so far been issued by the Government of India). This 90 per cent inflow of $4.5 billion can easily vanish, perhaps as quickly as it has come, after paying 10 per cent tax on capital gains after one year in all the three routes. We must remember that this bonanza has come into India's lap only because of low interest rates in the USA in 1993, coupled with an equally historic drop in Bombay Sensex to around 1600 points (after having demonstrated the capacity to go beyond 4000 points – during Harshad Mehta's heydays).

But this 4000 points Sensex is the optimal limit, beyond which any further portfolio investments would start yielding only sub-optimal returns for the foreign institutional investors and holders of Indian GDRs abroad. Therefore, no further similar astronomical growth of foreign indirect investments can be expected during 1994-95 and in the coming years. At best the growth, if any, would be only gradual. In fact there is even a danger of some net outflow from out of these portfolio investments, with the gradual rise in US interest rates. In a typical year, the US, the Dutch, the Japanese, and the UK institutional investors (including Banks and Pension Funds etc.) mop up $50 to 60 billion fresh accretions in a calendar year. India could attract more than its fair share during 1993-94 because of the low Sensex just at the right time. But, from 1994-95 onwards, India should be extremely lucky to see net positive portfolio investments of even two per cent of the total annual increase in world's portfolio investments (i.e. around $1 billion per year). Even this level of net inflow would continue if the Sensex remains well below 4000 points at the Bombay Stock Exchange. And, this can only be ensured by forcing the Indian Financial Institutions to unload their abnormally large holdings of shares of the already established and well-run companies, thus increasing the availability of the floating shares in domestic capital markets (so that they can absorb the further inflow of fresh capital from within the country and abroad), and also in the process increasing the flow of funds from them for promoting fresh investments in newer companies. As on today, too much money is chasing too few floating shares in the Indian Capital Markets, and there is no salvation (and solution for long term growth) without unloading the massive stocks on which these Financial Institutions are sitting (in a most unproductive – rather, counterproductive – manner).

As regards the direct foreign investments, the position is likely to emerge better gradually, but only very gradually. At around $500 million net inflow of FDI during 1993-94, we have been able to attract just around one per cent of the world's total FDI flows annually. On the basis of the approvals given for foreign direct investments since July 1991 so far, it can be safely assumed that FDI inflow would cross $1 billion during 1994-95 and may even touch $1.5 billion if the State Governments cooperate by speeding up the necessary approvals at their ends. But the FDI levels would not go up appreciably beyond these limits without an acceptable exit policy being put in place. But, politically, an exit policy of the type being demanded by foreign direct investors does not appear to be possible in the near future. As the Prime Minister very wisely said in his "middle path" speech at the World Economic Forum meeting at Davos in February 1994.

> "In the new-found enthusiasm for change, Governments should not go overboard and plunge large chunks of their people into mass misery; they have no right to do so."

But, we can certainly continue to pursue all other types of economic reforms and deregulation measures, as already promised by the PM and the Finance Minister repeatedly, on many occasions, the latest being at the Euromoney Conference in New Delhi, in end March 1994. It is only in regard to Exit Policy that we have been caught in a chicken-and-egg syndrome, as an Exit Policy cannot perhaps come till the industrial growth is of such an astronomically high level that the employment spurred by that growth can nearly eliminate unemployment in a country as populous and poor as India, and such high growth of industry and employment cannot come without massive inflow of foreign direct investments, which is itself possible only after a very flexible Exit Policy has been put in place.

Fortunately, such dilemmas do not confront us regarding other policy measures, which can be easily and surely pursued in our pursuit of foreign direct investments. And, we must pursue these measures since $15 billion is not a very comfortable level of foreign exchange reserves for a country of the size of India, specially when more than half of it is comprised of the $1.5 billion volatile portfolio foreign indirect investments, the $1.6 billion worth liability in respect of India Development Bonds, which would see an outflow of more than $2 billion very soon, around $1.5 billion liability on account of the Foreign Currency Convertible Bonds which can become pure debt instruments at the option of the foreign investors, and substantial amounts in the Foreign Currency Non Resident (FCNR) deposits belonging to the NRIs, which are presently repayable at the end of three years maturity periods only. This simple arithmetic itself shows that we must continue to doggedly pursue foreign direct investments, and must continue to try to make the investment climate in India as much more attractive for them as we can, without sacrificing our poor, and our national honour.

But, it is not as if the foreign investors would be having a cake-walk in India (after the Government's red carpet welcome). Two very interesting news items appeared in the *Economic Times* recently, which deserve a mention. On March 22, 1994, in a story datelined the previous day by one Shri Jaideep Lahiri, it was described very interestingly as to how "The humble potato and (desi) bhujiawala (have) rattle(d) Pepsi's bottomline". And in the lead story on March 28, 1994, a PTI dispatch "The quick bite: Desi restaurants vs. fast foods", described as to how the Indian restaurant owners are not in the least unsettled by the big names in fast food chains entering India. If quality Indian products are available, and are within reach, it would be impossible to change the taste buds of Indians, as can be proved even by the success of Indian restaurants abroad.

Indians have already established a presence and a reputation, in the Silicon Valley and Wall Street in USA, and own and control a substantial chunk of the wealth of UK. Singapore and Hong Kong owe a major partion of their trade, investments, and wealth to the Indians settled there. It should therefore be possible to attract high technology and foreign investments into India by welcoming back these Non-Resident Indians, and place NRI sponsored foreign investments on a higher pedestal than other foreign investments. In the recent two budgets, very little has been done for the NRI foreign direct investments. In fact the superiority of tax concessions etc. enjoyed by NRIs till 1991 has been totally eroded, and they are presently finding foreign investors being equated with them, or sometimes even preferred. Even the percentage limits of portfolio investments are five times higher for the foreigners than the 1 per cent/ 5 per cent limits allowed for NRI portfolio investments.

Conclusion

In the long run, there is no better alternative for India than to try to attract foreign direct investments, and to maintain the measured pace of economic reforms and deregulation which we have followed so far. And, it would be all the more better if this FDI inflow is in the form of NRI foreign direct investments.

There is also a need to maintain the present incentives allowed to foreign indirect investors, so that a constant trickle of net inflow of foreign portfolio investments is maintained in the long run. We must bring NRI portfolio investment limits at par with the limits allowed for foreign institutional investors (that is, upto 5 per cent of the issued capital of a company for the individual NRI portfolio investors, and upto 24 per cent of the issued capital of the company for all the NRI portfolio investors in the company put together). Let there be no protection offered by the Government to Indian family based managements (which tend to be inefficient, and lead to companies being used and treated as personal or family properties, rather than the property of the shareholders in general). When such a protection is not being offered against potential foreign corporate invaders, why should such a protection be available against NRIs?

With the set of irreversible reforms already put in place so far, we have already been assured of India no longer remaining an island in the world of the International Capital Markets. We would certainly get our due share fair of inflows of capital, directly, or indirectly. But we can hasten the pace of such inflows, and their quantum, by further pursuing the process of reforms. It is not a very long way off for the full convertibility of the rupee on capital account, which would bring back that wealth of this nation which is presently rotting away clandestinely in the Swiss Banks, and which would lead India on a further growth path after it returns.

Summary of Discussion

In the ensuing discussion the example of MOTOROLA which has not yet been given the final clearance, the original application for which was submitted in September 1991 was cited. It was observed that if the GOI had acted with speed on this case, this would have had the required demonstration effect on other investors.

Similarly, expressing concern over the failure to attract Japanese investments, especially in the infrastructure sectors like electricity, a need to identify further step. Mr J. L. Bajaj wanted to know what steps required was felt. Mr Sudhir Kumar, in his reply, said that the Japanese have set up three separate committee, each to look into the social, political and economic aspects of investments in India, respectively. The Japanese do not yet find the investment climate friendly enough. It was however, felt there appears to be deeper reasons why the Japanese are not investing; perhaps, they hope to extract more.

The issue of GOI's guarantee to provide 16 per cent dividends in dollar terms as annual returns on investments in the power sector was also raised. This was considered, quite alarming since in the event of possible devaluation this would tantamount to a 30 per cent dividend payments in rupee term. This would hardly leave these enterprises with any reserves for expansions etc.

It was also felt that the 10 per cent capital gains tax is a deterrent for the inflow of foreign investments. However, Mr Sudhir Kumar pointed out the foreign investors would be earning a great deal as capital gains despite taxes, because of the bullishness of stock prices in India. The problem is that there are not enough shares in the market commensurate to the portfolio investments from abroad. Whatever inflow of portfolio investments has been there, these have come in merely to raise the share holdings in foreign companies operating in India from the earlier level of 40 to 51 per cent, allowed under the NEP. This also shows that not much of industrial investments is taking place by way of foreign direct investments.

8

LIBERALISATION AT THE STATE LEVEL
A Study of Laws Affecting Forest Product Markets

N.C. SAXENA

Introduction and Role of Farm Forestry

Social Forestry Projects in India were originally designed to reduce the erosion of forest resources by increasing tree production on presently unproductive Government and community lands and to make fuelwood, fodder and small timber available to the rural communities. While this objective dominated the early structure and approach, the emphasis shifted by the early 1980s away from Government managed plantations to farm forestry, whereby the farmers were encouraged to plant trees on their own lands. The success of this approach in some States, notably in Gujarat, the Punjab, Haryana, western U.P. and Karnataka, opened up a vast potential for helping the farmers through the new activity of tree farming.

Theoretically speaking, there are several advantages in encouraging farmers to practice agroforestry and farm forestry on their lands. First, it saves marginal lands from further degradation and maintains or increases site productivity through nutrient recycling and soil protection. Second, it increases the value of output per unit of land through spatial or inter-temporal intercropping of trees and other species. Third, by supplying raw materials (such as left compost) to agriculture directly and indirectly, and by producing food and forage for human and animal consumption, it complements and supplements agricultural production. Fourth, it diversifies the range of outputs from a given area which increases self-sufficiency and reduces the risk to income from adverse climatic, biological or market impacts on particular crops. Fifth, it spreads the need for labour inputs more evenly seasonally, thus reducing the effects of sharp peaks and troughs in activity characteristic of tropical agriculture. Sixth, the technology is simple, labour intensive, and requires little outside technical or financial support. Seventh, trees have many useful characteristics as 'assets' for the poor-low investment cost, rapid appreciation, divisibility, flexible harvesting time, etc., and are available to meet unforeseen contingencies. Eighth, if there are strong and growing markets for tree products, a market oriented approach could enhance substantially the incomes of the poor farmers too. Ninth, it can be taken up as a part-time activity by households and does not require a change in the occupation of the landholder. Tenth, it promotes value-added activities in rural India, as several communities have traditionally been involved in supplementing their incomes through processing tree products. Eleventh, the programme of tree growing does not invite hostility from the rural rich, which is inherent in land reforms and other distributive programmes. And last, but not least, as rural women are involved in meeting daily survival needs of their households by collection of forest produce, decline in the country's natural vegetation has directly affected the rural poor women. An increase in fuelwood and fodder production through multiple nature trees on their own farm and leased lands will certainly reduce drudgery and save their labour for other productive occupations.

Thus, trees can be good investments as savings banks for the poor, enabling them to accumulate capital. But trees would become poor people's banks only when their right to ownership of trees is not disputed and impeded by law or bureaucratic regulations. Quite often this is not the case. Rights, which people have over trees planted on private lands, are often ambiguous. There is a widespread impression in the villages that if trees are planted on private lands, not only would be trees belong to the Government but land on which such plantation takes place would also revert to Government. In contrast to Africa (Ridell 1987:6), where trees are often planted to establish tenure rights, in India they are often removed to demonstrate claims to land. Even as late as 1987, a SIDA team touring in south Bihar encountered tribals' fears that if they planted trees their lands would be taken away by the Government (Government of Bihar, 1987). The fear is not baseless as the Bihar Private Forest Act and similar other enactments did precisely this in the past, by "nationalising" private trees.

Legal Controls on Disposal of Farm Trees

In most States people can cut trees only after going through a laborious process of getting a permit from designated minor functionaries – with consequences easy to imagine. There are three different sets of laws: a farmer cannot harvest trees without permission; a permit is required to transport them; and lastly some trees can be sold only to the F.D. Why were these laws enacted, what is the effect of these laws and how do they operate in practice?

The conceptual framework of Social Forestry Projects in India is based on the recommendations of the National Commission of Agriculture, which sought to explain deforestation as due to fuelwood and fodder needs of the people. It implicitly shared the perception of many foresters in India that excessive human and cattle population is an obstacle in preserving forest wealth. Since the people could not be removed from the vicinity of Government forests, it was necessary to create forests on common lands of the village so that the mounting pressure on reserve lands could be reduced. Thus, social forestry was, according to the Commission, to remove a serious impediments in the practice of production forestry, (GOI 1973:4).

The Governments in implementing the recommendations of the Commission went a step ahead. While tightening their control over forests and common lands (Forest Conservation Act, various Transit Rules, reduction in free supplies from forests to the people, nationalisation of forest products, and regulating supplies from common lands, etc.), many States decided to conserve the existing trees on private lands by banning or restricting felling of trees on such lands. It virtually amounted to nationalising timber from trees standing on private lands, while confining the rights of the people to usufruct, i.e., leaves, twigs, and fruits only. Legal provisions in some of the States are described below.

The Uttar Pradesh Protection of Trees in Rural and Hill Areas Act, 1976 provides that no person shall fell any tree standing on private land except after taking permission from the competent authority. He is also bound to plant two trees in place of every tree felled. Certain species like mango, neem, mahua, peepal and bargad have been declared as protected species which cannot be felled. Although another list of 26 species like eucalyptus, popular, etc., have been kept outside the Act to encourage its plantation, but here too the farmer requires permission under the Transit Rules if he wishes to transport the timber to the market.

According to section 4 of the Kerala Preservation of Trees Act, 1986 no person shall cut any tree without permission, which could be given only if the tree is a danger of life or property, the tree is diseased or windfallen, or the owner requires to construct his house. Thus, he is not entitled to permission if he requires cash for a contingency. Homestead lands of less than one hectare were so far exempt from this law. But with effect from 4.4.87 the State has decided through an administrative order that not only no tree shall be cut, but the trees already cut shall not be allowed to be removed.

The Maharashtra (Urban Areas) Preservation of Trees Act 1975 forbids anyone from felling a tree in the urban area, including private gardens. Seedlings of banyan, peepal and gular trees are also considered as trees and therefore their removal as weeds would invite punishment. The Government is also empowered to prescribe standards specifying the number and type of trees which will be planted on each piece of land.

Clause 3 of the Act states, "No such permission would be refused if the tree is dead". A Study (*The Times of India,* 27th July, 1986) observed that some unscrupulous people take advantage of the above clause to fell a tree. They first girdle the tree just above the ground level, by removing the bark all around the main trunk. This stops food supply to the roots. After a while roots starve and die. As a result the tree also lingers and dies. At this stage it is easy to get the permission, as it is obstructing ongoing agricultural activities.

There is yet another law, called the Maharashtra Land Revenue (Regulation of Right to Tree) Rules, 1967 according to which if a farmer wishes to fell a tree from his land where the tree density is less than 20 per acre or if the tree is within 30 metres of river, pond, stream or tank, the farmer requires permission from the Sub Divisional Officer.

The Tamil Nadu Hill Areas (Preservation of Trees) Act, 1955 forbids tree felling in the hill areas without permission from a Committee consisting of revenue and forest authorities.

The Orissa Timber & Other Forest Rules, 1980 gives the F.D. the power to exercise strict control over the movement and sale of forest produce, whether or not it originates in forest lands. There is yet another law, the Orissa Protection of Scheduled Castes and Scheduled Tribes (Interest in Trees) Act, 1981 which provides that no contract entered into by an owner of any specified tree for the sale of timber thereof shall be valid if the owner is a member of scheduled castes or scheduled tribes without prior permission of a range officer. Specified trees comprise of sal, teak, kendu, acacia, eucalyptus, and 23 other species.

Poor Information and Cumbersome Procedures

Several studies describe farmer's apprehension and fear in obtaining permissions from several departments for reaping benefits from trees they had planted. What was more striking was the lack of information about procedures. If some concessions were given recently, even the field staff was ignorant about them. For instance, Sections 240 and 241 of the Madhya Pradesh Land Revenue Code ban cutting of trees in private lands if such an act leads to soil erosion, or the concerned village is close to a Government forest. In addition, timber from certain specified trees like teak, sal, sheesham and khair cannot be sold in the open market, and have to be sold to the Government only. Despite these restrictions many senior forest officers were under the impression that farmers are free to sell their social forestry produce of four species, including eucalyptus, to any one they liked and there were no restrictions. However, the Revenue Department officials did not confirm this. According to them no recent change had been introduced in the Land Revenue code and if felling relates to the restricted category, written permission of the Collector will have to be obtained. However, the implication of this law is that in all other cases, the tree owner has to obtain a certificate from the revenue officials (which they will give after making dual field inquiries and referring the case to forest officials too for their opinion) to the effect that the case does not fall under one of the conditions mentioned above. The net result is that in all cases the tree owner has to go through a lengthy procedure.

In West Bengal it was noticed that the system of obtaining a permit for felling of trees was time consuming and involved bribes (Saxena 1991). The movement of an application through various channels was as follows:

Application →village panchayat and the pradhan → standing committee consisting of the B.D.O., Range Officer, and some elected members → Range Officer → local Land Reforms Officer to verify ownership of land →Range Officer to estimate the value of the plantation (this decides who in the forest hierarchy would issue permit) →the buyer to make an affidavit, and obtain a court order → now the buyer can cut trees, and apply to Range Officer for a transit permit → Range Officer (or his superior, depending upon the value of plantation) to inspect and hammer the trees, and issue the transit pass

What added to the harassment of agents, and consequently to the low prices to farmers was the fact that the officials involved were located in different places.

In Tamil Nadu too, restrictions on movement of wood are a major irritant. It takes three months to obtain a permit, in which time wood tends to lose weight. Many producers would like to market their trees themselves, and so would large urban merchants, but both have to depend on middlemen because of the permit problem. This increases the gap between producer price and the market price, For instance, Mahendran of village Abhasholai sold 35,000 trees at Rs. 300 per ton to an agent, who sold the same to a paper mill at Rs. 500 a ton. The only value added by the agent was through obtaining a valid permit to move wood (Saxena 1991).

Under the Bihar Forest Produce (Regulation of Trade) Act, 1984, farmers can sell wood to the State Trading Organisation only, and all sales in the markets are considered illegal. A study (SIDA 1990) revealed that getting permits from Government often required interventions from ministers, and sometimes even such recommendations did not expedite sales.

In many States, it is very difficult to obtain a new license for operating a saw mill, as Governments consider saw mills responsible for deforestation. There are many mills which operate without a license. In Mathura, U.P., it was observed (Saxena 1989) that license of the existing saw mills had not been renewed for the past two years. These cause uncertainty in the operation of the processing units and increase corruption. It is ironic that although industries worth billions have been de-regulated, establishment of a saw mill, requiring less than a lakh of Rupees, even in areas like western U.P., which has no Government forests, requires license. This too has to be renewed every year. In a recent survey (February 1994) in Muzaffarnagar it was noticed that out of eight saw mills only three had a valid license. Generally, the new license is not given for the amount and capacity applied for and this leaves room for corruption. All saw millers feared police and even if they wanted to expand their markets upto Delhi, they could not do so for fear of being checked and harassed by the police. The same survey revealed that even firewood *taals* require licenses which have to be renewed every year. The renewal fees is Rs 35, but the bribe demanded is Rs 100.

Impact of these Laws

Such forest laws leave villagers in doubt whether any wood they produce will belong to them. Perversely, the immediate impact of such legislation is always more destruction of private trees as people wish to cash their assets before the Government machinery to enforce laws is set up. For instance, in Maharashtra just before the Private Forest Acquisition Act, 1975 was enacted the holders of private forests cut and sold all the trees on their lands (Chambers *et al.* 1989). Besides, such laws make people indifferent to tree growing, depress their margins when they wish to sell trees, and encourage corruption and middle-men's profits. They also discriminate against poor farmers, as they are less likely to be able to obtain permissions at the time of need. The mid-term review of Andhra Pradesh Social Forestry Project (CIDA, 1988:82) rightly observed, "Majority of small and marginal farmers are not aware of the market value of their products. Intermediaries are already starting to reap the lion's share from the purchase and sale of such products."

A study of Pahela village in district Bhandara, Maharashtra (CENDIT, 1985) showed that although transport of wood within the village was not prohibited, in practice people were often harassed by officials. A poor farmer complained, "The contractors from Delhi, Hyderabad and Bombay come here and take away all the wood.. The F.D. officers go out of their way to be helpful to the contractors. And what happens to us? I can't cut even a branch of a tree on my field without the forest guard bullying me...If I go to the DFO to get permission to cut a tree growing on my own land, 'come back tomorrow', I am told every time."

A District Collector in U.P. conducted an enquiry into this problem. He obtained from the forest office the list of those who had received permits to sell their private trees. He then checked up in the field.

He discovered that the list of 17 names contained 3 which were either fictitious or of people who had not applied for permits. Clearly these were cases where permits had been obtained fraudulently by the contractors. Out of the remaining 14, two were marginal farmers who had obtained the permits on their own, without involving an intermediary. But when they took their permits to the local police station, they were asked to pay illegal gratification. On their inability to do so their permits were confiscated, and they were not allowed to fell their trees.

The remaining 12 admitted that they obtained the permit through the services of a middleman who "dealt" with the forest and police bureaucracy. The District Collector concluded in his report, "The consideration for these services rendered was adjusted in the sale price." He also observed, "It will not be an exaggeration to say that the marginal farmers and the poor tree patta holders will never be able to obtain a permit on their own from the forest department. Even if they do, they might not be able to 'convince' the local police. They will have to seek the protection of the local contractors."

In Moradabad, a prosperous district of western U.P., enquiries made by the Chief Development Officer (Kumar, 1987) revealed that in all cases except one, farmers applied for permission through intermediaries. In the isolated case, where a big farmer tried to do it himself, it took him 14 months to get permission as against a normal period of 2-3 months for contractors. He complained of harassment from F.D. as he had to spend more than Rs. 600 in travelling from his village to the forest office a number of times. In other cases trees were sold on as-is-where-is basis, and expenditure on felling and transport was borne by the middlemen.

In H.P. farmers cannot sell their commercial trees in the open market. All such trees have to be sold to the Forest Corporation, and that too only once in 10 years. Payment is made by the Corporation in four instalments spread over a couple of years. The logic is that as the Corporation is working on behalf of the farmers, it cannot, by definition, make losses, therefore, all overheads of the Corporation must be fully met before the last instalment is paid to the contractor. This results in low and delayed payments to the contractors, who in turn exploit farmers.

In one prosperous village in H.P. (Saxena, 1989) farmers had a number of Khair (*Acacia catetchu*) trees on their private lands. In 1983-84 this village was selected for felling of trees, according to the 10 years rule. A contractor on behalf of the farmers got permission for felling from the Forest Department, and moved an application in January 1984 to the Revenue and Forest Departments for joint demarcation of the trees. This took a long time, and ultimately the contractor could obtain the export permit only after 30 months, in July 1986. The whole process took about three years to complete. During the several months between the felling and getting permission to transport the trees, the wood must also have deteriorated. The farmers were only paid at the time of felling, in April 1986, which was almost two years after the settlement of the price. They got only 15 to 30 per cent of the estimated value of standing trees at farm site, as calculated by the Forest Department itself. The rest was lost because of long delays, uncertainty about payment by the Forest Corporation, the way farmers were kept in the dark about laws and procedures, poor publicity of market information, lack of competition leading to monopoly, and bureaucratic rents at various levels.

The rules concerning sandalwood trees present a striking instance of self-defeating regulation. Sandalwood is considered to be very auspicious for all religious ceremonies. Sandalwood and its oil are also used in perfumery and medicine. Despite increasing demand, sandalwood production in Karnataka has been declining. Its price of Rs. 12.50 a tonne in 1955 rose to Rs. 80,000 a tonne in the open market by 1988 (Roy, 1988). One reason for low production is absolute State control over sandal trees even on private lands. This means that an individual can derive no economic benefit from a sandalwood tree as he can neither cut it nor sell it. At the same time, due to the high price there is a lot of illegal felling of sandal trees from forest land. Thus, a vicious circle has been established leading to a price spiral. "Supply 600 times (600 times in real terms) has actually led to a decline in production! In the present scheme of things there are incentives only to the smugglers.

Compared with markets for other agricultural products, wood markets are still not developed for supply from farms (Saxena 1994). The contrast between tree marketing and agricultural crop marketing is sharp. For marketing agricultural products, the State Governments have set up vast infrastructure; remunerative procurement prices are announced several months in advance of the crop; generous subsidies are inbuilt into the system of Government purchase which absorbs surplus production and stabilizes prices; market yards have been set up to reduce exploitation; and middlemen's commission has been fixed. None of these interventions have been made with tree marketing. To the contrary, markets for forest products are dominated by cartels, shrouded in secrecy, and impeded by legal bottlenecks.

Whereas rural markets are small, localized, lack capital land hence buying capacity, as in most of the developing world (FAO 1988), urban markets are dominated by merchants dealing in construction timber, which is supplied by Government depots. Farmers, on the other hand, have no ready market. Legal restrictions on the transport of wood, designed to prevent illicit felling from Government forests, act against the interests of producers, and impede them from bringing their produce to urban markets. Forced to wait for the buyers to come to them, these rigid laws act as a barrier between the producer and the market, and bring uncertainty if not inherent inequity to sale transactions. Farmers' awareness about buyers, the prevailing market price, and Government rules is week. Due to these market imperfections, middlemen's margins are seemingly large, leading to high price differentials between what producers get and what consumers pay.

Due to Government restrictions on transport of private wood without a permit, farmers have been prevented from establishing direct contact with the market. As farmers are not able to get a permit on their own, they sell off standing trees to the traders in their fields. The experience of the farmers and the traders in western U.P. was that even if they had a valid permit from the Forest Department, Police still harassed them, and threatened them with arrests, on the grounds that the permission is false, or that the number of trees or its weight is more than what is written on the permit (Saxena, 1994).

Since the traders were used to dealing with the Police, it was routine them to go through the process of bribes, and get their stocks transported to the markets. Farmers have to do marketing only once in a while and hence prefer to sell standing trees to the traders, rather than face uncertainties of the police behaviour. The system works against the interest of small farmers who have smaller lots to sell, and hence the overhead charges of bribes become too high for them. To this should be added the cost of running to Government offices a number of times. Similarly, the system favours sale through agents who can combine the lots of several farmers, thus dividing the overhead charges.

In western U.P., I noticed that there was a tendency to transport eucalyptus on such routes which are not patrolled by the Police/Forest officials so as to avoid their gaze, with the result that inter-village sales within a distance of 10-15 km are quite common. While this reduces transport, handling and the number of intermediaries, it also brings in an element of uncertainty in operations, thus depriving the farmers of the true potential of their produce. Thus, farmers in western U.P. could not benefit from the high price of poles prevailing in eastern U.P., because longer the distance, more becomes the total incidence of bribe which has to be paid at each police barrier. Laws have led to fraudulent practices among all concerned, farmers, traders, and officials, and such practices either went undetected or were condoned.

One may add that in several other States the relaxations on harvesting and transit were reelected, but too late (in U.P. these were lifted in October, 1991, when most small farmers had already sold their produce), and it did not help in reviving the markets. Even field officials are not aware of these relaxations, much less the farmers. In any case, relaxations are a necessary but not sufficient condition for removing market imperfections in the free flow of wood. One needs to take an integrated view of extension, market information, publicity, Government support and laws.

State intervention thus has constrained the evolution of private markets for farm wood, depriving producers of the true market potential

(ORG 1990). A study done in 1987 in Gujarat (Wilson & Trivedi, 1988) showed that of the 45 producers who sold trees, only nine made a relative profit; 36 would have been better off sticking to agriculture. Jain (FAO 1988) reached similar conclusions in her studies of eucalyptus in the same State.

Such restrictions are based on assumptions about the behaviour of rural people which are widely shared by bureaucracies all over the world. They believe that farmers cannot be trusted with a resource which only yields income after a gap of several years. Such a prejudiced view has, however, no empirical basis. Besides, such controls act as self-fulfilling prophecies: they deter protection and promote irresponsible felling. To effect a change in the people's behaviour one should start by trusting them with trees, at least those on their own lands. Some decades back, similar apprehensions were expressed regarding giving poor people land and security of tenure: it was said that they would only produce for consumption and not for the markets, and that more land would make them lazy. Experience from all over the world has shown that once assured of security of rights, peasants have proved themselves worthy of trust through their hard work, rationality and market orientation.

Excessive regulations lead to corruption. A study of north Indian fuel markets (Chatterji, 1987) found that transporters carrying fuelwood to Delhi have to pay Rs. 500 per truck as "on-road considerations", a euphemistic phrase for bribes. These laws also keep the over-burdened bureaucracy busy in pursuits which (from the social point of view at least) are totally unproductive. Even when an officer is not corrupt, he is judged not on the basis of his help to small farmers, but whether he has been able to contain complaints of illegal fellings within "manageable" proportions. Yardsticks of performance get distorted, doing immense harm to social forestry programmes.

Awareness of laws and rules in India outside the bureaucracy is limited. They are generally shrouded in secrecy or in mystifying language. The cardinal principle governing the working of a Government office is that "a good decision is better than a quick one". Therefore movement of papers takes a lot of time, which is often independent of bribes involved. This has two implications for a tree farmer. First, because of lack of knowledge, he cannot on his own negotiate a permission; he needs a middleman to help him. Second, even the middleman does not know how much time the entire process is going to take; he therefore charges excessive margins. In the study of Delhi markets it was seen that taking all costs into consideration, including on-road bribes (which were generally Rs. 50 a tonne) and profits, fuelwood should be sold in the town of Delhi for Rs. 505 a tonne, whereas the actual retail price (less taxes) averaged around Rs. 800. The rest covered the risk or the uncertainty margin.

A political scientist may wonder, why have large farmers not been able to use their political clout with the State Governments to get these laws changed in their favour? The farmers are pitted here against two powerful lobbies. One is that of Government servants who have got accustomed to using controls as the only means to regulate economic activities. Even where legal powers do not exist these are often assumed. For instance, the U.P. Tree Protection Act does not apply to the towns, and yet even in Allahabad, which is famous for its legal luminaries, the city police checks all truck carrying timber, and harasses those who do not "behave".

The other lobby is those of environmentalists, academicians and members of the press who tend to see planting trees for economic gain in capital and cash as moral sin. People's participation, according to them, should mean planting trees for the next generation, or for meeting fuelwood and fodder needs of the people, or for supplementing agricultural production. A market orientation, in their view, harms the poor, as they are vulnerable to exploitation by middle-men, have little control over markets, and are likely to sell their trees for a so long before their optimal silvicultural and economic states is reached. People's participation is also equated with arousing collective spirit among the community, which along will ensure that the new wealth being created through the programme reaches the poor.

The influence of this lobby of mainly town-bred environmentalists on policy making in India should not be underrated. Their views have an aura of respectability and are readily accepted as defining desirable objectives. The standards set by them for evaluating the results of a programme become the accepted norms, and a contrary viewpoint is easily branded as an anti-poor stance.

The two lobbies, of officials and environmentalists, agree in seeing rules and controls as solutions. In the climate of opinion they have created, it makes good headlines if a Chief Minister announces that all tree cutting has been banned in a State; in contrast, a decision to liberalise tree cutting would be condemned as retrograde. But as we have seen, the tragic irony is that the rules and controls are self-defeating. They discourage tree planting and protection, and they discriminate against the poorer farmers, especially in marketing and prices.

The objectives of the environmental moralist lobby are not in dispute. Preventing environmental degradation and satisfying the consumption needs of the poor are laudable national objectives. Where we differ is not in the objectives but in the means. It is unrealistic as no private gains from what is being advocated. Beyond quite narrow limits, resource-poor realistic policy will seek ways in which ecological and social benefits are the by-products of tree growing. And tree-growing will be adopted because farmers see enhanced capital assets and cash incomes as the main benefits. For resource-poor farmers, even more than for the resource-rich, this requires freedom from any legal restriction which gives officials or others the power to extract rents.

For many resource-poor farmers, trees are like savings banks (Chambers and Leach 1987) but with the advantage that they often appreciate in capital value much more rapidly than bank deposits. They provide reserves which can be cashed to deal with contingencies, such as costs of medical treatment, marriage expenses, a large purchase, or any sudden or large need for money. Where a good market exists for the products, they can provide an alternative to taking loans and indebtedness. They are also often a source of income from their produce. When resource-poor farmers are prohibited from felling trees on their own land, it is like a bank manager refusing a depositor permission to withdraw money from an account. A banker interested in net deposits does not tell a new account holder that he can only deposit money and not withdraw it. Bankers who acted in such a manner would not last long. When the movement of timber and timber and other tree products is restricted, it is like prohibiting people from taking money from one part of the country to another. Political leaders and officials who tried to introduce such a regulation would quickly find themselves in trouble.

Several factors are involved in determining farm gate prices; but the evidence accumulated, some of it presented above, leaves no doubt that the uncertainties, bribes, difficulties and delays involved in selling trees are linked with rules and controls, and are a major reason why farmers, and especially those who are poorer and weaker, often get such scandalously low prices for their trees and tree products.

Subsidised Supplies to Industries from Forest Lands

Till a few years back Government was the largest supplier of raw material to industries, but with the advent of farm forestry, farm wood is now competing with supplies from Government forests. Here farmers have to face unfair competition, as Government supplies are subsidised. This has been one of the most important reasons for the setback to the farm forestry programme, despite initial keenness on the part of the farmers. Until very recently highly privileged prices have been standard practice for industries. Although the element of subsidy has been greatly reduced lately, it still continues in many forms. Moreover, traders are sometimes able to get more trees than contracted for from Government through bribes, which reduces the unit cost of supplies. Bhabbar grass is sold by the UP Forest Corporation at Rs. 72.50 per quintal to rope-makers, but to industries at Rs. 40 per quintal. The UP Forest Corporation had calculated that during 1983-84 the actual cost of raising eucalyptus in Government forests was Rs. 220 per tonne, whereas it was supplied to the Saharanpur Paper Mill at Rs. 140 per tonne, and to the Nainital Mill at Rs. 196. The market rate for equivalent quality of eucalyptus, as judged from the auction prices, was between Rs. 500-700 per tonne during the above period (information based on Government records, and all prices are for dry and debarked wood). In A.P., the price that F.D. got by selling bamboo in the open market ranged from Rs. 800 to Rs. 1200 a tonne in 1990-91, as against Rs. 550 at which bamboo was supplied to the industry. Although transport cost need to be added to make the two prices comparable, yet it cannot be denied that an impression prevailed among the local population that produce grown in their area was diverted at a cheap price to outsiders. Forest leases in favour of private parties continue in Orissa despite the Forest Conservation Act.

As regards priority, Government has created new rights of industrialists through long term agreements to supply forest products at a low price. An ex-Forest Secretary of M.P. writes, "This is clearly discriminatory. The rights of a huge section of society cannot be wiped out in order to benefit a few industrialists. For instance, the Orient Paper Mills was promised a lakh tonne of bamboo per year from 4 districts of the State. This eliminated all bamboo from Rewa, Panna, Satna and Shahdol. When such a situation arises the F.D. tells the villagers to fend for themselves because there is nothing in the forests for them" (NCHSE, 1987). One wonders whether such unilateral abrogation of people's rights is not illegal. Sometimes industries, in order to maximise production use methods which are destructive to these plants. An obvious example is extraction of resin from pine trees. Where industries hold bamboo leases they utilise even the better bamboo for pulp, and the better quality should be sold to artisans. Furer-Haimendorf (1985) describes how a particular paper mill exploited bamboo in a tribal region by bringing in hundreds of labourers from different States and used methods of extraction which endangered future regeneration.

It is obvious that the market for industrial raw material is totally distorted by the present system of committed supply from Government forests at concessional rates. Its impact can be summed up as under:

(i) It leads to creation of over-capacity and inefficient use of material by industry. It increases sickness in the industry and prevents its technological upgradation;

(ii) Price difference in open market and concessional rates lead to undesirable practices. There are reported cases of concessional supplies being siphoned off to open market for quick money by some concessionaries;

(iii) Arbitrary fixation of supply/quotas and prices to various units in similar business encourages corruption within the forest department at the cost of industrial efficiency. At the same time the State loses valuable revenue;

(iv) It discourages development of private efforts at tree plantation because of depressed market prices and low market demand from consuming industries; and

(v) Since there is a lagged response of forest product supplies to the current signal of price, and expectation of change in Government policy (such as allotment of forest land to industry, or new partnership arrangements with FDCs), there is a tendency on the part of industry not to take any initiative, and 'wait and see' becomes the safest policy.

Nationalisation of Non-Timber Forest Products (NTFP)

The nationalisation of several NTFP commodities forcing the gatherers to sell only to Government and not in the open market, done in different States in various years from 1960s to the end of 1970s, presumably with the intention of helping the poor, has affected their interests adversely. It has also reduced the incentive to collect.

Tendu leaves, as one of the most important NTFPs, are a case in point. In M.P. the production of tendu leaves fell from 5.10 million bags in 1981 to 3.9 million bags in 1985-86 (GOMP, 1987:33). In Orissa, despite nationalisation, production of tendu leaves over a longer period has remained stagnant. After nationalisation the collection of sal seeds fell in India from 2 lakh tons in 1979 to only 60,000 tons in 1987 (GOI, 1988)

Production of lakh, another nationalised item, had gone down from an average of 32000 tonnes per year during 1961-70 to 16000 tonnes during 1981-86 (GOI, 1988).

From the point of view of the poor, it is not just volume but remuneration that matters. After meeting all expenses and profits, tribals should be paid Rs. 1.31 a kg for collection of sal seeds in Madhya Pradesh, but the Government pays them only 55 paise a kg (GOI, 1988:55). In the case of tendu leaves in Orissa, during the twelve years 1967-79, increases in the unit price led to a twelvefold increase of gross revenue per ton (5.5 times at constant prices), from Rs. 297 to Rs. 3514 (Gupta and Guleria, 1982); but over the second half of the period, from 1973-79, workers' wages per quintal collected remained stagnant at current prices at Rs. 35-36 (*ibid*:84), which was a drop in real terms of 50 per cent. Nor was remuneration anywhere near equivalent to the minimum statutory wage: during 1979-80 the average daily wage obtained by workers for 8 hours of work in Orissa came to Rs. 1.61, whereas minimum statutory wages were Rs. 4 (*ibid*: p 85-86). It increased to Rs. 5.25 in 1984, (Fernandes *et. al.*, 1988:141) but was still only a little over half of the minimum wage. A Government Commission was told (Bhatt, 1988:xxv) by the tribal women in M.P. that when they walked a long distance to the office of the Forest Corporation to sell to the traders at only 20 per cent of the Government price.

Before nationalisation, the tribals could sell the produce of their own trees to anybody, but under the new system produce from trees on private land has to be sold to the Forest Department only. In almost all cases the Forest Department has appointed agents formally or informally (GOI, 1987). This has put the tribals at the mercy of two different sets of people, the contractor as well as the Government department, and whatever payment that tribals get has to be routed through both of them. Private trade in sal seeds is illegal in M.P., but shopkeepers manage to exchange it with tribals for daily necessities at a low price. They then sell it to Government bodies, thus defeating the very purpose of nationalisation (GOI, 1988). This results in delay, and makes tribals indifferent to trees on their own private land.

Prosopis juliflora juliflora occurs throughout the semiarid lands of India and has solved the fuelwood crisis in these areas. Its twigs can easily be converted into charcoal which can be transported easily. However, two controls exit on this cottage industry. First, one cannot establish a kiln without a license and secondly charcoal cannot be transported without a transit permit. Thus the potential for expansion of a labour intensive industry is killed, which could have provided good employment in agriculturally degraded areas.

Nationalisation and controls reduce the number of legal buyers, choke the free flow of goods, and delay payment to the gatherers, as Government agencies find it difficult to make prompt payment. This results in contractors entering from the back door, but they must now operate with higher margins required to cover uncertain and delayed payments by Government agencies, as well as to make the police and other authorities ignore their illegal activities. This all reduces tribals' collection and incomes.

Diversion of NTFP and Industries

Some NTFP items, like sal seeds, have become important for industrialists. This reduces the consumption of NTFP as a stable food and medicine for the tribals, especially when the total supply from forests has declined because of deforestation (Fernandes *et al.*, 1988: 105). As their consumption declines they are forced to borrow more and at a high rate of interest from money lenders for buying grain. Then even if they would like to consume minor forest produce they are not able to do so as pressure from moneylenders forces them to sell.

Sometimes industries, in order to maximise the collection of NTFPs, use methods which are destructive to these plants. An obvious example is extraction of resin from pine trees. In tendu tree areas, contractors slash all undergrowth to promote a better growth of tendu leaves. In the process, many fruits, roots and medicinal plants get destroyed. Besides, it causes soil erosion (Dasgupta, 1986). Where industries hold bamboo leases they utilise even the better quality bamboo for pulp, although according to rules only inferior quality bamboo should be used as pulp, and the better quality should be sold to artisans. Furer-Haimendorf (1985) describes how a particular paper mill exploited bamboo in a tribal region by bringing in hundreds of labourers from different States and used methods of extraction which endangered future regeneration.

Exploitation in Marketing

Products collected by tribals and others from forest lands are sold to businessmen or Government corporations. The terms of the transactions are often severely to the disadvantage of the sellers. In Sarguja (M.P.) tribals get only 50 paise for every kg. of mahua that they sell, but to buy the same mahua flowers during the lean season they have to pay Rupee one per kg. (Fernandes *et al.*, 1985:105). In Madhya Pradesh and Orissa the price, which tribals get for tamarind, is as low as Rs. 1.40 to 1.75 per kg. whereas it sells for Rs. 9-11 per kg. in the Bombay market. Sometimes the traders follow a barter system by offering 1 kg of sweet potato costing less than a rupee for 1 kg. of tamarind (GOI, 1988:40).

Nor do Government interventions appear to have been generally successful. This has been admitted in number of Government reports (GOI, 1982; GOI: 1987), and has been well documented in 6 volumes of evaluation studies undertaken for the Department of Tribal Development, Government of India (GOI, 1988). In 50 out of 68 villages of Orissa, it was found (Fernandes *et al.*, 1988:140) that government agencies had not managed to eliminate middlemen. On the other hand, the same middlemen who till recently exploited the tribals as moneylenders and merchants continue their work in the garb of agents of Government bodies.

The result is that the price tribals get for their produce is very low, when compared with its price in the neighbouring markets. Still it illustrates the fact of exploitation at the hands of procuring organisations.

A workshop on marketing of NTFP held in May, 1979 at Hyderabad recommended that there should be competitive procurement and marketing by public, cooperative and private agencies. This would generate healthy competition. The reverse seems to be happening. Government agencies like to deal only in commodities where they have a monopoly and profit margins are assured. Ten years back, the number of items handled by GCC (AP) and TDCC (Orissa) was more than twenty. Now it has come down to the two or three most profitable ones (GOI, 1988). Where Government alone does marketing it is inefficient; and where it is left to private trade, it is exploitative.

Conclusion and Policy Recommendations

The following changes in law and policy have been suggested in this chapter:

Transit and Harvesting Rules etc.

A great source of market imperfections in wood markets is the legal and procedural framework which makes cutting and selling privately owned trees difficult, irksome and complicated, besides unremunerative. Therefore, these restrictive laws should be abolished.

A fear is often expressed that giving complete relaxation, specially in heavily forested States like MP or AP, might increase theft from Government forests. There are several ways of tackling this. First, popular species for farm forestry, i.e. fast growing commercially in demand species like eucalyptus should not be grown on forest lands, which should be given more priority to multi-purpose trees. This will also help in reducing competition between farmers and Government, and help the producers in getting a better price, and not face a glut situation. Second, to begin with, relaxation in rules may be attempted in such areas which are remote from Government forests. Third, relaxation may be given only for certain modes of transport, like headloads and bullock carts, so that farmers may take their produce free from fear to the markets, and not be dependent on traders. If the will to help farmers is there, a way can surely be found.

Intervention in Markets

Government should stop subsidies on Government supply of wood to industries, thereby forcing industries to buy from the farmers at a remunerative price. Even better would be if Government stops supplies to industries altogether for a couple of years. Supplies could be resumed when the farm forestry source dries up, as there has been little planting on farm lands after 1987, and farm supplies will dwindle after 1994.

Marketing

For marketing NTFPs, Government should not have monopoly. Nationalisation reduces the number of buyers and does not help gatherers in the long run. Monopoly purchase by Government requires sustained political support and excellent bureaucratic machinery. It is difficult to ensure these over a long period and hence nationalisation has often increased exploitation of the poor.

In commercial areas, private trade is relatively efficient, and hence can function without Government intervention. In tribal and subsistence areas markets are generally exploitative. Here it is better for Government to regulate private trade, and to act as a watchdog rather than try to eliminate it. Where Government alone does not market it is inefficient;

and where it is left to private trade, it is exploitative. It is better to allow private trade and Government buying to co-exist, as it happens in the wheat purchase scheme in north India. At the same time Forest or the Tribal Development Department should undertake the responsibility of informing tribals and gatherers about the prices prevailing in different markets, improve marketing practices and act as a watch-dog.

Primacy of Rights

People's rights of access and their rights to tree products are restricted, vague, or not known to them. Sharing arrangements in social security plantations or community forestry schemes are ill-defined or not publicised, or poorly implemented. There appears to be general reluctance on the part of the field machinery to define clearly what people are to get, at what time, and at what price, in exchange for the participation expected of them. But participation of the poor is improbable unless their benefits are secure.

Therefore, we suggest that outside each forest coupe or social forestry plantation there should be a notice board publicising what rights people have as regards collection. The colonial tradition of secrecy or a wide gap between policy and implementation must be given up. A simple notice that, "these trees belong to the community, and not to Government", may in itself, encourage people to get involved in managing public resources. Where rights are individualistic in nature, as in social security schemes, agreements must be entered in writing with the beneficiaries informing them about their entitlement.

Many civil servants blame traders for making unreasonable profits, and for low prices of wood and wood products. After reviewing the market research that has been carried out in developing countries, Stevens and Jabara (1988) concluded that there were very few empirical studies to confirm the stereotyped beliefs and traders. 'Much of what passes as analysis in the marketing literature represents little more than a repetition of the conventional wisdom about middlemen behaviour with little or no empirical content'. Our enquiries into the nature of markets are in sympathy with this view point (Saxena 1994). Monopsony conditions involve barriers to entry of new buyers, and to no close substitutes for the product (Colman and Young 1989). If these conditions are not met, monopsony would be a short-lived phenomenon. In the case of NTFPs, monopsony conditions were created by Government. For farm forestry too, Government's policies in themselves were a source of market imperfections. Thus, Government laws and policies must change for creating free and equitable market conditions.

SUMMARY OF DISCUSSION

Following the presentation, a number of issues were raised by the participants. There was an apparent consensus about the necessity of ensuring people's participation in forest management and simplification of various Government rules and regulations to release people's initiative with regard to development and maintenance of forests. With regard to the suggestion made by Dr Saxena about adoption of the sugarcane model it was pointed out that the monopoly status enjoyed by sugarcane producers by way of preventing new factories to come in the areas of their respective operation should not be overlooked. It was noted that the policy prescriptions that may be suggested in case of forest may not exactly be so with regard to non-forest areas.

It was also pointed out that in view of a new policy if the cropping pattern is to be changed, the probable impact on food security should also to be kept in mind. In view of liberalization regarding land in urban sector whether Land Ceiling Acts are to be changed or not too needs to be considered.

Dr Saxena was of the strong opinion that the question of land ceiling must be understood at two different levels, since the dimensions are not the same in urban and rural areas. Rural India, in his opinion, till now continues to have the need for continuation of the existing land ceiling provisions both on equity and productivity grounds. The following points were reiterated.

(a) People's participation is non negotiable;
(b) Joint forest management needs strengthening and encouragement; and
(c) The interest of the tree growers are to be always kept in sharp focus.

9

SOME ASPECTS OF MANAGING ECONOMIC REFORMS

J. L. BAJAJ

In the 1980s India experienced a G.D.P. growth of 5.5 per cent per annum: However it became increasingly evident from the emerging patterns of growth that the planning strategy and the mode of financing called for some crucial modifications. Towards the end of the decade the areas that needed reforms were quite apparent: inflation, adverse balance of payments, profligacy of expenditure by the Union and State Governments, tax reforms, industrial licensing procedures and trade policy. Far reaching changes have taken place in industrial policy; licensing requirements have largely been removed, import duties reduced, a number of tax reform measures implemented accompanied by new trade and agriculture policies. The response to these steps has been very encouraging. The annual rate of inflation has been brought down from 17 per cent which was prevailing in 1991 to about 8 per cent in 1993-94. Foreign Currency reserves now exceed $ 14 billion and the current account deficit is likely to be about 0.5 per cent of G.D.P. in 1993-94. The inflow of foreign direct and portfolio investment will rise to $ 2.5 billion in 1993-94. Stock of foodgrains are at a record level and industrial production is picking up. Overall economic growth in 1993-94 is likely to be 3.8 per cent as against 1.1 per cent in 1991-92.

So far the major initiatives in policy reforms have been taken by the Union Government. However, there are major areas of economic policy in which the role of the State Governments is very important. Industrial liberalisation measures would be successful if procedures to gain access to available infrastructure are simplified. The State Government would also have to improve tax administration, undertake effective expenditure control and restructure public enterprises.

This chapter looks at some aspects of fiscal and industrial policies and administrative practices in State Governments, with special reference to Uttar Pradesh, having implications for the New Economic Policy.

In recent years, the growing imbalance in revenue and expenditure has been a cause of considerable concern to the State Governments. The share of States in total expenditure of Central and State Governments in 1991 and 1992 was estimated at about 53 per cent and the share of States in expenditure on social and economic services at 85 per cent and 56 per cent respectively. States raise about 60 per cent of their own resources to finance their expenditure while about 40 per cent is received by way of share in Central taxes, grants or loans. The Constitution provides for fiscal adjustment through sharing of some taxes levied by the Central Government, and provision of grants-in-aid to States. Such adjustments are effected through the recommendations of the Finance Commission. The Finance Commission assesses the expenditure requirements of the Union and State Governments every five years and makes recommendations about revenue sharing and grants-in-aid.

The revenue receipts of the State Governments in 1980s increased at the rate of 15.5 per cent per annum while revenue expenditure increased at the rate of 17.6 per cent. In the same period, the increase in capital expenditure at current prices was 9.6 per cent per annum only. However, during the 1980s the growth in capital expenditure at constant prices decelerated to (–) 1.2 per cent per annum. The imbalance in State finances has accentuated with the overall budgetary position of the State Governments deteriorating between 1991-92 and 1993-94.

The consolidated budgetary position of State Governments as reflected in the Accounts for 1991-92 showed an overall deficit of Rs. 96.3 crores. The State Budgets estimate this deficit to increase to Rs. 3128 crores in 1993-94. If the States realise the revenue expected from additional resource mobilisation measures the deficit will still be Rs. 2640 crores. (Table 9.1).

Transfer to States in the form of share in tax revenue, small savings, non-plan loans and grants and Central assistance was Rs. 53,163 crores in 1992-93. The revised estimates for 1993-94 expect these transfers to be Rs. 59,464 crores and in 1994-95 budget provides Rs. 59,854 crores for transfer to States. Central Assistance for State and UT Plans which was Rs. 21,014 crores in 1993-94 (RE), will be only Rs. 19,304 crores in 1994-95. States share in Small Savings will also decline from Rs. 5,700 crores (BE 1992-93) to Rs. 5,152 crores (BE 1994-95), and transfer on account of Central and Centrally sponsored schemes from Rs. 8,096 (RE) in 1993-94 to Rs. 7,601 crores in 1994-95.

TABLE 9.1 : **Consolidated Budgetary Position of State Governments**

Items	1991-92	1992-93	1992-93	1993-94
(1)	(2)	(3)	(4)	(5)
I. Revenue				
Account	80,538.7	89,989.4	91,433.9	1,00,562.1
Receipts		(87,616.4)		1,00,073.5
Expenditure	86,186.4	93,506.4	95,550.7	5,086.53
Surplus (+),	–5,650.7	3,517.0	4,116.8	4,524.2
Deficit(–)		5,890.0		(–5,012.8)
II. Capital Account				
Receipts	34,349.4	29,342.6	29,905.1	30,322.1
Disbursement	28,795.0	25,737.2	27,044.8	28,437.6
Surplus (+), Deficit(–)	+5,554.4	+3,605.4	+2,860.3	+1,864.5
III. Aggregate Receipts	1,14,885.1	1,19,332.0	1,21,339.0	1,30,884.2
		(1,19,332.0)		1,30,395.6
IV. Aggregate Disbursement	1,14,981.1	1,19,243.6	1,22,595.5	1,33,523.9
V. Overall Surplus (+), Deficit (–)	-96.3	+88.4	1,256.5	2,639.7
		(–2,284.6)		(–3,128.3)
VI. Financing of Surplus (+) Deficit (–)				
1. Increase (+)/ Decrease (–) in cash Balances(Net)	–629.1	+311.5	89.3	2,567.0
		(–2,061.5)		(–3,055.6)
2. Addition to (+)/or Withdrawals from (–) Cash Balance Investment Account (Net)	+685.4	–150.1	–396.3	–72.7
3. Repayment of (+) or Increase in (–) Ways and Means Advances and Overdrafts from Reserve Bank of India (Net)	–152.6	–73.0	70.9	–

Source : Reserve Bank of India Bulletin, October 1993.

The Union Ministry of Finance in their paper on 'Economic Reforms: Two years after and the Task ahead' have, taking the Centre and States together, set the fiscal deficit target at around 5 per cent of GDP in 1996-97. This would require a very sharp decrease in the Central

TABLE 9.2 : **Resources Transferred to States & Union Territories**

	1994-95	1993-94 (RE)	1993-94 (BE)	1992-93 (RE)	1992-93 (BE)
States Share of Tax Revenue of	24394	22244	22049	20525	19992
which Income Tax	8205	7771	7136	6060	5869
Excise Duty	16189	144473	14913	14465	14123
Share of Small Savings Collections	5152	5000	4500	4400	5700
Non Plan Grants	2538	3302	2485	3262	2755
Non Plan Loans	76	9	71	468	100
Total	2614	3311	2414	3730	2855
Central Assist. for State & UT Plans	19304	21014	18010	17339	16111
Assistance for Central & Centrally Sponsored Schemes	7601	8096	8681	6991	6111

Government fiscal deficit as its target of 4.7 per cent for 1993-94 has slipped to 7.3 per cent and even in 1994-95 the fiscal deficit is estimated at 6 per cent of GDP. If the target of 5 per cent fiscal deficit in the operations of Central and State Governments is to be achieved, the States will have to accord considerable attention to controlling expenditure and augmenting both tax and non-tax revenues, as well as improving the performance of State enterprises.

In the next section we illustrate the need for fiscal correction by reviewing the budgetary transactions of Uttar Pradesh–the most populous State in the country (see Table 9.3).

For the first-three-years of the 1980s revenue receipts in Uttar Pradesh exceeded revenue expenditure, thereby providing revenue surplus for undertaking capital expenditure. The last year when there was a revenue surplus was 1987-88. Since then the revenue deficit annually has exceeded Rs. 1000 crore and in 1992-93 revenue deficit reached 8.7 per cent of the revenue receipts. The seriousness of the problem of revenue deficit is also reflected by the fact that as a

TABLE 9.3 : **Budgetary Position in U.P.**

(Rs. in Crores)

Year	Revenue Receipts	Revenue Expenditure	Revenue Surplus (+) Deficit (–)		Col. 4 as per cent of Col. 2
1	2	3	4		5
1980-81	1,899	1,716	(+)183	(20.3)	(+) 9.6
1981-82	2,260	1,906	(+)354	(27.0)	(+) 15.7
1982-83	2,556	2,364	(+)192	(21.6)	(+) 7.5
1983-84	2,665	2,761	(–)106	(*)	(–) 4.0
1984-85	3,145	3,292	(–)147	(16.4)	(–) 4.7
1985-86	3,877	3,808	(+) 69	(12.7)	(+) 1.8
1986-87	4,172	4,349	(–)117	(**)	(–) 4.2
1987-88	5,332	5,080	(+)252		(+) 4.7
1988-89	5,652	6,257	(–)605	(33.2)	(–) 10.7
1989-90	6,623	7,654	(–)1,031	(28.8)	(–) 15.6
1990-91	8,310	9,538	(–)1,22	8(26.7)	(–) 14.8
1991-92	9,675	10,399	(–)724	(30.4)	(–) 7.5
1992-93	11,676	12,691	(–)1015		(–) 8.7

Notes: 1. Figures in parentheses in Col. 4 are percentage shares in all States, Figures in "*" and "**" are shown nil because all States figures are not available. Figures in these years are +Rs. 218 crore and Rs. +21 crore respectively.

Source: 1. Bulletins of Uttar Pradesh *Ay-Vyayak Ki Roop Rekha*, Finance Department, U.P.

proportion of all States revenue deficit, U.P.'s deficit was 33.2 per cent in 1988-89, 28.8 per cent in 1989-90, 27.7 per cent in 1990-91 and 30.4 per cent in 1991-92. As a percentage of State's domestic product the revenue deficit in U.P. was about 2.5 per cent in 1989-90 as compared to an average of 1.03 per cent in all States.

Another serious development has been the consistent increase in the revenue portion of Plan expenditure. In 1984-85 half of the State's budget was spent on capital outlay while the other half met revenue expenditure. Since then, the share of capital outlay has been declining. It came down to 29 per cent in 1992-93, as will be evident from Table 9.4.

A major reason for growing fiscal imbalance in the State is the relatively slow growth in revenue receipts. The average annual growth in the States tax and non-tax revenue was 16.1 per cent between 1980-81 and 1992-93. Total revenue receipts including share in Central Taxes increased at 16.3 per cent per annum in this period. The corresponding annual growth in revenue expenditure however was 18.1 per cent. In case this trend continues revenue deficit will necessitate still larger diversion of capital receipts to finance revenue expenditure, thereby lowering the capacity of the State Government to finance fresh investments.

TABLE 9.4 : **Shares of Revenue Expenditure and Capital Outlay in State's Budgets**

Year	Revenue Expenditure	Capital Outlay
1980-81	60	40
1981-82	54	46
1982-83	54	46
1983-84	56	44
1984-85	50	50
1985-86	53	47
1986-87	61	39
1987-88	65	35
1988-89	76	24
1989-90	73	27
1990-91	63	37
1991-92	62	38
1992-93	71	29

TABLE 9.5 : **Share of Revenue Expenditure and Capital Expenditure**

	1980-81 (Rs. in Crores)	1992-93 (Rs. in Crores)	Average Annual Growth %
Revenue Receipts			
Own Tax Revenue	645	3886	16.2
Own Non-Tax Revenue	243	1421	15.9
Own Total Revenue	888	5307	16.1
Central Transfer to the State	1011	6369	16.6
Total	1899	11616	16.3
Revenue Expenditure	1716	12691	18.1
Capital Expenditure	1135	5191	13.5
Total Expenditure	2851	17882	16.5

Another consequence of the increase in borrowing for financing Plan outlays is the accelerated growth of interest payments. The average annual growth in interest payments was 28.2 per cent in 1993-94 over 1980-81. The share of interest payments in total current expenditure increased more than three times from 6 per cent in 1980-81 to 19.4 per cent in 1993-94.

One area where the State's expenditure has increased considerably is wages and salaries. In addition to the salary of Government employees, the State Government is meeting the entire expenditure on the salaries of teachers and employees of recognised educational institutions. It also meets 30 per cent of the salary expenditure of the employees of local bodies. Table 9.6 shows the increase in salaries of Government employees, employees of educational institutions and State's share in salaries of the employees of local bodies. As compared to 1980-81 the expenditure on employees of different categories increased by above five times in 1991-92. This excludes the expenditure on wages and salaries of State Electricity Board, public sector corporations and cooperative institutions. In terms of numbers (excluding the above mentioned categories), there has been an increase of 24 per cent in employees of different categories. The largest increase has been in Government employees followed by local bodies. The lowest increase in these categories has been in the number of teachers. (Table 9.7).

TABLE 9.6 : **Expenditure on Education**

	1980-81 (Rs. in crores)	1985-86 (Rs. in crores)	1991-92	Increase in 1991-92 Over 1980-81 (Percent)
1. Government Employees	466.01	934.22	2741.79	488.2
2. Teachers and Employees of Recognised Educational Institutions	204.31	441.41	1167.30	471.3
3. 30% expenditure on Salaries of employees of local bodies which is being borne by the State Government	10.55	12.50	42.00	294.4
Total	680.97	1388.13	3951.09	480.2

TABLE 9.7 : **Number of Employees in Education Sector**

	1980-81	1987-88	Percentage increase
1. Government Employees	614965	832007	35.00
2. Teachers and Employees of Recognised Educational Institutions	499112	550003	10.00
3. 30% expenditure on salaries of employees of Local Bodies which is being borne by the State Government.	98842	127043	29.00
Total	1212919	1509053	24.00

The increase in the expenditure on employees has taken place largely since 1987-88. In 1987-88 Government of India accepted the Report of the Fourth Pay Commission, which substantially increased salaries and introduced a new formula for payment of dearness allowance for neutralizing the increase in the cost of living for the Central Government employees. State Governments, including U.P., have adopted the pay scales and allowances being paid to the Central Government employees. Of the expenditure of 3951.09 crores in 1991-92, on wages and salaries of employees about 10 per cent was on Plan and the balance on non-plan account. The total non-Plan expenditure of the State Government for that year was Rs. 8218.7 crores. This included Rs. 1874.83 crores as interest payment on loans. Excluding this, the balance non-Plan revenue expenditure was Rs. 6343.91 crores. Of this, the expenditure on employees constituted 56.5 per cent.

The magnitude of the problem can be assessed by looking at the establishment expenditure of two major construction departments, i.e., Public Works Department and Irrigation Department. The Public Works Department is responsible for the construction and maintenance of major roads and Government buildings and the Irrigation department for the construction and maintenance of irrigation works like canals and State tubewells. The total expenditure of Public Works Department between 1988-89 and 1991-92 increased from Rs. 347.86 crores to 442.17 crores. In the same period establishment expenditure increased from about Rs. 90 crores to Rs. 139.65 crores. Total Plan and non-Plan expenditure on irrigation works between 1989-90 and 1992-93 increased from Rs. 737.64 crores to Rs. 790.51 crores while the expenditure on employees during the same period increased from 229.35 crores to Rs. 300.14 crores. The latter constituted about 38 per cent of the total expenditure. Thus, nearly 40 per cent of the total expenditure in Public Works and Irrigation Departments is consumed by establishment charges (Table 9.8 and 9.9).

Another significant feature of administration is that 98 per cent of Government employees belong to Class-III and Class-IV. That an overwhelming proportion of Government employees belong to the category of peons, clerks, and those having similar government features reflects the quality of administration at the implementing level.

TABLE 9.8 : **Public Works Department**

	1988-89	1989-90	1990-91	1991-92	1992-93
Works Portion					
A. Plan Expenditure	207.33	197.80	243.66	240.41	268.17
Non-Plan Expenditure	140.53	127.42	206.98	183.76	124.27
	347.86			424.17	442.44
Establishment Charges					
B. Plan Expenditure	25.03	25.03	31.16	25.81	30.89
Non-Plan Expenditure	64.89	82.00	108.34	113.34	77.79
	89.92			139.65	108.68
'B' As percent of Work Expenditure					
Plan	12.10	12.70	12.80	10.70	11.50
Non-Plan	46.20	64.40	52.30	62.00	72.50

TABLE 9.9 : **Irrigation Works Portion**

	1988-89	1989-90	1990-91	1991-92	1992-93
A-Plan Expenditure		625.42	626.20	527.40	600.90
Recoveries		–329.30	–312.37	–330.43	–369.72
NET	409.43	296.12	313.83	196.97	231.18
Non-Plan Expenditure		470.38	451.59	586.56	594.15
Recoveries		–28.83	–26.49	–43.93	–34.82
NET	252.15	441.55	425.10	542.63	559.33
Establishment Charges					
B-Plan Expenditure	84.40	90.48	104.89	35.35	118.74
Non Plan Expenditure	200.12	138.87	149.50	236.96	181.40
B As percent of Works Plan Expenditure	20.60	30.60	33.40	18.00	51.40
Non-Plan	79.40	31.40	35.20	43.70	32.40

While unmitigated growth of Public expenditure is a matter of serious concern, the low growth in revenue of some of the backward States like Bihar and U.P. needs particular attention. The share of tax revenue in States own revenues. is about 75 per cent. U.P.'s own tax revenue in 1980-81 (Rs. 645 crores) was 9.7 per cent of the tax revenue of all the States that year, as against its share in GDP of 12.7 per cent (Table 9.10). While it is not necessary that the percentage share of State taxes in all State average of tax revenue should equal the share of State in total GDP, yet a large difference between the two indicates that there is scope for additional resource mobilisation. This becomes even more evident when we consider that the share of a low income State like Madhya Pradesh in all States tax revenue in 1980-81 was higher than its share in total GDP and that the difference in the share in two other low income States like Rajasthan and Bihar is less than that of U.P. Even more significant is the fact that the share of U.P. and Bihar in all States tax collection declined between 1980-81 and 1990-91.

TABLE 9.10 : **Share of States in National Income and all States Own Tax Revenue**

State	1980-81 Share in National Income Revenue	1990-91 Share in All States Own Tax Revenue	Difference in Col. 3 Over Col. 2	Share in All States Own Tax
Backward States				
1. U.P.	12.7	9.7	(–) 3.0	9.4
2. Raj	3.7	3.5	(–) 0.2	4.0
3. Orissa	2.9	2.0	(–) 0.9	2.2
4. M.P.	5.5	5.8	(–) 0.3	6.0
5. Bihar	5.5	4.2	(–) 0.8	3.8
Some Rich States				
6. Punjab	4.0	5.3	(+) 1.3	4.6
7. Maharashtra	13.7	17.0	(+) 3.3	16.9

Another indication of the resource raising capacity in State is the percentage own of tax revenue collected as a percentage of per capita income. The per capita own tax revenue in U.P. in 1988-89 was 5.7 per cent of State per capita income which was lower than the effort of all other major States except Bihar and Orissa.

Non-tax receipts in U.P. increased from Rs. 704.65 crores in 1988-89 to Rs. 1102.56 crores. However the share of non-tax revenue in total receipts declined from 12.5 per cent in 1988-89 to 11.6 per cent in 1991-92.

In Uttar Pradesh, as in most States, user charges for providing services like irrigation, medical and health are very low. Table 9.11 gives the financial results of the State's irrigation works, which include gravity canals, pump canals and State tubewells.

TABLE 9.11 : **Financial Results of State Irrigation Works**

(Rs. in crores)

	1990-91	91-92	92-93	93-94
1. Gross Receipts	4.77	51.17	46.51	84.98
2. Current Expenditure	302.57	490.71	433.27	438.37
3. Interest Charges	245.62	260.86	273.34	360.02
Total	548.17	751.57	706.62	798.39
Not Receipt	504.42	700.40	660.11	713.41

It would be seen that while receipts from water charges are about 85 crores, the total expenditure (including interest on capital works) amount to Rs. 800 crores. Water charges were last revised in 1983 and since then the increase in salary and maintenance cost has increased considerably leading to a deficit of over Rs. 700 crores per year in the operation of irrigation system in the State. The average per hectare receipts from pump canals, tubewells and canal system was Rs. 137.5, while the average expenditure amounted to Rs. 1132 per hectare. The gap between the cost incurred and the user charges collected was about Rs. 1000 per hectare of irrigated land.

The fees charged for veterinary services in the State dispensaries have remained at the level at which they were in 1950. For the treatment of cows and buffaloes only 20 paise per animal is charged while the cost of providing these services is estimated at Rs. 10 per animal. For artificial insemination Re 1 per animal is charged as against the cost of Rs. 20 and for vaccination ten paise per animal is charged while the cost of this service is Rs. 10 per animal. Today coins of 10 and 20 paise are not easily available but fees continue to be charged at this rate. The result of prescribing fees at such abysmally low level is that the quality of service provided by these State institutions is quite poor.

In this State there has been a substantial increase in number of Public Enterprise and investment therein. By 1991 the number of State enterprises in Uttar Pradesh had increased to 64 involving a gross investment of Rs. 10,720 crores. Major part of this investment amounting to Rs. 7,154 crores was contributed by the State Government. The largest public enterprise in the State is the State Electricity Board with the investment of about Rs. 7,000 crores. At the end of 1990-91 the State Government's investment in the State Electricity Board is Rs. 5,126 crores; in the remaining enterprises the State investment Rs. 2,027 crores by way of equity and shares. As in other States, the experience of public enterprises in Uttar Pradesh has not been favourable with the most frequent criticism being that of inefficient management and inappropriate investment in terms of comparative advantage. These enterprises represent a significant drain on the government budget. The only social purpose being served by continuing the loss making enterprises is protection of jobs. But this social purpose is being achieved at a very high cost. In addition to the financial losses, real resources such as land and other unutilised assets remain locked up in these enterprises. The present situation is that the State Government is not only not getting any return on equity and loans but is forced to borrow at high cost to finance the huge losses of these enterprises.

It will, therefore, be appropriate if the Government were to make a concerted programme of handing over these enterprises to workers' cooperatives. The State Government's share holding may be transferred at zero cost and all loans by the Government may be written off. In turn, the Government should have no further obligation for the management and financing of these enterprises. The scheme may be acceptable to workers only if permission to sell the land of these enterprises is given to them, otherwise, they would not be able to generate resources required for operating these enterprises.

A number of State enterprises have been referred to BIFR as their net worth has become negative. The fate of these companies is not likely to be decided soon, and till then the State Government will have to continue to meet their losses. Fifteen Public Sector undertakings have been closed down which include Chalchitra Nigam, U.P. Hortico, Divisional Development and Area Development Corporations, offer for sale of U.P. Instruments was invited in 1990 but few inquiries were received. U.P. Textile Corporation and U.P. Cooperative Federation invited offers for three closed Cotton Spinning Units situated at Akbarpur, Fatehpur and Kampil and Woollen Spinning Mills at Bhadohi. As serious offers were not received, Fatehpur and Kampil have been reopened on the basis of jobwork. The negotiations for the sale of Bhadohi Mill have run into trouble. Similarly, the MOU was signed for the sale of equity of the Coloured Picture Tube Factory, a subsidiary of UPTRON but the offer has been withdrawn by the prospective buyer. Recently, offers have been invited for the purchase of eight sugar mills belonging to the U.P. Sugar Corporation. In case of U.P. Cement Corporation the State Government sold 51 per cent of its equity to M/s Dalmia Industries in 1991. This step was opposed by a number of labour unions and political parties. In the face of this opposition the decision was rescinded. The accumulated loss of U.P. Cement Corporation at the end of 1991 was about Rs. 180 crores. By the end of 1993-94 the loss is likely to increase to about Rs. 290 crores. The decision to take over the Corporation in the Public Sector again has already cost the State exchequer over Rs. 100 crores in a period of two years. On the other hand, in case of Auto Tractors Ltd., the sale of equity to the private sector has improved its performance and the unit has been turned around from a loss making to a profit earning unit. For accelerating power development in the State MOU's have been signed for Vishnu Prayag Hydro Electric Project with JP Industries, ROZA Thermal Project (3x250MW) with Indo Gulf Fertilizers and Jawahar Hydel Scheme (3x250 MW) with Pacific Electric Development Corporation.

In the Industrial Sector the process of economic reform is slowly percolating to the States. Every State Government is entering the race for attracting more investments from within and outside the country. Earlier too the State Governments were providing fiscal incentives for new investment but now high pressure and active marketing is also being resorted to by these Governments. The States are also reviewing their procedures for setting up new industrial units and are opening up infrastructure like power and roads to private sector. In Karnataka it has been decided to release investment subsidies through the agency sanctioning financial assistance; after the expiry of lease period the stamp duty on land is to be charged on the original allotment price; for conversion of agricultural land for industrial use in identified zones, no prior approval of Government is required. Similarly, in Maharashtra, agricultural land upto 10 hectares can be transferred to any person for bonafide industrial use on the condition that within five years of the date of purchase the proposed industrial unit would be established. Where total area of land is more than 10 hectares permission is to be granted by the Development

Commissioner (Industries) or an officer authorised by the State Government. However, in some of the less developed States like Uttar Pradesh, the procedures are still cumbersome and the approval process requires considerable effort on the part of the investor. Annexure 1 gives the details of the formalities required to be completed for setting up an industrial unit in the State. As can be seen, the requirements are many and the procedures are forbidding. There is not a single place, including developed industrial areas like NOIDA, Kanpur and Lucknow, where all the requirements can be completed under one shed and infrastructure facilities like power connection and telephone made available. One can very well imagine the situation in industrial estates of backward areas. The Empowered Committees are still symbolic and the industrial estates are only earmarked pieces of land without even minimum facilities. Unlike Karnataka and Maharashtra the conversion of agricultural land for non-agricultural uses requires the permission of the Assistant Collector incharge of the division. Section 143 of the U.P. Zamindari and Land Reforms Act 1950 provides that where a holding is not being used for agricultural, horticulture or animal husbandry, the Assistant Collector incharge of a division may, on an application after making inquiries, make a declaration to that effect. If land is owned by a person belonging to a scheduled caste he has no right to transfer the land by way of sale, gift or lease to a person not belonging to a scheduled caste except with the prior approval of the Collector. There are also restrictions on the purchase of land by foreign nationals. Section 154-A of the same Act states that no foreign national shall acquire land by sale or gift without permission in writing from the State Government. Thus, getting land for setting up an industrial enterprise takes about six months unless land is purchased from the State Industrial Development Corporation or the District Industries Centre. Similarly, the procedural complexities in obtaining the permission of Pollution Control Board, Electricity Board and other bodies are enormous. The total number of cases pending for sanctions in different offices of the State Government in October 1993 are given in Table 9.12.

An area where almost no reform has taken place is the procurement system of Government departments. In Uttar Pradesh the Stores Purchase Rules were framed in 1935. These still form the basic framework for store purchase by the Government departments. The purchase system is heavily centralized with the requirement that all plant and machinery shall be purchased by the Government departments only through the Director of Industries. Rule 5 of the Stores Purchase Rules provides that even in the case of work contracts, a provision should be made in the contract agreement that the contractor must obtain articles required for the construction of such works from firms with which the Director of

TABLE 9.12 : **Number of Pending Sanctions with the State Government**

Sanction Required	No. of Pending for Sanctions (as in October, 1993)
1. Sales Tax Temporary Registration	9
2. Power Sanction	460
3. Power Release	3554
4. Land Allotment	712
5. Term Loan	2518
6. No Objection Certificate	116
7. Working Capital	816
8. Permanent Registration	4
9. Sales Tax Permanent Registration	24
10. Registration Under Factory Act	18
11. Food Department	9
12. Land Possession	1351
13. State Plan Section	34
14. Consent from Pollution Control Board	28
15. Sales Tax Exemption	169
16. State Capital Subsidy	349
Total Pending Cases	10992

Source: Department of Industry, Government of U.P.

Industries has made arrangements. Even in case of emergent situations a Head of office and a Head of the Department can purchase articles upto Rs. 20,000 and Rs. one lakh respectively. However, in every such case they are required to mention in the order the reasons for making use of emergent powers. There is a further requirement that articles of general use can be purchased directly only upto a limit of Rs. 5,000 by Head of office and upto Rs. 25, 000 by Head of Department without permission of the Store Purchase Section of the Directorate of Industries. Stores purchased beyond Rs. 1 lakh have to be purchased through the Director of Industries. If the items purchased exceeded Rs. 1.25 crores, the approval of the State Government is required before the supply order can be placed. The general principle laid down in the Government Order for purpose of rate contracts is that a unit set up in the State will be given priority over a unit outside the State. The price preference available to the products produced within the State is ten per cent.

There are certain items which are required by the Government departments every year. One hundred and seventy seven of such items of general use are broadly grouped under thirteen categories. Purchase of these items is decided by the Directorate of Industries on the basis of rate contract with the manufacturing units. Items which are not covered under rate contract but are required occasionally are purchased by the Director of Industries on the demand of one or more department by inviting tenders. This contract is known as Quantity Contract. For this, the Government departments are expected to send their indent to the Directorate of Industries by 1st November every year. Thereafter, the Directorate invites tenders and takes a decision on the price and the quantity to be offered to each of the firms whose tenders are accepted. The Government departments can make purchases only from the notified firms. Public Works, Irrigation and other construction departments continue to take the responsibility for supplying cement, steel, pipes etc. to contractors. This system had some justification when the price of these items was controlled and they were allocated to Government departments by the manufacturers on a preferential basis. Now that these and other materials are available freely in the open market, there is little justification in continuing these practices. The present system relieves the contractors from the responsibility of mobilising materials and gives them an opportunity for claiming price escalation whenever there is a delay in this. Studies carried out in the Government show that the present purchase procedures are time consuming, cumbersome and raise costs. They also are one of the factors delaying the timely completion of projects.

Deregulation of licensing requirements has had an immediate impact in Uttar Pradesh. In 1990-91, 159 medium and large industrial units were set up involving a capital investment of Rs. 1,372 crores. In 1991-92 while the number of units established increased to 205, capital investment declined to Rs. 511 crores. In 1992-93 the number of units has come down to 55 only while capital investment has further fallen to Rs. 476 crores. It would, thus, be seen that in a period of two years capital investment in medium and large industrial units in the State has declined by over 65 per cent. Similarly, the number of sick SSI and non-SSI units have increased by 22.57 per cent and 29.76 per cent between 1990-91 and 1991-92 respectively. The State-wise list of sick SSI units shows that some of the worst affected State are Karnataka, Rajasthan and U.P.. In non-SSI sector Kerala, Orissa and Uttar Pradesh are amongst the most affected States.

TABLE 9.13 : **State-Wise List of Sick Industrial Units in India**

	SSI Units Per cent				Non-SSI Units Per cent			
State	1990	91	92	Change	1990	91	92	Change
Uttar Pradesh	27862	27477	34150	22.57	84	94	109	29.76
West Bengal	37448	30748	32002	14.54	195	185	197	1.03
Andhra	30103	29487	29586	1.72	122	135	145	18.85
M. P.	16716	17146	22333	33.60	47	48	59	25.53
Maharashtra	19208	20332	20153	4.92	322	301	301	–6.52
Karnataka	10252	12858	17316	68.90	82	93	92	12.20
Kerala	15239	17973	14883	2.34	32	34	48	50.00
Rajasthan	9987	12196	14420	44.39	46	52	54	17.39
Tamil Nadu	9891	10757	9797	0.95	133	127	124	6.77
Orissa	7194	7443	8415	16.97	28	35	37	32.14
Bihar	5007	5171	7823	56.24	40	38	44	10.00
Gujarat	6174	6240	6581	6.59	155	154	155	0.00
Punjab	5938	5288	5485	7.63	28	32	32	14.29
Assam	4512	4892	5317	17.84	8	7	7	2.50
Delhi	4346	4364	4705	8.64	24	20	22	8.33
Haryana	3186	2720	3467	8.82	46	49	55	19.57
Manipur	771	2278	2277	195.33	–	–	–	–
H.P.	824	848	1481	79.73	15	15	22	46.67
Goa	1210	1148	1066	11.90	14	14	5	64.29
J & K	1819	720	769	57.72	1	2	2	100.00

Note: Percent change is between March, 1990 and March 1992.

The major agencies providing loans for industries in the State are PICUP, UPFC and commercial banks. PICUP sanctioned loans worth Rs. 167 crores and Rs. 228 crores in 1991-92 and 1992-93 and disbursed loans of Rs. 141.62 crores and Rs. 147 crores in 1991-92 and 1992-93 respectively. The loans sanctioned by the UPFC declined from Rs. 228 crores in 1991-92 to Rs. 190 crores in 1992-93, while loans disbursed fell from Rs. 146 crores to Rs. 143 crores in the same period. The level of bank lending in the State at Rs. 414 per capita is much lower than at Rs. 859 per capita at the national level. The credit deposit ratio is barely 42 per cent.

The industrial Sector in the State generates employment for about 97.3 lakh workmen and 35.2 lakh casual workers. Public sector employs about 21.42 lakh persons whereas 18.09 lakh persons are employed in family enterprises. About 218 lakh persons are employed in the agricultural sector out of which about 80 lakh workers come in the category of agricultural labourers. The list of labour laws enforced by labour department of the State along with details of inspections required to be carried out by various functionaries is listed at Annexure 1.2. Labour laws in the State may be classified as:

1. Laws relating to working conditions of workmen.
2. Laws for the regulation of service conditions of workmen.
3. Laws relating to regulation of service conditions of workmen.
4. Laws relating to social security of records and furnishing of various returns.

Besides the officials of Labour Department, industrial establishments are also inspected by inspectors of Health, Electrical Safety, Weights and Measures. Food and Civil Supplies, Provident Fund and Pollution Control Board etc. There is a general feeling among managers that labour laws need to be made less stringent and the number of inspectors reduced. For example, Punjab has introduced a self inspection system for industrial units reducing the need for multiple inspectors. This could be emulated by other States too.

Notwithstanding the profligation of public expenditure and vast manpower, the present delivery system is fraught with several shortcomings. Some of them are:

(a) Lack of motivation owing to many reasons ranging from a lack of substantive recognition for any good work done to transfers for subjective reasons.

(b) Lack of prioritization stemming mainly from lengthy job descriptions for officials as well as functionaries, e.g., The Chief Development Officer in a district in Uttar Pradesh overseas 38 departments and chairs about 20 committees, and the Village Development Officers are entrusted with 64 different activities.

(c) Prescriptive Programmes such as JRY and IRDP are implemented uniformly without any recognition of local realities.

(d) Weak linkages between the Secretariat through the district and block down to the village level, as well as horizontally at each level between various departments, officials and functionaries.

(e) Centralization of functions such as purchase and sale strangulates initiative, causes delays and fails to catalyse integration at the local level.

(f) Game of numbers becomes the litmus test of the development efforts while overall goal of a programme recedes.

The present administrative ethos is such that everyone there is a multiple layer of officials, all superintendending over a very large but mainly class III and class IV employees who are insufficiently trained and poorly motivated.

The management by few, and not supervision by many will be a necessary pre-condition for efficiency maximization. The State Governments have to design and setup a delivery system, some of the attributes of which should be :

(a) Greater transparency;
(b) Meaningful planning;
(c) Rationalization of functions;
(d) Improved personnel management; and
(e) Need based efforts at various levels.

Political, social and economic environment in India is changing fast. Every change requires adjustment. State Governments that respond quickly and effectively will be able to minimize this cost. An important task before the State Governments is to reduce their budgetary deficits. Governments in States at low level of economic development may have particular difficulty in controlling budgetary balances for three reasons: spending pressures, low private savings and low tax revenue. Emergence of strong local opinions has been identified as a major pressure on Governments of low income States. Education, modern communication, international migration have all contributed to these pressures. Governments of low income States also face the difficulty in reducing expenditure as many types of recurrent expenditure is impossible to reduce. In fact it has a minimum built-in growth due to periodic wage revisions, inflation and development commitments. Despite these problems there is enough scope for State Governments to exercise expenditure control improve tax revenues through widening of tax base and better collection, enhance user charges and cut down losses of Public Enterprises.

At the level of the Central government entry restrictions in industries have been relaxed considerably. But the same cannot be said of the State Governments. A recent survey by NCAER reports that about 60 per cent industrialists feel that there has been no change in the procedures at the State and municipal levels. There is a desire to improve the industrial environment but the attitudinal change has to percolate to the lower levels of bureaucracy. In States the role of civil service in providing internal security is very important. Economic reforms require stability and security if domestic and foreign investment is to increase. Therefore, the traditional role of the civil service in law and order will continue to be important. There is no substitute to civil service in this. Also, the civil service has to provide an effective delivery system for effective implementation of antipoverty programmes. They have to assist in dismantling old and archaic rules and procedures and set up an effective mechanism for providing services at the grass-root level. This cannot, however be attained by the civil service alone. The political executive has an important role to play here. A responsive and accountable bureaucracy is possible only if there is political and administrative stability, and the political executive and civil service understand and recognise each other's role.

ANNEXURE 1

DETAILED CHART OF FORMALITIES TO BE DONE REGARDING UNITS

SL. NO.	DEPART-MENTS	REQUIRE-MENT OF THE DEPTT.	FORMALITIES/ STEPS	PROCEDURE	PURPOSE	TIME TAKEN NORMALLY
1	2	3	4	5	6	7
1.	D.I.C	Temporary Registration of the Unit	Submission of Project Report	Submit to D.I.C to G.M., D.I.C	1. Margin Money 2.Recognition by other Deptt.	1-2 Weeks
2.	D.I.C	Permanent Registration	Submission of Report of Pro-duction in DIC	To D.I.C	1. Licences From Different Deptt. 2. Registration by Other Deptt.	
3.	Pollution Control Board	There are Four Categories of Industries :				
		1. Small Scale Industries other than Restricted 17 Categories	Only consent Required appli-cation to be Sent to Poll-ution Control Board.	Letter to Pollu-tion Control Board	To Obtain	—
		2. 179 Other Non Pollut-ing Industries.				

		3. 50 Less Polluting Industries	Empowered Committee to give Approval	Letter to Dist. Empowered Committee	N.O.C From Pollution Control Board	3 Months
		4. More Polluting Inds.	Regional Officer PCB to Give NOC	Letter to R.O. Pollution Control Board.		6 -12 Months
		5. Diesel Genarating set	Sanction is Given by the State Government	Letter to R.O. and State Government	To Authorise Purchase of Items on Form-31 Form C Form-3 (B).	6 months Onwards
4.	Land Allotment	There can be Three Categories of Land :				
		1.Own Land	Transfer of Land for Other than Agricultural Use to Done Under Section 143/154 A of ZA Act of SDM	Apply in the Court of SDO with Relevant Paper.	To Make Use of Land for Indl. Purpose	3 - 6 Months
		2. Land Purchased From Agriculture				
			3. Indl. Estate of : (1) UPSIDC (2) DIC	Allottment by UPSIDIC/DIC		

(Contd.)

ANNEXURE 1 *(Contd.)*

(1)	(2)	(3)	(4)	(5)	(6)	(7)
5.	D.I.C.	Possession of Land	After Sanction of Loan or After the Order is Placed for Machine.			
6.		Sanction of Map	It is Required From 5 Different Offices.			
		1. Deputy Director, Factories Under Factories Act/ Shop Act.	Application to D.D Factories and to Sanction Stability of Building & Licence Under B(2-A), Factories Act.	To Sanction Building Plan		3 - 6 Months
		2. Industrial Dev. Authority/Town Dev. Authority/ Prescribed Authority Under RBO Act/ Municipal Board	To Apply to the Prescribed Authority Under Urban Ceiling Act. To Get Maps Passed Application is to be Sent to Dev. Authority Under RBO Where Master Plan for a Dist. is Sanctioned.	To Get NDC		3-1 Year
		3. UPSIDC/DIC	Where (2) Not Applicable			3 - 6 Months

		4. Fire Brigade	Fire Officer		3-6 Months
		5. U.P. Road Side Control Act	Approval Collector		6-12 Months
7.	Electricity Board	1. Sanction of Empowered Committee upto 100 HP or	Application Before Empowered Committee	Prescribed Time Estimate to be Given Within 6 Weeks	24 Months
		2. Sanction Beyond 100 HP by State Government Electricity Board	Approval of Board District Level Officer	Connection Within 3 months of Money Deposit.	3-6 Months
		3. Sanction of Load for Temp Purpose of Construction is Also Given by Empowered Committee			6 -12 Months
8.	ESI Act. Registration.				
9	Central Excise Act. Licence : 1. Food Deptt. 2. Drug Controller. 3. Food Product Order 4. Explosive Act. 5. Others.				
	Raw Material Registration : 1. Indian Oil Corporation 2. Registration UPSIC 3. Iron 4. Coke 5. Store Purchase.				

ANNEXURE 1.1

LAWS APPLICABLE TO LABOUR AND OTHER PROVISIONS GOVERNING THE FUNCTIONS OF THE OFFICE OF THE LABOUR COMMISSIONER, U.P.

1. Minimum Wages Act, 1948
2. Motor Transport Workers Act, 1961
3. U.P. Dookan Aur Vanijya Adhisthan Adhiniyam, 1962
4. Bidi & Cigar Workers (Conditions of Employment) Act,
5. Child Labour (Prohibition & Regulation) Act, 1986
6. Equal Remuneration Act, 1976
7. Inter-State Migrant Workers (Employment, Regulation & Conditions of Service) Act, 1979
8. Contract Labour (Regulation & Abolition) Act, 1970
9. Sales Promotion Employees (Conditions of Service) Act, 1976
10. Plantation Labour Act, 1951
11. Industrial Employment (Standing Orders) Act, 1970
12. U.P. Industrial Establishments (National Holidays) Act, 1961
13. Payment of Gratuity Act, 1972
14. Payment of Bonus Act, 1965
15. Factories Act, 1948
16. Payment of Wages Act, 1936
17. Maternity Benefits Act, 1961
18. Trade Unions Act, 1926
19. U.P. Industrial Disputes Act, 1947
20. Industrial Disputes Act, 1947
21. Workmen's Compensation Act, 1923
22. Working Journalist & Other Newspaper Employees (Conditions of Service & Miscellaneous Provisions) Act, 1955
23. Working Journalist (Fixation of Rates of Wages) Act, 1958
24. U.P. Industrial Peace (Timely Payment of Wages) Act, 1978
25. U.P. Labour Welfare Fund Act, 1965
26. Indian Boilers Act, 1923
27. Bonded Labour System (Abolition) Act, 1976
28. U.P. Employment of Substitute Workmen Act, 1978
29. U.P. Industrial Housing Act, 1955
30. U.P. Industrial Undertakings Special Provisions for Prevention of (Unemployment) Act, 1966
31. U.P. Public Premises (Eviction of Unauthorised Occupants) Act, 1972.

ANNEXURE 1.2

LABOUR LAWS WHICH PROVIDE FOR INSPECTIONS BY THE AUTHORISED FUNCTIONARIES OF THE LABOUR DEPARTMENT

1. Minimum Wages Act, 1948
2. Motor Transport Workers Act, 1961
3. U.P. Dookan Aur Vanijya Adhisthan Adhiniyam, 1962
4. Bidi & Cigar Workers (Conditions of Employment) Act, 1968
5. Child Labour (Prohibition & Regulations) Act, 1986
6. Equal Remuneration Act, 1976
7. Inter-State Migrant Workers (Employment, Regulation & Conditions of Service) Act, 1979
8. Contract Labour (Regulation & Prohibition) Act, 1970
9. Sales Promotion Employees (Conditions of Service) Act, 1976
10. Plantation Labour Act, 1951
11. Industrial Employment (Standing Orders) Act, 1946
12. U.P. Industrial Establishments (National Holidays) Act, 1961
13. Payment of Gratuity Act, 1972
14. Payment of Bonus Act, 1965
15. Factories Act, 1948
16. Payment of Wages Act, 1936.
17. Maternity Benefits Act, 1961.
18. Working Journalist & Other Newspaper Employees (condition of Service & Miscellaneous Provisions) Act, 1955.
19. U.P. Labour Welfare Fund Act, 1965.
20. Indian Boilers Act, 1923.

ANNEXURE 1.3

LABOUR LAWS WHICH PROVIDE FÓR INSPECTIONS BY DESIGNATED OFFICERS

Sl. No.	Name of Labour Law	Section	Designated Officer	Responsibility
1	2	3	4	5
1.	U.P. Dookan Aur Vanijya Adhisthan Adhiniyam, 1962.	4-B	Labour Enf-orcement Officer	Registration of Shops & Commercial Establishments.
		4-C	-do-	Renewal of Registrat-ion of Shops & Commercial Establishments.
		5	-do-	Timings of Opening and Closing of Shops.
		6	-do-	Fixation of Working Hours and Overtime for Workers.
		8	-do-	Weekly Rest
		13	-do-	Timely Payment of Wages
		21	-do-	Prevention of Empl-oyment of Child Labour
		32	-do-	Maintenance of Atten-dance Register and Leave Register.
2.	Minimum Wages Act,1948.	12	-do-	Timely Payment of Fixed Wages and Prosecution in Case of Less Than Stipulated Wages.

(Contd.)

ANNEXURE 1.3 *(Contd.)*

1	2	3	4	5
		13	-do--	Fixation of Working Hours.
		14	-do-	Overtime
		18(26)	--do-	Payment of Wages Register, Maintenance of Muster Roll in Form IV, Displaying of Notice No. 1 to 6 andEnsuring Issuance of Pay Slips to Workers.
3.	Motor Transport Wokers Act, 1961	3	Labour Enforcement Officer	Registration of Motor Transport Organisations.
		8	-do-	Provision of Canteen for Units of 100 or More Workers
		12	-do-	Provision of Primary Health Facilities
		13	-do-	Fixation of 8 Hours' a Day Work and not More Than 48 Hours a Week
		21	-do-	Prevention of Employment of Child Labour and Overtime Wages.
4.	Bidi & Cigar Workers (Conditions of Employment) Act, 1966.	4	-do-	Registration
		8 to 15	-do-	Provision Regarding Health and Welfare of Workers
		17	-do-	Provision for Ensuring not More Than 9 Hours' Work Every Day and not More Than 48 Hours a Week
		18	-do-	Overtime Wages to be paid @ Double Daily Unit Rate

(Contd.)

ANNEXURE 1.3 *(Contd.)*

1	2	3	4	5
		20	Labour Enforcement Officer	Ensuring that Work is Not Spread Over More Than 10 Hours a Day
		21	- do -	Weekly Rest
		24	- do -	Prevention of Employment of Child Labour
		26	- do -	Provision for Annual Leave with Wages
5.	Child Labour (Prohibition & Regulation) Act, 1986	3	- do -	Ensuring that Children Below the Age of 14 Years are not Employed
		7	- do -	Regulation of Child Labour in Selected Industries and Ensuring Minimum Facilities Required Under Law
		8	- do -	Weekly Rest
		11	- do -	Maintenance of Register Containing the Details of Child Labour
		12	- do -	Extracts of Sec. 3 & 4 to be Displayed on the Notice Board
6.	Equal Remuneration Act, 1976	4	- do -	Payment of Equal Wages to Women
		7	- do -	Prevention of Discrimination to Women
		9 (16)	- do -	Maintenance of Register in Form 'D' by Employers

(Contd.)

ANNEXURE 1.3 *(Contd.)*

1	2	3	4	5
7.	Inter-State Migrant Workers (Employment Regulation of Service) Act, 1979	4	Labour Enforcement Officer	Registration of Organisations Dealing with Inter-State Migrant Lab ur Force.
		8	-do-	Insurance of Licence to Contractors Dealing with Migrant Labour
		12	-do-	Ensuring Issuance of Pass Books to Workers and Furnishing of Returns to Prescribed Authorities
		13	-do-	Rates of Wages, (To be Given by the Employers)
		14	-do-	Displacement Allowance (To be Given by the Employers)
		15	-do-	Traveling Allowance (To be Given by the Employers)
		16	-do-	Other Benefits (To be Given by the Employers)
		23	-do-	Maintenance of Prescribed Registers
8.	Contract Labour (Regulation & Abolition)	7	-do-	Registration
		12	-do-	Issuance of Licences Act, 1970.
		10	-do-	Payment of Wages at the Same Rate as Offered by Principal Employer to Others Doing Similar Work.

(Contd.)

ANNEXURE 1.3 *(Contd.)*

1	2	3	4	5	
		16 17	Labour Enforce- ment officer	Canteen Rest Room	Ensuring That These Facilities are Made Available
		19	-do-	Primary Health Care	
		29	-do-	Register of Contr-actors	
		Rule 74 Rule 75	-do-	Contractors Responsi-bility to Maintain Register of Contract Workers	
		Rule 76	-do-	Employment Card	
		Rule 78	-do-	Muster Roll, Paybill Register, Deduction Register, Overtime Register, Fines Register and Advances Register Ensuring that These Registers are Maintai-ned in the Prescribed Manner	
		Rule 80	-do-	Displaying of Notices	
9.	Sales Promotion Employees (Conditions of Service) Act, 1976	7 & Rule 23	-do-	Form 'B' Form 'C' Form 'D' Form 'D' Concerning With Attendance, Leave & Service Book	Ensuring Mainte-nance of These Provi-sions

(Contd.)

ANNEXURE 1.3 *(Contd.)*

1	2	3	4	5	
		4,13,16 17,19 & 20	Labour Encorce-ment officer	Ensuring that Various Leave is Made Available Or is Permitted to Employees	
10.	Plantation Labour Act, 1951	8		Drinking Water	Ensuring Enforcement these provisions
		10	-do-	Medical Facilities	
		11	-do-	Canteen	
		12	-do-	Creche	
:		15	-do-	Housing Facility	
		19	-do-	Regulation of Working Hours	
		20	-do-	Weekly Rest	
		21	-do-	Mid-Day Rest	
		22	-do-	Spread Over	
		25	-do-	Prohibition of Employment of Children of 12 Years Age	
11.	Industrial Employment (Standing Orders) Act, 1946	3	-do-	Certification of Dft. Standing Orders	

(Contd.)

ANNEXURE 1.3 *(Contd.)*

1	2	3	4	5
		9	Labour Enforcement officer	Displaying of Certified Standing Orders on the Notice Board
		12-A	-do-	Adoption of Model Standing Orders Till Such time Dft. Standing Orders are Not Certified.
12.	U.P. Industrial Establishments (National Holidays) Act, 1961	3	-do-	Provision of Holidays on National Holidays
		5	-do-	Maintenance of Register in Form II Registered National Holidays
13.	Payment of Gratuity Act, 1972	3	-do-	Ensuring Payment of Gratuity as Per Law
		10	-do-	Payment of Minimum and Maximum Bonus
		19	-do-	Payment of Bonus Within 8 Months of the Close of the Financial Year
		26(4)	-do-	Calculation of Allocable Surplus in Form 'A' Set off & Set on in Form 'B' and Details of Bonus Due in Form 'C' to be Maintained in Registers.
15.	Payment of Wages Act, 1936	5	-do-	Ensuring Payment of Wages in Time

(Contd.)

ANNEXURE 1.3 *(Contd.)*

1	2	3	4	5
		7	Labour Enforcement officer	Ensuring That No Dedution Other Than Authorised are Made and Prosecution in Case of Violation
		26 Rule 3,4,5	-do-	Ensuring Maintenance of Fines Register, Deduction Register & Wages Register
		Rule 6-B	-do-	Ensuring that Notice of Wage Rates and Extracts of the Act are Displayed
16.	Maternity Benefits Act, 1961	Sec. 4 & 5	-do-	Ensuring Maternity Benefits
		19	-do-	Ensuring that Extracts of Act & Rules are Displayed on the Notice Board.
		20	-do-	To Ensure Maintenance of Prescribed Register
17.	Trade Unions Act, 1926	1	-do-	Enquiries into the Changes in Executive Body of Regd. Trade Union
		2	-do-	Enquiries Regarding Declaration of Protected Workman Under Indl. Disputes Act, 1947
18.	U.P. Industrial Disputes Act, 1947		-do-	Conciliation Proceedings and Intervention in Respect of Strikes, Lock-Outs, Retrenchment and Dismissals

Note: Summary of discussion is included along with the discussion on the paper by Nitish Sengupta.

10

NEW ECONOMIC POLICY AND ITS ADMINISTRATION

Nitish Sengupta

The Indian government's on-going programme of economic reforms and structural adjustment since July 1991 have highlighted the visible inadequacies of the country's existing administrative structure to serve as an effective change agent.

The new economic policies are seeking to restore government's fiscal balance move towards de-regulation of government's regulatory and administrative functions in economic administration vacating for the public sector huge chunks of industrial activity hitherto reserved for it, greater and greater reliance on private sector initiative for industrial and commercial development and, last but not the least, exposing Indian economy to the pulls and pushes from the global economy, in other words the process of globalisation. These tasks are formidable and involve a complete change of the mind-set on the part of people in our administrative and political system who, for a whole generation, have been nurtured in a tradition of government's omnipresence in the economy, and also on India's traditional policy of self-reliance rather than an outward looking economy. This is not proving to be an easy transition. There are vested interests resisting having to part with power and authority. But more than these there are many not able to comprehend the significance of the breath-taking changes sweeping across our country.

Our administrative structure is essentially a survival from the colonial times when the entire emphasis was on regulation rather than growth, procedural perfection rather than achieving results. The assumption was that people in government know what is best for the country and, therefore, entrepreneurs, businessmen and managers should, by and large, follow the dictates from the government ministers and bureaucrats. This colonial tradition was further intensified as a result of the traditions of populism and socialistic intervention in economic matters which grew up in the year after independence. This essentially conservative machinery, when called upon to move with the mind-boggling policy changes which have taken place in the last 2-1/2 years, and to carry them forward naturally resists and is found to be an unwilling instrument.

The industrial, trade, fiscal and financial policy changes since June 1991 have brought about a complete metamorphosis in the business scenario in India. These changes have posed for Indian industry both a great challenge and great opportunities. The challenge consists in the fact that, for the first time since the 1950s, Indian economy has been deregulated both in respect of allowing domestic competition, and permitting liberal imports. Indian industry needs to learn to operate in this deregulated environment where it is required to compete not only with domestic competitors but also with foreign firms which could not hitherto send their goods to India on account of import barriers and prohibitive customs duties. To tackle this challenge, Indian industry needs to show all its competitive efficiency, marketing skills and quality improvement. Also Indian management needs to show its innovative potential. Those who can successfully tackle this challenge will not only reap a rich harvest in the domestic economy, but will also become big global players in the world economy. The opportunity consists in the fact that entrepreneurial decision making which, for about four decades, was a close preserve of government authorities--ministers and bureaucrats – has now been returned, by and large, to the entrepreneurs to whom it rightfully belongs. Except for a few industries, industrial licensing has been abolished and this puts up new horizons for industrial entrepreneurs. Also, government is giving utmost thrust on exports which have been given lot of incentives. Under the previous policy regime in a sheltered domestic economy, most of the industrial enterprises did not feel the need to go to the overseas market for selling their products as they were making enough profits from the huge and sheltered domestic market. In the changing context they need to build up a compulsive export culture, both in their own interest and the national interest.

Major Changes

The key changes in the industrial policy are the following:

Reduction of the number of industries or activities reserved for the public sector under the 1956 Industrial Policy Resolution from 29 (17 industries in Schedule A+12 industries in Schedule B) to only 8 (vide

Appendix I of the Industrial Policy Statement, June 24, 1991). This means that a vast range of industries, which were closed to private sector initiative from 1956 onwards will now be open to it for setting up new projects or expanding existing enterprises. The significance of this vast change in sectors such as steel, power, etc., cannot be over-estimated. Indeed, this will have enormous implications for the future growth of the private sector industry.

The abolition of industrial licensing except for 18 industries listed in Annexure II of the Industrial Policy Statement of July 23, 1991. Since this announcement, at least 4 of these areas have been further declined *viz.* motor cars while goods like refrigerators for Air conditioners, mining of most of the minerals, and molasses. Delicensing of several other items, like sugar, are also reported to be under consideration. As already stated, the policy of industrial licensing for all practical purposes will transfer entrepreneurial decision-making from the lap of ministers and bureaucrats, with whom it rested since 1951, back to the entrepreneur himself. The entrepreneurs will no longer be required to visit Delhi for obtaining industrial licences and go through a very round-about administrative procedure which was time consuming, full of uncertainty and meant a lot of administrative and economic costs. They can straightaway formulate their project on the basis of their assessment of the market, approach financial institutions for term loans or approach the capital market and go on implementing the projects. Needless to say that this will also mean much greater responsibility for entrepreneurs in term of alternative investment proposals and eventually taking correct investment decisions.

The new policy on small-scale industry, for the first time, allows SSI units access to overseas technology and also permits foreign equity investment upto 24 per cent. This policy change opens up new horizons for small scale industry units.

The new policy has openly welcomed foreign direct investment. It promises automatic approval to direct foreign investment upto 51 per cent foreign equity in a list of 34 high priority industries. The significance of this announcement, both from the point of view of foreign companies seeking to come to establish joint ventures in India and Indian entrepreneurs seeking foreign collaborators in establishing joint ventures in India, is not to be under-estimated. Also significant is the announcement that foreign equity proposals need not necessarily be accompanied in future by foreign technology agreement, and the announcement that majority foreign equity holding upto 51 per cent will be allowed to trading companies primarily engaged in export activities, and the formation of a specially empowered Foreign Investment Promotions Board for negotiating with large international firms and approving direct foreign investment proposals in selected already.

Along with a generally open foreign open investment policy, the procedure for foreign technology agreement has been made much simpler and easier. The policy announces automatic permission to foreign technology agreement in all the Annexure III industries upto a lumpsum payment of Rs 1 crore, 5 per cent royalty for domestic sales and 8 per cent for exports over a 10 years period from the date of agreement or 7 years from commencement of production. It also assures automatic permission to all foreign technology agreements in industries other than in Annexure III if there is no requirement of free foreign exchange. It abolishes the need for government permission for hiring foreign technicians.

The abolition of Chapter III of the MRTP Act has bedeviled large industrial houses ever since its commencement in 1971. The 91 Policy suggested that in future the MRTP Act will only be concerned with controlling and regulating monopolistic restrictions and unfair trade practices. The required amendment in the MRTP Act has been carried out since then and Chapter III has been abolished for all practical purposes. This frees corporate industry from an irksome restrictive system, almost an additional licensing system to which it has been subjected since 1971.

The introduction of partial convertibility by the 1992 budget, of full convertibility of rupees on trading account in the 1993 budget and of full convertibility on current account in the 1994 budget have also opened up new vistas for the future development of industry. Firms, which are earning foreign exchange by export of their goods and services, will be permitted to realise full value of their earning and use part of it to meet their own foreign exchange requirements. This is again for export-efficient units, although the units accustomed to full foreign exchange allocation from the government will no longer get this benefit and will be constrained. There are indications that convertibility on capital account may also come about soon. Enterprises should prepare themselves for it.

The drastic changes in the Foreign Exchange Regulation Act in 1992 are of great significance for companies with more than 40 per cent foreign share-holding. For all practical purposes all these irksome restrictions imposed on them in 1973 like prior permission of RBI for a whole range of business activities such as expansion, diversifying appointment of foreigners and even purchasing houses have been removed. The Act returns to its original form in 1947. Also 527, which prohibited Indians from accepting directorships, etc., in foreign countries, is removed. This was a great obstacle to internationalisation of our business.

Since the budget of 1991 there has been a general trend towards the lowering of customs duties and removal of blanket ban on imports. The 1994 budget has carried this process much further in its wide-spread customs duty reductions (from a general level of around 200 per cent to a general level of 65 per cent). While this is partly inevitable in the interest of meeting the IMF loan conditionalities and in the interest of exposing Indian Industry to external competition so as to raise its competitive efficiency, this has also brought about great difficulties for enterprises in a wide variety of industries. Indian Industry has been traditionally subjected to lots of quantitative controls and other difficulties such as prohibitive duty on capital goods import, and prohibitive cost of term loan and working capital loan. Industrial licensing has subjected our enterprises to scale restrictions. Overseas competitors have not been suffering from these disabilities. If Indian market is suddenly thrown open to overseas competitors, it will be difficult for some of our industries to survive in open competition. After all competition has to be among equals and not among non-equals. This reduction or removal of customs duties and import barriers must therefore be not an event, but a process spread over three to four years during which time Indian industry should be encouraged, persuaded and pressurized to improve its efficiency, to take advantage of the incentives being offered and to reach a level of international competitive efficiency. Those enterprises who can do that will no doubt succeed. But many others, hitherto nurtured in a sheltered atmosphere, free from competition, may have to close down. This aspect of globalization is therefore both a serious constraint and a great opportunity. But Indian Government must take care to see that globalization should not be at the cost of destroying our national industrial capabilities built up over a period of 4 decades without giving our industry a fighting chance.

The 1993 and 1994 budgets have also broken new ground by seeking to create demand by substantial reduction of central excise duties on a very wide variety of goods. Indian industry must take advantage of this. The benefit of this should be passed on to the consumers in full fledged manner so that they can feel encouraged to buy these products at substantially reduced prices. The Ministry of Finance should be congratulated for adopting this approach for demand regeneration through reduced levies. An aspect of this that should necessarily be borne in mind is that the substantial reduction of import duties will have a bearing on foreign direct investment, for the obvious reason that if multi-nationals can import their own final products into this country by paying a minimum duty or by not paying any duty at all, they will neither feel compelled to nor will have incentives to take the route of foreign direct investment and starting joint ventures in our country.

The launching of the Eighth plan (1992-97) also marks a sea-change in the business scenario. It marks a switch from detailed physical planning to indicative planning, from predominant government percentage share in plan expenditure to a larger percentage share for the corporate private and household sectors, and from an emphasis on pure spending to emphasis on productive efficiency and return. The Eighth Five Year Plan was launched in April 1992 with its emphasis on productive efficiency at all levels, vacating government presence from all areas where it is not in public interest for it to be present, greater reliance on private sector initiative, utmost national emphasis on population control, promotion of literacy, balanced human development, agriculture, exports and globalisation. All this also provide excellent background for an economic and industrial upswing in the coming years further reinforced by the improvement in the BOP situation, and the containment of inflation (between 6 and 7 per cent). The Plan also emphasises the generation of adequate employment in order to achieve near full employment level by the end of the century and strengthening the infrastructure (energy, transport, communication and irrigation) in order to support the growth process on a sustainable basis. This will also provide fillip to further economic growth. The acceptance of a clear policy not to subsidise losses in industrial enterprises and the gradual withdrawal of budgetary support from public enterprises, mark a watershed. Clearly, public enterprises must stand on their own feet and substantially improve their performance, improving their goods and services and changing over from resource-guzzling enterprises to surplus generating units. This will call for tremendous degree of management capability, innovation, change and results. Also, the private sector has to learn to operate in a de-regulated and internationalising business environment.

Need for Export Compulsive Culture in all Enterprises

Both the public sector and the private sector must give priority of emphasis on improving their export performance. If Indian economy has to get over the current impasse, there must be a spectacular improvement in exports. An export inhibition in our attitude needs to be replaced by a compulsive export culture. This again will mean full attention to quality control and assurance, product improvement, improved design and packaging. In short, a reorientation of our production management and shop floor culture which have been in general a dark area in our management system. In his book *'Out of the Crisis'*, Edwards Deming shows that 85 per cent of defective products come from defective production process, and gives his famous 14 points by which managers can bring about substantial improvement in quality or productivity To quote him "Innovation, the foundation of the future, cannot thrive unless top management has a declared and unshakable commitment to quality and productivity." Much of the performance of China in recent years has been on account of her spectacular increase of exports. Both China and India were exporting at roughly the same level around 1971-72 (China exported goods worth US $ 2.2 billion). While Indian exports have risen to the level of US $ 20 to 25 billion now, Chinese exports have already crossed US $ 85 billion and are fast approaching US $ 100 billion. There is no reason why India's exports cannot also rise up proportionately. But we need to shed off our pessimism, adopt a bold vision and follow it up by energetic action in building up export surplus, improving the quality of our goods and their brand name, providing vigorous marketing and after-sales service and showing greater integration with emerging regional markets such as the Asia-Pacific Region, the Gulf countries, the European community and the North American free trade area.

The collapse of the former Soviet Union and with it of the pattern of bilateral Rupee trade are often mentioned as the major reasons for affecting India's current export performance. We should not any longer lament the passing away of the old USSR but try to seek new opportunities in the future growth of Russia and the other successor republics. They have many things to give us e.g. arms and armaments, petroleum and technology. We also have many things to give them e.g. foodgrains, processed agricultural and horticultural commodities, light engineering goods and consumer products of any variety. That satisfactory currency and institutional arrangements have not emerged for bilateral trading, is no reason why we cannot resort to barter trade or counter trade which should enable us to survive the transitional period of uncertainty and free-for-all. Surely, we have greater potential than the West has in fulfilling some of the needs of some of these countries. The entire situation should, therefore, be regarded more as an opportunity than as a constraint.

On-going Constraints for Growth

Despite the sea changes in policies, these changes have not yet been reflected in procedural simplification and in bureaucratic attitudes. Many of the procedures from the old order still survive. Also, the old attitude of control, regulation and patronage still prevails among many politicians and bureaucrats, in particular among lower functionaries in the Central and State Governments who refuse to part with their power of patronage and, therefore, still insist on following the old procedure and practices (e.g. Motorola case). Industry must help the Government in transforming the old attitudes at all levels and discarding the prevailing counter-productive and bureaucratic procedural bottlenecks. Unless this is done we cannot really show any visible and spectacular improvement in our production, exports, foreign investment promotion and import liberalisation.

Public Sector Reform and Turn-Around

One of the major challenges facing India's economy today is how to turn the public sector enterprises from being non-performing assets to performing assets. According to the latest report of the Department of Public Enterprises, the aggregate assets of the 246 central public sector enterprises as on 31.03.91 would amount to Rs 113,234 crores. According to Comptroller & Auditors General's report tabled before Parliament in April 1993, out of 238 public sector units, 187 declared no dividend in 1991-92. The rest gave only Rs. 367 crores i.e. less than one per cent of the total investment of Rs. 40,121 crores in these public sector units. Nationalised banks gave only Rs.54.59 crores on an investment of Rs. 2,979 crores i.e. 1.83 per cent. This excludes the investments in departmental undertakings such as Railways, Post Offices, Telecommunications, Ports, Atomic Energy and Space. If the investments in these enterprises are added to the earlier figure, these will become much higher. If the State Government undertakings, including chronically loss-making State Electricity Boards, are added to it, one could easily put the aggregate figure of investment in the Public Sector to anything around Rs 300,000 crores. If these enterprises would have given a return of even 10 per cent that itself would substantially improve the currently miserable state of public finance in our country. Only a handful of these enterprises are giving a reasonable return of the investment, most of them again, operating the oil sector or other monopoly areas. The great majority of them not only fail to give a return on the massive investment made, but go on drawing on budgetary support every year at considerable cost to other priority sectors which are starved of investment. According to the latest figures available their profitability works out to a disappointing percentage of 0.9 per cent on the capital employed and 1.6 per cent on the sales turnover. This non-performance of the public sector is one of the principal reasons for India's lack-luster growth record and prevalence of so many ills such as chronic budgetary and fiscal deficit, inflationary pressure and steep price rise. Also, these public sector enterprises control many essential imports and raw materials in industry. On account of their inefficiency, the administered prices of these products have to go on increasing from time to time in order to cover their losses and this further aggravates the Government's fiscal and financial situation and adds to spiralling inflation. Clearly, the successful turn-around of PSUs is one of the top priorities of our economy today. While utmost priority should be given to management improvement, cost cutting, aggressive marketing, quality control, after-sales service, etc, groups of professional managers and private sector industrialists should also come forward to take charge of management of some of these enterprises which have promise of return to profitability and performance with better management. There needs to be a total change of culture and acceptance of competition, ability to eventually stand on their own feet rather than continuing to rely on budgetary support from Government and an attitudinal transition from distribution of products, sometimes of patronage to marketing and at times have aggressive selling. There is a related question of redundancy. This should be solved by taking the trade unions into confidence and relying on the National Renewal Fund which could follow a vigorous programme of retraining, redeployment, golden handshake and, in general, a social safety net. Unfortunately, Government has not yet done anything to free PSUs from the traditional bureaucratic stranglehold over their free functioning. The ongoing deregulation programme has affected only the private sector and left PSUs untouched.

Globalisation – An Irreversible Trend

Globalisation or internationalisation of our economy had become an irreversible phenomenon. In today's environment of superfast communication and breaking down of geographical barriers, no country can live in splendid isolation from the rest of the world. Inter-dependence rather than self-reliance has become the key word. True self-reliance which many people in the past confused with total avoidance of any import from outside and complete reliance on domestic market and domestic sources of supply can, in today's context, only mean concentrating on a country's own strengths and not hesitating to import whenever it is cheaper to do so than relying purely on supplies from domestic sources maintained at a high cost to the national economy.

The process of globalisation relies primarily on private sector initiative, aided by the evolution of the global information network. Government has a very important supportive or facilitating role in connection with macro adjustments, maintaining efficient infrastructure and, thirdly, promoting human development including anti-poverty programmes.

In the West there are many outstanding examples of corporations which have shaken up and changed their top management with a view to bringing about a "turn-around" e.g. General Motors, American Express, Westinghouse, IBM. All these companies and many others are feverishly engaged in identifying and working out key elements of turn-around, cost cutting, reengineering operations, laying off surplus people and entering into strategic alliances across the globe. Also, they are trying their best to close down all uneconomical operations and enter into new lines of business which promise growth and profit. There is a feverish surge for the best technology around the globe, cheaper sources of finance and markets that promise higher selling prices. To quote Peter Drucker: "The years ahead will be years of repeated changes in technology, in markets and market segmentation, consumer values and consumer behaviour, in finance, in political and geographical realities, in economic and trade policies. They will, therefore, steadily make existing theories of business obsolete. In fact, the most probable assumption is that no currently working business theory will be valid 10 years hence – at least not without major modifications. And yet, few executives accept that for a turn-around a company requires fundamental changes in the assumptions on which the business is being run. It requires a different business. It is not only businesses that will have to learn to turn themselves around, almost any large organisation will find itself in stagnation, frustrated, ailing, none more than the Government. Almost every large organisation will have to rethink its business theory"[1]. If the first-half of the current century witnessed the end of separate histories for separate countries and separate regions, the last decade is witnessing another profound change, what someone has picturesquely called the end of geography. The phenomenal inventions in the field of information technology, satellite communication and related fields have not only killed distances between various countries but have made it possible to shift strategic information and also funds across the globe at a moment's notice. Also, there is a breaking of the barriers between frontiers of communication, computer software, space satellites, TV and videos leading to the emergence of a powerful multimedia approach. These are aspects of globalisation our administration cannot afford not to take notice of. In fact, our administrators and managers, must familiarize themselves and become adept at seeing themselves as parts of the global information network and to conducting their operations accordingly. Globalisation is essentially an attitudinal change that does not confuse markets or areas of operation with national geographical boundaries and looks upon the whole world as the legitimate field of operations. Here money can be obtained from where it is the cheapest, raw materials should be procured from any source that promises the least price, the best technology should be obtained from wherever possible across the globe and, lastly, finished products are marketed wherever one gets the highest price. People in so called multinational enterprises should stop thinking in terms of a parent holding company and subsidiaries but look upon themselves as global players with no particular attachment to any single country. At the same time, they should get accustomed to working as a team of transitional managers recruited from all over the world. The end of geography paradigm is still psychologically a difficult concept to accept, but is fast becoming a reality.

The key areas for concentrated attention and concern in formulating a response strategy are: cost control and cost cutting at all levels; identification of redundant manpower and re-training, redeployment and good compensation packages for retirement and scheme self-employment/resettlement through the National Renewal Fund; close look at the existing product mix and willingness to shed off the chronically non-profitable activities and diversify into newer promising areas; close attention to the shop floor and production management with a view to improving the quality of products, the brand image and R&D; technological upgrading and modernisation; attention to after-sales service and aggressive marketing strategy both in exports and for the internal market; and effective HRD strategy with a view to improving the work ethos, all round productivity and morale; taking full advantage of the convertibility of the rupee on trade account by sourcing of inputs from outside the country wherever it is obtainable the cheapest and selling finished products overseas markets wherever one gets the highest price; and taking advantage of the abolition of the licencing system to attain economies of the scale through appropriate expansion with a view to meeting global competition. There has to be a corporate vision that includes strategic choices and organisation re-positioning wherever necessary. Private sector enterprises must evolve a strategy to fill the vacuum caused by the withdrawal of the public sector from a whole range of activities hitherto reserved for the public sector. For public sector enterprises there must be a strategy for converting the non-performing assets, wherever they are, into performing assets. When, after weighing the pros and cons, it is observed that a turn-around cannot be brought about in an enterprise on account of reasons beyond anybody's control, there should be no hesitation in closing down such enterprises without unnecessarily throwing people out of their jobs. Proper exploitation of the assets need to be made for giving the employees appropriate compensation packages on retirement and suitable resettlement benefits. Trade Unions should be taken into confidence as partners in a turnaround strategy. Those politicians, bureaucrats and industrialists, who had a vested interest in the licencing and permit regime of the last four decades and are still hoping that these reforms are a temporary phase and that we will soon return to the old order, must reconcile themselves to the fact that these reforms and adjustments are irreversible, no matter whichever be the government in power, and that the sooner they fall in line the better. A successful continuance of the same policy should ensure that India attains what can truly be a phenomenal technological and economic quantum jump by the time we step into the 21st century.

To understand this problem of interfacing between new tasks and the existing administrative apparatus, one has to analyse some of the features of the prevailing system:

1. Authority in the government is horizontally defused among large number of ministries and agencies and no single ministry or agency is competent enough to take the final decision in any important matter. Everybody needs to be consulted and there needs to be a broad agreement, even if not complete unanimity to get any policy change.
2. Authority is also structured vertically along a long line of hierarchy. In the Secretariat hierarchy starts with a lower level functionary called the Section Officer and moves along Under Secretary, Deputy Secretary, Joint Secretary, Additional Secretary, Secretary, Minister of State and Cabinet Minister. There is little of level jumping or a decision being taken at the same level where a

reference from outside is received. Many important cases need to go to the Prime Minister's Office or even to the appropriate Cabinet Committee.

3. There is an overwhelming reliance on administrative controls implying individual decision on individual cases by the prescribed authority, rather than legislation or budgetary type of indirect control. This again means arbitrary decisions in individual cases and inevitable delay on account of the requirement of the prescribed application to be submitted in individual cases to the prescribed authority.
4. The Secretariat appeared to have appropriated a large proportion of decision-making power in individual cases which normally should have been left with authorities lower down or authorities locally available.
5. The system of Parliamentary control or supervision over executive action also means the requirement of lots of administrative work, paper work and discussion which run directly contrary to the concept of high speed decisions.
6. The so-called principle of accountability or responsibility, specially accentuated in the last 2-3 decades, induces a general tendency on the part of officials to avoid taking decisions and playing safe in general so that they are not eventually made accountable and subjected to inquisitorial action.
7. There are several other factors: Our administrative machinery is divided between the Secretariat and the Directorate, the former concerned with policy making and the latter concerned with implementation of decision. This itself is a reason for avoidable delay and procrastination whereas, in general, the distinction between policy making and implementation is increasingly getting fuzzed.

We therefore have to think seriously of drastic orientation:

(i) in organisation structure;
(ii) procedural simplification, and
(iii) in our manner and style of functioning.

The policy changes during the last 2-1/2 years have brought about a complete metamorphosis in the administration-cum-business scenario in India. Gone are most of the administrative and quantitative government controls which, for decades, dominated the commercial and industrial landscape of the country. But the procedural and bureaucratic hangover still persists. There is an imperative need to get away from the traditional control-oriented mind-set to the psychosis of promotion, assistance and motivating in general. People in administration need to shed off the traditions of colonial governor or socialist regulator and to move on to a new role of facilitator for industry and business. Also, we need to give up many of the old laws which still clutter our industrial and commercial landscape, but have by and large outlived their utility. Even some of the essential laws which need to remain must be drastically overhauled. We need to ruthlessly axe a large number of ministries, government agencies and other offices which also have outlived their functions in this era of de-regulation, not necessarily by throwing people in these organisations out of employment, but by retraining them, re-deploying them in newer activities and in encouraging many of them to turn to self entrepreneur-ship. Examples of such organisations are : DGTD, DGS&D, Ministries of Electronics, Bio-technology, Textile Commissioner, Jute Commissioner, Iron & Steel Controller, Chief Controller of Imports and Exports, Bureau of Public Enterprises.

As State Government personnel are still unaware of the significance of the reform process and its inevitability it is necessary to launch a mass communication movement to indoctrinate and motivate them and to help them transform themselves into their new role of facilitators rather than controllers.

We need to give up the present hierarchical, overmanned administrative organisation and turn to flat, cellular or modular organisations which can be flexible and, therefore, adjusted suitably with changing times. Many of the problems which come to administration today are without precedents in the sense that the problems, which arose in the past and were dealt within particular ways, do not provide adequate guidance. There has to be, an end to the tyranny of Government by precedents. Also, there has to be, less of the insistence on governance through written files and much more of governance through oral communication. The new information technology has speedily cut across hierarchical and geographical boundaries and has made the old type of levels and hierarchies largely redundant. It is thus no longer necessary, nor desirable, to mechanically adhere to old norms about prescribed channels of communication such as from the Ministry to the Directorate or the Ministry to the Chief Secretary and the Chief Secretary to the concerned Secretary of the State Government, from the Secretary to the Head of Directorate, from the Head of the Directorate to the District Officer and from the District Officer to the subordinate authorities. The new multi-media information technology under which it is possible to send information or messages in seconds and minutes across the continent makes such outdated mechanisms superfluous and time-consuming. We have to accept that our procedures and practices are very often survivals from the 19th century, while the tasks and functions are almost anticipatory of the 21st century. Can we not avoid having to deal with 21st century issues and problems with 19th century tools and apparatus?

There is a general lack of awareness among State employees of the need for economic reforms and structural adjustments and of their inevitability and, for that matter, irreversibility. This ignorance pervades even in the minds of many officials in the central ministries. The State Government officials are still living in oblivion. Schemes are being prepared, new demands for funds are being made and such demands are still being dealt with in the old style and old manner of functioning, blissfully unaware of the fact that our Government, Centre and the States, are in the throes of unprecedented critical financial difficulties, and that Government is not likely to have in the near future the kind of funds which are needed to meet the existing deficits or to meet the new demands being made. De-regulations, de-bureaucratisation and greater reliance on private initiative are, therefore, the prime needs of the hour. The sooner we all realise this and are willing to give up our authority and power of yester years and reconcile ourselves to smaller Government, flatter Government and to a situation where control is reduced to the very minimum and promotional work will be given prime importance, the better for the nation. To quote from Machiavelli's Prince "Nothing is more difficult than initiating a new order of things . . . If you will always be doing what you did in the past you will also be getting what you got in the past".

SUMMARY OF DISCUSSION

To start with, it was observed that the two presentations make it clear that response of the states and the bureaucracy to the economic reforms is not what it ought to be. It was also the need for a more systematic and streamlined actions following the policy both in form and content was found crucial. It was pointed out that reforms merely in administration without complimentary restructuring of the legislature and the judiciary would not serve the desired goals and objectives. In response to the question as to how to make the reforms an agenda for the nation, it was noted that Panchayat Raj Institutions could be an instrument of achieving this objective.

The observations made in the course of the discussion stressed:

(a) that the need for administrative reforms is not dependent on the economic reforms, although the reform process adds on urgency to it;
(b) the need to review Centre-State financial relations in the context of liberalization and globalization trends;
(c) the need for substantive legal reforms; and
(d) the need for meaningful decentralisation which would give greater autonomy to the States and the grassroots for raising, spending and distribution of their resources.

NOTE

1. Asian Wall Street Journal, February 4, 1993 (p.8).

11

MANAGING CHANGE IN THE CONTEXT OF THE NEW ECONOMIC POLICY
Post Script

V. K. AGNIHOTRI and H. RAMACHANDRAN

Introduction

A one week modular programme was designed for a pre-identified group of senior officers representing selected areas such as trade, export promotion, industry, public sector, finance, fiscal and power sectors and organised from 23 to 28 May, 1994 at the Lal Bahadur Shastri National Academy of Administration, Mussoorie, which was coordinated by the authors of this chapter. Fifteen officers participated in the programme. The programme was structured to include five one-day modules covering: (i) Globalization; (ii) Financial and Fiscal sectors; (iii) Industry; (iv) Public Enterprises; and (v) Power sector.

The programme was designed with the following objectives:[1]

(i) discuss and debate implications of the New economic policy;
(ii) grasp the nuances of the interface among selected sectoral policy changes and administration;
(iii) develop an agenda of follow-up changes in procedures and regulations; and
(iv) demarcate areas, levels and nature of intervention in sectors such as industry, finance, fiscal, public enterprises and power.

Globalization – Opportunities and Threats[2]

In this overview module on Globalization – Opportunities and Threats, issues relating to three broad themes were identified for deliberation:

(a) Threats to and from Globalization process, (b) GATT and related Issues, and (c) Globalization and State Governments.

The participants identified that the forces of globalization would face hurdles from various segments and also in turn may affect the poor adversely. The kind of threats that the globalization process faces were identified, which essentially came from the bureaucracy, industry, trade unions and political compulsions. One common theme of threats emerging from the above quarters is that of 'fear' – in the case of bureaucracy it was identified as the fear of loss of power and importance; in the case of industry it might be the fear of inability to face competition from foreign producers; in the case of trade unions the loss of jobs and demands of increased productivity; and in the case of politicians of losing 'patronage influence'.

The participants, therefore, stressed on an effective action plan, arising out of historical considerations of Indian administration, polity and economy, wherein a system of controls pervaded. The necessary actions to be taken in order to overcome the hurdles posed by various quarters would include:

(a) attitudinal change in bureaucracy to be brought about by orientation and training programmes;
(b) accountability by making the administrative system more transparent;
(c) revamping the organization structure on rational lines;
(d) policy initiatives and incentives to make Indian industry more competitive;
(e) withdrawal of the government from uneconomic enterprises; and
(f) creation of suitable economic-political environment by imparting right information to the public at large.

The participants noted that the poor, would be one of the adversely affected segments as a result of globalization. The impact would be manifested in loss of employment, purchasing power and impact, of inflation in the short run. However, to minimize the negative impacts it would be necessary for the State to intervene effectively and efficiently in the core social sectors such as education, infrastructure, health etc. Such interventions would imply: Increased outlays in social service sectors viz. Education, Health, Rural Development, Social Security, Employment Guarantee Scheme, effective Public Distribution System and adequate credit to rural sector at reasonable rates. And these would call for, transparency in administration, proper Training and Reorientation, attitudinal change towards common man/consumer, accountability, computerization and redeployment.

The Agenda for Action suggested by the participants include the following :

(i) policy initiatives to make Indian industry competitive globally;
(ii) modifying import tariffs on raw materials, intermediate and capital goods in that order of priority ;
(iii) dismantling licensing further;
(iv) encouraging foreign investments;
(v) lower interest rates;
(vi) tax reforms: Vat/Octroi;
(vii) encouraging technology upgradation, R & D;
(viii) roviding better infrastructure: power, transport, communication;
(ix) withdrawal of Government from un-economic enterprises;
(x) devising a proper exit policy;
(xi) rapid employment generation to absorb redundant labour;
(xii) mobilizing public opinion and consumer groups to demand cheaper and better quality products and efficient services;
(xiii) cutting out delays; and
(xiv) reducing inventory carrying costs.

The second issue which came up for discussion related to GATT. The participants felt that GATT was a necessary and inevitable step in the consolidation of the process of globalization. The major advantages of the agreement were deliberated upon which include – integration of the Indian economy with the world economy, export-led growth strategy, abolition of tariff/non-tariff barriers etc. It was pointed out that negotiations with the developed countries should be undertaken collectively rather than individually.

Action agenda here would, among other things, include:

(i) cutting tariffs of industrial and farm goods;
(ii) services -- non-discrimination of (financial, professional) 'services' with few exceptions; and
(iii) anti-dumping – goods to be identified and necessary legislation to be enacted.

The extra theme which came up for discussion was Globalization and the State Governments. The participants were of the opinion that a substantial shift in terms of policies has to take place at the State level, keeping in mind the State's advantages. Related to this was the issue of regional disparities, wherein the role of the State still cannot be undermined. The most important point which was suggested as a measure to overcome this problem was to promote a healthy alliance among States on matters related to the economy.

Agenda for State Governments should include:

(i) Demystification of the globalization agenda to various sectors of the Government;
(ii) Review of systems and procedures of various Departments and elimination of hidden costs and redundancies in the system;
(iii) Review of all subsidies;
(iv) Identification of comparative strengths in resources/technologies building upon them and marketing them;
(v) Review of strengths and weaknesses in the agricultural sector;
(vi) Optimization and professionalization of manpower;
(vii) Upgradation of infrastructure to provide competitive effective production facilities for Indian Industry along with a time bound action plan;
(viii) More freedom to be given for exploitation of local natural resources along with a more suitable central policy on distribution of resources and royalties on natural resources.
(ix) Export of technology by way of joint ventures;
(x) Rational policy on privatization of PSUs; and
(xi) Action points for less developed State (resource rich but with poor infrastructure) including : (a) Strategic alliances between States; (b) Dismantling of inter-State barriers and; (c) Identification and building on competitive strengths.

Financial and Fiscal Sector Reforms[3]

The main issues which were raised and discussed included: (a) Resource mobilization by the Centre and States; (b) Fiscal situation in the country; and (c) Privatization as a means of achieving fiscal and financial stability.

With regard to the issue of resource mobilization and improvement of tax administration, the participants identified certain pre-requisites, the most important being the political will accompanied by an efficient and effective Government machinery. The philosophy under which such reforms could take place has to be "to encourage compliance and discourage evasion". It was noted that a substantive widening of the tax base, which was considered very much possible, along with a greater fiscal discipline would go a long way in helping the Governments at both Central and State levels to raise resources for development. The participants felt the need to charge for the "services" provided by the State, as such services were more often viewed as "free". It was pointed out that a "low rate and broad-based tax structure" with little exemptions should be practiced. The participants identified certain new service (other than goods which were already subject to taxation) which needs to be brought under the levy. For example financial services, marketing services, real estate services, manufacturing services etc. On the issue of subsidy to the PSUs, it was noted that a thorough overhauling through dis-investment, minimum rate of return and so on should be undertaken to check the increasing fiscal indiscipline

The participants, while discussing the state of fiscal position of the country identified certain "doomsday indicators" and "indicators of light". The prominent indicators of the former type included – high fiscal deficit, inflation, black money, lacklustre performance of industries, specially the PSU's and lastly the infirmities in the tax system. On the other hand, the participants pointed out certain promising situations, for instance a spurt in the exports, accompanied by an increase in the foreign exchange situation, a comfortable foodgrain buffer stocks, and lastly but perhaps most importantly an improving investment climate in the country. To cash on these advantages, the participants stressed on an action plan which pointed out the need to reduce non-plan expenditure, improving revenue receipts (by introducing presumptive tax, broad-based tax structure, taxes on services/agricultural land etc.), curbing black money, and to build political and public awareness on the urgency to have a streamlined fiscal policy.

The third issue pertained to the privatisation of PSUs, as a means of bringing about fiscal stability and discipline in the economy. Here, the participants identified various types of PSUs based on the type of industry, such as – Consumer goods, Service, Infrastructural and Core. The participants felt the need to have different responses to each of the types of PSUs. For instance in the case of Consumer sector it was pointed out that there was no option but to dismantle the PSUs, while in case of others the policy of dis-investment/privatization should be pursued in a phased manner.

The participants felt that adequate attention may well be directed towards those who would get adversely affected or marginalised as a result of such policies. A close co-ordination between the academicians, bureaucrats/planners and the politicians was viewed as imperative for better implementation of the new economic policy. Agenda for action suggested are as follows :

(i) Reduce Non-Plan Expenditure through: phased reduction of subsidies by about half in next three years; restructuring of PDS to cover only vulnerable sectors; reducing administration expenditure; down-sizing bureaucracy by 20 per cent in next 5 years; and social audit of Government expenses.

(ii) Improve Revenue receipts by: widening tax base; presumptive taxation; taxation of services/ agricultural land; and by introducing Expenditure Tax and VAT.

(iii) Curb black money formations by effective enforcement of laws, institution of ID Cards and computerised monitoring of purchases of cars, CTV, Urban Property, etc.

(iv) Curb inflation by: limiting Government borrowings from RBI; cutting on non-development expenditure of Government; and resorting to imports of essential commodities when needed.

(v) Disinvestment of PSU equity/revival or privatisation of PSUs and using receipts to liquidate debts.

(vi) Guidelines to direct capital raised by industry to productive uses away from speculative uses.

(vii) Streamline tax administration system.

(viii) Building public awareness and involvement through public debate.

Impediments to Reforms in the Industrial Sector[4]

The module on Industrial sector delved into the following issues: (a) Responses of Indian industry to import liberalization; (b) Means to promote Foreign Direct Investments; and (c) Protection of Small Scale Sectors

One of the key questions which was brought out in the course of discussion was – What will be the state of Indian industry with the result of import liberalization? The group dealt in detail with the strengths and weaknesses of Indian industries. One of the chief weakneses of the Indian industries identified by the participants was its very inward looking and insular characteristics. This along with poor management (specially in the case of PSUs), too much controls, presence of rigid labour laws were identified as the impediments to industrial sector reforms and also as the reason for the present state of Indian industry.

It was noted that despite the Indian industry's advantages, such as cheap labour, large skilled manpower and so on the industries were hardly competitive at the global level, for reasons already outlined. Naturally the central issue shifted to "how to make the Indian industry globally competitive?" As a response to this the participants stressed the need to address availability of infrastructure, administrative reforms, technological and fiscal initiatives which should be built on the strengths of Indian industry. The need was felt for the Indian industry to come out of their inward looking State protected regime to a market driven and outward looking approach.

The second key issue in this day's module focused on the existing gap between the promised FDI in India and the actual inflows. The question addressed was what is stopping the FDIs in India in a manner similar to other Asian "tiger" countries. The participants identified a number of reasons, the major ones being (a) lack of publicity/information on our new economic policy; (b) concern about the political and social climate; (c) rigid labour laws; and (d) lack of social and physical infrastructure. It was stressed by the group that a conscious effort towards spreading the information on new economic policy should be undertaken besides undertaking reforms in other sectors, especially administrative where "simplification" in procedures was noted as the need of the hour.

Another key issue was to assess the viability or rationality of extending protection to small scale industries. The participants noted that such reservation measures were often misused. Overcrowding and duplication of production items were also noted in the reserved SSI sector. Therefore, it was felt that "reservation"/ protection cannot be a rational measure to counter the market imperfections.

Agenda for Action suggested by the participants are as follows :

(i) More efforts needed to spread the message: Publicity, Seminars, Meetings with investors, economic advisors/academics; encourage research on Indian economy in the context of the new economic policy;

(ii) Centre has prepared enabling environment and the States have to take further lead (for example, Maharashtra, Gujarat, Haryana).

(iii) States to cut and simplify procedures: single window mechanism; one application for all permissions/approvals; escort officer/monitoring could be introduced;

(iv) Retrain and reorient bureaucracy down to cutting edge level;

(v) Identify priority areas for FDI particularly in infrastructures – which is a pre-requisite for industrialisation; identify and investigate specific investment projects such as roads, ports, airports, industrial estates, telecom, tourism and other potential areas (of power and petroleum sectors);

(vi) Amend laws to bring a suitable exit policy, repeal/abolish laws like abolishment of contract labour;

(vii) Train to impart needed skills: upgrade existing skills, multifunctional skills, enforcement of discipline on shop floor absenteeism, loss of time, involve labour in productivity improvement; and

(viii) Concentrate on successful implementation of a few pioneering projects as in China.

Public Sector Undertakings and the New Economic Policy[5]

The role of public sector, which has been an important input since the inception of Indian Planning process, was the theme selected for the fourth days module. Three key issues selected by the participants for detailed discussions were : (a) The future role of Public Sector; (b) accountability, autonomy and performance evaluation of PSUs; and (c) issues involving privatisation of PSUs.

One of the key issues which came up for discussion was the legitimacy and viability of the PSUs in a decentralised market economy. The discussions covered the initial objectives underlying the establishments of public sector, through changes in the economic environment and finally to a restricted, nevertheless crucial, function of the State in shaping the role of the public sector. The catalyst force which marked the shift from our earlier logic of creating PSUs were identified, which included the rise of the domestic private sector; a disturbing fiscal situation; ever increasing encroachments on the economic activities which are not necessarily "key" or "basic" in nature; and lastly, the changing [open] nature of the world economy.

The participants stressed on the need to restrict the PSUs to sectors which are of strategic / national importance. Further, it was considered imperative to allow the existing PSUs to be run on private (economically efficient) and on professional lines. In order to do so, the participants felt that substantive deregulation and reduction of the State's influence/ interference in running of a PSU should be undertaken.

The second key issue revolved around the organisational principles of accountability, autonomy and performance evaluation. The participants felt that in case of PSUs it would not be possible to evaluate or assess purely on economic criteria, as the PSUs also served certain social/ promotional objectives. The participants, therefore, felt the need to assess the PSUs on both quantitative and qualitative criterias. On the vexing issue of accountability and autonomy a need was felt to create a statutory body, with substantive powers in the area of recruitment, investment and monitoring. Such a body, the participants felt, would be more transparent, less bureaucratic and should be made directly accountable to the Parliament. New statutory body will mean more freedom of operation and autonomy. It will also devise new methods and support enhancement of powers for PSUs, deployment of workforce – retrenchment and compensation. However, the body will only issue guidelines. It should be prohibited from regulating PSUs in any way and only go by evaluation. Similar framework was also suggested for the State PSUs.

The third and the last issue which came up for discussion by the participants was related to the "Issues in Privatisation of PSUs". The modalities for such a transfer were also discussed. The need for such a change was essentially due to heavy loss incurred by PSUs over the years, gross inefficiency and lack of entrepreneurship in the area of resource mobilisation. On the modalities involved in such cases, the participants broadly agreed on the policies of dis-investment, followed by open and transparent bids, based on assessment/valuation of property at the current market rates. However, the participants noted that the policy of dis-investment has to be gradual, selective and on a case-by-case basis. The participants entered a note of caution by stating that any such exercise should consider the rights/claims of the concerned parties like the State, Financial Institutions and workers, and that it should not be an exercise in profiteering/speculation by private enterprises.

Modalities of privatising should take care to ensure that only such of the PSUs should be privatised which do not come under the protected list, and only those consumer and service industries which do not impinge upon security or strategic needs of the country. While disinvesting, care should be taken that the management is not controlled by a single or group of people detrimental to public interest. Disinvestment should be gradual. It was suggested to adopt the following strategy:

(a) Sick unviable PSUs – to be sold off/liquidated.
(b) Healthy PSUs – disinvestment upto 49% of equity i.e. to hold only 51 per cent equity.
(c) Healthy Consumer Industry – disinvestment suggested upto 74 per cent of equity, i.e. PSU should hold only 26 per cent P.C. share of equity.
(d) Preliminary pre-disinvestment action to be initiated on administrative and legal issues, financial issues, redeployment or exit policy.

Having decided to disinvest, logical steps should be the following: assessment/ valuation of property at current market rate, inviting bids, evaluating bids/disposal, transparency on all activities and to follow the strict procedures laid by the law of the land i.e. BIFR/SICA etc. Possibility of involving the trade union/workers during negotiation may be experimented to remove bottlenecks.

Reforms in Power Sector [6]

The issues taken up for detailed deliberation were : (a) Restructuring of SEBs; (b) Privatisation of SEBs; (c) Tariffs and subsidies; and (d) Procedure of global tendering.

Restructuring of SEBs could be done on (a) geographical basis which will lead to fissiparous tendencies and increased costs, or (b) Functional basis which will lead to problems of coordination and recovery of costs. Therefore, the possible alternatives are as follows:

(i) Convert existing SEBs into an independent company with government retaining not less than 51 per cent shares.
(ii) Encourage different consumers to contribute remaining shares with stipulation but not more than 2 per cent or 5 per cent will be held by any single party;
(iii) Fix the tenure of Chairman and Directors to be not less than 5 years. Lay down the procedure for removal;
(iv) Give the company complete control over generation and transmission; and
(v) For distribution, encourage private companies or subsidiaries. In areas where no Distribution company comes forward, the reconstituted SEB will be responsible for distribution too.

The participants noted that privatisation would imply entry of private finance on project basis for investment in generation/transmission or distribution. This can be in the following forms: (i) Build, Own and Operate; (ii) Build, Operate and Transfer; (iii) Outright sale of power plants; and (iv) Built by private party and leased to SEB. Issues/controversies regarding privatisation include:

(a) Inflated capital costs : which can be handled through proper procedure for cost scrutiny, publication in official gazette and local newspapers inviting representations, scrutiny by SEB/State government and scrutiny by CEA;

(b) Loaded in favour of private developers, e.g. (i) Very high guaranteed return although this is linked to performance of 68.5 per cent PLF. However, this is not very unique because NTPC is allowed 12 per cent post-tax return. IRR has to be above 20 per cent to attract foreign capital in view of the competition with other LDCs in attracting capital. (ii) Protection against FE fluctuations : a project financed through foreign funding, either debt or equity, has to service its foreign currency obligations. Foreign equity investors would, therefore, require protection of their earning from FE fluctuations. MIGA membership provides some security; however, direct compensation is sought for. All countries provide for it. Some denominate the entire tariff in US dollar, while India permits only 16% to be FE indexed;

(c) Excessively high cost of power (i) If SEBs had to resort to commercial borrowings and not government budgetary support, our costs would also be high, (ii) Present cost by SEBs would not be very much less, specially if time and cost overruns are included.

(d) High PLF will force SEBs to back down their own plants and hence increase their losses; this depends on the requirement of power. In the present situation of acute shortage, the demand for more power would mean that private companies would be asked to perform at highest possible PLF.

The third issue the group deliberated upon concentrated on the debate about tariff and cross-subsidies. They noted that in the present system as per Electricity (Supply) Act, Tariff is to be determined by SEBs so as to earn a minimum 3 per cent rate of return on fixed assets. SEBs generally follow cost plus basis with some considerations of equity.

However generally the State governments consider the proposals and determine the tariff. Various political considerations come into play. Generally agriculture and very small domestic consumers are heavily cross-subsidised at the cost of HT/Commercial consumers. Hardly any regulatory mechanism under Electricity (Supply) Act; exists although Consultative Council represent, various interests.

In view of this, the participants suggested that:

(i) Some subsidy to agricultural consumer and to very small single light households – but overall no subsidy to Domestic sector;
(ii) Supply at not less than 50 per cent of cost of supply which in besides are considered or tariff should cover atleast variable cost or certain percentage of total revenue (say 10%) can be used to cross subsidies; and
(iii) Regulatory mechanism should include Statutory Tariff Commission, consisting of experts/economists, as well as public hearing. Commission should determine normative costs (Rate of Return), take into account special conditions, determine cost of supply, fix indexation for inflation/fuel cost increase and review basic tariff once, say, in three years.

The fourth aspect that was covered relate to procedures for global tendering in power sector. The group felt that in preparation and evaluation of bids the following features have to be insisted upon:

1. Cost of construction/plant: strict evaluation to exclude 'non-essentials', to avoid excessive capital investments.
2. Process of evaluation: identification of key parameters – 'marking' procedure – may be adopted to determine an overall index.
3. Technical specifications to be unambiguous.
4. Capacity estimation to take note of time-lag and projected use of power by new industries.
5. Generation in excess of normative PLF (68.5%) – operation at higher levels should be on demand by SEB –
   – in case of demand-adequate compensation
   – in case of shortfall – to be adjusted in the same tariff year.
6. Training of personnel for preparation /evaluation of Bids – including legal aspects.
7. Bids to be evaluated on the basis of unit electricity rates.

8. Reduced counter-guarantees.
9. Cost of escalation on account of exchange rate for imported equipment.
10. PPA – should not be for more than 20 years from the date of commercial operation.
11. No direct supply to consumers to the extent possible.

NOTES

1. The course was designed for senior officers and as such structured to be highly interactive. In each day's module the internal faculty and the guest speakers initiated the discussion on the theme during the first session. Subsequently, the participants were divided into groups to work intensively on various issues identified in order to prepare an agenda of action and each group presented its agenda in the plenary session each day. The agenda was thus discussed by the participants in a plenary session that included guest speakers, internal faculty and the programme coordinators.
2. The day's proceedings were coordinated by Prof. Brij Pal Singh. The groups of participants associated with preparation of action agenda on various sub-themes are as follows :

   Threats to and from Globalisation : Mr. Paul Antony, Mr. R. Yadav, Mr. A.V. Mago and Mr. H.S. Brahma.

   GATT and Related Issues : Mr. S. Ray, Mr. Rajan Kashyap and Mr. B.D. Seth.

   Globalisation and State Governments : Mr. P.R.A. Ramanan, Mr. R.C. Agarwal, Mr. B. B. Bhasin, and Mr. Tej Singh.
3. The day's proceedings were coordinated by Mr. K.K. Sharma. The group of participants associated with the preparation of action agenda on various sub-themes are as follows :

   Resource Mobilisation by Centre and States : Mr. A.M. Nimbalkar, Mr. Paul Antony, Mr. B. Bhasin and Mr. Rajan Kashyap.

   Fiscal Situation in the Country : Mr. S. Ray, Mr. B.D. Seth, Mr. Tej Singh and Mr. R. Yadav.

   Privatisation as a Means of Achieving Fiscal and Financial Stability : Mr. L.N.S. Mukundan, Mr. A.K. Mago and Mr. R.C. Agarwal.
4. The Day's proceedings were coordinated by Dr. Sharat Kumar. The group of participants associated with the preparation of action agenda on various sub-themes are as follows :

   Responses of Indian Industry to Import Liberalisation: Mr. S.B. Mishra, Mr. Paul Antony, Mr. A.K. Mago, Mr. Tej Singh, Mr. S. Ray, Mr. R. Kashyap, Mr. B.D. Seth and Mr. Ajit Sharan.

   Means to Promote FDI : Mr. L.N.S. Mukundan, Mr. A.M. Nimbalkar, Mr. H.S. Brahma and Mr. R. Yadav.

   Protection of SSI : Mr. P.R.N. Rahahan, Mr. B.B. Bhasin and Mr. R.C. Agarwal.
5. The day's proceedings were coordinated by Dr. Atindra Sen. The group of participants associated with the preparation of action agenda on various sub-themes are as follows :

   The Future Role of PSUs : Mr. P.R.N. Ramanan, Mr. B.B. Bhasin, Mr. R. Kashyap and Mr. R. Yadav.

Acceptability, Autonomy and Performance Evolution of PSUs : Mr. L.N.S. Mukundan, Mr. S.B. Mishra, Mr. Tej Singh and Mr. Ajit Sharan.

Issues Involving Privatisation of PSUs : Mr. H.S. Brahma, Mr. Paul Antony, Mr. B.D. Seth and Mr. A.M. Nimbalkar.

6. The day's proceedings were coordinated by Dr. H. Ramachandran. The group of participants associated with the preparation of action agenda on various sub-themes are as follows :

Restructuring of SEBs : Mr. A.M. Nimbalkar, Mr. Paul Antony, Mr. B.D. Seth and Mr. S.B. Mishra.

Privatisation of SEBs : Mr. S. Ray, Mr. R. Kashyap, Mr. Tej Singh and Mr. Ajit Sharan.

Tariffs and Subsidies : Mr. A.K. Mago, Mr. R. Yadav, Mr. L.N.S. Mukundan and Mr. B.B. Bhasin.

Procedures in Global Tendering : Mr. H.S. Brahma, Mr. P.R.V. Ramanan and Mr. R.C. Agrawal.

LIST OF PARTICIPANTS

Agnihotri, (Dr.) V.K.
Joint Director, Lal Bahadur Shastri National Academy of Administration, MUSSOORIE - 248 179

Ahuja, A.S.
Joint Secretary, Ministry of Environment & Forests, Paryavaran Bhavan,CGO Complex, NEW DELHI - 110 003

Bajaj, J.L.
Agricultural Production Commissioner, Government of Uttar Pradesh, Council House, LUCKNOW - 226 001

Basu, (Dr.) Kaushik
Executive Director, Centre for Development Economics, Delhi School of Economics, DELHI - 110 007

Kumar, Brijesh
Joint Secretary, Ministry of Civil Aviation and Tourism, Department of Civil Aviation, New Delhi.

Purohit, (Dr.) M.C.
Professor, National Institute of Public Finance and Policy, 18/2, Satsang Vihar Marg, Special Institutional Area, (Near JNU), DELHI - 110 067

Pandit, V.N.
Professor of Economics, Delhi School of Economics, University of Delhi, DELHI- 100007

Ramachandran, (Dr.) H.
Professor & Faculty Co-ordinator, Centre for Micro-Planning & Regional Studies, Lal Bahadur Shastri National Academy of Administration, MUSSOORIE - 248 179

Ramachandran, (Dr.) Nira
Co-ordinator, Centre for Sustainable Development, Lal Bahadur Shastri National Academy of Administration, MUSSOORIE - 248 179

Rao, J. Mohan
Visiting Associate, National Institute of Advanced Studies, Indian Institute of Science Campus, BANGALORE - 560 012

Ramani, R.
Joint Secretary (Training), Ministry of Personnel, Public Grievances and Pensions, Department of Personnel and Training, Block 11, CGO Complex, Lodi Road, NEW DELHI - 110 003

Rao, V.M.
Member, Commission for Agricultural, Costs and Prices, NEW DELHI

Reddy, (Dr.) Y. Venugopal
Additional Secretary, Ministry of Commerce, NEW DELHI - 110 011

Saxena, (Dr.) N.C.
Director, Lal Bahadur Shastri National Academy of Administration, MUSSOORIE - 248179

Sengupta, (Dr.) Nitish Kumar
Director General, International Management Institute, B10, 30 & 31, Qutab Institutional Area, Tara Crescent, NEW DELHI - 110 016

Sen, (Dr.) Atindra
(Economics Faculty) Lal Bahadur Shastri National Academy of Administration, MUSSOORIE - 248 179

Sen, (Dr.) Tapas Kumar
Professor, National Institute of Public Finance Policy, 18/2, Satsang Vihar Marg, Special Institutional Area, (Near JNU), NEW DELHI - 110 067

Sharma, K.K.
Sr. Dy. Director, Lal Bahadur Shastri National Academy of Administration, MUSSOORIE - 248 179

Singh, (Dr.) Brij Pal
Professor, Lal Bahadur Shastri National Academy of Administration, MUSSOORIE -248 179

Srivastava, Ravi
University of Allahabad, ALLAHABAD

Sundaram, (Dr.) K.V.
641, Sector A, Pocket C, Vasant Kunj, NEW DELHI - 110 030

Tripathi, S.C.
Commissioner, Agra Division, Commissioner's Office, AGRA - 282 001 (U.P.)

Vyasulu, (Dr.) Vinod
Director, Institute of Public Enterprise, Osmania University Campus, HYDERABAD - 500 007

CHAIRMEN/ MODERATOR AND RAPPORTEURS

Chairmen/Moderator	Rapporteurs
N.C. Saxena	Atindra Sen
J. Mohan Rao	Harsh Mander
Ravi Srivastava	Brij Pal Singh
R.K. Dar	K.K. Sharma
Vinod Vyasulu	Sharat Kumar
Arun Kumar	P.S. Datta
A.S.Ahuja	S. Mendiratta
J.L. Bajaj	V. K. Gupta
V.K. Agnihotri	
Kaushik Basu	
Nitish Sengupta	

REFERENCES

Ahluwalia, I.J. (1993) Industrial Policy, Reform of Public Sector Enterprises and Privatisation in India, Paper presented at the Conference on Indian Economic Reforms, Merton College, Oxford, June 27-29.

Ahluwalia, I.J. (1991) *Productivity and Growth in Indian Industries,* Oxford University Press, Delhi.

Ahmed, E and N.H. Stern (1984) The Theory of Tax Reform and Indian Indirect Taxes, *Journal of Public Economics,* 23: 259-98, No. 3.

Ajit, D (1992) Industrial Growth and Employment : An Analysis of Labour Absorption in Manufacturing Sector in India RBI Staff Studies, DEAP, RBI, Bombay, Dec.

Alchain, Armen (1995) The Basis of Some Recent Advances in the Theory of Management of the Firm, *Journal of Industrial Economics,* pp : 30-41.

Anant, T.C.A., Gangopadhyay, Shubhashis and Goswami, Omkar (1993), Industrial Sickness in India: Characteristics, Determinants, and History, 1970-1990', Mimeo: I.S.I., Delhi.

Anthony, R. Boote and Janos Somogyi, (1991) Economic Reform in Hungary Since 1968, IMF Occasional Paper No. 83, July.

Baer, W. and I. Kerstenetzky, (eds), (1964) *Inflation and Growth in Latin America,* Yale University Press, New Haven.

Bagchi, Amaresh and Pulin B. Nayak (1994) A Survey of Public Finance and the Planning Process: The Indian Experience.

Bagchi, Amaresh and Nayak, Pulin (1990) Public Finance and the Planning Process, Paper presented at the International Seminar on Public Economics, January.

Balakrishnan, P. (1991) *Pricing and Inflation,* Oxford University Press, New Delhi.

Baran, Paul and Paul Sweezy (1967) Monopoly Capital, Review Press, New York.

Bardha, Paranb (ed) (1989) *The Economic Theory of Agrarian Institutions,* Clerendon Press, Oxford.

Basu, Kaushik (1984), The Right to Give up Rights *Economica,* Vol. 51.

Basu, Kaushik (1989) Technological Stagnation, Tenurial Laws and Adverse Selection, *American Economic Review*, Vol.79.

Basu, Kaushik (1992) Markets, Laws and Government, in Jalan (1992).

Basu, Kaushik (1993) Rural Credit and Interlinkage: Implications for Rural Poverty, Agrarian Efficiency and Public Policy, DERP Working paper, London School of Economics.

Baumol, William, J. (1990) Entrepreneurship: Productive and Destructive *Journal of Political Economy*, Vol. 98, No 5.

Baviskar, B.S. and D.W. Attwood (1991) Fertile Grounds: Why Do Co-operatives Flourish in Western India? *IASSI Quarterly*.

Baviskar, B.S. and D.W. Attwood (1992) The Political Economy of Co-operation in Rural India, Vols. I & II. Report of International Development Research Centre, Ottawa.

Bhagavan M.R. (1985) The Capital Goods Sector in India, *Economic and Political Weekly*, Vol. 20, No. 10, March 9.

Bhagwati, Jagdish and T.N. Srinivasan (1993) India's Economic Reforms, Ministry of Finance, New Delhi.

Bhagwati J.N. and Chakravarty S. (1969) Contributions to Indian Economic Review, Supplement, September.

Bhatt, Ela (1988) *Shramshakti:* National Commission on Self Employed Women and Women in the Informal Sector. Department of Women & Child Development, Government of India, New Delhi.

Bhattacharya, B.B. and M. Lodh (1990) Inflation in India: An Analytical Survey, *Artha Vijnana*, Vol. 32, No. 1, 69-87.

Bromley, Daniel (1992) Reconstituting Economic System : Institutions in National Economic Development, (Draft) University of Wisconsin, Madison.

Boyce, J.K. (1986) Kinded Exponential Models for Growth Rate Estimation, *Oxford Bulletin of Economics and Statistics*, Vol. 48, No. 4.

Brahmananda, P.R. (1982) *Productivity in the Indian Economy : Rising Inputs for Falling Outputs,* Himalaya Publishing, Bombay.

Buiter, W. and Patel, M. (1992), Debt, Deficits and Inflation: An Application to the Public Finance in India, *Journal of Public Economics*, Vol. 47, No. 2.

CENDID, (1985b) The Maharashtra Social Forestry Project in Bhamdara District : Case Studies of three Gram Panchayats, Centre for Development Instructional Technology, New Delhi (Memo).

Chakravarty, S. (1988) *Development Planning: The Indian Experience,* Oxford University Press, Delhi.

Chakravarty, Sukhamoy, (1987) *Development Planning : The Indian Experience*, Oxford University Press, New Delhi.

Chambers, Robert and Melissa, Leach, (1987) Trees to Meet Contingencies: Savings and Security for the Rural Poor. IDS Discussion Paper 228. Institute of Development Studies, Sussex.

Chambers, Robert N.C. Saxena, and Tushaar Shah (1989) *To the Hands of the Poor: Water and Trees,* Oxford and IBH, New Delhi and Intermediate Technology, London.

Chandrasekhar, B.K. and S. Chatterjee (eds) (1993) The Dunkel Draft, Design for Disaster, *Nava Karnataka*, Bangalore.

Chary , S.N. and Vinod Vyasulu (eds), (1992) *Managing India's Planning,* 2 Vols, Printwell, Jaipur.

Chelliah, Raja J.(eds.) (1993) Growth of Indian Public Debt, in Jalan, Bimal, *Indian Economy: Problems and Prospects,* Viking.

Coase, Ronald (1937) The Nature of the Firm, *Economica,* No. 4, pp. 386-405.

Collis, Maurice (1937) *The Land of the Freat Image, The New Directions,* Paperback, New York.

Comptroller and Auditor General of India, (1992) Report Nos. 8 and 13, Tabled in Parliament on May 12, 1992, New Delhi.

Conway, Frederick J. (1987) Case Study : The Agroforestry Outreach Project in Haiti, Conference on Sustainable Development, International Institute for Environment and Development, London (Mimeo) February.

Cuthbertson, K. and M.P. Taylor (1987) *Macroeconomic Systems,* Basil Blackwell, Oxford,.

Dasgupta, Subhachari (1986) Forest, Ecology and the Oppressed. People's Institute for Development & Training (PIDT), New Delhi.

Demsetz, Harold (1967) Some Aspects of Property Rights, *Journal of Law and Economics,* 9, pp. 66-83.

Dhar, Biswajit (1992) The Decline of Free Trade and US Trade Policy Today, *Journal of World Trade*, December.

Dilip, K. Das (1992) *Korean Economic Dynamism,* Macmillan Academic and Professional Ltd.

Eisenhardt, Katheleen M (1989) Agency Theory : An Assessment and Review, *Academy of Management Review,* Vol. 14, No 1.

EPW Research Foundation (1993) India's External Debt, Special Statistics: 1, *Economic and Political Weekly*, June 26.

FAO (1988) Case Studies of Farm Forestry and Wasteland Development in Gujarat, FAO, Bangkok.

FAO, (1986) Forestry Extension Organisation. FAO, Forestry Paper No. 66, Rome.

Fernandes, Walter and Geeta Menon (1988), Deforestation, Forest Dweller Economy and Women, Indian Social Institute, New Delhi.

Fernandes, *et al.* (1988) Forests, Environment and Tribal Economy: Deforestation, Impoverishment and Marginalisation in Orissa. Indian Social Institute, New Delhi.

Fields, Gary (1993) Changing Labour Market Conditions and Economic Development in Hong Kong, Korea, Singapore and Taiwan, (Mimeo) Cornell University.

Friedman, M. (1968) The Role of Monetary Policy, *American Economic Review,* Vol. 58, 1-17.

Frisch, H. (1983) *Theories of Inflation,* Cambridge University Press, London.

Ghosh, Arun, (1993), Power Generation, Foreign Investors and Money Market Borrowers, *Economic and Political Weekly,* June 26.

Ghosh, Jayati (1993) The Dynamics of New Economic Policy : Implications for Women, Keynote Address, at The Sixth National Conference of Indian Association For Women's Studies, Mysore, 30th May.

GOB (1987), Study on the Participation of Women in the Social Forestry Project, Forest Department, Government of Bihar, Patna (Mimeo).

Government of India (1976) Report of the National Commission on Agriculture, Part IX, Forestry, Ministry of Agriculture and Cooperation, Government of India, New Delhi.

Government of India (1982) Report of Committee on Forest and Tribals in India, Ministry of Home Affairs, Government of India, New Delhi.

Government of India (1969) Report of the Industrial Licensing Policy Inquiry Committee (ILPIC), New Delhi.

Graham Bird, (1992) *Economic Reform in Eastern Europe,* Edward Elgar Publishing Ltd., England.

Guhan, S., Centre and States in the Reform Process, Paper Presented at the Conference on Indian Economic Reforms, Merton College, Oxford, June 27-29.

Gulati I. S. (1993), Tackling the Growing Burden of Public Debt, *Economic and Political Weekly*, May 1.

Gupta, Anirudh (1992) *Minorities on India's West Coast: History and Society,* Vikas Publishing Co, Delhi.

Haymin, Y. and V. W. Ruttan (1971) *Agricultural Development: An International Perspective,* : John Hopkins Press, Baltimore.

Hazari, R. K. (1985) *Essays in Industrial Policy,* Concept Publishing Co., Delhi, 1985.

India (1992) Report of the Tax Reform Committee (Chairman : Raja, J. Chelliah), Ministry of Finance, New Delhi.

India (1989) Report on the Current Economic Situation and Priority Areas of Action, Economic Advisory Council, Government of India, New Delhi.

Institute for Social and Economic Change (1993) RBI Unit: A Report for the Five Years Ending, Bangalore, (mimeo), March 3.

International Labour Organisation (1991) Social Dimensions of Structural Adjustment in India, ARTEP, New Delhi.

Jaime, De Melo & Andre Sapir (eds), (1991) *Trade Theory and Economic Reform,* Basil Blackwell, Inc., USA.

Jain, L.R. and S.D. Tendulkar (1992) Inter-temporal, Inter-Fractile Group and Rural-Urban Differential in the Cost of Living, Real Level of Living, Inequality and Poverty for All-India, 1970-71 to 1988-89, *Journal of Indian School of Political Economy,* Vol. 4, No.3, 456-483.

Jalan, Bimal (ed), (1992) *The Indian Economy: Problems and Prospects,* Viking, Penguin, India.

Jalan, B. (ed), (1992) *The Indian Economy,* Viking-Penguin, Delhi.

Jha, Shikha and Srinivasan P.V., (1988) Indirect Taxes in India : An Incidence Analysis, National Institute of Public Finance and Policy.

Kalecki, M. (1971, Selected Essays on the Dynamics of the Capitalist Economy, Cambridge University Press, Cambridge.

Khan, Mohsin S., Peter J. Montiel and Nadeem U. Naqvi, (eds.) (1991) *Macroeconomic Models for Adjustment in Developing Countries,* International Monetary Fund, Washington.

Kornai Janos, (1986) The Hungarian Reform Process, Visions, Hopes, and Reality, *Journal of Economic Literature,* Vol. XXIV, December, pp. 1687-1737

Krishna, Kumar T. (1993) Fund Bank Policies of Stabilisation and Structural Adjustment: A Global and Historical Perspective, *Economic and Political Weekly,* April 24.

Krishnamurty, K. (1984) Inflation and Growth: A Model for India, *Indian Economic Review,* Vol. 19, No. 2, 16-111, Reprinted in Krishnamurty and Pandit (1985).

Krishnamurty, K. and V. Pandit (1985) Macroeconomic Modelling of the Indian Economy: Studies on Inflation and Growth, Hindustan Publishing Corporation, Delhi.

Krishnamurty K., V. Pandit and T. Palamivel (1994) Price Behaviour During The Eighties, in V.N. Kothari (ed), *Indian Economy During The Eighties*, M.S. University of Baroda, (Forthcoming).

Krueger, Anne, O. (1974) The Political Economy of the Rent Seeking Society, *The American Economic Review*, June.

Kumar, A. (1988) Diminishing Returns of an Unchanged Fiscal Policy Regime, *Economic & Political Weekly*, April.

Kumar, Praveer (1987) Marketing of Trees in Moradabad. Office of the Chief Development Officer, Moradabad (U.P.) (Typescript).

Laidler, D.E.W. and M.J. Parkin (1975) Inflation – A Survey, *Economic Journal*, Vol. 85, 741-809.

Lance, Taylor, (ed) (1993) *The Rocky Road to Reform - Adjustment, Income Distribution, and Growth in the Developing World,* United Nations University Press, Tokyo.

Lipsey, R.G. (1960) The Relationship Between Unemployment and the Rate of Change of Money Wage Rates in the UK, 1862-1957: A Fuller Analysis, *Economica*, Vol. 27, 1-32.

Mahalanobis, A. (1982) P.C. Mahalanobis, National Bank Trust, New Delhi.

Mallick, S.K. (1993) Capital Formation in Indian Agriculture: Trends and Factors, Unpublished Paper QAU, ISEC.

Mani, Sunil (1991) *Foreign Collaboration in the Public Sector,* Oxford & IBH, New Delhi.

Minhas, B.S., Jain, L.R. Jain and S.D. Tendulkar, (1991) Declining Incidence of Poverty in the 1980s: Evidence Versus Artifacts. *Economic and Political Weekly*, pp. 1673-82.

Mohan, Rakesh (1992) Industrial Policy and Controls, Jalan.

Mohanty, Deepak (1992) Growth and Productivity in the Indian Economy, RBI Occasional Papers, Vol 13, No. 2.

Mundle, S. and M. Govinda Rao (1992) "Issue in Fiscal Policy" in Bimal Jalan (Ed), The Indian Economy Problems and Prospects, Viking Publications, New Delhi.

Mundle, Sudipto and Rao M Govinda (1991) Volume and Composition of Government Subsidies in India - 1987-88, *Economic and Political Weekly*, May 4.

Munshi, K.M. (1935) *Gujarat and its Literature,* Bharatiya Vidya Bhawan, Bombay.

Myrdal, Gunnar (1957) *Economic Theory and Under-Developed Regions,* Methuen, London.

Nag, A.K. and G.P. Samanta (1994) Inflation in India During the Eighties: An Analytical Review, *Economic and Political Weekly,* Vol. XXIX, No. 8, 431-440.

Nagaraj, R. (1991a) Increase in India's Growth Rate, *Economic and Political Weekly,* April 13.

Nagaraj, R. (1991b) Public Sector Performance in the Eighties: Some Tentative Findings, *Economic and Political Weekly,* December 14.

Nayyar, Deepak (1993) Indian Economy at the Crossroads: Illusions and Realities, *Economic and Political Weekly,* April 10.

North, D. C. (1989) Institutions and Economic Growth: An Historical Introduction, World Development, Vol. 17, No. 9, pp. 1319-1332

Nurkse, R. (1953) *Problem of Capital Formation in Underdeveloped Countries,* Oxford University Press, New York.

Panchamukhi,V. R. (1992) (ed): *Fiscal Management of the Indian Economy,* Interest Publications, New Delhi.

Pandit, B.L.(1992) *The Growth and Structure of Saving in India,* Bombay, Oxford University Press, New York.

Pandit, V. (1978) An Analysis of Inflation in India, 1950-1975, *Indian Economic Review,* Vol. 13, No. 2. 89-115.

Pandit, V. (1984) Macroeconomic Adjustment in a Developing Economy : A Medium Term Model of Output and Prices in India, *Indian Economic Review,* Vol. 19, No. 2,112-157. Reprinted in Krishnamurty and Pandit (1985).

Pandit, V. (1985) Supply, Demand and Monetary Policy in LDC: An Empirical Analysis for India, Discussion Paper No.85.01, Centre for the Analysis of Developing Economies, University of Pennsylvania.

Pandit, V. (1992) Inflation is Here to Stay, *Financial Express,* June 14.

Pandit,V. (1993) Controlling Inflation : Some Analytical and Empirical Issues, *Economic and Political Weekly,* Vol. 34, Nos. 1 and 2, 39-42.

Patnaik, Prabhat (1990) *Economics and Egalitarianism,* Oxford University Press, Delhi.

Phelps, E.S. (1967) Phillips Curves, Expectations of Inflation and Optimal Unemployment Over Time, *Economica,* Vol. 34, 254-281.

Phillips, A.W. (1958) The Relationship Between Unemployment and the Rate of Change of Money Wage Rates in the United Kingdom 1861-1857, *Economica,* Vol. 22, 283-299.

Porter, Michael (1991) The Competitive Advantage, *SPAN*, XXXII (9), September

Porterm, Michael (1990) *The Competitive Advantage of Nations,* Mac Millan, New York.

Prebisch, R.(1961) Economic Development or Monetary Stability : The False Dilemma, Economic Bulletin for Latin America, Santiago, Economic Commission for Latin America.

Radhakrishna, R. and A. Sharma (1976) Inflation and Disparities in the Lends of Living, *Indian Economic Journal*, Vol. 23, No. 4.

Raghuram, Shobha (ed), (1992) Development Policies: Issues and Challenges for the 90's, HIVOS, Bangalore.

Raj, K.N. (1966) Price Behaviour in India, *Indian Economic Review*, Vol.1, New Series, 56-78.

Rajagopalan, R and Tushaar Shah (1992) The Power of Design : Sugar Cooperatives as on Engine of Member Economic Growth Paper presented at the international Symposium On Management of Rural Co-operative at IRMA, December. 7-11.

Rakshit, Mihir (1991) The Macroeconomic Adjustment Programme: A Critique, *Economic and Political Weekly,* August 24.

Rangarajan, C., A, Basu and N. Jadhav, N. (1990) Dynamics of Interaction between Government Deficit and Domestic Debt in India, Paper presented at the International Seminar on Public Economics, New Delhi, January.

Rao, V.K.R.V. (1953) Deficit Financing Capital Formation and Price Behaviour in an Underdeveloped Economy, *Indian Economic Review*, Vol.1, No.3, 55-91.

Rao, M.G. and Sen, T.K. (1993) Government Expenditure in India: Level, Growth and Composition, (Processed), National Institute of Public Finance and Policy, New Delhi.

Ray, P. and Kanagasabapathy (1992) Industrial Inflation in India During the Eighties", RBI Occasional Papers, Vol. 13, No. 1,1033.

Ray, Amal *et al.* (eds) (1991) *The Nehru Legacy*, Oxford and IBH, New Delhi.

Richard, N. Cooper (1992) *Economic Stabilization and Debt in Developing Countries,* The MIT Press, Cambridge, England.

Riddell, James C. (1987) Land Tenure and Agroforestry: A Regional Overview in John B. Raintree (ed) *Land Tree and Tenure,* ICRAF and the Land Tenure Centre Nairobi and Madison.

Rosentein-Rodan, P.N. (1943) Problems of Industrialisation of Eastern and South Eastern Europe, *Economic Journal*, June-September, p. 202-211.

Roy, S.N. (1988) Depleting Sandalwood Production, *Economic Times*, 12th January.

Rudiger, Dornbusch (1993) Stabilization, Debt, and Reform, Harvester Wheatsheaf, England.

Samuelson, P.A. and R.M. Solow (1960) The Problem of Achieving and Maintaining a Stable Price Level: Analytical Aspects of Anti-Inflation Policy, *American Economic Review*, Vol.50, 177-194.

Saxena, N.C. (1991) Marketing Constraints for Eucalyptus from Farm Forestry in India. Agroforestry System, 13 (1), 73-81.

Saxena, N.C. (1992) Farm Forestry and Landuse in India – Some Policy Issues, *Ambio*, 21(6).

Saxena, N.C. (1992a) Adoption of a Long-Gestation Crop: Eucalyptus Growers in North-West India, *Journal of Agricultural Economics*, 43(2):257-267.

Saxena, N.C. (1988) Who Owns the Trees? Tree Harvesting Laws in India and its Implications for Forestry Extension, in Shingi, P.M. and Veer, C.P. (eds.) *Planning Forestry Extension Programmes:* India Bangkok: Regional Wood Development Programme in Asia, FAO.

Saxena, N.C. (1994) *India's Eucalyptus Craze: The God that Failed*, Sage, New Delhi

Shroff, Manu (1993) Indian Economy at the Crossroads, *Economic and Political Weekly*, July 25.

Shah, Tushaar and 150 IRMA Students, (1992a) Seeking Sailience: Governance and Management in Indian Co-operatives, Workshop Document Prepared for the International Symposium on Management of Co-operatives at IRMA, December 7-11.

Shah, Tushaar and Others (1992b) Design for Democracy : Building Energetic Farmer Organisations, Workshop Document Prepared for the International Symposium on Management of Co-operatives at IRMA, December 7-11.

Shah, Tushaar and Michael Johnson (1992) Informal Organisations for Rural Financial Intermediation : Chit Funds, Vishis and Self-help Groups, Anand: IRMA, Working Paper No. 28, April.

Shah, Tushaar (1993) *Groundwater Markets and Irrigation Development*, Oxford University Press, Bombay.

Shah, Tushaar and S. Bhattacharya (1992), Farmer Organisation for Lift Irrigation : Irrigation Companies and Tubewell Co-operatives of Gujarat, Paper Presented at the International Symposium on Management of Co-operatives at IRMA, December 7-11.

Shetty, S.L. (1990) Investment in Agriculture : Brief Review of Recent Trends, *Economic and Political Weekly*, Feb. 17-24.

Shetty, S.L. (1978) Structural Retrogression in the Indian Economy, *Economic & Political Weekly.*

Shultz, T. W. (1968) Institutions and the Rising Economic Value of Man, *American Journal of Agricultural Economics*, Vol. 50, No. 5, December.

SIDA, (1988) Andhra Pradesh Social Forestry Project: Mid-Term Review, Canadian International Development Agency, New Delhi.

SIDA (1990) Evaluation of the Social Forestry Project, Bihar, SIDA, New Delhi.

SIDA (1990) Report on Pilot Market Studies of Farm Forestry Produce in India. SIDA, New Delhi.

Singh, Ajit (1993) The Plan, The Market and Evolutionary Economic Reform in China, United Nations Conference on Trade and Development Discussion Paper No. 76, December.

Singh, Jaivir (1993) Monopolistic and Restrictive Trade Practices: Comments on the Anti-Monopoly Legislation in India, Delhi School of Economics, Working Paper, 93-02.

Singh, M. (1991) Keynote Address in Workshop on Social Dimension of Structural Adjustment in India, by ILO and WEP, New Delhi, December 10-11.

SSM Unit, ISEC (1991) Strengthening the Credit Delivery System, Report Submitted to NABARD.

Taylor, L. (1988a) *Varieties of Stabilisation Experience,* Clarendon Press, Oxford.

Taylor, L. (1989) *Stabilisation and Growth in Developing Countries : A Structuralist Approach*, Harwood Academic Publishers, London.

Taylor, (1988b) Macro Constraints on India's Economic Growth, *Indian Economic Review,* Vol. XXIII, No. 2, 145-166.

Tobin, J. (1980) *Asset Accumulation and Economic Activity,* Basil Blackwell, Oxford.

Tyabji, Nasir (1990) *The Small Industries Policy in India,* Oxford University Press, New Delhi.

Upendranath, C. (1993) SAP and Education: Issues related to Equity, *Economic and Political Weekly* (Forthcoming).

Vaidyanathan, A. (1993) Fertilisers in Indian Agriculture, L. S. Venkataramanan Memorial Lecture, ISEC Bangalore, February 16.

Vanek, Jaroslov (1971) *The Participator Economy,* Cornell University Press, Ithaca, NY.

Vani, B. P. and Vinod Vyasulu (1993) A Disaggregated Analysis of Agriculture Production in Karnataka – Ongiong Study, RBI Unit, ISEC, Bangalore, Vol. 9 (4) : 82-99.

Vyasulu, Vinod, and G. Chakkalingam (1989) Growth Without Development, *Financial Express,* April, 3.

Vyasulu, Vinod (1992) Class and Surplus Value: Towards A Re-examination of Concepts, Unpublished Manuscripts, ISEC.

Vyasulu, Vinod *et al.* (1991) Towards a Political Economy of the Economic Policy Changes, *Economic and Political Weekly*, September 21.

Vyasulu, Vinod and M. Gadgil (1992), Subsidies Controls and the Use of Natural Capital in India, Paper Presented at the 2nd Meeting of International Society of Ecological Economic, at Stockholm University, Stockholm, Sweden August 3-6.

Vyasulu, Vinod (1993) The New Economic Policy and Technological Change: Towards New Initiatives, Paper presented in a Seminar at IPE, Hyderabad, March, 8-9.

Williamson, Oliver E .(1988) The Logic of Economic Organisation, *Journal of Law and Economics,* Vol. 4 No. 1, Spring.

Wilson, Patrick, H. and Trivedi Dipak (1988) *Eucalyptus – The Five-Year Wonder,* VIKSAT, Ahmedabad.

World Bank (1988) Adjustment Lending – An Evaluation of Ten Years of Experience Policy and Research Series.

World Bank (1984) Hungary – Economic Developments and Reforms, A World Bank Country Study.

INDEX

DIMENSIONS OF THE NEW ECONOMIC POLICY

VOLUME TWO
SOCIAL SECTOR

DIMENSIONS OF THE NEW ECONOMIC POLICY

Volume One	:	Economic Sector
Volume Two	:	Social Sector

About the Author

Dr. V.K. Agnihotri, an IAS Officer of the 1968 batch, belongs to Andhra Pradesh cadre of the service. Born on 25th August 1945, he obtained his Masters degree in English Literature and Political Science from the University of Allahabad, Allahabad. He has done his Ph. D. in Public Policy Analysis and Design from Indian Institute of Technology, Delhi. Before joining the IAS, he served on the Faculty of the Department of English Studies, University of Allahabad. He was the recipient of several awards and honours during his distinguished academic career, and has been a Visiting Fellow at the Queen Elizabeth House, University of Oxford, in 1991-92. Among several responsible positions with the State and Central Governments, Dr. Agnihotri, has held the posts of Collector, Visakhapatnam (Andhra Pradesh) and Development Commissioner for Handloom in the Ministry of Textiles, Government of India. He is presently Joint Director and Co-ordinator Public Administration Faculty at Lal Bahadur Shastri National Academy of Administration, Mussoorie. He is also the Chaiman of the Core Groups of the Centre for Micro-Planning and Regional Studies, SOFTRAIN and Village Study Unit at the Academy. His areas of specialisation are Public Policy, Rural Industries, Economic Reforms, Education and Panciayati Raj. He has several publications to his credit including books entitled *Environment and Development* (Concept), *Skills for Effective Administrators* (Vikas) and *Public Policy Analysis and Design* (Concept).

Dr. H. Ramachandran (bom on 15th September, 1947) is Professor and Faculty Co-ordinator in the Centre for Micro-Planning & Regional Studies, Lal Bahadur Shastri National Academy of Administration, Mussoorie. Prior to his joining the Academy he has been on the faculty of Department of Geography, Delhi School of Economics, Delhi University, and on the faculty of Institute of Social and Economic Change, Bangalore. His Publications include among others: Village Clusters and Rural Development (Concept, 1980), Behaviour in Space-Rural Marketing in an Underdeveloped Economy, (Concept, 1982), Schooling and Rural Transformation (Co-author), Environmental Issues in Agricultural Development (Concept, 1990) and Integrated Rural Development in Asia (Concept, 1991).

DIMENSIONS OF THE NEW ECONOMIC POLICY

VOLUME TWO

SOCIAL SECTOR

Editors

Vivek K. Agnihotri, *I.A.S.*
Joint Director
Lal Bahadur Shastri National
Academy of Administration
Mussoorie

H. Ramachandran
Professor & Faculty Coordinator
Centre for Micro-Planning & Regional Studies
L.B.S. National Academy of Administration
Mussoorie

Published for

United Nations Development Programme
&
L.B.S. National Academy of Administration

by

CONCEPT PUBLISHING COMPANY PVT. LTD.
NEW DELHI-110059

ISBN: 978-81-7022-603-1 (Set)
ISBN: 978-81-7022-601-7 (Vol. 1)
ISBN: 978-81-7022-602-4 (Vol. 2)

Edition 2025

Published and Printed by

Concept
Since 1974

Concept Publishing Company Pvt. Ltd.
A/15-16, Commercial Block, Mohan Garden,
New Delhi-110059 (India)
T: 91-11-41101460
E: publishing@conceptpub.com, *W*: www.conceptpub.com

FOREWORD

Since 1992 we have organised a number of in-service courses with a focus on the New Economic Policy at the Lal Bahadur Shastri National Academy of Administration, Mussoorie. The interest of the Academy in the New Economic Policy relates to the ways in which liberalisation affects State administration. In the last one or two decades the bureaucracy has expanded at a very fast rate and government seems to be functioning to a significant extent for government servants. No wonder that of the plan and non-plan budget of some states about 90 percent is spent on government servants.

It is necessary to make administration more responsive. There is a need, and an urgent one, to simplify procedures and perhaps delete a large number of laws and regulations which have outlived their use. I have had an occasion to study in depth some villages of western Uttar Pradesh where I found that although we have liberalised and can set up industries worth billions without much of a licensing hurdle we still require a large number of licenses when a farmer wants to set-up a rice shelling plant or a wheat flour mill or a brick kiln unit or a cold storage. If we can make administration responsive and if we can encourage local entreprenureship it would be easier and politically feasible to think of ushering in rapid changes required to face the challenge of globalization.

However, it is not only the speed - the slow speed - that is of concern but some times the direction which we are taking itself needs to be analysed. Some time last year in a workshop at the Academy on the status of Dalits in India many participants criticised some of the policies which are being advocated in the name of liberalisation, as these could affect the interest of the poor and increase disparities at various levels. Two suggestions which are often made are that why don't we do away with land ceilings or why don't we give forest land to industries. There is a lot more work that needs to be undertaken on these issues since apparently such suggestions are anti-poor and anti-equity.

Considerable literature has accumulated in the last two years contributing significantly to the debate on the New Economic Policy.

However, it is to be noted that a number of steps taken in the early 90's are irreversible and, therefore, the interface between economic policy and civil as well as development administration is of particular interest. It is with this view that a workshop followed by two modular programmes on the New Economic Policy - in fact on the management of the change - was organised by the Academy. The programme was financially supported by UNDP and sponsored by the Department of Personnel and Training, Government of India. My colleagues Dr.V K Agnihotri and Prof. H Ramachandran coordinated and edited the volumes based on the proceedings of the workshop and the two modular programmes on managing change in the context of the New Economic Policy.

N C Saxena
Director

December 1995

Lal Bahadur Shastri National Academy of Administration
Mussoorie

CONTENTS

LIST OF TABLES

LIST OF CONTRIBUTORS

Agnihotri, (Dr.) V. K., Joint Director, Lal Bahadur Shastri National Academy of Administration, Mussoorie, 248 179.

Ayyar, (Dr.) R. V. Vaidhyanatha, Joint Secretary, Ministry of Human Resource Development, Department of Education, Government of India, New Delhi.

Gadgil, (Dr.) Madhav, Professor, Centre for Ecologial Sciences, Indian Institute of Science, Bangalore, 560 012.

Ramachandran, (Dr.) H., Professor & Faculty Co-ordinator, Centre for Micro-Planning & Regional Studies, LBSNAA, Mussoorie, 248 179.

Ramachandran, (Dr.) Nira, Co-ordinator, Centre for Sustainable Development, LBSNAA, Mussoorie, 248 179.

Rao, (Dr.) V. M., Member, Commission for Agricultural Costs and Prices, New Delhi.

Reddy, (Dr.) K. N., Professor, National Institute of Public Finance and Policy, New Delhi

Sundaram, (Dr.) K. V., Former Joint Adviser, Planning Commission, Government of India, and Development Consultant FAO, 641 Sector A, Pocket C, Vasant Kunj, New Delhi, 110 070

Varghese, (Dr.) N. V., National Institute of Educational Planning and Administration, 17-B, Shri Aurobindo Marg, New Delhi, 10 016.

ABBREVIATIONS

ADB	Asian Development Bank
AICTE	All-India Council of Technical Education
ASEAN	Association of South East Asian Nations
BEP	Bihar Education Programme
BPL	Below Poverty Line
CABE	Central Advisory Board of Education
CGHS	Central Government Health Scheme
CIVE	Central Institute of Vocational Education
DIET	District Institute of Education and Training
DNP	Drought Nutrition Programme
DPEP	District Primary Education Programme
EAS	Employment Assurance Scheme
EC	European Commission
EFA	Education for All
EGS	Employment Generation Scheme
EFF	Extended Fund Facility
EME	Established Market Economics
EPW	Economic and Political Weekly
ESE	Economics of Europe
ESI	Employees State Insurance
ESIS	Employees State Insurance Scheme
ETDZ	Economic and Technological Development Zone
FAO	Food and Agriculture Organisation
FCI	Food Corporation of India
FPS	Fair Price Shop
FWP	Food for Work Programme
GATT	General Agreement on Trade and Tariff
GDP	Gross Domestic Product
GNP	Gross National Product
GOI	Government of India
HDI	Human Development Index
HYV	High Yield Variety
ICDS	Integrated Child Development Scheme
IDA	International Development Agency

IDS	International Development Society
ILO	International Labour Organisation
IMF	International Monetary Fund
JRY	Jawahar Rojgar Yojana
LJP	Lok Jumbish Project
MSP	Minimum Support Price
NCERT	National Council for Educational Research and Training
NCTE	National Council for Teacher Education
NGO	Non Government Organisation
NIEPA	National Institute for Educational Planning and Administration
NP	Nutrition Programme
NPE	National Policy on Education
NREP	National Rural Employment Programme
NRF	National Renewal Fund
NRI	Non Resident Indian
NRY	Nehru Rojgar Yojana
NSS	National Sample Survey
ODA	Oversees Development Agency
OECD	Organisation for Economic Co-operation and Development
PDS	Public Distribution System
PHC	Public Health Centre
POA	Programme of Action
PQLI	Physical Quality of Life Indicators
RLEGP	Rural Landless Employment Guarantee Programme
RPDS	Revamped Public Distribution System
SAARC	South Asian Association for Regional Cooperation
SAF	Structural Adjustment Facility
SAL	Structural Adjustment Loans
SECAL	Sectoral Adjustment Loans
SEZ	Special Economy Zone
SSN	Social Safety Net
TLC	Total Literacy Campaigns
TNC	Trans-National Corporation
UEE	Universalisation of Elementary Education
UGC	University Grants Commission
UNEP	United Nations Environment Programme
UNESCO	United Nations Educational, Scientific and Cultural Organisation
VFPC	Village Forest Protection Committee
VRS	Voluntary Retirement Scheme
WCED	World Committee on Environment and Development

INTRODUCTION

V.K. Agnihotri and H. Ramachandran

It is somewhat ironical that in many parts of the world there has been an unprecedented growth after World War II accompanied by greater intervention; but now, for the same reasons of economic growth, a reduction in state intervention is advocated. Perceptible change in the economic policy of India was ushered in during the 1980s, albeit hesitantly, with a small degree of deregulation and decontrol. The cost of regulations, on the one hand, had become abnormally high and, on the other, resulted neither in bringing about equity nor promoted indigenous development in technology and competitiveness. As a result, performance was at a discount. Where performance was good it was not rewarded and failure did not invite punitive action. In fact, often failure attracted rewards and performance attracted penalty. The changes were introduced cautiously with a hope that the rate of economic growth would increase. Instead they led to a balance of payment crisis in 1990 that reduced the choices that we had in the eighties and hastened the introduction of a crisis-driven package of structural adjustments and stabilisation programme.

However, India is not the first country to have faced such a crisis nor are the basic ingredients of the response to the crisis unusual. We have the experience of other countries before us. Unfortunately, these experiences vary considerably. Thus, the debate on the nature of economic reforms and their impact is continuing since 1990 in India, and will continue. It is also apparent that some of the changes brought about are not reversible unless the circumstances become abnormal. The change in economic policy is also not a one shot strategy and needs to be supported by policy changes in various sectors of the economy as well as administration.

* The views expressed in this chapter are personal to the authors. They do not reflect the opinions of either the Government or their organisations.

It is necessary to emphasise that reforms in many sectors, particularly in terms of improving efficiency, cost reduction, cut in administrative delays etc., need to be tackled irrespective of changes in the economic policy. At the cutting edge - the states and lower levels - there is an urgent need for reforms. Such reforms are not necessarily restricted to the economic sectors and economic policies but essentially include change in the administrative ethos and responsiveness.

It is against the back drop of these observations that an agenda of workshops, training courses and lectures was developed by the National Academy of Administration during 1993 and 1994. A number of issues relating to the reforms in various sectors, their sequencing and pacing, the problems of implementation, and action agenda that could be implemented to activate change at the cutting edge level were discussed in these programmes. The deliberations included both economic and social sectors. As a part of this agenda a Workshop on the New Economic Policy was organised by the National Academy of Administration in April 1994. The Workshop and two modular training programmes on Managing Change for serving officers from the higher civil services were funded by the UNDP and sponsored by the Department of Personnel and Training, Government of India. The material essentially generated during these programmes is being brought out in two volumes.

Adjustment Programme and the Social Sector

Social policies in India include policies on sectors such as health, education, housing, family welfare, youth and sports, welfare of weaker sections, water supply and sanitation, labour welfare and employment. The policies are designed by the respective ministries/departments at the national level, based on which the state governments, in some cases, formulate their own state policies. To translate the intentions of the policies into reality, various programmes and activities are formulated and implemented through the five year and annual plans.

It is widely believed that during structural adjustment, the poor suffer the most - as evidenced by a number of empirical studies of developing nations that had undertaken adjustment programme. The need for a safety net which will protect the vulnerable section of the population cannot be over-stated. No low income country could avoid a period of contraction. The Government of India, for example notes "..fiscal discipline forces limits on government spending and this may affect the pace of implementation of programmes in the social-sector which are especially critical for the well-being of the poorer sections. Economic restructuring may also involve loss of jobs in certain sick and unrevivable units as labour is redeployed into other expanding or new units" [GOI 1993a, p 19]. The implications are in terms of a need for fiscal discipline that forces the government to limit its spending which may affect the implementation of programmes in the social sector. While other sectors are regarded as "sensitive" and therefore expenditure on them cannot be cut, social sectors are receiving a low priority as is reflected in a decline in real per capita expenditure across the states on education and public health since the second half of the 1980s.

Figures given in Economic Survey 1992-93 also corroborate this. Although there was an increase in absolute terms, the percentage distribution of plan outlay to social services (education, health, family welfare, housing, urban development and other social services) declined from 16.3 per cent in 1991-92 to 15.9 in 1992-93. Similarly, allocations to rural development declined from 6.2 per cent in 1991-92 to 5.6 in 1992-93.

Performance in the Social Sector

The actual performance in the social sector has been brought out in an analysis by EPW Research Foundation (1993), the major findings of which are :

(1) There is a distinct declining trend in the country's natural growth rate in population which is attributable to the receding crude birth rate. The decline in birth rate as well as the natural growth rate has been sharper in urban areas than in rural areas.

Rapid increase in level of life expectancy, and decrease in maternal and infant mortality rates cannot be expected in the near future.

In rural areas health infrastructure is weak and is probably getting weaker year by year. The objectives of setting up primary health centres have hardly been fulfilled.

The daily caloric supply, and in particular the daily protein supply, per capita have registered a distinct decline during the 1980s and thereafter.

There are serious doubts about the feasibility of achieving the goals of child survival and safe motherhood scheme (launched in 1992-93) through, reduction of the infant mortality to less than 60 per thousand live births, child mortality rate to less than 10 per thousand children population and maternal mortality rate to less than 200 per 100,000 live births by 2000 A.D.

(2) There is a glaring disparity in educational status of men and women.

Although gross enrollment ratios are impressive, drop-out rates, especially among girl students, are very high at all levels.

Drop-out rates are higher in those villages where the incidence of child labour is high.

(3) Unemployment, measured in terms of person-days, showed a significant decline in 1987-88 and chronic unemployment measured by the usual status approach showed a gentle increase between 1972-73 and 1987-88.

As per the findings of an Expert Group of the Planning Commission, 302 million people (38% of the total population) were below the poverty line in 1987-88.

(4) There is an acute inter-regional and inter-state disparity in social development.

Tangible reductions in birth and death rates are not possible without a significant increase in literacy rates.

Literacy attainments, particularly amongst women, play a pivotal role in containing population growth.

Better participation of women in paid labour contributes significantly to a reduction in birth rates.

Literacy attainments and demographic achievements are necessary (but not sufficient) conditions to economic improvement.

Economic development by itself will not ensure social development.

There has been a distinct decline in per capita expenditures across the states on education and medical and public health since the second half of the 1980s.

The Components of the Safety Net

The government envisages [GOI 1993a, p 19-20] three components of a safety net :

(i) *National Renewal Fund* which will finance schemes for compensation, retraining and redeployment of workers affected by restructuring;

(ii) *Strengthening of Food Security*; and

(iii) *Stepping up of expenditure (relative) on social sector.*

However, as pointed out earlier, public expenditure on these very items is shrinking in view of resource crunch, while the government simultaneously argues for a higher priority to these sectors as a part of the safety net. Of the three components of the safety net outlined by the government, not much has been done about the National Renewal Fund. The public sector enterprises which were running in losses were to be pruned. For this purpose the government created the National Renewable Fund with three objectives:

(i) First, excess personnel should be retrenched; but since this would generate trade union resistance it was considered desirable that benefits under Voluntary Retirement Scheme (VRS) be offered so that excess staff could be persuaded to accept it.
(ii) The second objective was to train workers in new technology so that they could undertake hi-tech jobs.
(iii) Thirdly, it was felt that workers be retrained in the lines of production which were emerging as new areas so that they could be deployed elsewhere.

The problems with implementation of Voluntary Retirement Scheme compelled its withdrawal within a few months in many public sector undertakings but was reintroduced later. However, what is underlined by the experience so far is the need for selective VRS.

The second component, i.e. the food security, articulated largely through the Public Distribution Scheme (PDS) in operation in India, leaves much to be desired. The problems relate both to the inadequacy - low level of subsidy and lack of purchasing power in the hands of the poor - as well as of management and targeting - such as discrepancy in food habits and availability of rations, over-stressed and under-utilized Fair Price Shops, etc. The Revamped Public Distribution System (RPDS) which the government launched in January 1992 was extended to 1700 specially identified blocks. The aim is to provide a minimum quantity of foodgrains at specially subsidized rates to the most backward sections of the population residing in geographically difficult and remote areas. However, it has been found that the RPDS has run into the same difficulties as the existing PDS.

The importance of state expenditure on social sectors need hardly be overemphasized. Simple correlation coefficients computed between the variables (i) total real per capita expenditure (1990-91) and HDI; (ii) real per capita expenditure on social sectors (1990-91) and HDI; (iii) real per capita expenditure on education (1990-91) and HDI; and (iv) real per capita expenditure on medical, public health etc. (1990-91) and HDI for 15 major states in the country display a high degree of association between the levels of social development and state expenditure on social sector. That is, any cuts in social expenditure would result in slowing the present pace of social development.

Studies on expenditure pattern on social sector and human development in India indicate that it is at par with average levels in other Asian countries, yet the level of human development indices is low. Further, a synergistic relationship between education, health and nutrition is found which necessitates a simultaneous increase in allocation for these sectors. Intra-sectoral reallocations have also been recommended. For example, at present over 50 per cent of allocations in the education sector are towards elementary education. This is inadequate as India requires over 65-70 per cent allocations in all states. Similarly, in the health sector, less than 20 per cent of government health expenditures, are incurred towards public health. After including water supply and sanitation, the expenditure on an average do not exceed 40 per cent which again is found to be grossly inadequate.

The success stories of Korea, Malaysia and Thailand owe a lot to the existing pre-conditions in these countries vis-a-vis the quality of their human resource. For example, Korea had achieved a literacy rate of nearly 80 per cent by the early 1960s itself. Maternal mortality rates in 1980 per 100,000 live births was 34 in Korea, 59 for Malaysia, 270 for Thailand and 500 for India. However, in India the availability of resources for human resource development at the moment is dependent on the success of the New Economic Policy.

Since public funding for the social sector is likely to stagnate or decline in real terms at least in the coming few years, and the possibility of reallocation from other sensitive sectors such as defence in India (in per capita terms) is low, the feasible areas of evolving an efficient safety net lies in:

(a) re-prioritisation within each sub-sector;
(b) identification of areas of leakage and high overhead costs and the ways of dealing with them;

(c) application of an efficient system of user-charges;
(d) use of local institutions, such as Panchayats and Zilla Parishads, in the management of social sector programmes for improving their efficiency;
(e) identification of segments that are amenable to privatisation and private-public joint ventures which would go in tandem with the concept of user-charges;
(f) methods for coordination with labour unions with reference to re-deployment, re-training, VRS etc.; and
(g) appropriate mix of community-oriented and household-oriented programmes.

It is in this background that we have included in this volume papers that were presented in the Workshop on the New Economic Policy and the proceedings of the modular programmes on these themes at the Academy. We begin this volume with a paper on the next phase of anti-poverty programme by V. M. Rao. He observes that we are witnessing a reduction in the scale of anti-poverty programmes which, combined with inflation, means a significant decline in allocation. Various public policies in the past have responded effectively to provide relief in situations like drought and scarcity, but we do not have any significant response to protect the poor in a situation of inflation.

He finds that so far our tentative plan has been to provide relief to the poor but not to make them economically viable. There is no doubt that we have succeeded in establishing a delivery system for relief in times of distress. This is no mean achievement; we now have some link with the poor and also a working system which can provide an effective nucleus for change.

Rao further makes the point that in the pre-liberalization socialistic era, anti-poverty strategies were minimally conceived. According to him, so long as the economy was based on control by the government of the "commanding heights" of the economy and its critical sectors, the reliance on "minimal" strategy might have been an appropriate anti-poverty policy. But once the government decides to step down from the "commanding heights", it would not be enough for the government to ask who the poor are and what they lack. A battery of anti-poverty programmes are required, which have to go beyond relief measures and become a programme which enables a poor household to join the main-stream growth processes.

The employment based anti-poverty programmes as well as relief measures are crucial for providing food security. The role of such programmes is reviewed by Nira Ramachandran in the process of an analysis of sustainability of our food security in the background of the New Economic Policy. Achieving sustainable development for a country must of necessity involve the provision of an adequate food supply on a sustainable basis. Thus food security will remain an important item on the policy agenda in the foreseeable future. While it is well known that during the twentieth century the growth rate of world food production has exceeded that of the population by a comfortable margin, yet the problems of chronic food deficits and even famine remain unresolved.

At the country level, in India, the changed agricultural scenario from the mid-sixties onwards has resulted in marginal surpluses in good agricultural years. Over the last four decades, the country's foodgrain production has almost trebled rising from 51 million tonnes in 1950-51 to 170 million tonnes in 1988-89. The bumper wheat production in 1967-68 and the increasing production in the subsequent years enabled the Government to build up bigger stocks which helped the country through several periods of crisis without recourse to the international market on a large scale, a case in point, being the three successive years of drought during 1986-1988. Yet even today, about 37% of the population (below the poverty line) do not have access to adequate food supplies. The concept of food security thus implies not only sufficient levels and stability of supply, but also empowering the people with the means to purchase food. She points out that policy options encompass a range of choices from macro-economic decisions to welfare schemes aimed at supplementing nutrition levels and employment schemes with the objective of increasing the purchasing power of the people.

Since in India, like the other countries of Monsoon Asia, foodgrain production is characterised by a considerable degree of year to year instability, Nira Ramachandran critically reviews the options - the carrying of large stocks of foodgrain imports through food aid or trade. Another possibility in the context of the second option which needs further exploration is that of regional food security involving SAARC and ASEAN.

Moving on from issues relating to Food Security to those of health Dr. K. N. Reddy finds very little attention being paid to the reforms in the health sector. While substantial improvement in health status indicators are noted, he considers them unimpressive when compared with other countries such as China, Sri Lanka, Thailand and the Republic of Korea. He further notes that the fulfilment of Alma Ata declaration (1978) may remain a dream since, as of now, the system is beset with a number of weaknesses and is badly in need of reform.First, there seems to be misallocation of resources and it has been in practice for quite some time. Contrary to general opinion and worldwide view, larger share of resources is going to curative services. Very little has gone for capital formation. Second, rural areas have been neglected. Third, accessibility to health care is very poor. The system favours the elite and higher income groups. Be it medical care, or water supply and sanitation or be it any health related facility, poorer segments of the population are the last ones to receive them. Fourth, there exists a mismatch between the supply of and demand for health services, both at the Central and the States' levels. Fifth, quality of service in public hospitals (government hospitals) has been deteriorating fast, partly because of lack of adequate supply of medicines and equipment and partly because of faulty manpower planning and selection procedures. The delivery system has become bureaucratic and unaccountable. Sixth, the health care system is not cost effective. Seventh, there seems to be difficulty in allocating higher share of States' resources; to health care on account of (a) shortage of resources and (b) expenditure compressions. Finally, rapid developments in expensive medical technology and new drugs have inflated health care costs.

In this situation, what is the rationale for liberalisation or privatisation of health services? Reddy comments on some the major factors supporting privatisation. First, privatisation works out cheaper to government, because the dynamics of competition may compel the contractors to cut down their costs in order to win or retain contracts; contractors may provide services at lower cost, because labour may be cheaper for them as they are not bound by civil services hiring requirements or public employee pay scales. Second, privatisation affords flexibility. Whatever is not possible for government agencies due to political and administrative difficulties, privatisation makes it possible. It will facilitate the initiation of new programmes with existing staff and hire new staff. If government agencies have to provide 'services, they have to provide the same throughout the country and a degree of uniformity in standards has to be ensured - the option of taking local sentiments and local conditions into account will not be there. But if contracting the same service with non-profit organisations is made local requirements will be met as the latter are aware of local conditions. Further, it may enable changing direction or could be cut back quickly if the government priorities change. Quite often cutting back public employment is much more difficult and the consequences are much more severe.

As we move on from issues of reforms in health sector to those pertaining to education, Dr. R.V. Vaidyanatha Ayyar develops his analysis with the initial observation that public policy and research on the relationship between education and economic reform process is mostly monotonic, being limited to equity aspects. According to him it is now universally accepted that during the process of structural adjustment, effective policies should be put in place to protect the public expenditure on basic needs, as an integral part of the reform process itself rather than as a subsequent 'add on' component when the adverse impact of the reforms has already caused considerable damage. He argues, firstly, that expenditure on education can be stepped up during adjustment and secondly, while equity issues are important, the question to consider is not merely how economic reforms affect education but how education can accelerate the economic reform process.

Ayyar further stresses that the area which calls for particular attention is the financing of tertiary education (higher, general and technical education). India has 6,204 colleges and universities as compared to 1,075 in China, a country with a larger population and greater success than India in universalising elementary education. For every 100 students in secondary schools India has 8.34 students in higher education institutions; China has only 4.06. Given this large number of higher education institutions, the resource requirements are immense and impossible for the budgetary resources to meet them.

Varghese speculates the probable impact of recent economic reforms on the education sector. In the background of his analysis of the changing pattern of World Bank funding to the developing countries he deals with the recent economic reforms in India with a focus on a quick evaluation of the performance of the Indian economy during this period and attempts to draw some implications of adjustment policies for the education sector.

He notes that World Bank lending in the sixties and seventies was dominated by project lending where changes in the macro-economic policy variables were not directly addressed. Even when such issues were addressed, they were not conditionalities to approve or release the loans. The Bank loans of the recent past are more in the category of adjustment loans with the accompanying conditionalities. Education sector in India was relatively free from external funding. However, recently efforts are being made to get international assistance or loans for primary education under the Social Safety Net (SSN) programme of the World Bank. India has also received educational funds from many other bilateral and multilateral agencies in the recent past. There is every possibility to believe that external funding in the educational sector may go up in the coming years. Since these funds are routed through the government, public expenditure on education in India during the reform period may not decline.

Varghese further deals with the ways in which adjustment programme affects the recurring expenditure on education. He draws attention to the fact that at all levels of education, salary component forms the major share of recurring expenditure in education. At primary levels the share of salaries to the total recurring expenditure is over 95 per cent. In many countries, salaries cannot be cut and hence a reduction in the budgetary provision on this account is difficult to be effected. He underlines that search for policy options end more often with cost recovery measures and reduction of subsidies. He believes that private sector in education in India can be efficient and effective so far as it remains small. The private sector in India may not be in a position to manage a larger share of the system very efficiently. Hence privatisation of education on a large scale is not a viable solution in India.

K. V. Sundaram draws attention to the spatial disparities in development as a consequence of policies in colonial and post-independence India. Inspite of various attempts made by Government, development has not spread evenly over the entire country, but rather in a point-line-network. The New Economic Policy is weighted in favour of areas already having infrastructure, essentially medium and high development areas, and is likely to result in greater polarization. Sundaram cites the example of China where the recent open door policy for foreign investment is coupled with a conscious attempt at ensuring spatial equity.

He makes a case for indepth work in understanding the spatial implications of the New Economic Policy and advocates the "development from within" or auto-centric development approach which involves people organizing themselves into voluntary interest groups and taking the initiative for development. He suggests an agenda for achieving this and specifies the roles that the National and Local Governments would need to play to achieve this end.

An important area that falls largely outside the ambit of 'markets' is the issues relating to environment. Madhav Gadgil comments on environmental issues in the context of globalization-liberalization-privatization syndrome. According to him these developments have evoked two markedly different reactions. The prophets of doom foretell that the living wealth of India coming under control of avaricious multi-national corporations, who would patent, exploit, poison and finally wipe it out, leaving us worse off than ever before. Others more optimistically view the times as an opportunity to rid the nation of the stranglehold of the iron triangle of greedy politicians, corrupt bureaucrats, and unscrupulous businessmen, to inject some efficiency in our economic enterprises, to create wealth based on our biological heritage, to empower our people to serve as effective custodians of our natural resources and to share in the fruits of their utilization. Gadgil argues that in the ambiance of the new economic policy there is much merit in accepting this counsel of hope and working towards making it a reality.

His basic contention is that over the last four decades the process of development has degenerated into a process of the state sponsoring subsidized fluxes of resources to a narrow elite comprising organized industry and services and the more influential landholders. These have received water, power, forest and mineral resources all at large public subsidies in various forms, as well as license to pollute the commons without paying for the damage it inflicts. This has created an atmosphere in which manipulating the state machinery to get access to such favours has become the focus of all enterprise, throwing to the wind considerations of efficiency and sustainability. It has also encouraged continual borrowal of technology, without investing in innovation. Thus we have seen the coming into being of an iron triangle with its three vertices being made up of (1) organized industry, services and bigger landholders who benefit from state subsidies, (2) bureaucracy administering these subsidies, and (3) politicians deciding on who gets what level of subsidies.

Thus he finds that the new economic regime is a welcome development, hopefully promoting greater efficiency of use of natural resources. But since in itself the new set of policies will not promote more sustainable and equitous use of such resources, he suggests that in a more open, democratic atmosphere we must now craft other people-oriented institutions to promote sustainability and equity.

Be it environmental issues or that of poverty, education or health, the authors addressing these issues together attempt to identify an appropriate mix of possible role of State - in production, delivery, licensing, contracting, financing, subsidising and regulation.

1

COPING WITH LIBERALIZATION
The Next Phase in the Anti-Poverty Strategy

V.M. RAO

Anti-poverty Strategy : The Present Status

The anti-poverty strategy pursued so far in India has relied chiefly on Government programmes to reach employment, assets and basic needs to the poor. While there are controversies about the extent of poverty prevailing now, most researchers appear to agree that the anti-poverty strategy has brought about reduction in the level of poverty. Not only do the statistical estimates show the reduction but also field studies in areas affected by droughts and scarcity conditions provide convincing evidence of the beneficial impact of the anti-poverty programmes (Tendulkar, 1993, Acharya, 1989). It is reasonable to hope that the present strategy would bring about continuing reduction in poverty and that, eventually, its extent would reach a level which most might regard as modest.

Would this mean the end of the problem of poverty ? Hardly so. It is necessary to remember that our anti-poverty policies and programmes are based on what may be called the "minimal" concept of poverty focussed on providing relief to the poor rather than equipping them with skills, resources and infrastructures to make them economically viable. The policy pronouncements do indeed emphasise the latter objective. But, if one goes by what is observed on the ground and not by good intentions and resolves embodied in the policy documents, the following would be a fair assessment of the achievements so far of the anti-poverty strategy.

(i) The strategy has had considerable success in alleviating the widespread distress suffered by the poor during periods of scarcity.

Famines have been averted and, also, some progress has been made towards providing food security and off-farm employment to rural workers during the lean season (Jharwal, 1993, Chandramohan, 1992). Compared to the historical past, this could be regarded as a path-breaking achievement. However, the programmes are still on a scale too modest to provide a credible employment and minimum income guarantee to the rural poor and little has been done to "drought-proof" agriculture through improvements in land and water resources. Particularly glaring has been the failure of the strategy to mobilise the rural labour to carry out such improvements on a sustained basis (Rao, V. M. 1992);

(ii) A wide-spread extension has been achieved in the educational and health facilities though the quality of services provided by them remains poor and, given their harsh struggle for survival, the target groups of these facilities are hardly in a position to benefit from the facilities on the required scale (Asian Development Bank, 1993).

(iii) Unlike the wage-employment programmes which tend to be relief-oriented, creation of self-employment opportunities through provision of assets can, in theory, make the poor economically viable. However, in practice, the schemes for self-employment have operated like programmes distributing doles and, as a result, their contribution has been meagre both in reducing poverty and in adding to growth (Rao V. M. 1987); and

(iv) Possibly the least successful have been the programmes to reform land relations and to strengthen institutions like markets, cooperatives, etc. The ineffectiveness of these programmes implies that the institutional environment continues to be unfriendly towards the poor (Rao, V.M., 1988). It would be a formidable barrier in the way of the poor when they begin their struggle for much more substantive economic opportunities and resources than the modest benefits they are getting now. The recent political trends leave little doubt that such a struggle would emerge soon in many parts of the country.

Clearly, there has to be a next phase in the anti-poverty strategy going beyond its present "minimal" concerns. The new phase would have to pay pointed attention to dimensions of deprivation neglected so far viz. education, health, skills and assets. The development bureaucracy and delivery systems would have to be strengthened and reoriented. This, in a way, is only an extension of the present "minimal" strategy. However, given the change envisaged in the Indian economy towards thorough-going deregulation and liberalisation, the anti-poverty strategy would need a fresh perspective on poverty in tune with the reforms in the economy. The present strategy visualises bringing about reduction in poverty by identifying the poor households and providing them with the goods and services they lack. The new perspective would have to be a broader one looking at poverty as a characteristic of the larger society. While the new perspective would have room for identifying the poor to meet directly their critical needs, it would also have to take into consideration the features of the society which give rise to poverty in the first place with a view to eliminating, or at least progressively moderating, these features. So long as the economy was based on control by the government of the "commanding heights" of the economy and its critical sectors, the reliance on "minimal" strategy might have been an appropriate anti-poverty policy because, given the socialistic ideology, the development strategy as a whole is expected in such an economy to work towards achieving the goal of abolition of poverty. But, once the government decides to step down from the "commanding heights", it would not be enough for the government to ask who the poor are and what they lack. The anti-poverty strategy in a liberalised economy would have to be based on an understanding of the factors giving rise to poverty and the measures necessary to counteract them. It is argued in the section which follows that these factors have left their imprint on the economy even during the political regime professing socialism and that, with liberalisation and deregulation, they are likely to become far more strong and ruthless.

The Emerging Context

The factors causing poverty operate through depressing growth and keeping certain regions, resources and sections of population away from the growth processes. Our attempt in this section is to illustrate the impact of these factors on the economy with the help of a few suggestive trends and indicators. It is best to begin by taking a look at the growing gap between agriculture and non-agriculture which is a good proxy reflecting the rural-urban dualism in the Indian economy (See Table 1.1).

TABLE 1.1 : Per Capita Incomes in Agriculture and Non-Agriculture from 1950-51

(Rs. in constant 1970-71 prices)

Per capita income/Year	1950-51	1960-61	1970-71	1980-81	1990-91
(1)	(2)	(3)	(4)	(5)	(6)
Per capita net domestic product at factor cost					
1. In Agriculture	402	427	427	417	483
2. In non-agriculture	588	831	1.080	1,252	1,742
3. Total	462	551	626	687	951
4. Ratio of 2 to 1	1.46	1.94	2.53	2.93	3.61

Source : Bhalla, 1993.

Table 1.1 comes from a study prepared by Sheila Bhalla (Bhalla, 1993). Commenting on the gap, she observes "Low farm incomes on sub-marginal holdings combined with employment growth rates in the economy which have fallen increasingly below population growth rates place a large sub-set of the rural population in a situation where they have limited options". The interesting point to note is that the relatively faster "non-agriculture" income growth does not necessarily reflect the economic strength of this sector. Consider, for example, the following assessment of the modern industrial sector in India which is hardly flattering - "Indian industry has grown in an artificial environment of high protection, shortages ...... Many are overstaffed; and will not survive the emerging open and competitive environment" (Rao, S.L., 1994). This propped-up structure does not even have the saving grace of helping the rural poor : "A disturbing feature of the development process (in many developing Asian economies) has been the tightening of the labour market and the consequent increase in the wage rates in the non-agricultural sector" (Madhur, 1994). This has happened when the economy is "still having substantial surplus labour in agriculture .... (the economy is) hitting the labour-bottleneck at too early a stage of development".

While the industrial structure has been propped up, the development strategy has paid little attention to growth opportunities in agriculture which could have directly benefited the rural poor and helped in making the growth process more broad-based. This can be seen from Table 1.2 which shows that while all the major crops and crop-groups bear the evidence of growth in production during the post-Independence period, a sharp contrast has emerged among them in relation to the extent of increase in production, improvement in yields and extension of irrigation.

TABLE 1.2 : Production, Area and Yield of Important Crops/Crop-Groups

Crop	Production (million tonnes)		Area		Yield (million ht.)		% Irrigated Area (Kgs/hect)	
	I	II	I	II	I	II	I	II
Wheat	6.4	55.1	9.8	23.0	655	2397	31.5	78.4
Rice	23.5	73.7	30.5	42.3	771	1741	32.3	45.2
Cotton	2.8	9.8	4.9	7.7	95	217	8.2	33.6
Oilseeds	5.2	18.3	10.1	25.4	519	719	0.8	19.8
Coarse Cereals	16.8	26.3	38.8	33.8	433	778	8.5	9.3
Pulses	8.2	12.1	20.2	22.6	405	534	7.8	9.5

I = 1949-50, II = 1991-92

Source :Agricultural Statistics at a Glance, March, 1993. (Government of India).

The contrast is attributable to a number of factors including soil-climatic but an important contributor has been the pronounced policy bias towards the "green revolution" crops as indicated by the dramatic performance of wheat (a nearly nine-fold increase in production and a four-fold increase in yield along with a quantum jump in the extent of irrigation) and of rice. These crops have benefitted the most from the supportive policies for adoption of new technologies, intensified use of modern inputs and increased availability of dependable irrigation (Misra, 1993; Sinha, 1994). The next two crops in Table 1.2 – Cotton and oilseeds - are illustrative of the policy maker's attempts in recent years to move beyond the "green revolution" crops. Their performance is relatively modest as compared to wheat and rice. It also needs to be mentioned that their production and yield continue to remain unstable and, as a result, their markets often go through volatile and speculative price changes. However, the improvement in these crops is of particular significance for the future as it provides ground for hope that, with patience and perseverance, our policies do have the capacity to promote growth in situations which have been considered so far as uncongenial for modernised agriculture. Viewed thus, the last two crops Table 1.2 – whose performance in terms of increase achieved in production is poor – can be regarded as crops which have been neglected so far in our development policies for agriculture. The performance of pulses has been poor despite strong demand pressure and high and rising price levels. *Prima facie,* lack of policy support is the main hurdle faced by this crop group. As regards the coarse cereals, they are neglected by the policy maker as well as by the market as the demand for them is weak, their short shelf-life comes in the way of providing effective price support and the new technologies developed for them are modest in impact and need local adaptations.

The bias in the development strategy towards modern industry and the relatively prosperous parts of agriculture is often justified on the ground that it promotes faster growth in the economy. A consequence of the bias, which is of particular relevance to the theme of this chapter, is that both the government spending on anti-poverty programmes and their performance indicators appear to have decreased during the reforms for macro-economic stabilisation being implemented since 1991-92. It is necessary to remember that this period was marked by sharp rise in foodgrain prices, particularly in the prices of coarse cereals consumed by the poor and, hence must have been a period of acute distress to the poor. Deepak Nayyar describes the philosophy underlying the reforms for macro-economic stabilisation in an expressive phrase : "comfort for the rich and hardship for the poor" (Nayyar, 1994). It is our feeling that a fuller explanation of such biases in our policies needs consideration of influence wielded by diverse organised groups on policy-making in India. They have deeper hidden roots than merely the concern of the policy-maker for growth. It is enough for the purpose of this chapter to note that, since liberalisation and deregulation of the economy leave the relatively organised and modernised sectors free to operate through markets, there is a strong case for the government to focus its developmental activities on the resources and people comprised in the unorganised parts of the economy. This would provide a strong foundation for the next phase in the anti-poverty strategy which would have to shed the "minimal" perspective on poverty to look at the development needs of the poor in a more meaningful and adequate manner. Taking agriculture for illustration, the following section describes the poverty situations having good potential to contribute to both growth and poverty removal if the anti-poverty strategy is suitably "revamped".

Prospects for Agricultural Growth in Poor Areas: Some Illustrations

Agricultural scientists take the view that the Indian agriculture is still well within the limits imposed by our land and water resources. Unchecked population growth would indeed eventually push the economy closer to these limits and, hence, measures for demographic control would have to be a top priority item in the policy agenda. However, in the field of agriculture over the medium term, the focus would have to be on devising policies for acceleration in agricultural production without impairing the objectives of sustainability of growth and of conservation of resources. Scientists assure us that there are promising opportunities precisely of this kind in large regions across India which are still relatively untouched by policies for agricultural development. We can do no better in this chapter than describe a few illustrative cases.

Eastern India

Prof. M.S. Swaminathan has described the eastern region of India as a "non-green revolution" green area offering scope for substantially higher production within a reasonable time. Social science observers of the region have catalougued a number of institutional barriers inhibiting agricultural growth. Field visits to poor groups like small jute growers in backward pockets would leave an overwhelming impression of unrelievable poverty. Placed in an environment of shrinking export markets, sick manufacturing units, speculative traders and absence of new technologies, the jute growers indeed face a grim future. However, during the latter half of the Eighties substantial increase in agricultural production seems to have taken place in some areas in this region (Rao, C.H.H., 1994). The performance of West Bengal in recent years in agricultural and rural development has been impressive. Even the jute industry is showing some signs of revival through diversification of products and prospects of increased exports. On the whole, the indications are that the situation in the Eastern region might have reached a stage where determined policy efforts to increase production would evoke good response. The region needs major reforms in infrastructure, markets, credit and cooperatives. Once these preconditions for steady growth are established, it would be easier to tackle the other problems in the region like those connected with land relations.

Dryland Areas

The dryland areas in the central, western and southern parts of India have a weak and exhausted land base and poor water resources. While the relief needs of these areas during periods of scarcity receive prompt and even generous policy response, little success has been achieved so far in setting up stable arrangements for conservation and optimum use of land and water resources in the region and to insulate the farm economy from the disruption caused by periodic droughts. When this is done, the region would find it possible to absorb the new technologies which are being developed to suit the conditions of the region. There are already a number of successful experiments in this region where local leadership has organised people to improve farming through their own efforts and use of local resources. The main problem is to arrange for replication of such experiments on a sufficiently wide scale and to provide for the components of public sector investments in the region. While the region may not achieve quick and dramatic increases in agricultural production, considerable expansion in employment, sizeable improvement in levels of living and effective coping with weather-related instability would be feasible objectives for the region to achieve given the required policy support. Considering the proneness of this region to chronic poverty, progress in realising these objectives would be a major gain for our development strategy seeking to bring the poor within the mainstream economy.

Fallow and Waste Lands[1]

The land-use statistics show that even as recently as in 1989-90 fallow and waste lands totalled to 56 million hectares. They formed nearly 20 per cent of total reporting area (305 million hectares). The importance of their judicious use can be gauged from the fact that the Indian agriculture has the land base of only 140 million hectares of net area sown. While fallow and waste lands cannot support regular cultivation, putting them under tree cover would serve both the purposes of conservation of land and adding to agricultural production through increased output of tree-based and related products. The land-use statistics show that an active policy regime is yet to emerge for the fallow and waste lands. Land classified as current fallows increased from 11 million hectares in 1950-51 to 16 million hectares in 1989-90 and "other fallow land" after decreasing from 17 million hectares in 1950-51 to 9 million hectares in 1970-71 registered a small increase in later years to reach the level of 11 million hectares in 1989-90. As regards "culturable waste" land, its extent decreased from 23 million hectares in 1950-51 to 18 million hectares in 1970-71. But the decrease in the next two decades was quite modest and in 1989-90 there were still 15 million hectares of culturable waste lands. On the other hand, the land under tree crops decreased sharply from 20 million hectares in 1950-51 to 4 million hectares in 1989-90. The grazing lands and permanent pastures also decreased from 14 million hectares in 1960-61 to 12 million hectares in 1989-90. It needs to be mentioned that though fallow and waste lands occur in all regions, they are likely to be concentrated precisely in the regions having weak agriculture. Their development, preferably through grassroot level organisations of rural people, could bring many benefits to the backward areas, particularly to the poor in these areas. Where such organisations are not available, private enterprise might be in a position to develop the fallow and waste lands though care would have to be taken to see that the local people share adequately in the benefits flowing from the development of these lands.

Anti-Poverty Strategy in a Liberalised Economy : Critical Policies and Priorities

The agricultural growth achieved so far has relied chiefly on the potential of a small part of our resources located in the green revolution area. The new anti-poverty strategy based on promoting broad-based agricultural growth would need to shift towards resources in other regions requiring different technologies but also providing opportunities to spread agricultural growth far more widely and to make the development process genuinely participatory and poor-friendly than has been the case in the past. While this shift in emphasis would mean a growing and eventually large role for local people and voluntary organisations, the transition would need time and strong policy support to activate the development process at the grassroot level. Four policy areas which are likely to be of critical importance are described below.

Support Measures

While in the "minimal" strategy the approach has been to lift the poor above the poverty-line by delivering critical goods and services to the poor, the approach in the strategy appropriate in the context of liberalisation would have to be to enable the poor to become economically viable so that they can dispense with the continuing dependence on an external agency - even if it be the government - for their livelihood. This means they have to eventually function in markets and normal economic processes without outside props. A major handicap of the rural economy is that dispersed small producers, unless suitably organised for group action, find it extremely difficult to cope with volatile, unpredictable and, often, depressed markets. Consider, for example, the behaviour of wholesale prices in the five markets connected with cotton and its manufactures - Raw cotton and Handloom cloth where producers are rural, small, dispersed and unorganised and cotton yarn and cotton cloth (Mills and Powerloom) whose producers are urban-based and much better organised. (See Table 1.3).

TABLE 1.3 : Index Number of Wholesale Prices (Base 1981-82 = 100)

Month	Raw Cotton	Cotton Cloth (H.L)	Cotton Yarn	Cotton oth (Mills)	Cotton Cloth (P.L)	All Comm-odities
Sept. 1990	141.3	201.6	187.3	157.6	169.6	180.9
Dec. 1990	153.3	201.6	190.6	162.1	174.9	186.6
March 1991	171.9	200.6	195.4	166.6	192.7	191.7
June 1991	219.6	202.7	208.3	177.9	193.1	198.4
Sept. 1991	251.5	202.7	240.6	184.1	200.0	210.4
Dec. 1991	242.1	202.7	241.2	185.6	196.9	213.2
March 1992	231.1	213.1	258.2	196.9	196.9	217.7
June 1992	233.1	216.6	248.1	198.3	209.5	224.1
Sept. 1992	217.7	216.6	254.2	199.7	214.1	230.7
Dec. 1992	204.8	216.6	254.2	201.5	218.9	231.4
March 1993(P)	202.3	218.5	252.2	205.8	226.8	232.5

Source: Compendium of Textile Statistics, 1993, Office of the Textile Commissioner Government of India, Bombay.

P.L.=Powerloom; H.L. = Handloom; P = Provisional.

The period covered by Table 1.3 – September, 1990 to March, 1993– witnessed a sharp inflationary rise of nearly 30 per cent in the whole sale price index for "all commodities" from 181 to 233. There was a matching rise in the index for cotton yarn and cloth. On the other hand, the increase in the index was only 8 per cent in the case of handloom cloth indicating fall in its real price when the price of cotton yarn – its main raw material – was rising sharply. Even more alarming, the index for raw cotton increased by nearly 80 per cent from September, 1990 to September, 1991 and, thereafter, declined continuously from the peak level of 252 to 202 in March, 1993. Table 1.3 reflects well the hardships suffered by cotton cultivators and handloom weavers in marketing their produce. An implication of Table 1.3 is that such market-vulnerable producers would have to be given a measure of protection through price support and market intervention policies. Such policies are difficult to devise. By a convenient coincidence, the present state (in February, 1994) of the cotton market provides a good example of these difficulties. The high prices of cotton prevailing at the moment despite its comfortable availability in the economy have baffled both the government and the industry and the drastic measures like banning of exports of cotton being taken by the government reflect more a sense of panic than deftness in handling a tricky situation created by shrewd speculators.

Investment[2]

The gross capital formation in agriculture (at 1980-81 prices) which was in excess of Rs 5000 crores per annum in the late seventies is estimated to have declined to levels close to Rs 4000 crores per annum over the Eighties. The major reason for this decline has been the sharp fall in the public sector gross capital formation from nearly Rs 1700 crores in 1978-79 to less than Rs 1200 in 1989-90. There has been some decline in the private sector gross capital formation also and, considering its complementary relationship with the public sector capital formation, the situation may further worsen unless the latter revives. A plausible explanation for the decline in the public sector capital formation is that while the tempo of investment in the green revolution areas is slowing down, the other areas whose investment needs are large and pressing are yet to receive the attention they deserve. It is obvious that development of watersheds, conservation and productive use of common lands and provision of wide range of infrastructures for backward areas would all need substantial amounts of public investments. A systematic assessment of these needs and arrangements to meet them would have to be given priority to raise the public sector capital formation.

Panchayati Raj Institutions

Reaching investments and development inputs across large and widely spread areas needs active networks of grassroot level organisations. Those like cooperatives and voluntary groups have to emerge through the initiative of local people themselves and the government can only lend a helping hand. On the other hand, the institutions to bring about decentralisation in administration and in development planning and implementation have to be established and nurtured by the government. Without effective local-level integration of schemes, coordination in implementation, participatory mechanisms and continuous monitoring, it would hardly be possible to implement the development strategy for agriculture sketched in this chapter[3]. In large parts of areas to be reached, the situation is likely to be one of institutional vacuum. However, determined efforts would have to be made to establish the Panchayati Raj institutions and to put pressure on them to shoulder the tasks of decentralised development as is being done in a few states like Karnataka. The tendency among the policy maker is still to take it for granted that once priority is given to a sector in terms of larger allocation in the Five Year Plans, the development of the sector would automatically follow. In the case of agriculture (and rural development in general), ineffectiveness of the grassroot level organisations is likely to be a constraint which is far more difficult to overcome than the problems in enhancing the plan allocations for the sector.

Incentive Framework

There is a misconception that agriculture is a heavily subsidised and pampered sector. Scholars who have looked at the direct as well as indirect interventions of the government in the agricultural sector find that the net effect of all these interventions is equivalent to imposition of modest tax on agriculture rather than handling out large subsidies (Gulati & Sharma 1992). Others have pointed out that subsidies categorised as agricultural often reach manufacturers of inputs or meet the costs of employing expensive government bureaucrats (Tyagi, 1991). Terms of trade for agriculture which can be taken as a rough indicator of the incentive framework for agriculture and which remained at the level of

100 or above during the period mid-sixties to mid-seventies - have been below the level of 90 for all the years after 1976-77. Liberalisation implies freeing of domestic input and output markets and permitting exports and imports in response to the changing demand and supply conditions. Agriculture is still subject to numerous restrictions which would have to be progressively relaxed to improve the incentive framework for agriculture. The green revolution areas could give a lead in making agriculture a thriving industry dispensing with the crutches of subsidies. It would be important to see that their enthusiasm and drive are not curbed through controls and restrictions which are a legacy of the past but have become irrelevant in the emerging situation. If the four policy areas indicated above get the emphasis they deserve in our anti-poverty strategy, there is every reason to hope that the resulting agricultural growth in the coming years would be fast enough to help these areas and their poor as well as to sustain growth of the economy as a whole at an acceptable rate.

Conclusion

The anti-poverty strategy pursued so far has helped the poor mainly in the form of relief provided during periods of distress and schemes for giving a modest quantity of off-season employment. Despite "socialistic" planning, the policies to tackle the problem of poverty at the source have done little to remove the factors giving rise to poverty in the first instance. These factors are likely to acquire further strength and spread as liberalisation and deregulation open up the mainstream economy to market forces operating much more freely than now. In the emerging context, the anti-poverty strategy would have to focus its policies and programmes on building up the environs and the resource bases of the poor with a view to making them viable and self-reliant. There are large parts of Indian agriculture which provide scope for such a strategy. More hopefully, the recent growth experiences in agriculture seem to indicate that dispersed local foci of growth are emerging in many parts of agriculture which have remained stagnant so far. Thus, the conditions appear to be profitious for launching the next phase in the anti-poverty strategy though its achievements would depend on a number of imponderables including the pace and quality of the growth in the economy resulting from liberalisation.

NOTES

1. The statistics given in this paragraph are from *Agricultural Statistics at a Glance*, March, 1993 (Government of India)
2. The Statistics given in this paragraph are from *Economic Survey*, 1993-94, Government of India.
3. This chapter shares some portion with its companion study "Agriculture and Liberalisation: Some Implications for Development Policies" published separately (Rao, 1994).

2

HOW SUSTAINABLE IS OUR FOOD SECURITY ?

NIRA RAMACHANDRAN

Attaining of self-sufficiency in food production within two decades is an achievement that merits recognition and a justifiable sense of national pride, yet the goal of food for all still eludes our grasp. India, like most developing countries, cannot lay claim to having achieved food security. Despite concerted efforts at eliminating hunger, elaborate welfare schemes such as food for work, EAS, JRY, NRY and an extensive public distribution system, India's foothold on the ladder to food security remains a tenuous one. With the advent of the New Economic Policy and the globalisation of the economy, macro-level policy changes and their concomitant impacts down to grass-root level are inevitable. In this radically altered scenario, with its emphasis on withdrawing agricultural subsidies, and its known antipathy to welfare schemes, the goal of achieving food security for all becomes even more nebulous. Achieving sustainable food security in this context would necessitate rethinking issues, policies and methodology.

An attempt is made in this chapter to review existing food policies, action plans, and international aid and its impact on food security in the context of sustainability.

'Food Security' has been variously defined. The World Bank's definition of 'access by all people at all times to enough food for an active and healthy life' (World Bank, 1986) is a widely accepted one. It further brings in the concepts of 'chronic food insecurity' defined as a continuously inadequate diet caused by the inability to acquire food and 'transitory food insecurity' as a temporary decline in a household's access to enough food. The latter would imply a sudden shortfall of food as in the case of drought, floods or other natural or man made calamities and necessitate emergency measures such as rushing in food supplies. The former is what directly concerns us here and would involve long term strategies for achieving sustainable food security both at the macro and the micro level including increasing agricultural production, employment generation, infrastructure improvement, reduction of regional disparities, etc.

The FAO Committee on World Food Security, Council and Conference, 1983 emphasized three basic aims of food security at the Global level which could quite easily translate into national level objectives. They are ensuring production of adequate food supplies, maximising stability in the flow of supplies, and securing access to available supplies on the part of those who need them or in other words, production, availability and access.

Viewed from another angle, food security is an outcome (the object of the policy is to make people food secure), but it is more importantly an approach to development thinking. It is an organising principle. Effective food security analysis should direct the government to put in place those policies, investments and institution building efforts which are consistent with long term reduction of food insecurity (Hindle, 1990).

Dearden and Cassidy (1990) state that food insecurity is the most fundamental manifestation of absolute poverty. It is a less nebulous concept than poverty and it emphasizes more clearly the importance in understanding poverty, of perceived and actual risks of going hungry i.e. of vulnerability. Thus a food security approach to development planning can be more effective in two ways. First, food security indicators such as amount consumed or nutritional status reflect geographical, intra-household and inter-temporal variations in the prices and accessibility of food better than the standard per capita income estimates, and as poor people spend a high proportion of their income on food, using food security yardsticks would lessen the risk of overlooking the poor. Second, a focus on food security would lead more directly than conventional approaches towards the key economic and political factors, relationships and processes which make poor people vulnerable and which efforts to assist them must take into account. Also a food security perspective is less likely to overlook the indirect impact on the poor of macro level policies such as the effect of exchange rate devaluation and trade liberalisation on food production and consumption incentives

Based on the definitions authored above, it is evident that food security viewed as an approach to development planning may well form an innovative and effective tool for the planner. The level of food security existing in a country, however, is a complex of interactions operating at different levels from the macro to the micro or household level. The components of the system would include international trade and macro policies, the agricultural sector, the market economy, consumption patterns, and the micro economy or household incomes, urban rural differentiation, gender issues, etc.

Thus assessing the level of food security and its implication in terms of sustainability would involve a critical assessment of three major aspects : food production, assured supply and access to food.

Food Production

The production of foodgrains in the country underwent a radical change from the late sixties onwards. Prior to 1967-68, India was heavily dependent upon large-scale food imports. On an average, between 1946 to 1976, about four million tonnes of foodgrain were imported per annum. The annual gap between supply and demand of food in the period from the early sixties to the mid seventies was about 5.1 million tonnes

The advent of the Green revolution in the mid sixties was at a time when the availability of further land for agriculture had more or less reached its limits, the agricultural scenario changed from one of land reclamation to one heavily dependent on modern inputs. The introduction of HYVs which are heavily water and fertilizer dependent brought in a rapid increase in irrigation facilities, as can be seen from Table 2.1.

TABLE 2.1 : Irrigation Facilities

	1965-66	1973-74
Private Tube wells	100,000	820,000
State Tube wells	12,400	20,000
Pumping Sets	513,000	2,000,000

Source: Etinne, 1977.

The wheat areas of the north-west comprising the states of Punjab, Haryana and Western U.P. which already possessed an extensive canal irrigation system, displayed spectacular results with total wheat production increasing from 12 million tonnes in 1964-65 to 26 million tonnes in 1971-72. Together with the adoption of Mexican wheat, this region also absorbed a large portion of the new inputs especially tube wells and chemical fertilizers. In 1973-74, e.g, the consumption of nitrogen fertilizers was 56 kg/ha. in the Punjab, compared to 4.5 kg in Bihar or 6.5 kg in Maharashtra (Etinne, 1977).

With rice, however, no major breakthrough was achieved. The early varieties of rice including the IR-8 proved ill adapted. The diversity of conditions (rain fed and irrigated) and micro climates under which rice is grown, make the introduction of new varieties more complex than in the case of wheat. Besides monsoon crops are more vulnerable to the twin incidence of pests and disease. Thus while the production of wheat more than doubled in the period from the mid sixties to the early seventies, rice production during the same period recorded an increase of only four million tonnes (from 39 million tonnes in 1964-65 to 43 million tonnes in 1971-72).

Other major foodgrains like jowar and bajra did not register any visible impact mainly because they are concentrated in the non-irrigated, erratic-rainfall areas of the Deccan where high water and fertilizer-demanding varieties are not viable.

While the growth rate in agricultural production between 1964-65 and 1970-71 was 3.28 per cent per annum compared to 2.55 per cent for the proceeding fifteen years, it became extremely prone to fluctuation.

The two bad monsoons of 1972 and 1974, resulted in a fall of output to pre 1970-71 levels, with 1974-75 recording an output of only 100 million tonnes. Productivity of wheat in the green revolution areas began to level off. A variety of factors may be responsible for this. Seeds were not renewed every four to five years as required, power shortages affected irrigation adversely, and as the prices of imported fertilizers registered a steep hike, fertilizer consumption began to decline. In fact, between 1973-74 and 1974-75, the consumption of chemical fertilizers registered a decline of 300,000 tonnes. While fertilizer consumption rose again in 1975-76, it remained about 3 per cent below 1973-74 figures.

The experience of the eighties, however, shows an improvement in the growth rate of foodgrains when compared with the first decade of the green revolution. Crops such as rice and pulses whose growth rates had fallen below those recorded in the pre-green revolution period, showed higher growth rates (Rao,1994). Another positive aspect is that the eastern states of Assam, Bihar, Orissa, West Bengal and Madhya Pradesh where poverty is widespread and the growth of foodgrain output had slowed down in the seventies, have performed comparably or even higher than the all India average.

However, sharp fluctuations in agricultural output still persist. This can be explained in terms of several factors. Firstly, agricultural output in the post green-revolution period is highly dependent on yield, rather than on the more stable component of area. Thus in a year where rainfall is adequate and the water table favourable, yields are pushed up significantly and more area is allocated to foodgrains, while in adverse climatic conditions, the reverse situation holds (Rao,1987). Secondly, while 30 per cent of the country's cultivated area is under irrigation, a large portion of this is dependent on tanks and wells which are themselves sensitive to rainfall. Thirdly, concentration of output growth in limited pockets also tends to accentuate fluctuations in output.

As regards the future of foodgrain production in the country, stress must be laid on improving yields per crop and multi-cropping. Plan achievements with respect to increases in gross cropped area through multiple cropping have fallen short of expectations. This is largely due to the fact that potential areas for multi-cropping which have an abundance of labour and a predominance of small farmers like the eastern gangetic belt, lack sufficient supply of water, while the capital-intensive nature of the new technology makes it more suited to large farmers who are unwilling to employ the extra labour necessary for multiple cropping.

Thus it is obvious that water management will play a pivotal role in evolving a sustainable food production strategy. The development of irrigation from assured sources such as major and medium irrigation projects, the exploitation of ground water in high rainfall regions such as the eastern gangetic belt where the water table is favourable and less sensitive to rainfall, the provision of necessary incentives for private exploration of ground water, and the evolving of techniques for water harvesting and moisture conservation are likely to have the greatest impact in stabilizing the foodgrain output and ensuring a sustainable supply of food.

According to rough estimates it should be possible to reach a maximum net irrigated area of 70 million hectares, which with multiple cropping could be raised to 107 million hectares. Out of the latter, 72 million hectares would be irrigated through surface water sources, the remainder through ground water (GOI,1976).

Irrigated area devoted to cereals could reach 55 million hectares, of which 37 million hectares could be double cropped with a combination of wheat and rice, wheat and maize, rice and rice. (Etinne, 1977). Taking an average yield of 2000 kg. per hectare of rice or other cereal, production would total about 184 million tonnes of grain. (Table 2.2)

Unirrigated areas devoted to cereals and pulses (often jowar and bajra) would cover at least 60 million hectares.

TABLE 2.2 : Production and Productivity of Irrigated and Unirrigated Area

Irrigated Area		
37 million hectares (double cropped)	yield 2000 kg per hectare	148 million tonnes
18 million hectares (single cropped)	yield 2000 kg per hectare	36 million tonnes
Unirrigated Area		
40 million hectares	yield 500 kg per hectare	20 million tonnes
10 million hectares	yield 1000 kg per hectare	10 million tonnes
10 million hectares	yield 1500 kg per hectare	15 million tonnes
		229 million tonnes

Source : Etinne,1977.

In round figures, the estimated output could reach about 230 million tonnes by the year 2000. However, while the growth rate of foodgrain production (3.2 per cent) has so far exceeded the growth rate of population (2.5 per cent), food supply has been unable to meet the demand for food because of the increase in per capita consumption. It is further estimated that the demand for foodgrains is likely to grow at a rate of 3.5 to 4 per cent compared with the historical foodgrain growth rate of 2.9 per cent recorded by it during 1949-50 to 1989-90 (Bhalla,1993). With a population base of 844 million and the projected increase in demand for food, the problem of food supply now begins to assume even larger dimensions.

Assured Supply

Despite the break-through in the production of foodgrains and the marginal surpluses achieved in good agricultural years, ensuring a measure of food security to so large and economically disparate a population, distributed over so vast and diverse a country remains a formidable problem.

While total food output has increased substantially, per capita food output has not increased dramatically. Also, the increase in food production has led to reduction of imports and large buffer stocks, so that net aggregate consumption of food per head has remained remarkably constant for the last forty years (Dreze and Sen, 1989)

In a situation where supplies are less than the market demand, distribution of the overall short supplies can be carried out either through market channels or through controls or through a judicious combination of both (Chopra, 1988). Till the Bengal Famine of 1943, the distribution of foodgrains was left entirely to private traders. While in normal times, the market performed its functions efficiently, the tendency to hoard and raise prices, thereby creating artificial scarcity during years of crop failure, could not be ignored by the government. Thus the Foodgrains Policy Committee under the Chairmanship of Sir Theodore Gregory was set up in 1943 which recommended rationing to increase available supplies and statutory price control to check rising prices. The Committee's recommendations were broadly adopted and the emerging food policy of the country was based on them.

The Indian government has broadly adopted a mixed dual market arrangement of private trade and the public distribution system working side by side. On an average, about 9 to 15 percent of the total foodgrain production is channelised through the public distribution system, via a network of fair price shops (FPS). As on March 1992, there existed over 4 lakh FPS in the country, 3.05 lakh is rural areas and 0.94 lakh in urban areas. On an average, one fair price shop covers a population of about 2000 (Bhalla, 1993).

The bulk of the foodgrains distributed through the PDS consists of rice and wheat, though in a few states, some coarse cereals are also distributed. Over the forty year period from 1951 to 1992, the distribution of food grains has roughly trebled rising from about 8 million tonnes in 1951 to 22 million tonnes in 1992. Up to the seventies, wheat was the major foodgrain for distribution, but from the eighties onwards, nearly equal quantities of rice and wheat have been distributed (Table 2.3).

TABLE 2.3 : All India Distribution of Foodgrains Through PDS

Year	Production of Foodgrains (million tonnes)	Public Distribution ('000 tonnes) Rice	Wheat	Total
1951	51			7865
1961	82	950	2983	3977
1962	83	1134	3221	4365
1963	80	1361	3816	5178
1964	81	1859	6785	8665
1965	89	3586	5939	10079
1966	72	4131	8142	14085
1967	74	3010	7366	13166
1968	95	3287	5755	10221
1969	94	3405	5195	9385
1970	99	3050	5347	8841
1971	108	3230	4455	7816
1972	105	3688	7413	11396
1973	97	3206	7130	11414
1974	105	3753	3669	10790
1975	100	3211	7545	11253
1976	121	3643	5015	9174
1977	111	4589	6396	11729
1978	126	3328	6855	10183
1979	132	4049	7493	11663
1980	110	6057	8819	14993
1981	129	6402	6427	13014
1982	133	7500	7168	14768
1983	129	7853	8121	16206
1984	152	6739	6504	13326
1985	146	7231	8477	15799
1986	150	8460	8504	17269
1987	143	9825	8784	18700
1988	140	9695	8719	18580
1989	170	8566	7253	15903
1990	176	8659	6568	15325
1991	176	9610	9500	19100
1992	167	10360	10360	21720

Source : Bhalla, (1993)

Production figures relate to the agricultural year July-June :1951 figures correspond to the production of 1950-51.

The pattern of distribution is a fluctuating one with large amounts being distributed during lean years with a considerable drop in years when market prices are low. However, monthly variations are not very high. Regional variations in off take are considerable ranging from only

4,29,000 tonnes for Orissa to 1,736,000 tonnes for Kerala. The four states of Andhra Pradesh, Kerala, Maharashtra and West Bengal which have developed an efficient distribution network to distribute a large proportion of the procured foodgrain. Unfortunately, the poorest states like Bihar, M.P. and Orissa account for only a small proportion of the available foodgrains.

The establishment of the Public Distribution System (PDS) has no doubt contributed to relieving the misery faced in distress situations to a considerable extent. No famines of the Bengal magnitude have recurred after the food policy of 1943 was implemented. The role of the PDS as a price stabilizer particularly during crisis situations has been quite remarkable especially in comparison with the pre-independence period, for example, the drought of 1987-88 which led to a considerable decline in food production, resulted in an increase in foodgrain prices of less than ten per cent. This was largely due to the large scale sale of food through the PDS (Dreze and Sen, *op cit*). However, the efficacy of the system in providing food security needs further analysis. Table 2.4 reveals that the per capita distribution of foodgrains through the PDS ranges from a mere 7 kg per year in U.P. to 62 kg per annum in Kerala. Assuming a minimum foodgrain requirement of 1/2 a kg. per capita per day, the total supply of foodgrains through the PDS in states like U.P. would amount to 31/2 days of assured food in the year.

TABLE 2.4 : Per Capita Distribution of Foodgrains through PDS, 1984-88

STATE	Per Capita Distribution (kg. per year)
Punjab	9.459
Haryana	10.040
Maharashtra	22.701
Gujarat	21.802
West Bengal	32.749
Tamil Nadu	31.075
Karnataka	23.167
Andhra Pradesh	23.286
Kerala	61.893
Rajasthan	18.587
Uttar Pradesh	7.175
Madhya Pradesh	9.192
Orissa	13.340
Bihar	9.954
All India	21.739

Source : Mooij, 1994.

PDS foodgrains are not distributed to individuals but to families holding ration cards. Taking the example of Karnataka in 1990-91, there were 78,40,154 ration cards. If the foodgrains are shared equally among all these families, each family would receive 105 kgs per year, that is less than 9 kgs per month. An average household in Karnataka consists of 5.2 members. That means that an average household with a ration card would receive 1.75 kg foodgrains per person per month through the rationing system (Mooij, 1994). It is only in a model state like Kerala where the public distribution system is well organised and covers virtually the entire population, that foodgrain distribution meets about 30 per cent of the requirement or in terms of indirect financial benefit, provides a subsidy of about approximately Rs 40 per month for an average household (Mooij, 1994). This also tends to influence the open market price.

The impact of the public distribution system as a check on open market foodgrain prices and as a safety net for the weaker sections of society, is minimal in most other states, particularly where the per capita distribution is low and social and economic inequalities are more pronounced.However, if the Kerala PDS is taken as a model, with 30 per cent of the foodgrain supply through the PDS being accepted as a national norm, there would be an annual requirement of 46 million tonnes of foodgrain for distribution through the PDS, which is roughly about three times the amount distributed in 1990. This would require an increase in annual food subsidy from Rs. 2,800 crore to about Rs 8500 crore. While variations in the employment situation, consumption levels, percentage of the population below the poverty line, etc. between states are large and some states would not require the PDS to supply 30 per cent of their foodgrain requirement, other states might require considerably more. However, so large an expansion in the PDS is unlikely to take place.

A study by Reddy and Selvaraju (1992) based on NSS data, analyses the distribution pattern of the two staples wheat and rice through the PDS among different classes of consumers (based on monthly per capita expenditure). It reveals that food subsidy accruing to the higher income classes is higher than that accruing to the poor. This disparity is not merely confined to the rich and the poor, but also exists, and is widening between the urban poor and the rural poor. Taking the distribution pattern of wheat, it is clear that the bottom 40 per cent of the households (according to monthly per capita expenditure) account for 46.24 per cent of PDS users, but purchase only 24.31 per cent of total PDS supplies of wheat in rural areas. In urban areas, the picture is slightly better, with the lowest 40 per cent expenditure class accounting for 48 per cent of PDS users and consuming 35 per cent of total PDS wheat. Where rice is concerned, the distribution is more balanced with, the bottom 40 per cent of rural households accounting for 51 per cent of PDS users and purchasing 40 per cent of PDS rice, while the corresponding urban households account for 49 per cent of the users and 45 per cent of the purchases.

On the other hand, the top 40 per cent of the households (i.e. the highest income class) account for 32 per cent of the users and 62 per cent of the wheat purchases in rural areas, and 30 per cent of the users and 42 per cent of the wheat in urban areas.

In the case of rice, the figures are 30 per cent of the users and 38 percent of the purchase in rural areas, and 27 per cent of users with 27 per cent of purchases (of total PDS supplies) in urban areas (Table 2.5).

TABLE 2.5 : Percentage Distribution of PDS Users and Supplies

	WHEAT				RICE			
	RURAL		URBAN		RURAL		URBAN	
% of households according to per capita monthly expenditure	Users	Supplies	Users	Supplies	Users	Supplies	Users	Supplies
00-10	12.71	4.44	10.78	6.14	14.9	6.67	12.97	7.91
10-20	10.50	7.99	11.64	13.26	11.4	8.34	10.51	11.29
20-40	23.66	11.88	25.57	15.96	24.2	25.24	25.34	25.87
40-60	21.09	13.76	21.80	22.98	19.6	21.45	23.99	27.52
60-80	17.14	16.87	17.12	20.79	18.3	23.74	16.35	17.38
80-90	9.03	19.42	7.81	-	6.82	9.09	6.75	
90-100	5.87	25.64	5.28	20.87	4.49	5.47	4.09	10.03
Total	100.00	100.00	100.00	100.00	100.00	100.00	100.00	100.00

Source : Reddy and Selvaraju, 1992.

Other constraints to the effective functioning of the PDS which can be more easily tackled are :

The Viability of Ration Shops

As the organisation of the Public Distribution System is carried out through fair price shops, the economic viability of these shops is relevant to the efficient functioning of the system as well as a curb on malpractices such as the diversion of fair priced commodities to the open market. Mooij's study of Karnataka (Mooij, 1994) reveals that in 1990-91, only 2 per cent of the 16,980 fair price shops were run by the government, the rest were managed by co-operative societies and private individuals. On an average, each fair price shop sold 48,400 kgs. of foodgrains (1990-91) i.e. just over 4000 kgs. per month. The profit margin being fixed at 10 rupees per 100 kgs. meant an average monthly income of only Rs. 400. Additional sources of income from the sale of sugar which has a fixed profit of Rs. 350 per 100 Kgs. and gunny bags at a rate Rs. 7 per piece, result in a total monthly gross income of Rs. 800 only. With an average expenditure on rent, labour, travel to and from warehouses, electricity, stationery, tips and bribes totalling to about Rs. 200 per month, the net income amounts to only Rs. 600 per month.

Compared to these small earnings, the investment required by fair price shop owners comes to at least Rs. 15,000 and this amount is required in a lump sum, as the entire monthly allotment must be lifted at once.

Another problem is that, particularly in rural areas, the stock in the fair price shop is usually sold out within a few days, so that the trader has to wait for nearly one month before re-investing his earnings. Besides, the Food and Civil Supplies Department does not encourage fair price shops owners to have their own private business. The prevalence of illegal sales under such conditions is not surprising. If distribution is organised on a weekly basis, following the Kerala pattern, the invested capital would be continuously utilized, and smaller amounts of cash would be required at a time.

From the purchaser's point of view too, a weekly system of allotment would be more beneficial, as many of the really poor families cannot afford to purchase their whole entitlement in the few days when stock is available.

The Role of Public Awareness

The people can exercise an effective check and control on the functioning of the Public Distribution System as is evident from the example of Kerala. The existence of a large number of grassroot level organisations provide several fora for consumers' complaints, and complaints by card holders are usually taken seriously as there is always the danger of local organisations pursuing the matter with higher officials. Thus greater emphasis on consumer awareness, rather than official PDS vigilance committees may be more effective in streamlining the food distribution system.

The PDS is often cited as a safety net for the poor in view of the structural adjustment policies which have had and will have negative effects on the poorest strata of society. Under the Dunkel proposals, however, provisions regarding the 'supply of food to the poor' are subject to "clearly defined criteria related to nutritional objectives" which will be fixed by agencies like the IMF in the name of free trade (Thomas *et al.*, 1994), thus undermining the food security systems of the poor in many countries (Shiva, 1993).

The Dunkel proposal also requires that the PDS be maintained through purchase and sale at market price only, which effectively debars the government from interfering with the price mechanism. In times of shortages, this can jeopardise the country's efforts to procure and stock food and release it for consumption at a subsidised rate (Thomas *et al.*, 1994).

However, the government has issued frequent statements assuring the continuance of food subsidy and the strengthening of the PDS. The recent (1991) attempt at revamping of the PDS by selecting 1700 disadvantaged blocks (out of a total of 5,100 blocks) for special attention is a case in point. But, while the allocation of food to these blocks has been increased and a number of new fair price shops have been opened, the total amount of food in the PDS system has not been increased, and the beneficiaries of the new system are only gaining at the disadvantage of the relatively developed areas. How far this new approach to the PDS will succeed remains to be seen.

Buffer Stocks

The food security system of the country rests on the building up and maintenance of buffer stocks. In a country, where agricultural production is still largely monsoon-dependent and large scale year to year fluctuations persist, the options for providing a measure of food security are limited to large scale food imports or maintaining a buffer stock. Since India has chosen the path of self-reliance, the maintenance of a massive buffer stock becomes inevitable involving a huge cost to the exchequer. The validity of this policy has been criticised by many scholars and alternatives have been suggested to reduce stocks without seriously endangering food security.

The objectives of a buffer stock are three fold :

1. to cater for the lean years when a minimum level of consumption of food must be provided;
2. to ensure a continuous supply of foodgrain through the PDS throughout the year; and
3. to give price support to the farmer in a bumper crop year.

Grain surplus countries have a buffer stock for the sake of the producer, i.e. to protect his income by exporting. In deficit countries, it is necessary to protect the consumer's interest, at the same time not giving up the producer's interest in order to sustain the pace of production (Chopra,1988). Buffer stocks are built up by absorbing the excess production of a good crop year, or by setting aside a specified quantity out of imports every year, to be released during years of bad crop failures

The need for such reserves was stressed by various food policy committees appointed by the Government of India from time to time. The Foodgrain Policy Committee of 1943 recommended the creation of a central foodgrain reserve of not less than five lakh tonnes. By 1957, an emergency reserve stock of at least 2 million tonnes was mooted. The Foodgrains Policy Committee of 1966 suggested building up a stock of 4 million tonnes with a view to achieving inter-seasonal stability in supplies together with the stabilization of prices. Originally, the buffer stock was to be created out of imported grain. It was only with the Green revolution in the late sixties that the possibility of a buffer stock of indigenous grain began to take shape. The total quantum of stocks held currently is based on the recommendations of the Technical Group set up in 1975. After taking into account variations in food production from 1960-61 to 1975-76, and the gap between procurement and requirements under the PDS in different years, the Group recommended the creation of a buffer stock of 12 million tonnes. This recommendation was accepted by the government (Bhalla,1993).

This buffer stock of 12 million tonnes will be in addition to the operational stock required to maintain the Public Distribution System. On the basis of a normal level of 12 to 13 million tonnes of public distribution in a year, the size of the operational stock has been estimated for different dates, i.e. on 1 April at the beginning of the *rabi* season as 3.5 to 3.8 million tonnes, (consisting of 9 months requirements in rice and 3 in wheat) which may be adequate to take care of any delays in harvesting, marketing, procurement and transport of the new wheat crop, harvesting of which commences in mid April and the rice crop which is harvested in October. On 1 November at the beginning of the *kharif* season the operational stock requirements are estimated as 4.8 to 5.2 million tonnes

In poor crop years, the buffer stock will have to draw down to meet the needs of the PDS. However, that the buffer stock must not fall below 5 million tonnes has been recommended, with simultaneous replenishment of the stock being undertaken to take advantage of seasonal low prices in the world market.

With a buffer stock of 12 million tonnes, the total stocks with the government are likely to reach around 21 million tonnes during the peak season, thus involving a total storage capacity requirement of 23 million tonnes. The financial implications of this size of buffer stock were estimated by the group in December 1976 as Rs. 1715 crores (this investment had largely been made) with an additional investment of Rs. 360 crores for increasing storage capacity and a recurring maintenance cost of Rs. 258 crores per annum or nearly 15 per cent of the purchase price. In 1992-93, the food subsidy amounted to Rs. 2800 crores and is expected to rise to Rs. 3000 crores during 1993-94.

One of the problems with maintaining a buffer stock is that under Indian climatic and storage conditions, a 'turnover' of at least once a year is necessary for the health of the grain. This would imply some sort of compulsory or necessary sales on a regular basis through the Public Distribution System even in a market of plenty. Under the current situation of high growth rates in food production, together with the government's commitment to giving support prices, (almost 90 per cent of the public sector procurement of grain being obtained through price support), there can arise a situation when the grain procured in a particular year may far exceed the limits of the buffer stock and the operational stock requirements.

Two suggestions have been put forward to deal with such a situation (Chopra, 1988).

1. A free movement of grain may be allowed to give some relief in the matter of storage, but this would necessarily be coupled with a price support assurance, and will result in a set back to the off take of already stored grain.
2. Excess foodgrains in the buffer stock may be issued at highly subsidised rates to the weaker and vulnerable sections of the

population particularly in the tribal and backward areas, or distribution through the 'food for work' programme may be considered. As the holding cost of buffer stock grain has risen from Rs. 20 per quintal in 1976 to Rs 43 in 1984-85, such measures would serve the dual purpose of meeting both social and economic objectives.

The sustainability of the country's policy of maintaining such large buffer stocks has now to be reconsidered. Several important changes have taken place at both the national and international level which have a bearing on buffer stock management (Bhalla, 1993)

1. Domestic foodgrain production now plays the dominant role in the building up of buffer stocks.
2. The declining world prices of wheat and rice may soon be reversed following the withdrawal of agricultural subsidies after the signing of the GATT agreement.
3. The cost of maintaining buffer stocks has risen considerably, from an estimated maintenance cost of 15 per cent per annum over the purchase cost (1975) the actual carrying cost of the food buffer in 1992 was about 23 per cent of the purchase price. (GOI,1993)

A more sustainable strategy for buffer stock management in view of the above mentioned charges should hinge on the following suggestions put forward by Bhalla.

1. A buffer stock of 10-12 million tonnes a year should be carried. This would suffice to meet the requirements of the PDS in times of scarcity with marginal imports being resorted to for augmenting stocks during scarcity and controlling domestic prices.
2. The Food Corporation of India should enter into the international future markets with a view to reducing the buffer stocks and cutting down costs and subsidies. This would also help to curtail speculative stocks held by the traders during shortages.
3. Regional and international co-operation should play a major role in providing food security. New international initiatives like the IMFs Food Financing Facility which provides foreign exchange for food imports, the 1980 Food Aid Convention which has increased the annual food aid commitment to 7.6 million tonnes compared with 4.2 million under the earlier 1971 convention, the International Emergency Food Reserves of 0.5 million tonnes during 1981, the

Food Security Assistance Scheme of the FAO under which nearly $ 50 million have been pledged and the Global Information and Early Warning system of the FAO are all measures in the right direction, but as yet highly inadequate. Regional cooperation under SAARC and ASEAN to develop food security programmes could provide a less expensive option. A beginning has been made with the Asian Emergency Food Reserve under which a stock of 50,000 tonnes of rice is to be maintained.

International Trade in Food

The carrying of large buffer stocks and/or foodgrain imports are the two most common methods of stabilising the supply of food in a country. There is an obvious trade off between the two. While carrying large stocks is more costly than earmarking a part of foreign exchange reserves for food imports, scarce foreign exchange earnings and the long term depressing effects of food imports on domestic food production, make self-sufficiency a more reliable option.

In the period immediately before Second World War, India was importing about 5.9 million tonnes of foodgrain annually. This was largely in the form of rice from Burma. With the disruption in production during the war, food imports fell to just about 1.16 million tonnes (1948-52). This drying up of South Asian supplies, especially Burma, has been pinpointed as one of the causes of the Bengal famine of 1943 (Subramaniam, 1994). With the signing of the first PL-480 agreement of 1956, the scene changed, and India become heavily dependent on wheat imports which reached a high of 14.23 million tonnes in the two drought years of 1965-66 and 1966-67.

The negative impacts of such large-scale food imports can be seen in the downward trends in area and production of wheat during the peak import years. While the area under wheat had been continually rising from 9.5 million hectares in 1951-52 to 13.5 million hectares in 1956-57, i.e. a 43 per cent increase in five years, with the arrivals of large shipments of wheat during 1956-57, the acreage under wheat remained static during the Second Plan period, and actually declined to 12.57 million hectares in 1965-66. Domestic output of wheat which accounted for 74 per cent of the total supplies in 1956-57 fell to 62 per cent in 1964-65 and further to 54 per cent in 1965-66 (Shenoy u.d.).

Table 2.6 brings out the trends in cereal production vis-a-vis imports from 1948-52 to 1982-86. The bumper wheat production in 1967-68 and the increasing production in the subsequent years enabled the government to build up bigger stocks which helped the country through several periods of crisis without recourse to the international market on a large scale, a case in point, being the three successive years of drought during 1986-88.

TABLE 2.6 : Cereal Production and Trade : 1948-52 to 1982 -86

(in Million Tonnes)

Period	Production	Import	Export	Net Availability
1948-52	56.06	1.16	0.01	57.21
1961-65	87.55	5.38	negligible	92.93
1970-74	103.9	3.3	0.2	107.0
1976-80	133.9	1.9	0.5	135.3
1982-86	159.8	1.7	0.4	161.1
1988-92	133.14	0.78	?	134.16

Source : (Bhalla, 1993a)

However, in the present scenario of liberalisation of the domestic economy and increasing integration with the global economy, the question of self-sufficiency in food production versus increasing involvement in international trade is once again being opened. India's policy of total self-reliance and isolation from world markets is no longer realistic. Before delving deeper into the pros and cons of entering the world food market, one must accept the premise, that for a country of India's dimensions, basic food security will have to be provided through domestic production (Bhalla, 1993a). This is because of two reasons. Firstly, the total domestic demand in, say, one cereal, rice, is about 65 million tonnes, while the total annual world trade in rice is only 10 to 15 million tonnes per annum, so that even a mere 10 per cent shortage amounts to nearly three-fifths of the total world trade. Even a signal for imports of this magnitude can cause world market prices to soar. Secondly, in a country where the major part of the population is dependent on the agricultural sector, and 80 per cent of total agricultural production consists of foodgrains, fully exploiting domestic production of food would not only provide productive employment to the agricultural work force, but also ensure cheap food, the main wage good in the economy.

It is now clear that the government plans to liberalise international trade in foodgrain allowing domestic prices to reach international levels. At present, Indian prices for wheat are roughly 10 per cent less, for rice 30 per cent less and 10 per cent more for cereals and pulses. The GATT agreement is likely to push up the international relative price of wheat and coarse grains by 5 per cent, while bringing down rice prices by a similar amount (Brando and Marlin, 1993). A rise in domestic relative prices of foodgrain by about 15 to 20 per cent may be envisaged in the post GATT scenario, which would squeeze the foodgrain consumption of the poor, leaving the rich relatively unaffected. In this case, export surpluses of about 10 to 15 million tonnes may be possible in 2000 AD. While the effect of exporting food on domestic price and availability is direct and obvious, similar results would occur even if other non-food cash crop exports were encouraged in so far as these imply a shift in acreage (J.M., 1994). The Inter Ministerial Working Group's[1] estimates of foodgrain requirements suggest that there is already a surplus production of 20 million tonnes, which will increase over time, if production increases faster than population. The World Bank projects foodgrain demand in 2000 to 205 million tonnes which implies an exportable surplus of around 17 million tonnes, and thus recommends diversification of agricultural production and the opening up of agriculture to international trade. (World Bank, 1991).

The implications of agricultural exports on the food security of the country can be envisaged from the experience of other countries like Ghana, Nigeria, Chile, Peru and Mexico which enhanced production for exports at the cost of food self-sufficiency under the structural adjustment programmes with a resulting increase in hunger and malnutrition among the poor.

A recent study by the International Institute for Applied Systems Analysis, Luxembourg points out that by the year 2000, there would be 5.6 per cent more hungry people in India than there would be without liberalisation. The amount of agricultural produce consumed by the people would be reduced by 26.2 per cent (Thomas, *et al.*, 1994).

Access to Food

Over the last four decades, the country's foodgrain production has almost trebled rising from 51 million tonnes in 1950-51 to 170 million tonnes in 1988-89. While the rate of growth of food has outstripped the rate of growth of population, and in the, words of the Inter Ministerial Working Group constituted to assess total domestic requirement of food by the year 2000, the total per capita availability of energy, proteins and fat from indigenous production now exceeds the nutritional requirements of the entire population, in terms of attaining the objective of ensuring food security for every individual, we still have far to go. Even today, about 40% of the country's population or 300 million people still live in poverty with hunger as an accepted part of their existence.

How far the country has succeeded in attaining the objective of increasing physical and economic access to food since Independence needs to be analyzed, before prescriptions can be given for a future course of action. India has had a long history of famines with the last major one where 1.5 million people lost their lives occurring in 1943 in Bengal. To the credit of the country, no such large scale starvation has recurred since that time. In several years during the post-independence period, when the domestic production of foodgrain fell sharply, such as in 1955,1966-67,1973-75, 1979 and 1987, conditions were ripe for a famine, but each time the disaster was successfully averted. In this context, Tyagi (1990) quotes from Reutligner (1978), 'the Government of India was able to manage, by and large, this difficult situation by administrative means, mobilisation of extra grain supplies from abroad, and thereby avoid widespread catastrophic famine.'

Physical access to food can best be measured in terms of per capita availability of foodgrains. (Table 2.7). Although, there have been fluctuations in the year to year per capita availability of food, the underlying trend has been one of increase. From an availability of 355 grams of foodgrain per capita per day in 1951 which amounted to 88.75 per cent of the basic requirement of 400 gms. per day, physical availability has risen to 476 gms. which is 119 per cent of the requirement. In fact, a higher per capita availability is likely if the netting factor is adjusted in the light of the fact that after the Green Revolution, the yield per hectare of all important foodgrains have gone up, so that seed should account for a much smaller proportion of the total production.[2]

TABLE 2.7 : Availability of Foodgrains

Year	Pop (in millions)	Net Availability Foodgrains (million tonnes)	Per capita Net Availability of Food grains Per Day (grams)
1951	363.2	52.3	394.9
1956	397.3	62.6	430.7
1961	442.4	75.7	468.7
1966	493.2	73.5	408.1
1971	551.3	94.3	468.8
1976	617.2	95.8	424.3
1981	688.5	114.2	454.8
1986	766.5	133.8	478.1
1991*	851.7	158.6	510.1
1993*	883.9	150.2	465.6

Production figures relate to the agricultural year July-June : 1951 figures correspond to the production of 1950-51.
* Provisional
Source : Directorate of Economics & Statistics, Department of Agriculture and Cooperation.

Economic access to food can be measured by assessing the proportion of per capita income required to buy a unit of food. If over a period of time, this proportion reduces, it can be assumed that access to food in economic terms has increased. In India, in the seventies, as much as 12.9 per cent of per capita income was required to buy a quintal of wheat. By 1980, only 7 per cent of per capita income was sufficient to purchase the same quantity. This proportion further dropped to 6.4 per cent during 1984.

However, intra-group differences based on type of employment, social class variations and urban or rural locale still persist. For targetting to be functional, these differences must be taken into account whether the PDS system is retained or whether it is replaced by food coupons or some other type of subsidy. Table 2.8 A and B bring out the variations in urban and rural areas between various social and employment groups. It can be seen that, on an average, rural households spend about 64 per cent of their monthly per capita expenditure on food items of which 26 per cent is expended on cereals. Urban households on an average spend 56 per cent of their monthly per capita expenditure on food, of which only 15 per cent is spent on cereals. In both rural and urban areas, it is the casual labourer (lowest income group) who spends the largest proportion of his total expenditure on food, as much as 67 per cent (of which 33 per cent is on cereals) in the case of agricultural labourers in rural areas, and 64 per cent (24 per cent on cereals) in the case of casual labourers in urban areas. Both in urban and rural areas, social class contrasts persist with the scheduled tribes expending the largest proportion of their income on food in rural areas, while in urban areas, the plight of the scheduled castes seems to be at par or even worse than that of the scheduled tribes. Both these social groups, however, also correspond with the lowest income/expenditure class.

TABLE 2.8A : Average Monthly Per Capita Expenditure on Food in Urban Areas

House-hold Type	House-hold Group	Total Monthly Per Capita Expenditure (in Rupees)	Expenditure on Food (in Rupees)	Expenditure on Food (% to total)	Expenditure on Cereals (in Rupees)	Expenditure on Cereals (% to total)
1. Self Employed	S.T.	214.22	128.58	60.02	38.82	18.12
	S.C.	179.56	109.48	60.97	37.25	20.73
	Other	230.39	134.21	58.25	36.31	15.76
	Total	225.29	131.87	58.53	36.45	16.18
2. Regular Wage earner	S.T.	220.06	127.25	57.83	37.36	16.98
	S.C.	211.71	122.94	58.07	36.73	17.37
	Others	299.96	159.10	53.04	37.90	12.64
	Total	286.18	153.48	53.63	37.74	13.19
3. Casual Labour	S.T.	135.04	88.96	65.88	36.98	27.38
	S.C.	143.94	92.06	63.96	35.74	24.83
	Others	154.36	98.60	63.88	35.44	22.96
	Total	150.51	94.34	64.01	35.62	23.67
4. Other House-holds	S.T.	230.52	134.40	58.22	33.58	14.57
	S.C.	206.78	125.21	60.55	27.62	13.36
	Others	289.09	165.83	57.36	36.95	12.78
	Total	278.47	160.45	57.52	35.98	12.90
5. All House-holds	S.T.	201.79	120.19	59.56	37.35	18.81
	S.C.	185.03	111.55	60.29	36.26	19.60
	Others	256.50	143.30	55.87	36.95	19.97
	Total	245.72	138.56	56.39	36.88	15.01

Source : NSS 43rd Round (July 1987- June 1988).

TABLE 2.8B : Average Monthly Per Capita Expenditure on Food in Rural Areas

Household Type	Household Group	Total Monthly Per Capita Expenditure (in Rupees)	Expenditure on Food (in Rupees)	Expenditure on Food (% to total)	Expenditure on Cereals (in Rupees)	Expenditure on Cereals (% to total)
1. Self-Employed in non-Agriculture	S.T.	135.96	87.97	64.70	41.71	30.68
	S.C.	144.09	93.14	64.64	41.23	28.61
	Others	171.99	108.95	63.35	42.07	24.46
	Total	165.48	105.23	63.59	41.91	25.33
2. Agricultural Labour	S.T.	106.50	73.30	68.83	39.68	37.26
	S.C	118.96	79.29	66.65	36.02	32.80
	Others	126.20	84.43	66.90	40.04	31.73
	Total	121.12	81.21	67.05	39.63	32.72
3. Other Labour	S.T.	114.86	75.41	65.65	35.91	31.26
	S.C.	133.68	87.28	65.29	38.66	28.92
	Others	155.12	98.71	63.63	39.23	25.29
	Total	143.78	92.40	64.26	38.60	26.85
4. Self-Employed in Agriculture	S.T.	130.62	87.60	67.06	44.60	34.18
	S.C.	144.57	94.41	65.30	43.89	30.36
	Others	178.77	113.53	63.51	43.08	24.10
	Total	170.40	108.95	63.94	43.32	25.92
5. Other Households	S.T.	184.33	119.28	64.71	42.06	22.82
	S.C.	187.07	108.58	58.04	39.14	20.92
	Others	220.27	131.04	59.49	42.61	19.34
	Total	213.71	127.32	59.58	42.11	19.70
6. All Households	S.T.	123.04	82.62	61.96	41.65	33.85
	S.C.	133.35	86.97	65.22	40.35	30.26
	Others	169.23	107.53	63.54	42.02	24.83
	Total	157.66	101.06	64.10	41.67	26.43

Source : NSS 43rd Round (July 1987-June 1988).

Yet another way of measuring the trend in economic access to food put forward by Tyagi is to compare the increase in per capita income at current prices with the increase in the prices of food items. Between 1960-61 and 1970-71, per capita income in the country increased from, Rs. 305.60 to

Rs. 632.80, while the increase in the price index of food articles was from 100 to 195 only. The period between 1970-71 and 1980-81 registered an increase of 147 per cent in per capita income with a corresponding increase of only 124 per cent in the price index of food. Taking the two staple food grains, prices of wheat and rice have consistently risen more slowly than per capita income.

Thus, with reference to all the above measures, both physical and economic access to food in the country appears to have registered a substantial increase. However, even today 11.50 per cent of all rural households and 3.80 per cent of all urban households report inadequacy of food (Table 2.9).

TABLE 2.9 : Percentage Distribution of Households by Availability of Two-Square Meals a Day.

	Rural		Urban	
Households getting two square meals a day.	1983	1990-91	1983	1990-91
1. Throughout the year	81.09	88.30	93.25	95.50
2. Only some months	16.19	10.80	5.56	3.00
3. Proportion of households reporting inadequacy of food	18.54	11.50	6.63	3.80

Source : NSS 38th round (1983) and 46th round (1990-91).

In a situation where agricultural production outpaces population growth, and grain surpluses co-exist with widespread hunger, the food security problem can be better stated in terms of man days of employment, rather than in metric/tonnes of foodgrains (Swaminathan, 1981).

As far back as the mid-Nineteenth Century Col. Baid Smith, enquiring into the causes of the famine of 1860-61, concluded that the Indian famine was 'rather a famine of work than of food'. In the case of a pure peasant economy, a famine will occur only when there is a crop failure. However, in a monetized economy, famine can occur even without a decline in the availability of food. In a country like India, where agriculture forms the mainstay of the majority of the population, a drought sweeps away employment and incomes of agricultural labourers as well as all those in the related service sectors. Without remunerative employment, these sections of the population no longer have access to food. (Tyagi, 1990).

Lack of access to food can result from either a decline in the capacity to purchase food (through lack of employment and income) or a sharp increase in the prices of food without a corresponding increase in purchasing power. Measures have been initiated by the government to deal with both these root causes of hunger.

As regards, loss of purchasing power, employment generation schemes for those who can work and relief measures for those who cannot, were laid down by the Famine Commission of 1880, and have been largely followed with modifications from the experience gained from subsequent Famine Commission Reports. During the drought of 1987-88, central assistance was extended for the generation of employment for small and marginal farmers as well as for landless agricultural labourers. Of the total drought assistance of Rs. 16,173 million, Rs 8421 million was allocated for employment generation programmes in various states, Additional employment for more than 600 million man-days was generated under the National Rural Employment Programme (NREP) and the Rural Landless Employment Guarantee Programme (RLEGP) particularly during the agricultural season. These programmes provide relief to small and marginal farmers during periods of scarcity, and to medium farmers in areas facing severe drought. (Tyagi, 1990).

To meet the food access problem in the wake of the 1987-88 drought, the government announced the Food For Work Programme under which 2 kg. of foodgrain per man-day (3kg. per man-day in severely drought affected areas) were given as part payment to workers engaged in relief works.

The pattern of food distribution under various schemes and programmes of the government has registered a steady increase in the decade 1977-1987 as can be seen from Table 2.1. Drought years like 1980 and 1987 obviously record a much larger magnitude of foodgrain distribution under various programmes like Food for Work, NREP, RLEGP and Drought Nutrition Programmes. Moreover, more liberal norms are used to assess employment generation requirements in the severely drought affected regions.

As regards prices, the Government of India has been using monetary and regulatory controls to maintain domestic prices at the required levels. Under the Essential Commodities Act, the government has the power to control the price at which any essential commodity may be bought or sold as well as prohibit the withholding from sale of any essential commodity ordinarily kept for sale. By changing policies relating to credit controls (margin restrictions, culling restrictions), the government can also influence the buying behaviour of private trade. Through the Public Distribution System, an effective control on prices can be maintained by increasing the supply of foodgrains to the market as soon as the signals for increasing prices begin to emerge. With the wide regional variations in food prices, a major objective of the PDS is to equalise availability and thus keep a check on the regional variations in food prices.

While schemes like the Jawahar Rozgaar Yojana, Food for Work Schemes and Integrated Development Programmes aim at providing a measure of food security to the poorest of the poor who often get by passed by the PDS safety net, it must be remembered that poverty in this country is not confined to small and marginal farmers and landless labourers in the rural areas, but is matched by the large scale urban poverty among the unorganised labour and those engaged in the informal sector. Thus food security programmes must be aimed at both the urban and the rural sector.

Special nutrition programmes for disadvantaged and vulnerable groups like children, pregnant and nursing mothers, the old and the sick are needed if the aim of achieving food security for all is to be realised. A start has been made by the introduction of the midday meals programme for school children in Tamilnadu, drought nutrition programmes and other nutrition programmes of the government.

Yet another aspect to be taken into consideration is the seasonal variation in access to food. At the village level, particularly in rain fed areas, where only a single crop is harvested annually, the lean season often turns into a period of virtual starvation with villagers resorting to gathering forest produce in an attempt to assuage hunger. The Food For Work Programmes in the lean season in such areas would go a long way in eliminating the threat of hunger.

Early Warning Systems

The efficient functioning of the food security system is largely dependent upon an effective monitoring and communication network. Agriculture in India is ultimately dependent on the monsoon, with almost two-thirds of the area under cultivation being rain-fed. From past experience, the probability of a drought or crop failure (partial or total) occurring at least once in three years is extremely high. While the technologically advanced states like Punjab, Haryana and Western Uttar Pradesh may not be very vulnerable, the same cannot be said of other states. Thus an Early Warning System which reviews rainfall patterns, market prices and the level of draw down on the stocks held by both private trade and the government is an essential feature of the food security system (Subramaniam, 1994).

The Union Ministry of Agriculture closely monitors progress on the crop production front. Almost every week, a senior officer level committee reviews the progress of the monsoon in different agro-climatic zones and the growth of various crops in different regions. Based on this assessment, the Cabinet is kept informed of the situation as it develops.

This system permits an early assessment of impending food shortages. In areas, where rainfall in a particular season is below normal, close monitoring is done by the state government to assess the potential crop loss. This elaborate administrative arrangement not only provides an early warning system, but also helps in coordination of policy measures that are to be initiated as a consequence of the failure of the monsoon. (Tyagi, 1990).

The price behaviour of essential commodities is also under constant review. Wholesale and retail price statistics for all essential items of consumption are collected on a weekly basis from a large number of markets in different regions. Based on this data, policy makers are kept informed of the developing price situation on a weekly basis. Any unusual behaviour in the price of a commodity initiates action by the concerned government department.

This level of monitoring is not available in any other third world country with the possible exception of China, and the Indian system is ranked amongst the best in the world. However, at the regional level, there is considerable scope for improvement in the system.

Conclusion

The sustainability or otherwise of our food security system in all its dimensions has been reviewed above with reference to emerging trends and policy changes. However, in essence, the sustainability of the country's food security depends upon the sustainability of the environment.

Complementarities between food security and the environment are based on the inter-dependence between food availability and a healthy natural resource base, which is seen to promote mutually reinforcing practices. Conflicts arise if the pursuit of food security or policies to ensure

TABLE 2.10 : Foodgrains Distribution Under PDS and Other Programmes

(in hundred thousand tonnes)

Year	Rice					Wheat								Total
	PD	FWP NREP	RLEGP	EGS/ RUNP	Total	PD	NREP	RLEP	EGS/ RL	NP/ DNP	MILLS	Total	CG/PD	Foodgrains
1977	45.89				45.89	36.40					27.56	63.96	7.44	117.29
1978	32.29	1.00			33.29	35.50	1.00				33.05	68.55	0.99	103.83
1979	35.68	4.81			40.49	32.23	12.01				30.69	74.93	1.21	116.63
1980	50.25	10.32			60.57	41.24	10.52				36.43	88.19	1.17	149.93
1981	61.57	2.45			64.02	32.56	0.29				31.44	64.29	1.85	130.16
1982	74.29	0.71			75.00	38.69	0.17				32.82	71.68	1.00	147.68
1983	77.75	0.76		0.02	78.53	49.58	1.15		0.53		29.95	81.21	2.32	162.06
1984	66.29	0.80	0.06	0.15	67.30	32.64	0.84	0.19	0.02		31.36	65.05	0.91	133.26
1985	71.24	0.91	0.16	NEG		46.96	84.77	0.91	157.99					
1986	81.77	1.75	0.68	0.40	84.60	43.92	13.11	3.83	0.19	0.32	23.67	85.04	3.05	172.69
1987	(P)91.35	3.29	1.87	0.14	96.65	57.08	11.32	6.64	11.11			86.15	0.87	183.67

(P): Provisional
(RL) : Relief.
(MILLS): Roller Flour Mills.
(DNP) : Drought Nutrition Programme.
(CG) : Coarse Grain.
PD) : Public Distribution.
(NP) : Nutrition Programme.
EGS : Employment Generation Scheme/s.
(R) : Revised.
(NEG) : Below 500 tonnes.
(FWP) : Food for Work Programme.
(NREP) : National Rural Employment Programme.
(RLEGP) : Rural Landless Employment Guarantee Programme.

Source : (Tyagi & Vyas, 1990)

it entail inevitable costs to the environment or vice-versa. (Davies and Leach, 1991).

In the recent past, policy and planning concerns have tended to sway between achieving the two objectives, with environmental concerns dominating at certain times, only to be submerged under pressing food security concerns at others. In the post-colonial era, the development agenda has been largely dominated by first, production led and later, entitlement-focused policies for national and household food security. With the current focus on sustainable development, the link between food security and environmental concerns has re-emerged more strongly in the form of 'sustainable livelihood securities' or people's access to adequate stocks and flows of food and cash to meet basic needs (Chambers, 1988)

The sustainability of food production is heavily dependent on environmental factors like soil quality, containment of soil-erosion, and leaching, level of the water table, etc.

Negative environmental impacts have led to a levelling off in the productivity of even the most agriculturally advanced food producing regions of the country. R & D efforts in natural farming and organic farming systems are being carried out on a small scale, but large scale replicability may be necessary to ensure a sustainable system of food production in the future.

Stepping outside the confines of agriculture into the wider realm of natural resource conservation may be required if the production of food and of agricultural crops in general is to be maintained. Since the late 1980s, the idea that conservation or regeneration of the natural resource base is an essential pre-requisite for the future development of poor countries has gained currency (WCED, 1987). This has been informed to a large extent by the fact that since the mid 1970s drought has been a major contributory factor to food insecurity and natural resource degradation. (Downing *et at,* 1989). The recurring famines in Africa in the 1970s and 1980s have lent impetus to attempts to look beyond crisis drawn food security towards longer-term policies which promote sustainable food production and which do not degrade the environment (Davies and Leach, 1991a)

Turning to the question of access, the complementarity of food security and environmental concerns is even more evident. It is often the food insecure groups who are most vulnerable to the effects of environmental degradation, as it is the poorest groups that are most heavily dependent on natural resources to meet their needs of food, fuel and fodder. With the degradation of the resources on which their livelihood is based, they tend to move into the environmentally fragile frontier areas moving one notch forward in the cycle of irreversible environmental deterioration.

The poor are (thus) both victims and agents of environmental damage. Land hungry farmers resort to cultivating steepfy sloped, erosion-prone hillsides, semi-arid land where soil degradation is rapid, and tropical forests where crop yields on cleared fields frequently drop sharply after just a few years (World Development Report, 1992).

Traditional concerns with maintaining the environment such as following a jhum cycle of several years were rooted in the need to meet immediate and immediately foreseeable needs. Purely conceptual goals of being food secure in the distant future carry no meaning for a hungry person. Policies aimed at ensuring food security or conserving the environment must of necessity emphasize measures for interim food security, while retaining the longer term objective of sustainable livelihoods. Only if such measures are implemented will there be a move from a situation of conflict to one of complementarity (Greeley, 1991). Greeley's study of a doner-aided project in a rainfed tribal area of India brings out clearly the conflict between local food security and environmental sustainability. While watershed management planning in the project area emphasised the planting of trees on the slopes, the indigenous population of scheduled tribes had spread their cultivation of annual crops to the middle and upper slopes which were officially the property of the forest department. Lack of alternative sources of food made this a necessary survival strategy for them. In ignoring the local food security concerns, the project could achieve only limited success in meeting its own environmental objectives.

As regards the sustainability of assured food supplies, at the international level, environmentally conscious aid flows may mean reduced aid to poverty and food security. At the national level, 'green conditionality' may force governments to prioritise environmental concerns over those of food security, for example, cash crop development policies aimed at least in part, at improving food security by increasing access to food, may conflict with local environmental stability and access to food which are threatened if food crops are pushed onto ecologically marginal lands. Fulfilling national environmental objectives through the large scale increase in protected area may also entail costs to local food security (Davies and Leach, 1991).

Thus, policy must emphasize the need to pursue environmental conservation without compromising food security or vice versa.

NOTES

1. An inter-Ministerial Working Group with representatives from the Ministries of Agriculture, Food, Civil Supplies and Health, the Planning Commission, the National Sample Survey Organisation and the National Institute of Nutrition was set up by the Government of India to review domestic foodgrain requirements by the year 2000. The report of the Working Group on Foodgrain Requirements by the year 2000 AD was brought out by the Ministry of Agriculutre in April,1994.

2. Estimates of per capita availability in India are derived by calculating net production of foodgrains using a netting factor of 12.5 per cent for seed, feed and wastage (Tyagi, 1990).

3

LIBERALIZATION AND HEALTH

K.N. Reddy

Introduction

Although liberalisation may mean different things - such as decontrol, deregulation, delicensing, "load-shedding" and privatisation - to different people, its objectives are to improve efficiency of the system in the country and save costs for the government. During the past four years, ever since Narasimha Rao came to power as Prime Minister, considerable attention has been paid to economic reforms and considerable gains also have been achieved from them in sectors like finance, industry, trade, banking and foreign exchange. But, not much attention has been paid to areas in social sector. The least attention paid is that of health. It is high time that some attention is paid to health sector also.

An attempt is made in this chapter to describe progress made in health status and discuss possibilities of reform - to be specific liberalization - in health sector to provide health care for all in the next six years – i.e., by 2000 AD. In the second section, progress made in health status is reviewed briefly and weaknesses of the present system are mentioned to serve as a backdrop for the rest of the chapter. In the fourth section areas for liberalization are presented. And in the fifth and final section concluding observations are made.

Health Status and Weaknesses of the Present Health System

Measured in terms of (i) life expectancy at birth, and (ii) child mortality rate - the two most widely used indicators of health status - health status in India has improved during the past three decades, 1960-1990. Life expectancy at birth (in years) increased from 41.3 in 1960-61 to 55.9 in 1990-91 and 60.8 in 1992-93 (Government of India, 1994). Infant mortality (per 1000 live births) declined from 129 in 1971 to 80 in 1990

(Government of India, 1992), death rate declined from 22.8 (per 1000) in 1961 to 9.8 in 1991, birth rate declined from 41.7 (per 1000) in 1961 to 29.5 in 1991. Consequently, growth of population increased from 439.2 million in 1961 to 846.3 million in 1991 and 878.6 in 1993 (Government of India, 1994). In terms of average annual growth rate, it increased from 2.20 in 1961-71 to 2.22 in 1971-81 and declined to 2.14 in 1981-91 (Table 3.1). It is expected to decline to 1.78 in 1991-2001.

TABLE 3.1 : Growth of Population and Health Status Indicators for Selected Years

Year	Population per 1000 (million)	Birth rate per 1000 population	Death rate at birth population	Life expectancy (in years)	Infant mortality
1960-61	439.2	41.7	22.8	41.3	146 (1951-61)
1970-71	548.2	36.9	14.9	45.6	129
1980-81	683.3	33.9	12.5	54.4	110
1990-91	846.3	29.5	9.8	55.9	80 (1990)
1991-92	865.5	N.A	N.A	60.3	NA
1992-93	878.6	N.A	N.A	60.8	NA

Sources: 1. Government of India, Ministry of Health and Family Welfare (1992), Health Information of India.
2. Government of India, Ministry of Finance, Economic Division (1994), Economic Survey, 1993-94.

But these improvements are not impressive when compared with other countries. It can be seen from Table 3.2 that life expectancy at birth in India has gone up by 23.40 per cent only as against 60.46 per cent in China, 24.13 per cent in Sri Lanka, 30.76 per cent in Thailand, 32.08 per cent in Republic of Korea, 28.26 per cent in Indonesia and 36.96 per cent in "demographically developing group" and child mortality rate decreased by 45.96 per cent in India as against 79.52 per cent in China, 84.29 per cent in Sri Lanka, 75.84 per cent in Thailand, 76.69 per cent in Republic of Korea, 48.13 per cent in Indonesia and 53.13 per cent in demographically developing group during 1960-90. If the pace of improvement in health status continues to be the same, several years will be taken to provide health care for all. The fulfilment of Alma Ata declaration (1978) may remain a dream. As of now, the system is beset with a number of weaknesses and is badly in need of reform. Before contemplating about its reform and its associated liberalization an overview of the weaknesses of the existing system may be useful.

TABLE 3.2 : Health Status Indicators for Selected Countries

	Life expectancy at birty		Percentage increase in 1990 over 1960	Median age at death	Child Mortality		Percentage decrease in 1990 over 1960
	1960	1990			1960	1990	
Sub-Saharan Africa	43[w]	52[w]	20.93	5[w]	251[w]	175[w]	30.28
India	47	58	23.40	37	235	127	45.96
China	43	69	60.46	64	210	43	79.52
Other Asia & Islands	50[w]	62[w]	24.00	42[w]	182[w]	97[w]	56.70
Sri Lanka	58	72	24.13	73	140	22	84.29
Philippines	59	64	8.47	49	103	62	39.81
Thailand	52	68	30.76	71	149	36	75.84
Malaysia	58	72	22.41	63	106	20	81.13
Korean Republic	53	70	32.08	71	133	31	76.69
Indonesia	46	59	28.26	63	214	111	48.13
Latin America & the Caribbean	54[w]	70[w]	29.63	55[w]	161[w]	60[w]	62.73
Middle Eastern Countries	44w	61w	38.64	24w	242w	111w	54.14
Formerly Socialist Economics of Europe (ESE)	66w	72w	09.09	72w	68w	22w	67.65
Established Market Economics (EME)	70w	76w	08.57	75w	36w	11w	69.44
FSE And EME	69w	75w	08.70	74w	46w	15w	67.39
Demographically Developing group	46w	63w	36.96	39	226w	106w	53.10
World	53w	65w	22.64	35	195w	96w	50.77

Source: World Bank: World Development Report 1993, pp. 200-201.

TABLE 3.3 : Structure of Health Care Expenditure by Purpose and by Level of Government: 1974-75 to 1990-91

	Level of Government/ Purpose	Direction[1] & administration	Curative[2]	Preventive[3]	Miscellaneous[4]	Total
	1974-75					
a	Central government	4.79	57.43	19.65	18.13	100.00
b	State governments	6.45	64.72	22.91	5.91	100.00
c	Union territory govts.	8.01	82.73	3.49	5.76	100.00
d	All governments (a+b+c)	6.35	64.46	22.34	6.86	100.00
	1978-79					
a	Central government	4.00	56.45	23.22	16.33	100.00
b	State governments	4.67	62.50	25.21	7.62	100.00
c	Union territory govts.	2.92	74.29	11.11	11.66	100.00
d.	All governments (a+b+c)	4.59	62.26	24.81	8.42	100.00
	1982-83					
a	Central government	3.02	55.00	22.85	19.13	100.00
b	State governments	5.03	60.45	27.18	7.34	100.00
c	Union territory govts.	3.18	75.26	10.94	10.62	100.00
d	All governments (a+b+c)	4.82	60.26	26.51	8.34	100.00
	1986-87					
a	Central government	2.46	64.07	21.12	2.35	100.00
b	State governments	5.01	57.20	32.03	5.76	100.00
c	Union territory govts.	3.18	82.47	10.62	3.08	100.00
d	All governments (a+b+c)	4.73	58.50	30.41	6.36	100.00
	1990-91					
a	Central government	2.66	62.58	25.54	10.22	100.00
b	State governments	5.12	59.19	27.14	8.55	100.00
c	Union territory govts.	4.63	86.12	6.76	2.48	100.00
d	All governments (a+b+c)	4.88	60.25	26.33	8.53	100.00

Notes:

1. Includes Direction and Administration under (a) Medical, (b) Public Health and (c) Family welfare.
2. Includes expenditure on Medical Relief. Employees State Insurance, Central Government Health Scheme, Medical Education Training Research, Other systems of Medicine - Ayurveda, Homeopathy, Sidda Unani, etc. - under **Medical.**

First, there seems to be misallocation of resources and it has been in practice for quite some time. Contrary to general opinion and worldwide view, larger share of resources is going to curative services. As of 1990-91, a little more than 60 per cent of the resources had been allocated (by the Central, State and Union territories government combined) to curative services, 26 per cent had been allocated to preventive services and the remaining had been allocated to administration and miscellaneous services (Table 3.3). Similarly 97.02 per cent of the resources had been devoted to consumption expenditure (that is, 58.97 per cent for salaries, 2.58 per cent for office expenses and 35.47 per cent for materials and supplies, medicines, rents, taxes, festival advance, scholarship and stipends, travel, petroleum, etc.) and 2.97 per cent only to machinery and equipment, basic to health care in the long run (Table 3.4). Very little had gone for capital formation (Reddy, K.N. and V. Selvaraju, 1994). How can future generations be ensured with proper health care if due allocation are not made for capital formation?

Second, rural areas are neglected. A greater chunk of resources have gone to urban areas. As of 1990-91, 66.96 per cent of the resources spent on health care had gone to urban sector (having 25.7 per cent of the population), while 33.04 per cent of the resources had gone to rural sector (having 74.30 per cent of the total population) (Table 3.5). In terms of per capita allocations, urban sector received 5.8 times more than what the rural sector received. It is a pity that health care did not reach the people for whom it was meant.

TABLE 3.3 *(Contd.)*

3. Includes expenditure on (a) Prevention and control of diseases, prevention of food adulteration, drug control, minimum need programme under **Public Health** and (b) Rural Family Planning Services, Urban Family Planning Service, Maternity and Child Health compensation and Other Services and Supplies under **Family Welfare**.
4. Includes expenditure on (a) International cooperation, medical stores department, department of drugs, school health scheme, other health schemes and tribal area sub-plan under Medical, (b) Training, health statistics and research, public health laboratories, health transport, international cooperation under Public Health and (c) Transport selected area programme, education, training, research and statistics research and evaluation, awards tribal area sub-plan and international cooperation under Family Welfare.

Source : Reddy, K.N. and V. Selvaraju (1994), Health Care Expenditure Government in India: 1974-75 to 1990-91, National Institute of Public Finance and Policy, New Delhi.

TABLE 3.4 : Structure of Health Care Expenditure* by the Government by Economic Categories in Nominal Terms: 1974-75 to 1990-91 (the Central, the State and the Union Territory Governments Combined)

(In Percentage)

Year	Salary	Office expenses	Machinery & equipment	Others**	Total (1+2+3+4)
	1	2	3	4	5
1974-75	39.93	4.37	2.85	52.86	100.00
1978-79	40.11	3.61	3.20	53.09	100.00
1982-83	51.14	4.58	2.91	41.37	100.00
1986-87	52.41	3.55	3.34	40.70	100.00
1990-91	58.97	2.58	2.97	35.47	100.00

Notes: * Health care expenditure here refers to expenditure on medical relief, hospitals and dispensaries and family welfare only as data for other items are not available.

** Others include materials and supplies, travel expenses, motor vehicles (purchase, maintenance, cost of fuel), hospital accessories, medicines, rents and taxes, festival advance, petroleum, oil lubricants, stores and equipment, scholarships and stipends, cost of text books to the children of low paid government servants, etc. They vary from state to state.

Sources :1. Reddy, K.N. and V. Selvaraju (1994), Health Care Expenditure by Government of India: 1974-75 to 1990-91, National Institute of Public Finance and Policy, New Delhi.

Appendix Tables A.40 to A.44.

Third, accessibility to health care is very poor. The system favours the elite and higher income groups. Be it medical care, or be it water supply and sanitation or be it any health related facility, poor are the last ones to receive. According to a study conducted by the author (Reddy, K.N. and S. Sudhakar, 1989) per household benefits to the poor were Rs. 20.42 only as against Rs 39.97 to middle income and Rs 726.17 to high income group. Perhaps, for this reason and other associated reasons, it has been observed that "the failure of the present system is not on account of financial and human resources or of infrastructural facilities or shortages of drugs...but in their skewed distribution" Antia, N.H. (1993).

Fourth, there exists a mismatch between the supply of and demand for health services, both at the Central and the States' levels. Under the Constitution of India, States are responsible for provision of health care, but are not able to cope up with demand for health services. The devolutions made, at the behest of Finance Commissions and Planning Commission are not able to meet their requirements. Nor are the states able to allocate higher percentage of their resources to health care. A glance at the allocation pattern of expenditure on health care will reveal marginal decline, and in some states significant decline too (Table 3.6). There seems to be a snag in the very arrangement of financial resources for health care. The paradox of national policies is that when it comes to the question of political stability and safeguarding the sovereignty of the country, States are treated as Union of the States, and when it comes to the provision of basic services, e.g., health, sanitation, nutrition, etc. – the same States are asked to fend themselves. I am wondering whether other federations are having such awkward national policies. Canada, Germany, Australia, Switzerland are having national (social) insurance with accessibility to every one. Even the United States of America, the hard core believer in private competition, provides accessibility to poor under Medicaid programme and to old and disabled under medicare programme. It needs no mention that in most of the federations, health care (upto a particular point) is the concern of the Centre as well as the States and not completely the responsibility of the states. The kind of system in India and the transfers made for centrally sponsored programme to the states do not address the basic problem of assuring medical care.

Fifth, quality of service in public hospitals (government hospitals) has been deteriorating fast, partly because of lack of adequate supply of medicines and equipment and partly because of faulty manpower planning and selection procedures. The delivery system has become bureaucratic and unaccountable. It is more so in primary health centres and sub-centres in rural areas. According to the findings of some researchers, whether at the sub-centre or at the primary health centre, health workers remain unaccountable to the community which they are supposed to be. "Doctors posted at PHC have no proper training; they are more thorough in recognising and treating cardiac failure, but

TABLE 3.5: Percentage Shares of Rural and Urban Sectors in Health Care Expenditures by Level of Government: 1990-91

Levels of Government	Rural	Urban
A. Central Government	**29.00**	**71.00**
B. State Government		
Andhra Pradesh	31.80	68.20
Assam	35.60	64.40
Bihar	42.73	57.27
Gujarat	29.03	70.97
Haryana	37.44	62.56
Kerala	34.13	65.87
Madhya Pradesh	35.33	64.67
Maharashtra	33.62	66.38
Orissa	36.33	63.67
Punjab	38.61	61.49
Rajasthan	31.31	68.69
Tamil Nadu	30.89	69.11
Uttar Pradesh	35.87	64.13
West Bengal	30.83	69.17
State Governments (Total)	**33.79**	**66.21**
C. Union Territory Governments	22.55	77.45
D All Governments (A+B+C)	**33.04**	**66.96**

Source: Reddy, K.N. and V. Selvaraju (1994), Health Care Expenditure.

TABLE 3.6 : Percentage Share of Health Care Expenditure in Total Expenditure (Centre, States and Union Territories Combined)

Year	Medical and public health	Family Welfare	Total
1974-75	3.89	0.54	4.43
1978-79	4.05	0.48	4.53
1982-83	3.66	0.75	4.41
1986-87	3.09	0.78	3.87
1990-91	3.14	0.64	3.78

Source: Reddy, K.N. and V. Selvaraju (1994), Health Care Expenditure by Government of India: 1974-75 to 1990-91, National Institute of Public Finance and Policy, New Delhi.

ignorant about the treatment of rheumatic fever. Medical officers posted at primary health centres do not have adequate experience in simple tasks like giving injections, I.V. fluids, and resuscitation" Muley, Y.P. (1993). In the words of Praful Bidwai (1992), "going to a public hospital remains a nightmarish experience, big crowds, long queues, confusing maze – like layouts, incomprehensible instructions, tedious procedures, casual diagnosis, rough handling by sullen staff, rude physicians, bribe taking by touts, complete absence of accountability and unconscionable delays. Most working people think twice about visiting hospital O.P.D. simply because it means missing a day's work and wages... Most public hospitals are inherently patient - unfriendly and hopelessly mismanaged".

Sixth, the health care system is not cost effective. This is evident when compared with other countries, for example, China, Japan and the United Kingdom had been able to ensure health care to all their people by spending 3.5 to 6 per cent of their GDPs while India had not been able to do so with the same (Reddy, K.N., 1994) (see Table 3.7). This is a sad commentary on the performance of our health care system.

Seventh, the system - rationing by queue - has outlived its usefulness. It was alright when India was under the foreign rule. Continuing with the same system is unfortunate and to my mind has worked in favour of the elite and employees of organised sector. Witness, for example, per capita expenditure on medical care of the employees of government and other organised sectors as against those of unorganised sector. Employees of Central government are looked after by the Central Government Health Scheme (CGHS) and employees of the organised sector are looked after by the Employees State Insurance Scheme (ESIS) to a large extent. CGHS provides comprehensive medical care - that is, free medical care and supply of medicines, laboratory and X-ray investigations, domiciliary visits, emergency treatment, ante-natal care, advice on family welfare, specialist consultation and hospitalization facilities in government hospitals as well as in hospitals recognised under CGHS. Similarly, ESIS provides for sickness, medical care, maternity and employment injury benefits to the employees of all factories (with a few exceptions) by contributions from their employees. As of 1991-92, 65 lakhs persons were insured under ESIS and Rs 241 crore were spent on their medical care in 1991-92. In terms of per employee, the State governments spent Rs 370 on medical care, which is 5 times more than per capita expenditure incurred on people in the unorganised sector. The point is that, with the share of expenditure on health care in the State budgets remaining constant or even declining, any increase in the number of employees in government and organised sector will severely affect per capita availability of services in rest of the sectors. This indeed is what had happened for the past one and half decades.

TABLE 3.7 : Health Expenditure in Selected Countries: 1990

	Per capita Health expenditure (official exchange rate dollars)	Health expenditure as percentage of GDP		
		Public Sector	Private Sector	Totall
	(1990)	(1990)	(1990)	(1990)
Sub-Saharan Africa	US$ 24	2.5	2.0	4.5
India	US$ 21	1.3	4.7	6.0
		(1.65)	(2.09)	(3.75)
China	US$ 11	2.1	1.4	3.5
Other Asia & Islands	US$ 61	1.8	2.7	4.5
Sri Lanka	US$ 18	1.8	1.9	3.7
Philippines	US$ 14	1.0	1.0	2.0
Thailand	US$ 73	1.1	3.9	5.0
Malaysia	US$ 67	1.3	1.7	3.0
Korean Republic	US$ 377	2.7	3.9	5.0
Indonesia	US$ 12	0.7	1.3	2.0
Latin America & the Caribbean	US$ 105	2.4	1.6	4.0
Middle Eastern Countries	US$ 77	2.4	1.7	4.1
Formerly Socialist Economics of Europe (ESE)	US$ 142	2.5	1.0	3.6
Established Market Economics (EME)	US$ 1860	5.6	3.5	9.2
FSE and EME	US$ 1340	5.4	3.4	8.7
Demographically Developing-group	US$ 41	2.3	2.5	4.7
World	US$ 323	4.9	3.2	8.0

Note: Figures within brackets are the estimates made by us (See Reddy, K.N. and V. Selvaraju, 1994).

Source: World Bank: World Development Report 1993, pp. 200-201.

Public Sector Expenditures include government health expenditure, parastatal expenditure, foreign aid, making the figures comparable with those for OECD countries. Private sector expenditures for countries other than OECD members are based on household surveys carried out by the ILO and other sources, supplemented by information from United Nations National Accounts, World Bank studies, and other studies prescribed in the scientific literature (World Bank 1993, p.197-198).

"Health expenditure includes" outlays for prevention, promotion, rehabilitation and care; and emergency aid specifically for health. It does not include water and sanitation. Per capita expenditures are based on World Bank Mid year population estimate.

Eighth, there seems to be difficulty in allocating higher share of States' resources to health care on account of (a) shortage of resources and (b) expenditure compressions. States are facing intense competition from many other worthy programmes (i.e. agriculture, industry, roads, communications, education, power, etc.) for limited funds. Moreover, expenditure compressions practised for the past three years have resulted in underfunding of existing hospitals, primary health centres, sub-centres and maintenance of the buildings, equipment and of staff.

Finally, rapid developments in expensive medical technology and new drugs have inflated health care costs. Even the middle and higher income people are turning to government hospitals, unmindful of the meagre facilities and chaotic situations prevailing there. As a result, government is finding extremely difficult to cope up with the demand. Those who can afford to wait in the queue and lose their day's wages they are benefited; but those who cannot afford or are afraid of losing their day's wages by standing in serpentine queues, are forced to go to the private sector. The system is gradually and surely working against the majority for whom health services are badly needed.

In short the present system is beset with a number of weaknesses and cannot continue as it is. It has to give way to a better system and has to be evolved. What type of system is needed? What reforms are needed in the existing system? are the questions that have to be addressed. But before doing so, more important thing is to know about reforms itself. The reforms are by and large in the nature of liberalisation or privatisation and have to be understood in proper perspective. We shall address to these in the next section.

Liberalization in Health Sector

Public discourse on liberalisation has been going on for the past one-and-half a decades in the West and most of the Socialist countries. It is of very recent interest in India. Thanks to the Finance Minister's Budget Speeches and implementation of reforms in the fields of industry, banking, foreign exchange and finance and subsequent discussions in Parliament and intensive debate in newspapers during the past three years, liberalization is well known. Nevertheless, it is useful to describe briefly what liberalization is all about in regard to health.

Liberalization - delicensing, deregulation, decontrol - consists of two interconnecting themes - (i) "competition" theme and (ii) "load-shedding" theme. The "competition" theme emphasizes efficiency of market dynamics. It promotes the notion that, wherever possible, private sector should be made responsible for the distribution of goods and services; for, competition fosters innovation, minimises production costs, and saves resources. In contrast, monopolistic government bureaucracies tolerate inefficiency, destroy initiative and push up health care cost. Without competition, government programmes may languish with little care for quality of services or the cost of producing them. "Load-shedding" theme connotes transfer of functions carried out hitherto by public agencies to private sector or contracting with non-profit or profit organisations. But it does not specify which function of government should be transferred to private sector and which function should be retained with it.

What are the rationales for liberalisation or privatisation of health services? There are several rationales; but the most important ones are as follows: First, privatization works out cheaper to government, for, the dynamics of competition may compel the contractors to cut down their costs in order to win or retain contracts; contractors may provide services at lower cost, because labour may be cheaper for them as they are not bound by civil services hiring requirements or public employee pay scales. Second, privatisation affords flexibility. Whatever is not possible for government agencies due to political and administrative difficulties privatization makes it possible. It will facilitate the initiation of new programmes with existing staff and hire new staff. If government agencies have to provide 'services they have to provide the same throughout the country and a degree of uniformity in standards have to be ensured - the option of taking local sentiments and local conditions into account will not be there. But if contracting the same service with non-profit organizations is made local requirements will be met as the latter know local conditions. Further, it may help change direction or cut back quickly if the government priorities change. Quite often cutting back public employment is much more difficult and the consequences are much more severe. Third, privatization would allow government to extend services without generating growth in government workforce, and divert criticism on government growth to taxes, expenditures and other related issues not genuine to health (Smith and Lipsky, 1992).

To what extent these rationales stand the test of scrutiny is a matter for empirical verification. Since India does not have any experience in the matters of privatizing health care, it is worth experimenting. However, there are certain fears which need to be cleared before embarking upon it.

First, it is feared that the efficacy of competition may get blunted if there are few providers. Privatisation can work efficiently if there are large number of providers. Looking to the number of doctors produced every year and the number of corporate hospitals coming up, there may not be scarcity of providers. Given the opportunity, several NRI medical professionals will come and float non-profit organizations.

Second, it is feared that the dependence of public agencies on private providers may create vested interests, and the so called saving in cost may turn out to be nil. This has been illustrated by Smith and Lipsky (1992) exceedingly well. I quote:

> "If local public health centre depends upon State contracts for half of its revenue, public officials will be reluctant to jeopardise the fiscal health of the agency if they are dependent upon the health centre for some of its services. If the centre is one of the only providers in a small city, officials will be very cautious about taking actions that might jeopardise the existence of one of the few organisations with the capacity to deliver private services. The need to retain a capacity to treat certain classes of clients creates an incentive to continue contracting with important providers rather than seeing each contract period as a fresh opportunity to buy this year's bundle of service requirements. In considering defunding the centre, public officials must confront the political pressures, particularly from powerful community supporters, that will be brought to bear to ensure that the centre has a reasonably stable funding stream. Further, most contracts are renewed, if providers seek renewal. A few are adjusted upward toward good performance or as expressions of changing public priorities. Some are marginally reduced to sanction inadequate performance. Major shocks to the provider network tend to be avoided and this is more

the case the more government depends on particular providers for services delivery".

Third, it is feared that assessment of performance of contracting agencies may be difficult. According to Smith and Lipsky (1992), performance based contracting is opposed by providers, for they fear that the measures to be employed are unrealistic or not reflective of effective practice. Providers also worry that they will be held to performance standards without being given the resources to achieve their quotas. In the event of not insisting on the performance standards, government will be not knowing whether they are getting value for which it pays. Even if government knows what it is wanted, it will be defeated in monitoring the providers. Monitoring the providers is a great problem.

Areas for Liberalization

What areas of health sector be considered for liberalization? What priorities should be followed? What programmes be subjected to which type of liberalisation - delicensing, decontrol, deregulation and load-shedding?

Activities of Government in Health sector are numerous - ranging from cradle to grave. Broadly speaking, they fall into curative, preventive, administrative and miscellaneous services which again fall into several programmes and sub-programmes. Under curative services there are activities like medical relief, Employees' State Insurance Scheme (ESIS), Central Government Health Scheme (CGHS), medical education, training and research, etc. Under preventive services there are prevention and control of diseases, prevention of food adulterations, drug control, health education and publicity, minimum needs porgramme, etc. Under direction and administration and miscellaneous there are rest of the activities. Keeping aside the last two types of activities for their essentially and indivisibility, attention is required on the first two types namely – curative and preventive.

Let us take up the second one first as it belongs truly to the category of public-cum-merit good. The preventive services affect the entire society and consumption of these goods, e.g., prevention of tuberculosis, control of malaria and filaria, leprosy, eradication of Aids and sexually transmitted diseases – benefit every one and cannot be contracted out. Similar is the case with respect to family welfare, whose effective implementation benefits the entire society. Coming to curative services

- hospital based services, diagnostic services, surgery, maintenance of hospital buildings, and medical equipment, catering, cleaning, and supply of medicines, CGHS and ESIS - the same thing cannot be said. They account for 65 per cent of total health expenditure (Table 3.8). The scope for privatisation, in each of these areas (curative) is substantial. But to what extent the savings are likely is difficult to estimate. No studies are available on the hospital finances, and cost structure of hospitals. Nor, reliable information is available on the socio-economic background of the users of the hospitals.

Information about cost structure and socio-economic background of users would help to develop models of liberalisation, suitable to our country. Pending availability of such studies and development of liberalisation models, discussion on the following issues is worthwhile.

- What is wrong with our health care system? Does it need change? If so, in which direction, i.e., delicensing, decontrol, deregulation and load-shedding.
- Should we interpret it in the sense of contracting out services to non-profit organizations? Would it reduce the costs of government?
- Would not liberalization create vested interests? If vested interests develop, what precautions are necessary to ensure efficiency and quality of care and accessibility?
- Would not liberalization (without governmental subsidy) aggravate inequities in accessibility to health care and affect poor adversely?
- Is it not the responsibility of government to provide minimum health care to one and all? If Constitution of India could say about provision of elementary education to one and all, and some action is on the way towards it, cannot we ask for a similar mandate for primary health care?
- Does liberalization involve pricing of medical care? What systemic changes are needed then? Should not India go in for national health insurance as Canada did or U.K. did or Germany and Japan did?

May it be noted that liberalisation is inclusive of relaxation or removal of controls and regulations on the entry of foreign nationals and multinational corporations in production of pharmaceuticals and provision of medical care. To what extent these liberalizations effect domestic pharmaceutical industry, private hospitals and domestic corporate hospitals is a question that has to be discussed.

TABLE 3.8 : Composition of Expenditure on Medical, Public Health and Family Welfare, by Major Items and by Level of Government: 1990-91

Programmes		Central Govt. Total	States Total	Union Terri. Total	All Govts. Total
1		2	3	4	5
	MEDICAL - 2210				
1.	Direction and administration	1.25	1.40	3.01	1.44
2.	Medical relief	10.26	41.12	76.74	39.30
3.	Employees State Insurance	0.00	4.98	0.00	4.39
4.	Central Govt. Health Scheme	16.24	0.02	0.00	1.50
5.	Medical Edn Training Research	35.57	8.51	7.14	10.94
6.	Other systems of medicine				
	i. Ayurveda	0.32	2.50	1.11	2.26
	ii. Homoeopathy	0.12	0.56	1.06	0.53
	iii. Other (incl. Siddha, Unani etc.)				
	Total	0.50	2.48	2.24	2.29
7.	Medical Expenditure	0.04	3.31	1.71	2.97
A	**MEDICAL - TOTAL**	**63.87**	**63.90**	**90.85**	**64.66**
	PUBLIC HEALTH - 2210				
1.	Direction and administration	0.42	2.42	1.58	2.22
2.	Prevention & control of diseases	5.10	11.78	4.86	10.98
3.	Prevention of food adulteration	2.27	0.70	0.95	0.67
4.	Drug control	0.30	0.40	0.31	0.39
5.	Health education and publicity	1.05	0.38	0.30	0.44
6.	Minimum needs programme	0.00	0.98	0.00	0.86
7.	Other expenditures	3.78	1.56	0.75	1.74
B	**PUBLIC HEALTH-TOTAL**	**10.91**	**18.23**	**8.75**	**17.30**
TOTAL MEDICAL & PUBLIC HEALTH (A+B)		**74.78**	**82.13**	**99.59**	**81.95**
	FAMILY WELFARE - 2211				
1.	Direction and administration	0.99	1.29	0.04	1.23
2.	Rural family planning services	0.06	6.97	0.15	6.15
3.	Urban family planning services	0.52	1.21	0.00	1.11
4.	Maternity and child health	8.26	2.61	0.02	1.52
5.	Compensation	0.26	2.61	0.08	2.32

(Contd,)

1	2	3	4	5
6. Other services & supplies	8.79	1.24	0.10	1.89
7. Other expenditures	6.40	3.68	0.02	3.82
C **FAMILY WELFARE**				
TOTAL	**25.22**	**17.87**	**0.41**	**18.05**
MEDICAL & PUBLIC HEALTH AND FAMILY WELFARE (A+B+C)	100.00	100.00	100.00	100.00

Source : Reddy, K.N. and V. Selvaraju (1994), "Health Care Expenditure by Government of India: 1974-75 to 1990-91", National Institute of Public Finance and Policy, New Delhi.

Concluding Observations

Health status in India is among the lowest in the world. The progress achieved so far, although considerable, is far inferior to the progress achieved by comparable developing countries. Health care system is beset with a number of weaknesses – misallocation of resources, neglect of rural areas, inequity in distribution of medical care, lack of accountability in medical staff, inadequate allocation for infrastructure and maintenance, lack of motivation, over centralisation, inappropriate manpower policy and above all lack of incentives. Its organizational pattern – rationing by queue – is oppressive to the poor, exploitative to the taxpayer, frustrating to the honest medical professional and wasteful to the nation. In the context of present income distribution and rising prices, the following observations assume importance.

> "With the increase in doctors' fees and prices of medicines, the average man today finds it virtually impossible to get any satisfactory medical treatment. In fact the situation is so bad that even upper middle class people, including senior company executives, find it difficult to manage within the medical reimbursement limits offered by their employers.
>
> Government hospitals and ESI hospitals are the only alternatives for the common man. Unfortunately, most of these are in deplorable state of hygiene, understaffed as far as doctors and nurses are concerned, perhaps overstaffed with clerks and admin-

> istrators, perpetually mismanaged, full of corruption - in short, hardly places that would cheer up a sick person. Despite all these handicaps, these places are invariably overcrowded - a north Delhi hospital recently reported patients of 10 times the number of beds it is equipped for - because there are no options... There is regular pilferage in the purchase of medicines, consequently life saving drugs are rarely available and, in times of need, the attendants and relatives have to run to private chemists and obtain them at their own cost.
>
> Private hospitals and doctors are beyond the reach of even the upper middle class. The house call fees of doctors go up to Rs 500 in case of general physicians and up to Rs 2000 for well known specialists. A room in a small, well equipped overcrowded private nursing home costs around Rs 1000 per day and this is just the room rent everything else, namely, doctors' visits, medicines, intensive care facilities, etc. is extra" (Krishan Kalra, 1994).

Under the circumstances, whether liberalisation would solve the problem is a big question mark. In my opinion, it may improve efficiency slightly but not solve the basic problem. The reason is that due attention has not been given to management of health care and resource allocation. What is perhaps needed is that of thorough reform in financing, organisation and delivery system of health care. Social security models of Japan and China – based on compulsory contributions from beneficiaries - or Canada and Germany need be examined and adapted suitably to our cultural, financial and climatic conditions. The goal must be towards self supporting system of medical care with human face and not towards total dependence on government. It may mean decentralization, it may mean community financing or it may mean national compulsory health insurance as in Canada, Germany, Japan and China. Under no circumstances, the present system should continue which is fast moving towards American model without its positive features, e.g., "medicare" and "medicaid". According to international surveys, the American system is scoring lowest in terms of consumer satisfaction, although no other country spends as lavishly on health care" (Reinhardt, Uwe E., 1992; and Hsiao, William C., 1992).

4

EDUCATION AND THE ECONOMIC REFORM PROCESS

R.V. VAIDYANATHA AYYAR

Mission of the Ministry

Till the 42nd amendment of the Constitution (1976), education was in the State List, except for certain specified items in the Union List like determination of standards in institutions for higher education or research, and establishment and maintenance of central universities. It was in pursuance of these powers that the University Grants Commission (UGC) and the All India Council of Technical Education (AICTE) were set up as statutory bodies. The objective of incorporating education in the Concurrent List was to facilitate evolution of all-India policies in the field of education. Though the parliament was thereby empowered with the authority to legislate on education, the centre has been relying on persuasion and consultations. The concept of concurrency was given an operational meaning by the National Policy on Education, 1986 [NPE]. This policy envisages concurrency as a "meaningful partnership between the Centre and the States" and placed on the union government a larger responsibility in regard to the national and integrative character of education, quality and standards, manpower planning, research and advanced study, and international aspect of education, culture and human resource development. The mission of the Department of Education is to promote educational development in this true spirit of concurrency.

Policy Frame

Since 1986, educational development is being attempted within the framework laid down by the NPE. The NPE was the culmination of an intensive consultative process which included the publication of a candid critique of educational development since independence, entitled the *Challenge of Education,* a nation wide debate of that critique and consideration of the draft policy by the Central Advisory Board of Education (CABE), the National Development Council and the Parliament. Through a similar process NPE and its Programme of Action (POA) were reviewed and updated in 1992. In 1990, a committee under the Chairmanship of Acharya Ramamurti reviewed the NPE; the report of this committee was examined by a CABE committee on Policy under the chairmanship of Shri Janardhana Reddy, the then Chief Minister of Andhra Pradesh. The CABE committee came to the conclusion that while very little of the policy itself required reformulation, the POA needed to be revised considerably. The revised policy was tabled in the Parliament on 7th May, 1992 and its POA on 19th August, 1992.

The NPE addresses all aspects of education: equity, efficiency, relevance, quality, content and process, linkages with culture, values, society, polity and economy, resources and management. The NPE seeks to tilt the balance away from quantitative expansion of institutions towards quality and equity. At all levels of education importance is being given to curriculum renewal, improving teacher competence and other aspects of pedagogy having a bearing on quality, context and process. Consolidation and protection from degradation of higher educational institutions is postulated as an important policy objective. Complementary to this objective is vocationalization of secondary education. By the year 2000, twenty-five per cent of the secondary students are to be covered by the vocational stream, thereby reducing the pressure on higher education. In technical education the focus is on modernisation of facilities and courses, with particular emphasis on emerging areas of technology. Being a cost effective, flexible and innovative system, distance education mode is increasingly being promoted as suited to the needs of a large developing country like India.

The NPE, gives the highest priority to UEE (Universalization of Elementary Education) and Adult Education. There is universal recognition that basic education [or the catchy phrase Education For All (EFA) encompassing universal elementary education, universal literacy and post-literacy and continuing education] is a pure public good with several positive externalities in diverse areas such as productivity, demography, health, nutrition, and empowerment of women and disadvantaged groups. The strategies for achieving UEE and universal literacy proceed from the premise that a host of measures, both on the supply side and demand side, are required to complement higher allocation of resources. The NPE postulates in the field of basic education are path breaking in several aspects and have shaped international thinking in this area. It anticipated the declaration and framework adopted by the World Conference on Education For All in 1990 (more well known as the Jomtien Conference). The NPE recognised the organic unity of early childhood education, primary schooling, non-formal education, adult education and post-literacy and lifelong continuing education. The policy conceives education as a dynamic, cumulative life-long process, encompassing a wide diversity of learning opportunities, applying to all people, but laying stress on girls, children and youth, particularly, those belonging to disadvantaged groups. Even while stressing school effectiveness, it boldly sought to address the more difficult aspects of access to education of millions of children who are beyond the pale of the school system. To reach out to these millions it had postulated a large and systematic programme of non-formal education as an integral component of the strategy to achieve Universalisation of Elementary Education. It perceived education as an agent of basic change in the status of women, of playing a positive, interventionist role in their empowerment. It also laid stress on teacher training, convergence of primary education and other related services like Integrated Child Development Scheme (ICDS) and primary health, participative processes and decentralisation of education management. The years since NPE 1986, have witnessed major interventions such as, the operation blackboard which was conceived for improvement of primary schools and provision of support services, the District Institutes of Education and Training which provide institutional infrastructure for teacher training, the programme of non-formal education which as the objective of enabling learners to learn at their own pace, the National Curricular Framework, the laying down of Minimum levels of learning and so on, the vocational education programmes at the secondary stage, the Academic Staff Colleges for providing inservice training to teachers in colleges and universities, the schemes for modernization and removal of obsolescence in technical education and for developing technical manpower in other areas of technology.

Education and Adjustment

The impact of adjustment on social sectors like education has been a subject matter of controversy. The controversy is not a little due to:

(i) imprecise use of expressions such as 'structural adjustment.', 'stabilization', and 'economic restructuring',
(ii) the divergent economic beliefs,
(iii) the pitfalls inherent in any attempt to generalise from diverse country experience, and
(iv) the frequent failure to address the counterfactual but highly relevant question: How things would have turned out in the absence of adjustment?

It is well known in public policy that the answers to questions depend upon the conceptual frame adopted – the basic assumption, the categories used and the angle of vision. The conceptual frame not only fixes figuratively, the mesh of the net that the analyser drags through the material in order to explain a particular phenomenon; it also directs him to cast his net in select ponds, at certain depths, in order to catch the fish he is after.

One needs to differentiate between the two parts of the economic reform process: (i) short term stabilisation and (ii) the medium-to-long term structural adjustment. The immediate objective of stabilisation is to restore balances in the country's fiscal and trade accounts while the objectives of structural adjustment are to improve resource allocation, economic incentives (i.e., prices, wages and salaries) and increase competition in the markets by reducing or eliminating factors that tend towards market distortions.

Country experience of the impact of adjustment on education has been varied. In many African and Latin American countries there has been a decline in enrolment arising from the simultaneous decline in public expenditure and household incomes; on the other hand, there are a good number of adjusting countries which choose to increase education spending as a percentage of GNP. In general, countries have generally found it difficult to maintain public spending on social sectors in the face of the compulsive austerity enjoined by stabilization. The country experiences would vary under structural adjustment. Countries do have a choice as to how they treat education within adjustment or in how the education sector itself adjusts to new economic realities. For this reason countries should formulate appropriate policies and international financing agencies should support contextual adjustment policies rather than prescribe standard formulations.

World over the consensus now is that adjustment should have a human face, that social services, particularly those catering to basic needs, should be protected during the adjustment process and that the focus of adjustment should shift from short term crisis management and stabilisation (which dominated the 1980s) to the more fundamental issues of long term growth, development and poverty reduction. It is this consensus that was articulated in the Delhi Declaration, issued by the recent EFA Summit of Nine High Population Institutions:

> "We therefore call upon:
>
> *international financial institutions, in the context of structural adjustments, to recognise education as a critical investment without imposing predetermined ceilings on such investments, and to promote an international environment to enable countries to sustain their socio-economic development;...*"

In fact, there exists a strong case for enhancing investment in education as a concomitant of the economic reform process. Restructuring of government budgets is often associated with the economic reform process. Efficiency and equity are simultaneously furthered, if public expenditure is redirected towards education and, within education, towards the poor, basic education, skill development, technical and management education. Social sectors like education now expect a restructuring dividend from the economic reform process akin to the peace dividend that developed countries expect from the cessation of the cold war. The higher allocation for education needs to be complemented by better utilisation of resources. Internal efficiency needs to be augmented by better linkages with the world of work.

Impact of Adjustment on Financing of Education

Conceptually there are four main variables that are of crucial importance in determining the effects of adjustment on education:

(i) government budgets, in the light of changes both in total level of government expenditure and the relative priority given to education, training and other social investment,

(ii) household income and expenditure, particularly the level of private household expenditure on education and training,

(iii) the level and distribution of employment and unemployment, together with shifts in the labour markets and employment pattern, and

(iv) the level of company profits and taxation, which affects expenditure by private and public enterprises on training.

In India, Government (centre, states and local bodies put together) has come to provide a higher and higher share of the income to educational institutions. Over the period 1950-51 to 1983-84 the share of government increased from 68 per cent, notwithstanding the fact that private managed institutions account for over 60 per cent of the senior secondary schools, colleges and technical institutions. This anomaly is explained by the fact that except for the so called "self-financing" technical institutions all other are dependent on the government for grant-in-aid which generally covers not only maintenance costs but also partly capital costs. Hence the impact of adjustment on education expenditure is to be perceived in the trends of government expenditure on education. Immediately after NPE, 1986 there was indeed a steep step-up in public spending on education by the centre as well as the states. However, this momentum, particularly in the plan outlays, could not be sustained thereafter, though there was a continuous nominal increase in public spending even after the stabilisation process was initiated (Table 4.1).

TABLE 4.1 : Expenditure on Education (Centre & States)

(rupees in crore)

Year	Centre		States/UTS		Total	Centre	
	Plan	Non-Plan	Non Plan	Plan	Plan	Non-IUT	States
1986-87	302.84	345.39	676.36	7125.73	979.20	7471.12	8450.32
1987-88	746.62	430.13	774.73	8478.71	1521.35	8908.84	10430.19
1988-89	839.19	710.82	1125.58	9733.13	1964.77	10443.95	12408.72
1989-90	781.00	681.05	1626.87	11955.27	2407.87	12636.32	15044.19
1990-91	833.18	760.53	1297.54	14302.41	2130.72	15062.94	17193.66
1991-92(BE)	977.00	771.17	1709.90	14920.90	2686.90	15692.07	18378.97
1991-92(RE)	959.38	771.17	1660.71	15618.03	2620.09	16389.20	19004.29
1992-93(BE)	950.78	771.04	2132.28	16895.99	3083.06	17667.03	20750.09
1992-93(RE)	1011.30	812.89	N.A.	N.A.	N.A.	N.A.	N.A.
1993-94(BE)	1309.30	850.03	2327.98 (Approved Outlays)	N.A.	3637.28	N.A.	N.A.

N.A. : Not Available.

Note: The Eighth Plan allocation on education is higher than the Seventh Plan expenditure by over 313 per cent. The policy priorities are reflected in the intra-sectoral allocations (Table 4.2).

TABLE 4.2 : Intra-Sectoral Allocation of Resources

(figures in percentage)

	Share in	
	Seventh Plan Expenditure	Eighth Plan Outlay
Basic Education	49.6	55.7
Higher Education	11.4	6.7
Technical Education	10.0	16.1

At a more disaggregated level, stabilization did affect the Central plan outlay. The 1992-93 outlay (BE) at Rs. 951 crore was lower than that of the 1991-92 (BE) outlay by Rs.25 crore. This decline followed the decision of the Government to enhance central assistance to State plans even while freezing the total budgetary support for State and Central plans at the 1991-92 BE level. However, as the year progressed, the Central plan outlay was increased, no doubt facilitated by the Social Safety Credit Adjustment Loan offered by the IDA. In the next year, 1993-94, the Central plan outlay on education received a further boost, the largest since 1987-88.

As of now, public expenditure on education is of the order of 3.5 per cent of GDP which compares favourably with that in other Asian developing countries including China (1.9), Pakistan (2.6), Bangladesh (1.6), Indonesia (0.8), Philippines (2.6), Korea (3.3) and Thailand (3.1). However, it still falls short of the norm of 6 per cent set as early as 1968 and also of the resource requirements of education. In the years to come an important indicator to gauge the impact of economic reforms would be the level of resource support for education.

Resource support need not be limited to budgetary support; nor resources to financial resources. The NPE itself speaks of the nation as a whole assuming the responsibility of providing resource support for achieving the objectives it laid down. It also postulates resources, to the extent possible, being raised by mobilising donations, raising fees at the higher levels of education, effecting some savings by the efficient use of facilities and levy of a cess or surcharge on user agencies. All these measures are sought to be undertaken not only to reduce the burden on State resources but also creating a greater system of responsibility within the educational system. The total Literacy Campaigns offer a telling example of how substantial non-budgetary resources can be mobilised. As of now, four million volunteers, most of these being women, are engaged in these campaigns trying to impart functional literacy to millions of learners. If quantified, the opportunity cost of this voluntary work is at the minimum of Rs. 6180 million or roughly seven per cent of the eighth plan allocation on adult education.

An area which calls for particular attention is the financing of tertiary education (higher and technical education). India has 6,204 colleges and universities as compared to 1,075 in China, a country with a larger population and greater success than India in universalising elementary education. Given this unbridled proliferation of institutions, the resource requirements are immense if only to prevent further deterioration of the higher education system, not to speak of augmenting the quality of higher education and of meeting the challenge of international competitiveness. It would be well nigh impossible for the resource requirement of this order being met by budgetary resources. Several reports, including that of the West Bengal Education Commission (1992), had observed that the fees are archaic and bear little relation to the relevant unit costs. There is a case for raising fees together with appropriate support to the needy students. However, nowhere in the world is higher education financed solely by fees. In fact, there is no magic or single solution to the problem of financing higher education. It is not a question of either budgetary resources or non-budgetary resources, but one of harmoniously harnessing all possible sources of funding. Financing policy should, therefore, seriously encompass a mix of reinforcing and consistent measures. Another important issue in this context is providing for the special needs of institutions of national importance in a manner consistent with principles of equity. Experience in India and elsewhere bring out the fact that steering of the reform of higher education calls for navigational skills of no mean order.

It is in this background that the UGC appointed a Committee under the chairmanship of Justice Punniah to consider the step that can be taken to mobilise additional resources for higher education, to bring about a better balance in the funding of institutions of higher education and research, and to improve the cost efficiency of the university system. The Committee recently submitted its report.

The 1993-94 Budget provided concessions, under section 80 G of the Income Tax Act, to donations to Universities and institutes of national importance. As a follow up the Indian Institutes of Technology, the Indian Institutes of Management and the Indian Institute of Science have taken a major initiative in mobilising non-budgetary resources. Each of these institutes would set up an endowment fund, which cumulatively would amount to Rs. 200 crore over the next four to five years. If the idea gains larger acceptability, the endowment funds could be of a much higher order as well. Each fund would be in the nature of a corpus and the institute would be free to utilize the interest and the accruals from the corpus in the manner it deems fit. Government proposes to provide additional incentives to the institutes, over and above the tax incentive, by agreeing to:

(i) maintain the block grants without deducting the proceeds related to the corpus, and
(ii) conferring greater autonomy in their internal administrations.

During the 1980s there was enormous growth of "self-financing" professional colleges in some States like Maharashtra, Karnataka and Tamil Nadu. They mainly cater to the excess private demand for professional education. Efforts by State Governments to regulate such institutions in the matter of admissions, facilities and fees have not been effective. An important development in 1993 was the landmark judgment of the Supreme Court in the case of Unnikrishnan and others *V.S.* State of Andhra Pradesh. Though a few issues are still pending consideration by the Supreme Court, it can be said that the judgement has paved way for an effective regulatory framework for professional colleges in the country. The regulatory frame would be complete once the Accreditation mechanism is set up by the AICTE and all pending issues before the apex court are judiciously resolved.

The 1994-95 Agenda

Even while pushing forward the implementation of NPE, POA, 1992 and all the attendant schemes, the Department of Education, GOI, has identified five thrust areas: adult literacy, primary education, decentralisation of educational management, vocationalisation and technical education.

In adult education the momentum of the Total Literacy Campaigns (TLCs) would be further built up and the Hindi heart land would receive particular attention. So far 216 TLC projects have been approved involving 240 districts (either fully or partially) in the States of Andhra Pradesh, Bihar, Gujarat, Haryana, Himachal Pradesh, Karnataka,

Maharashtra, Madhya Pradesh, Orissa, Punjab, Rajasthan, Tamil Nadu, Uttar Pradesh and West Bengal. Currently, approximately 31 million learners in the 9-45 age-group are learning but it is estimated that about 15 million of them have already acquired the threshold level of literacy and numeracy. Post Literacy and Continuing Education activities are being launched even as TLCs make significant progress in an area. The objective to cover 345 districts during the Eighth Plan and make 100 million people functionally literate. Over the last few years the efficacy of TLCs was demonstrated in states with different endowments; with the emergence of TLCs it is now increasingly being perceived that universal adult literacy is no longer a hopeless dream but an achievable task.

In the area of primary education, the major initiative would be implementation of District Primary Education Programme (DPEP). The POA 1992 and the Eighth Five Year Plan enunciate the strategy of disaggregated target setting and decentralised planning as the main strategy for achieving UEE. The Social Safety Net (SSN) credit offered by IDA was used to conceptualise this strategy through DPEP. The DPEP had elicited keen interest of the external donor agencies. The DPEP seeks to channelise the keen interest evinced by international agencies to support basic education in a way consistent with national capacity building. The cost for civil works component would be limited to 24% and management cost to 6 per cent of the total project investments. In other words, bulk of the investments (about 70%) would go to improve the quality of teaching and learning processes and enhancing school effectiveness. The DPEP moves away from the earlier schematic piecemeal approach and takes a holistic view of elementary education, emphasises decentralised management, community mobilization and undertakes district and population specific planning. The programme also builds upon experience gained from the Bihar Education Project (BEP), Lok Jumbish Project (LJP) in Rajasthan and the planning of U.P. Basic Education Project.

The special features of DPEP are:

(i) Local area planning with district as the unit;
(ii) Focussed targeting to improve access and retention;
(iii) Stress on education for girls and socially disadvantaged groups;
(iv) Emphasis on qualitative improvement in schools to ensure minimum standards of learning;

(v) Development of creative alternative to formal schooling so as to cater to the learning needs of out-of-school children;

(vi) Sustaining a genuine community involvement in primary education;

(vii) Building local and state level capacities to sustain planning, implementation, monitoring and evaluation; and

(viii) Building a network of education, management and social science research organisation at the national and state levels with a view to supporting the programme with professional input.

The programme targets on the educationally backward districts with female literacy below the national average as well as districts where TLCs have been successful leading to enhanced demand for elementary education. DPEP will eventually cover all states and districts in a phased manner. To begin with eight states which are not already covered by externally aided basic education projects are being taken up under the programme. In the first year, 46 districts in Assam, Madhya Pradesh, Haryana, Karnataka, Maharashtra, Tamil Nadu and Kerala and Orissa are proposed to be covered under DPEP. During the Eighth Five Year Plan, the DPEP would be extended to 110 districts.

While the quantum of funding would vary with reference to the specific needs of the individual districts, the level of investment per district is expected to be between Rs. 30 crore to 40 crore over a 5 to 7 year period. The participating State Governments would provide 15 per cent of the total project outlay while Government of India (GOI) would meet the balance 85 per cent to be received from external funding. The World Bank has indicated interest in financing DPEP to the tune of US $ 200 m - 250 m per year over the coming years. The European Commission (EC) has pledged assistance amounting to ECU's 150 m (equivalent to Rs. 585 crore) spread over in four years (1993-94 to 1996-97).

The DPEP would be implemented in a mission mode through a registered state level autonomous society. The need for a society is rooted in the experience gained from the Bihar Education Project and the U.P. Basic Education Project and the belief that existing administrative structures have shown an inadequacy to implement specific time-bound educational programmes. Furthermore, a society provides an appropriate forum to foster a meaningful partnership between the government machinery, voluntary agencies, teachers unions, parent-guardian groups who can help to implement and guide the programme. It also helps to forge linkages between the National Resource Institutions like NIEPA and NCERT ensuring professional rigour and inputs to the programme. In essence, the DPEP seeks to bring about a qualitative transformation in primary education scene the way TLCs have done in adult literacy.

Another thrust area would be decentralization of education system. Immediately after the enactment of the 73rd and 74th Constitutional amendment bills, a CABE Committee on Decentralised Management of Education was set up under the chairmanship of Shri M. Veerappa Moily, to consider the whole question of decentralization of educational management. The report strikes a balance between decentralization of administration and maintenance of academic standards. It provides a great deal of flexibility to the state to harmonise the recommendations with their situational imperatives. The report of the committee has since been endorsed by the CABE and commended to the states. The Department of Education, GOI sets great store by implementation of the report as it is only through devolution to local communities of powers and responsibilities that the goals of UEE would be achieved. Equality as well internal efficiency of the primary education system would be fostered by decentralization.

Vocationalization of secondary education has been a priority area since 1986. The initiatives in 1994-95 would be two fold; (i) operationalization of Central Institute of Vocational Education (CIVE) set up this year in Bhopal, and (ii) introduction of vocational courses at the undergraduate stage. The CIVE is expected to provide a strong institutional support for development and revision of curricula and textual material appropriate to the changing manpower needs of the economy. A welcome development has been its association with the network of institutions being set up under UNESCO's programme.

In the area of technical education the three major initiatives would be: (i) operationalization of AICTE as a regulatory-cum-development body, (ii) manpower development in computer software, and (iii) technical education missions. In the current year the organisational requirements of AICTE were studied in great detail and necessary approvals accorded so that AICTE can effectively fulfil the regulatory and developmental role expected of it. The Departments of Electronics and Education have jointly developed a manpower development strategy for the computer software sector. Among others, the strategy envisages development of Centres of Excellence in software engineering and upgrading the existing programmes in different institutions.

Professional Observations on Educational Economic Reform Process

Jagdish Bhagwati and T.N. Srinivasan in their review of macro- and micro-economic reforms entitled *India's Economic Returns* observe that they do not address issues such as primary education and population not because they attach low priority to these questions but because they just do not fit well into the economic architecture that our reforms seem to create and whose dimensions we wish to focus on. Doubtless, the Finance Minister's colleagues in charge of these other portfolios will pursue them with equal energy and steadfastness.

There is no reason why education should not be integrated with economic reforms; nor is there any reason for such integration to be consigned to individual departments. In its treatment of Human Resource Development, the Discussion Paper brought out by the Department of Economic Affairs, *Economic Reforms: Two Years After and the Task Ahead* only two issues are perfunctorily touched upon viz, higher budgetary allocation for primary education and reduction of subsidy in higher education. As the experience of countries, developing and developed, would bear out, there is more to the education-economic reform linkage than isolated issues of equity. The question to consider is not merely how economic reforms affect education but how education can accelerate the economic reform process. We need to address the issues of training, retraining, continuous education and technical and management education with the same ferocious intensity one notes in countries pursuing international competitiveness. International competitiveness is no longer rooted only in size or in endowment of natural resources, but in the quality of human resources.

The National Renewal Fund (NRF) has made a beginning in coping with the human resource dimensions of industrial restructuring. These efforts need to be carried further and intensified. The key requirement is flexibility. Training systems need to be expanded; they should be more responsive to changing economic trends and pay greater attention to self employment, in-service training and reaching large number.

The building of international competitiveness calls for greater attention to technical and management education, with an intensity akin to the Total Literacy Campaigns. Empirical evidence from the East Asian Countries as well as the new strategic trade theories demonstrate the desirability of countries positioning themselves in emerging areas of technology.

It would be fallacious to equate the economic reforms process with privatisation. As the World Development Report, 1991 puts it:

> "Governments need to do less in those areas where markets work, and can be made to work, reasonably well. In many countries, it would help to privatise many of the State-owned enterprises. Governments need to let domestic and international competition flourish. At the same time, Governments need to do more in those areas where markets alone cannot be relied upon. Above all, this means investing in education, health, nutrition, family planning and poverty alleviation; building social, physical, administrative, regulatory, and legal infrastructure of better quality; mobilising the resources to finance public expenditure; and providing a stable macro economic foundation, without which little can be achieved."

Therefore the State has to play a major role in strengthening the educational underpinnings of the economic reforms. It is no longer a question of the State *Vs.* the markets but of State and markets working together. The question is no longer one of whether the State should intervene but one of devising appropriate forms of interventions that minimise governmental as well as market failures, and promote., social objectives at minimal social costs.

5

ECONOMIC REFORMS AND PROSPECTS FOR THE EDUCATIONAL SECTOR

N.V. VARGHESE

Introduction

The decade of eighties was a period of severe economic crisis in many developing countries and many of them had to borrow heavily from the World Bank to overcome domestic economic problems and balance of payment difficulties. The World Bank loans to these countries were conditional to the reform measures to be adopted by the countries. The reform measures or adjustment policies had their implications for all sectors including education. This chapter is an attempt to briefly discuss the reform measures initiated in India and to speculate on the probable impact of recent economic reforms on the education sector.

This chapter is organized as follows: Section 2 captures the changing pattern of World Bank funding to the developing countries. Section 3 deals with the recent economic reforms in India with a focus on a quick evaluation of the performance of the Indian economy during this period. Section 4 attempts to draw some implications of adjustment policies for the education sector in general and the final section attempts to make some observations as conclusions of this chapter.

From Project Lending to Adjustment Loans

The eighties was a period of severe economic crisis in many countries of the developed and developing world. Many developing countries, especially of the African and Latin American region, witnessed unprecedented balance of payments difficulties. The major initiative of the domestic policy makers was to get out of the immediate difficulties arising from the balance of payment problems and invariably many of them approached the World Bank for loans. The Bank did introduce new forms of loans, specifically taking into account the immediate requirements of the developing world with a commitment from the recipient countries to introduce long term policy changes. Because of these conditionalities attached to these types of loans, they are broadly called adjustment loans.

World Bank lending in the sixties and seventies was dominated by project lending where changes in the macro-economic policy variables were not directly addressed. Even when such issues were addressed, they were not conditionalities to approve or release the loans. The Bank loans of the recent past are more in the category of adjustment loans with the accompanying conditionalities. These loans are essentially for two purposes: stabilisation and structural adjustment programmes. According to the World Bank (1988a) stabilisation loans are non-project lending to support policies to achieve sustainable fiscal balance, to overcome balance of payment deficits and to reduce inflation. Similarly, structural adjustment loans are non-project lending to support programmes to effect changes in policy and institutional arrangements necessary to modify the structure of an economy to maintain sustainable growth rate and viability of its balance of payments in the medium term (Michalopoulos: 1987).

The Bank introduced a number of credit arrangements (Jones: 1992) to meet the ever increasing loan requirements of the developing countries within the framework of the adjustment loans: (i) structural adjustment loans (SAL) introduced in 1979 essentially to help the needy countries to come out of the impending balance of payment problems; (ii) sectoral adjustment loans (SECAL) introduced in 1980 to finance structural adjustment in specific sector; (iii) structural adjustment facility (SAF) introduced in 1986 to finance medium term policy reforms; and (iv) the extended fund facility (EFF) which is in existence from the seventies with a provision for 2 or 3 years of lending facility.

Unlike project lending, the structural adjustment loans are characterised by their conditionalities with respect to the reform measures that are to be undertaken by the recipient government. These conditionalities are to be strictly adhered to. In fact there are two distinguishing characteristics of these conditionalities - front loading of conditions and tranching. 'Front loading' means the commitment shown by the recipient government to fulfil the conditionalities attached to the loan. 'Tranching' means that the release of subsequent instalments of the loan is subject to the fulfilment of the conditionalities. This implies that the subsequent instalments will not be released unless and until the recipient government fulfills that part of the conditionality or reform which was committed to be completed within the time limit. These measures are meant to ensure that the conditionalities are strictly adhered to. In general, the reform measures suggested as part of the structural adjustment loans include policies pertaining to demand restraints, financial reforms, import liberalisation, devaluation, switching of resources from non-tradeables to tradeables.

Recent Economic Reforms in India

Central to the recent economic reforms in India is the need to redefine the role of the state in development. Ever since the beginning of the planning era, the state played an important and dominant role in the economic development of the country, essentially through the mechanisms of planning and public policy. Even under the mixed-economy framework, which we had adopted, public actions defined the boundaries of market operations; and public control mechanisms were effective tools in limiting the free play of market mechanism. The current reform measures try to alter the existing division of labour between the state and the market (Sinha, 1994).

The assumption underlying all the reform effort is the firm conviction to rely on market forces to effect efficiency in allocation and use of scarce resources. The belief is that the existing controls exercised by public authorities constrain efficient functioning of the market. Hence the first step is to remove the restrictions to make the market effective i.e. to reduce or remove controls to liberate the market forces.

The new economic reforms initiated in India essentially consist of two stages: (i) stabilisation; and (ii) structural adjustment programmes.

Stabilization deals with demand side of the economy. Stabilization seeks to use macro-economic, fiscal and monetary policies to deflate demand so as to reduce resource gap between aggregate demand and short-run aggregate supply. It addresses these problems through the following policy measures: (a) devaluation to correct balance of payment imbalances; (b) control of inflation through restrictive monetary policy facilitated by increase in interest rates to reduce investment demand and to increase savings; and (c) curb on public spending to check fiscal deficits through cuts in subsidies, cuts in non-essential spending etc.

Structural adjustments, on the other hand, entail major policy shifts to allow markets to determine prices, to allocate resources, introducing institutional reforms, trade liberalisation, free flow of foreign capital etc. (Bajpai: 1993; Sinha: 1994). The economic reforms initiated in India envisaged both stabilisation policies and structural adjustment programmes. In fact, the programme was envisaged to lay primary emphasis on stabilisation policies in the initial stages with fiscal restraints and currency devaluation taking the leading role, followed by structural adjustment programmes to ensure growth of the economy (Bajpai: 1993).

It is only four years since the reform measures have started in India and hence it is too early to come to any definitive conclusions about the long-term effects of the programme. However, some trends are visible which give enough scope for realistic speculation. One of the major achievements of the reform measures is the steady improvement in the balance of payments reserve; similarly inflation has also shown declining trends; efforts were also made to reduce the fiscal deficit, at least in the first year of the reform programme. Except the balance of payments reserves, achievements in all other fronts were of a very temporary nature. For example, in the year 1993-94 GDP growth rate was only 3.8 per cent as against the target of 5 per cent; inflation which came down to around 8 per cent, has already shown a tendency to further move upwards. It was expected that the fiscal deficit will be brought down to 4.7 per cent, but at present it remains at 7 per cent of the GDP.

What is worse, is the performance of the economic sectors. Agricultural production has declined: the growth rate of agricultural production (1993-94) is negative (–0.9%); the growth rate in food supply has also declined with a negative growth rate of –0.5%. Hanumanta Rao (1994) notes that agriculture can work as the biggest safety net during periods of adjustment by softening the rigours of inflation and raising employment and income for the vulnerable sections of society. Therefore, a reasonable growth of this sector is essential especially in the short run. What has happened in India is just the reverse.

Industrial production grew at a meagre rate of 1.6 per cent. Imports have stagnated in dollar terms; exports have grown by about 20 per cent in dollar terms. Many economists agree that by all indications there has been a slowing down of economic activities ever since the reform programme started. Some note that this slow down is to be seen in the light of the fact that the really hard prescriptions are yet to come (Sinha: 1994).

The future growth potential of the economy can be seen in the light of the present capital investments and future prospects to increase the levels of investment in the economy. The capital expenditure of central government has virtually remained stagnant from the very beginning of the reform programme. For example, it was Rs. 31,782 crore in the year 1990-91 and it is Rs. 32,888 crore in the budget for the year 1994-95. The gravity of the situation is more clear, if it is expressed in terms of the share of the GDP. Capital expenditure as a share of GDP declined from 6 per cent in 1990-91 to around 3.6 per cent in 1994-95 (Sen, Rao and Ghosh: 1994).

According to the budget estimates for the year 1993-94, 45.13 per cent of the revenue receipts were to go into interest payments (domestic and international) and the revised estimates show that the percentage is around 49.23 because of the fall in the revenue receipt. The budget for the year 1994-95 has set aside nearly 53% of the estimated revenue receipts for payment of interest. There is more to this exercise. In 1993-94, the interest payments (Rs. 38,000 crore) really exceeded the net borrowings of Rs. 32,645 crore i.e. the entire net borrowing and much more went into interest payment leaving nothing for new investments. However, in the previous year we could avoid this situation of repayment of interest exceeding the borrowing because of larger borrowing (Rs. 49,491 crore). It constituted only 75.7 per cent of the net new borrowing. In 1994-95 the interest payments are projected to be 94 per cent of the net new borrowings. This shows that we are entering into a debt trap, that is, one has to borrow even to pay the interest on the earlier borrowing, leaving little possibility of repaying the principal amount (Dandekar: 1994). Continued net borrowing increases the liability of the government. Assets as per cent of liabilities are continuously declining ever since the reform programmes started. Assets constituted 61.17 per cent of the liabilities in 1991-92 and they have declined to 56.41 per cent in 1994-95 budget. During the reform period, the liabilities are around 77 per cent of the GDP (Dandekar: 1994). All these figures show that all is not well with the reform programme even on economic performance.

The adverse effects of adjustment programme to the vulnerable groups of society necessitated many to argue for 'Adjustment with a Human Face' (Cornia *et al.* 1987). The social impact of the reform programme in India needs to be seen in the light of the employment prospects in the coming years. Estimates by Mudle (1992) show that the rate of unemployment will be increasing during the period of adjustment in India. Employment situations in the organised sector has already shown declining trends. The estimated strength of central government establishments has already declined from 4.14 million in 1991-92 to 3.99 million in 1994-95. The retrenchment policies, recruitment freeze and golden hand-shake policies can only accentuate the deteriorating employment situation. A sustained growth in agriculture would have acted as a safety valve under these conditions. However, this requires stepping up of public investment in irrigation, research extension and in education and skill development (Rao: 1994). One doubts whether such possibilities are proposed to be exploited adequately. As of now, the growth rate in agricultural sector has shown negative trends.

The public distribution system which is another institutional arrangement to facilitate supply of essentials at subsidised prices, is under strain. The food price subsidies are reduced and the prices of essentials supplied through the public distribution system have been increasing. Now, perhaps, there is an effort to target the public distribution system only to the poorest of the poor. All this may amount to making the public distribution system less effective in influencing the prices of commodities in the open market. To sum up, what is happening, perhaps, is a decline in employment and income at the household level and an increase in prices of essentials which make the living conditions of the poor still worse. This may be compounded by the changes in social sector spending.

Adjustment and the Education Sector

In the eighties a larger number of adjustment loans went to African and Latin American countries. The first set of countries to receive educational sectoral loans were Ghana and Morocco in 1986 and Senegal in 1987. A larger number of countries which received adjustment loans had their impact on the education sector, either directly or indirectly. It may be interesting to see the impact of these loans in other countries with longer years of experience in borrowing. Given the similarities in conditionalities imposed by the Bank, the impact of adjustment loans in these countries may provide us rich experience to avoid many of the initial problems of implementation of the adjustment programmes.

One of the impacts which is shared by a larger number of borrower countries is the decline in public expenditure. In fact, between 1980 and 1984 real government expenditure per capita fell in many countries (Cornia *et al.* : 1987; Lewin and Berstecher : 1989). The implications of a declining public expenditure on education are very severe since education in many of the developing countries is essentially a state funded activity. There are two dimensions to this issue : (i) a decline in the public expenditure itself; (ii) a decline in the share of the reduced public expenditure to education. In fact both these things have happened simultaneously in many countries. A reduction in public expenditure is a conditionality for the adjustment loans. When public expenditure is to be reduced, in many countries the social sectors are going to be more adversely affected; hence the possibility of a reduced share of the reduced public spending in education is plausible and it did happen in many countries. In fact in many countries the actual spending (at constant prices) on education has declined. In India the central government expenditure has not declined in absolute terms. During four years preceding the reform programme, the public expenditure (central government expenditure) grew at a rate of 11.4 per cent and in the four years of the reform period the growth rate is only around 8 per cent. In other words, in India the growth rate in public expenditure has declined. If we consider, in real terms, it can be found that the total public expenditure has been either stagnant or declined in India too.

One of the immediate impacts of a decline in public expenditure is a decline in the allocations to social sectors in general and education sector in particular. This has happened in many of the African and Latin American countries where adjustment programmes were introduced (Tibi: 1989; Lewin and Berstecher: 1989; World Bank: 1988; Tilak: 1993 and Woodhall: 1991 for a summary). When public expenditure on education is reduced, it is the capital expenditure on education that gets affected in the first instance. This means that no more construction of buildings and provision of equipments. As one knows very well, the condition of school buildings is very poor in many of the developing countries, any cut on capital expenditure, therefore, will have serious repercussions for the quality of services provided in the educational sector in the long run.

Adjustment also affects the recurring expenditure on education. At all levels of education, salary component forms the major share of recurring expenditure in education. This share, in general, is inversely related to the levels of education. At primary levels the share of salaries to the total recurring expenditure is over 95 per cent. In many countries, salaries cannot be cut and hence a reduction in the budgetary provision on this account can be effected through not making any adjustment for inflation in the salary in the subsequent years. This will imply that the real salary may be declining. In many countries, the real salary of teachers has declined and they are forced to take up second jobs for their survival. At times the governments have legitimised these second jobs. Another way of effecting a cut in the recurring expenditure is to reduce the number of teachers employed. This is also a difficult proposition on practical grounds since many a governments may not find it politically feasible to dismiss any of the existing teaching staff. What can normally be implemented with least resistance is to do away with the temporary teachers. The best option by which the government can reduce the number of teaching staff is to stop recruiting new teachers in place of those who are retiring every year.

Some of the other measures attempting to save expenditure on education include multi-shift schools and multi-grade teaching. These measures may save space and teacher salaries. These would be very poor reform measures, if at all attempted in India. The general norm in the rural schools in India is multi-grade teaching; single grade teaching is almost an exception. Many schools used to have only one teacher in India. Only after the 1986 policy on education, the minimum number of teachers for a primary school was compulsory fixed at two and the operation blackboard scheme tried to improve the teaching strength of the rural schools to at least two. Under these conditions, it is not possible to reduce the number of teachers in the primary schools in India.

Another reform measure which is very often suggested is distance mode of education. This is already prevalent, especially at the school level and at university levels in India. We have a national open school. Similarly we have correspondence courses attached to many universities. In addition, we have open universities at the national and some of the state government levels. However, one is not very sure of the effectiveness of such modes of delivery, especially at the primary levels of education.

Major policy interventions in altering the funding pattern pertain to cost recovery measures in education. There are various measures suggested in this context all of which come under the category of reducing subsidies to education. Some of these measures are introducing student loans; introducing graduate taxes and increasing fees (for a summary of these options see Tilak and Varghese: 1991). Each of these measures has its own logic and the general logic being withdrawal of the state from direct financing of education. However, most of these measures are applicable more in the field of higher education. What is expected is to transfer the amount so saved at higher education level to lower levels of education. Various measures to this effect are already in operation. For example, at one point of time, UGC attempted to freeze the grants to colleges and universities at the current levels; many universities have increased student fees, although most of them did not touch the tuition fees; professional colleges are introducing capitation fees and management institution are becoming self-financing. It can be very realistically argued that the fees in Indian Universities have remained at a very low level and the cost-fee disparities have increased over the years. Therefore, there is a strong case to enhance fees. But the question is how fees can be used to mobilise additional resources without adversely affecting the equity dimensions. We have argued elsewhere (Tilak and Varghese, 1992) that a discriminatory pricing policy in education is more reasonable than a uniform increase in the fee rates.

A significant measure that captures many of the reform efforts is privatisation of education. It is suggested that state being the dominant partner of the educational process in India it should be blamed for the inefficiency of the system. The easy way suggested at times to save the system is to privatise the provision of education. It is argued by many that the private sector in education in India is very efficient and hence the best way to improve the efficiency of the system is to increase the share of private schools. I have argued elsewhere (Varghese: 1993) that private sector in education in India can be efficient and effective so far as it remains small. The private sector in India may not be in a position to manage a larger share of the system very efficiently. Hence privatisation of education on a large scale is not a viable solution in India. At present private sector constitutes only a small share (nearly 8%) of the school education sector. No realistic assessment can project its share to increase substantially in the immediate future. Therefore, in my view, privatisation is not a viable proposition to improve educational provision in this country.

Concluding Observations

India has initiated economic reforms in the nineties with emphasis on stabilisation and structural adjustments. These reforms are at their infancy and hence any assessment at this stage may not be very realistic. However, the broad trends in the performance of the economy have given adequate scope for reasonable speculation. The growth rate in public expenditure at current prices has declined. Capital expenditure has stagnated and as a share of GDP it has declined from 6 per cent in 1990-91 to 3.6 per cent in 1994-95. The growth rate in agriculture has become negative and that in industry continues to be very low. Projections show a higher rate of unemployment, atleast in the initial stages. Public subsidies are being withdrawn and hence the prices of essentials have been rising and the economic condition of the poor is worsening.

Allocations to education in the eighth plan show that the share of education is around 4.9 per cent of the total plan outlay which is higher than its share during the seventh plan. Even in terms of allocations within the education sector, there is an apparent shift towards the primary levels of education. The increase in allocation to education which was witnessed in 1993-94 over 1992-93 has slowed down for the year 1994-95, at least in case of the plan outlay of the centre. As can be seen from the Table 5.1, between 1992-93 and 1993-94, the increase in allocation to elementary education was Rs. 158 crores; between 1993-94 and 1994-95 the increase in investments in elementary education has declined to Rs. 81 crores. The corresponding decline at the secondary level is from Rs. 96 crores to 28 crores; at higher education level it is from Rs. 47 crores to 9 crores and for adult education it is from Rs. 58 crores to Rs. 36 crores.

TABLE 5.1 : Plan Outlay on Education (Centre)

(Rs. in Crores)

Level	1992-93	1993-94	1994-95
Elementary	284.0	442.2	523.0
Secondary	209.0	305.3	334.0
Higher	124.0	161.0	169.0
Adult Education	120.0	178.0	214.0

Source: Budget documents for the respective years.

The non-plan expenditure on education (centre) has shown a decline in absolute terms from Rs. 945 crores in 1993-94 to Rs. 932 crores in 1994-95. In real terms the decline may be more steep. In other words, one is not sure whether public expenditure on education will be maintained atleast at the same level in real terms. Some argue that there is a decline in educational effort during the reform regime (Tilak: 1993a: Chalam: 1994). Given the fact that education in India is essentially a state funded activity, any decline in public expenditure on education may have far reaching implications.

Educational sector in India was relatively free from external funding. However, recently efforts are being made to get international assistance or loans to primary education under the Social Safety Net (SSN) programme of the World Bank. India has also received educational funds from many other bilateral and multilateral agencies in the recent past. There is every possibility to believe that external funding in the educational sector may go up in the coming years. Since these funds are routed through the government, public expenditure on education in India during the reform period may not decline. Most of the externally funded educational projects are targeted to the primary education sector. Hence primary education may also be protected, at least partially, from the adverse effects of reforms. It needs to be mentioned that these loans are mostly for primary education sector and that too for certain selected states and within the states to certain selected districts. In other words, the positive effects of maintaining the same level of expenditure or improving it marginally may not be shared by all regions but may be confined to the project districts only. Hence there is a possibility that new forms of disparities may emerge between these project districts and non-project districts during the reform period. However, the sustainability of state expenditure after the project period even in the project districts is something to be worried about.

With the decreasing employment prospects and reduced food subsidies, the purchasing power of the poor may worsen. Under such conditions, any efforts towards shifting the financial burden of education to the household level may not be a viable proposition. Hence state has to continue its dominant role. Thanks to the external funding the educational sector may be in a position to maintain the system at its present levels of operational efficiency. However, one is not very optimistic about its fate once the flow of funds to this sector from the external sources gets exhausted. Other levels of education, for example, higher education which is not at present receiving external funding, has already shown signs of stress during the reform period. What gives strength to the educational sector at present is the borrowed money. This strength may be very temporary and the system may be paralysed in the long run if effective measures are not initiated to protect the level of public expenditure on education from domestic sources.

6

LIBERALIZATION AND OTHER NEW ECONOMIC POLICIES AND THEIR IMPACT ON REGIONAL AND LOCAL DEVELOPMENT

K.V. SUNDARAM

Introduction

Too much of the writing on the economic crisis and policy reforms in India is pitched at the macro level. There is a woeful lack of adequate analysis on the distributional consequences of the current structural adjustment policies. This has tended to underestimate their impact on the spatial and social aspects of the development problem by governments. We must recognise the importance of the fact that national policy objectives must not be pursued at the expense of regional and local welfare.

This chapter focuses on the impact of the current reforms on regional and local development and seeks to provide an agenda for spatial equity. The structure of this chapter is as follows: First, the substance of India's economic reforms is broadly stated. The emphasis is on the central thrust of policy, not on the details. Second, the problem of regional disparities in development in the country is set out and the current status examined. As the promotion of industrial dispersal through financial concessions and tax incentives to entrepreneurs in the industrially backward areas in the country is a crucial factor in the achievement of balanced regional development, how the 'reforms in place' and the 'reforms in prospect' would affect the spatial disparities problem are specifically examined. Thirdly, the importance of the endogenisation of development is stressed. Given the present situation, the need for operationalising the concept of 'Development from within' and promoting a fully decentralised management of economic affairs is recognised as crucial and imperative. This calls for 'Reinventing Governments' at the regional and local levels and building entrepreneurial public organisations which are "catalytic, community-owned, competitive, mission-driven, results-oriented, customer-driven, enterprising, anticipatory, decentralised and market-oriented."

The Substance of India's Economic Reforms

Since June 1991, the Government of India has initiated certain economic reforms "with the objective of putting the Indian economy on a sustainable path of high growth"[1]. The strategy of economic reform was based on a combination of measures aimed at economic stabilisation to restore balance of payments equilibrium and to control inflation as well as structural reform to stimulate growth and competitiveness. Stabilization was a short-term fire-fighting affair for one year and a half, while structural reform is a medium-term exercise spread over three years. In this 'three years two - step strategy' for economic adjustment, the focus has been on slashing down demand in the first-half and then addressing the supply side through structural reform. The first phase of stabilisation has been accomplished, according to the government with great success and on schedule. The principal instruments of stabilisation were fiscal policy and monetary policy used in conjunction with exchange rate adjustment, which sought to reduce the level of aggregate demand in the economy. According to the Finance Minister's statement in the *Economic Survey* (1992-93) "Substantial progress has been made in bringing about fiscal correction reflected in the deceleration of inflation in the course of the year. But a great deal remains to be done". Critics have pointed out that in the course of stabilisation, the government had taken the soft option of squeezing public investment (more precisely, gross capital formation) relative to gross domestic product, which makes the remaining tasks of supply augmentation so much more difficult. Other options like a temporary compression of consumption have not been considered, which would have had no negative impact on growth potential of the economy.) Deepak Nayyar is somewhat sceptical about the results of stabilisation, whether considered in relation to the problem of inflation or the balance of payments situation. According to him, "much of the stabilisation is now attributable to borrowing and, therefore, may not be sustainable in the long run'[2]).

As regards structural adjustment, this is being sought to be achieved through four instruments :

(i) Trade reforms
  (a) By eliminating restrictions on imports, except for consumer goods; and
  (b) By progressively reducing tariff levels.

(ii) Increasing the openness of the economy
  (a) By the liberalisation of trade, capital and technology flows.

(iii) Industrial Policy Reform
  (a) By the removal of barriers to entry of new firms;
  (b) By the removal of the limits on growth in the size of existing firms; and
  (c) By cutting out state intervention in investment decision.

(iv) Deregulation in the financial sector of the economy in stages.
  (a) By fully deregulating interest rates;
  (b) By eliminating directed loan programmes;
  (c) By removing controls on capital movements; and
  (d) By allowing entry of foreign institutions into domestic financial markets.

In general terms, the structural reforms rest on the tripod of liberalisation, privatisation and globalisation. In particular, reforms have to be pushed forward in critical micro-economic areas such as industrial and trade licensing reform, wider opening up of the economy and the acceptance of the Dunkel Draft, privatisation of large public sector enterprises, the institution of a flexible hire and fire labour policy and the freeing of the financial sector. Second, structural reform is essential to fight the twin problems of poverty and unemployment. The Government's accomplishments have been mainly in two directions viz.

(i) The dismantling of the licensing system that governed industrial and trade decisions along with the restoration of the rupees (trade account) convertibility, and
(ii) The opening of the economy wider to trade along with a favourable shift in the attitude and a major shift in the policy towards direct foreign investment.

Reforms in other areas have been relatively slow. Bhagwati and Srinivasan who studied the progress of reforms (upto July 1993) have opined that "the reforms have much further to go in other critical areas, chiefly the privatisation of the large public sector, the institution of a flexible labour hire-and-fire policy and the freeing (simultaneously with the necessary social regulation) of the financial sector."

In the Finance Minister's statement in 'Economic Survey (1992-93)', the words "The phase of crisis management is over ...... But a great deal remains to be done" are quite significant and noteworthy. According to S.P.Gupta, "Solving them (i.e. macro-economic imbalances of the economy) only via a macro frame based almost exclusively around the central budget without any in-depth analysis of the states and many micro/sectoral economic activities covering technical, institutional and other factors will be highly risky". One of the weaknesses of the Reforms Policy is the fact that it has not so far, attempted to draw the sub-national areas into its fold. It seems that the central government is working on the premise that the complementary state-wide efforts would automatically fall in place and get incorporated into the scheme of reforms. Such a parallel process of mutual adaptation and effective sequencing, however, rarely synchronise. If the reforms do not trickle down, they may even prove to be dangerously counter-productive. Citing the substantial delicensing of trade and industry and the virtual restoration of current account convertibility, which have led to the possible creation of appropriate market incentives in the economy, Bhagwati and Srinivasan point out that the "State-level restrictions are still in place, and there is much bureaucratic machinery in place with consequent delays and transaction costs that damage the economy, despite much delicensing". The bureaucracies which have long been engaged in regulation and enforcement have to adapt to far-reaching changes. They have to develop the capability to serve as efficient functionaries of a state which facilitates the market and plays a promotional and enabling role. All macro policies must ultimately get translated into reality in space. This transition involving a spatial ordering of the elements of development (e.g. their location and spatial relations) is a crucial one and unless these are planned and steered in a careful manner, the reforms are likely to cause distortions in the territorial pattern of development of the economy.

Changing Spatial Structure of the Economy in India

Since our focus in this chapter is on the impact of economic reforms on regional and local development, we may start our probe with an analysis of the changes in the spatial structure of the economy in the country since independence[3]. In the colonial era, economic activities were mainly centered around the major ports of Bombay, Calcutta and Madras, leading to a geographical division of labour between these segments of the dependent colony and the metropolitan economy of the imperial power. This is described as 'enclave economy' with the port towns, the plantation areas and the mining areas constituting the 'enclaves' and the rest of the country relegated to the position of "a hinterland of primary production". After the attainment of independence, changes in the regional structure of the economy and consequential modifications in the geographical division of labour took place. During the 50's and 60's, a major thrust was given to industrialization based on the premises that heavy industry was fundamental to rapid growth and for a self-reliant and self-generating economy. This led to the setting up of capital intensive industries and power projects in the public sector using modern technology. Some of the major industrial projects, which are resource based were located near the source of raw-materials, which happened to be the industrially backward states of Bihar, Orissa and Madhya Pradesh. But many of these giant projects became merely another set of "enclaves", which had no relationships with their hinterlands and on the other hand, positively disrupted the traditional occupations and economic and social life in their immediate neighbourhood. Thus this rapid industrialization strategy led to certain adverse consequences of "geographic dualism".

At the same time, developments undertaken in the agriculture sector envisaged three major types of changes :

(i) Vast increases in irrigated areas brought about by the large multipurpose and irrigation projects;
(ii) The intensification of agricultural production; and
(iii) The intensification of agricultural specialisation within the physical zones and states.

All these changes were expected to act as important 'region forming forces' leading to the development of internal territorial specialisation and forging of economic links among regions. However, the capital-intensive, multi-purpose and irrigation projects failed to build up utilization capacities, leading to poor returns on the capital invested in them. Similarly, the green revolution strategy pursued vigorously during the late sixties accentuated the regional disparities by benefiting the elite class of farmers and certain preferred locations only.

Thus the spatial structure of development in India in the early seventies revealed an uneven growth pattern of a "localised" and "patchy" character in the interior. The growth processes were certainly permeating in the interior, but in an uneven manner. This is typically characteristic of the way development spreads and the closure of the regional gap takes place in an underdeveloped country (i.e not like how oil spreads, but through a leapfrogging and infilling process). Development starts at certain discrete points in space (as scattered droplets of investment in space) and then multiplies along a line (axial development), where natural resource endowments and physical and social infrastructure provide the stimulus and then such accretions in investment tend to saturate the region and close the gaps in space, completing the "net work". In the field of development planning, as in many other constructive fields, two different stages repeatedly appear, the one in which the development experiment makes some new dents and the next phase, when the knowledge and experience gained from such experiments are consolidated and systematically ordered. The spatial structure of the Indian economy was typically following this trend and was moving from "points" to the "line". In course of time, given a favourable policy environment, it would have continued in this progression to close the spatial gaps in development.

Industrial Incentives and Backward/Area Development Policies

Since the Fourth plan, India has been making a systematic effort towards the accelerated development of backward areas and initiated certain specific programmes for development dispersal. For the dispersal of industries in backward areas, incentives have been offered by the central government subsidy, central transport subsidy and backward area development allowance. Another scheme intended to encourage industrial dispersal is the one of 'freight equalisation', according to which the prices of certain critical industrial raw materials like cement, steel and coal were made uniform at all locations. We may collectively call these incentives as, "equilibrating mechanisms".

Besides the central incentives, state governments, in turn, have also offered several incentives to attract enterprises to backward areas[4]. The range and coverage of these incentives/facilities vary widely among the states. It is worth inquiring into the impact of these policies.

A recent study by Awasthi on the dynamics of regional industrialization in India, by looking into the regional industrial structures and shifts therein over a period of 18 years between 1961 and 1978/79 has offered conclusive evidence that interregional inequalities in the level of industrialisation have declined over time in the country.

Another study by Aggarwal and Sondhi has specifically inquired into the impact of the central incentive schemes on balanced regional development. The study has concluded that the various incentive schemes along with the necessary infrastructural facilities have played a significant role in the dispersal of industry to backward areas and their growth.

During the current plan period and more or less synchronising with the commencement of the new economic reforms, the industrial incentive schemes have undergone lot of changes in their content. The central investment subsidy has been withdrawn. The freight equalization scheme has also been done away with. Thus most of the 'equilibrating mechanisms' have virtually disappeared, although the transport subsidy, continues. The trends in industrial dispersal and the performance of the industry-incentive schemes reveal that the developed states in the backward areas have proved to be more attractive for industrial investment than the backward states in developed areas, emphasizing the importance of the infrastructure element (both the producer-oriented tertiary as well as the consumer-oriented tertiary as the crucial determinant on the siting of industries[5])

In response to these findings, the growth centre approach has been accepted by the government as a suitable measure for industrial dispersal. During the Eighth Plan period, the establishment of seventy (70) growth centres with full infrastructural facilities costing Rs. 30 crore in each growth centre is proposed to be established. The pattern of financing would be as follows : Rs. 10 crore by the centre, 5 crores each by the state government and the financial institutions and the rest 10 crore would be raised through market borrowings. Undoubtedly, the programme overstretches the fiscal ability of the government and raises doubts about its effective implementation. What the central government's approach to industrial dispersal means is that the new incentives proposed would not be individual-centre, but place (infrastructure) centred. How the incentives being provided by the state governments will now change in their content in view of the liberalization policies is difficult to guess. But one may be reasonably certain that in the states also, the 'investment subsidy' type of incentives will vanish. The establishment of industries will be determined more by market forces. Entrepreneurs are not likely to go to areas, which lack the necessary infrastructure. Industrial investment will therefore tend to concentrate in and around the better developed areas, where it can find adequate ancillary services, sub-contractors and already skilled employees. This would mean that the resulting development will tend to accentuate regional disparities. Dualistic structures of production will be re-inforced and recreated. It will tend to cause a sharp dichotomy between regional standards of living, leading to inter-regional frictions.

The unhappy part of this spatial trend of polarised growth will be the growth of big industrial agglomerations, where the events of the past have already assembled people and industry together and have thus created economies of scale. This will naturally deprive peripheral regions of potential growth. Should such a trend prevail, our national goal of prosperity-cum-equity would be more difficult to attain. Liberalisation and globalization will set in motion a new territorial division of labour reflecting itself in international dependency, interregional cleavages and spatial dualism. The growth centre strategy contemplated in the Eighth Plan is good in theory as an antidote, but difficult in practice. This has been the experience in many countries.

The Impact of Direct Foreign Investment

The other problem that we have to contend with here is the fact that liberalisation will bring in its wake, several trans-national corporations (TNC's) with external investments, whose adverse effects would be felt by indigenous enterprises and residents of the region in which they would be located. It cannot be assumed that these externally stimulated growth mechanisms either produce all of the benefits claimed for them or that the benefits will automatically stimulate the development of the region in which they operate. According to Sricharatchanya, such industries "seek out cheap labour, require low-skilled workers, pay relatively low wages, base their production on high import content and generate low domestic value added. Being mobile, they are able to exert maximum pressure on governments by threatening to pull out unless maximum benefits are provided". From this statement based on country experiences, it is clear that external investments can generate self-sustaining regional development only if ways can be found to improve the region's physical resources, to build local entrepreneurial skills, to improve the quality of regional labour force and to expand the amount of investment capital available within the region. The location and spatial configuration of investments will be determined by the TNC's in their own global interest and we would have no choice but to accept the resultant outcome. As Ghosh points out very realistically "The process of 'opening up' releases forces which will be difficult, if not impossible, to mould to any desired pattern". Negative controls and incentives, the so called 'stick and carrot' policy, by the state governments can go a long way in influencing the spatial pattern. But whether the states will have the financial and administrative edge as well as freedom to exercise such controls in an effective manner is a moot question. In any case, the TNC's, given their undisputed command over resources, technology and knowledge will try to bypass these restrictions. "They will never take any chances in the production or servicing of their integrated networks, unless they have complete dominance in the matter of cost and quality and flexibility of operation". The argument for what is vaguely being referred to as a 'level playing-field' may have some relevance; but in the context of the ongoing process of reform, the indigenous enterprises have to face the challenges of the TNC's either by increasing their competitiveness or by accepting the dominance of the TNC's and playing an obliging and submissive role. In this context, how the Chinese have tackled the regional consequences of foreign investment by a carefully guarded open-door development strategy is quite interesting and illustrative.

China has utilised 'export-oriented zones' as mechanisms to introduce open-door policies to promote significant reforms. The largest was at Shenzhen. The area had no special advantages. There was very little infrastructure, practically no industrial base and an almost exclusively peasant labour force. The proximity to Hong Kong and the belief that Hong Kong was a door that could be opened wide on both sides made Shenzhen a viable candidate for regional development. Throughout the 1980's, virtually the whole of China's east coast has been opened up to foreign investment and, while Shenzhen was one of the first important sites of foreign investment, it is now one among the many. Foreign investment has been directed in steps. In 1984, fourteen (14) coastal cities were opened for foreign investment. These had some industrial base and traditional link with outside world. In 1985, the programme was expanded and fifteen (15) Economic and Technological Development Zones (ETDZ) were opened. They were eligible for some preferential treatment including tax and other benefits. In 1988, China opened its three (3) river deltas - viz the Yellow river, the Yangtse and the Pearl river. Agricultural and industrial development were promoted in these river deltas. In 1990, China opened its fifth Special Economy Zone (SEZ) at

Hainan. It is now the largest Special Economiy Zone. China's strategy has been to start with the coastal cities and then move into the interior, where there was little infrastructure. The foreign firms were encouraged to build the infrastructure for which special incentives were given. In July 1992, China opened twelve (12) river cities along the Yangtse river for infrastructure and industrial development. The whole experiment in Directed Foreign Investment was organised as a step-by -step open-door development strategy and carefully monitored. There is not much literature in English setting out the regional consequences[6]. However, it is understood that upgrading of the local labour force as well as the transfer of technology and building up of infrastructure have been the major gains. While China could not really dictate what type of foreign investment should take place, the country, by and large, seems to have bent foreign investment to her requirements.

The Special Area Development Programmes

Apart from the incentive programmes for industrial dispersal, special area development programmes in certain specific areas of acute backwardness are also being implemented during the last 15-20 years in India. These include the programmes for the Hill areas, the North-East region, Border areas and Desert areas. These are specific regional programmes.

The backward area development strategy adopted here is one of 'transition growth', which means initially making a deep dent into the identified problem areas and gradually enlarging the effort in a definite progression along a development continuum. In terms of allocation of development funds to the backward areas, it means a progressive increase until development gets saturated. If we look at the Indian experience, some components of the backward area programme like the tribal development programme, small Farmers' Development Programme etc. have already been phased out and incorporated into the Integrated Rural Development Programme, which is showing diminishing trends in overall allocations. If we look at the year-wise allocation of special central assistance to a backward area programme like the hill areas, for instance, the static nature of these allocations, and hence of developmental trends is revealed. With such a trend in the pattern of allocations, the 'take-off' stage for backward areas will be an illusion and a mirage. The following figures are illustrative.

Allocation of Special Central Assistance under Hill Area Development Programme.

TABLE 6.1 : Allocation of Special Central Assistance
Under Hill Area Development Programme

(Rs. Crore)

Year	Amount
1989 - 90	267.81
1990 - 91	287.00
1991 - 92	290.00
1992 - 93	290.00

Source: Table 17.2, Eighth Five Year Plan (1992-97), Volume II, pp. 437.

The static nature of the allocations since 1991 may be particularly noted. This is a clear evidence of cut-backs of state expenditures on regional and social programmes and consequently of a general decline in living standards and services that are taking place at the sub-national levels in the country. Here Deepak Nayyar's observations are quite relevant. "A scaling down of public investment would squeeze supply responses in the medium term not only because it would cut back on infrastructure but also because it may dampen private investment". "Safety nets" are being talked about, but for all their rhetoric, the reality is that the country will not have adequate resources for this purpose. Bhagwati and Srinivasan have perhaps sought to soft pedal the impact of the reforms by their statement "the reforms are thus aimed at taking the government out of some areas and concentrating energies on others. They aim to refocus policy intervention". Among the micro-economic reforms where new steps must be taken boldly, they have not specifically touched on the aspect of complementary spatial policies. They have, however, emphasised the need for enlightened state level intervention that would complement the nation's economic reforms. For instance, if industrial delicensing is to be achieved effectively, liberalisation measures at the central level alone will not do; the simultaneous dismantling of state level restrictions is also needed. Ghosh's observations are quite relevant. "The long term interests of the country, politically, economically and strategically demand a positive and supportive state policy of not only preserving but developing actively the core of what we aimed at and sought to achieve in the past four decades".

The Core Objectives of Subnational Development and the Coping Strategies

The core of what we wanted to achieve at the Subnational levels through planned development effort may be broadly summed up as follows. Firstly, we wanted to achieve greater efficiency in the spatial economy through more optimal locational patterns for growth maximisation, achieving a more rational spatial division of labour, and articulating a system of spatial markets for capital, labour and commodities. Secondly, we sought to increase the equality of access to the bases of social power among the constituent populations (rural and urban) of the national territory. The instrumentalities to achieve the above were through state policies and programmes concerned with balanced regional development, poverty alleviation, decentralisation and development of indigenous local level institutions. As a result of these policies and programmes, the spatial structure of the economy has been changing. The colonial pattern of the space economy had virtually broken up with tentacles of growth pushing into the interior from the growth agglomerations around the coastal metropolitan centres. A process of regional economic integration was starting, as domestic industrialization made a dent into backward areas. Some changes in the inter-regional division of labour was becoming clearly visible. It is at this juncture that the macro economic crisis with its decelerating effect on the development of sub-national areas has struck and the tempo of changes in the spatial economy has received a serious set back. In this context, it is to be noted that even otherwise, the introduction of a strong spatial perspective into public sector policy-making is extraordinarily difficult. Sectoral policies are rarely explicit on spatial equity goals. To a degree, one can sympathise with the "sectoralists" who fail to provide a spatial orientation because the case for spatial policies on efficiency grounds has not been demonstrated adequately and forcefully. If such policies can only be championed on redistributive grounds, the temptation will always be great to let spatial policies take a back seat in preference to national priorities such as fighting inflation or closing the balance of payments gap. The central government, in its preoccupation with macro economic adjustments and meeting the obligation of international debt repayments, will have neither the time nor the resources to tackle at its own level, the problem of regional disparities within the country. In a federal country like India, the states and the local administrative areas below the state are the area levels at which this problem has to be squarely tackled. Also by necessity, the central government will be unable to provide adequate development resources to the regional and local areas, and these latter areas will have to mainly shoulder the burden of development on themselves and take the major initiatives in this regard. For enabling them to do so, decentralization and devolution with its parallel ideas of local resources mobilization and people's participation are quite relevant. Thus decentralization must be conceived as one of the important policies implemented as part of the economic reforms to spread its benefits in space, outwards to rural areas and downwards from the metropolis to the small rural communities. Such an approach will widen the opportunities of individuals, social groups and territorial organised communities at small and intermediate scales to mobilize the full range of their capabilities and resources for their common benefit. It is now evident that for solving our present economic problems, a policy of structural adjustment with transformation must be consciously pursued. To implement such an approach, improvements at the macro level alone will not do. Economic progress in the country must be based on far reaching internal reforms at the regional and local levels and much more cost effective use of resources. Studies on the African crisis and experiences with structural adjustment programmes have made it abundantly clear that internal policy reform and institutional change constitute the main factors within human control to foster economic growth. In this context, it is considered important to encourage regional and local initiatives and the work of regional and local government organisations to promote self-sustaining regional and local development. This is the strategy of "Development from within", which is now being vigorously advocated for sub-Sharan African development. What it really means is the setting in motion of a process that would channelise the great spurt of awakening and consciousness for change among the regional and local communities, enable grassroots organizations and non- government bodies to take charge of regional and local community affairs, unburden the bureaucracy from unnecessary accretions to its duties and responsibilities and enable the regional and local communities to mend matters for themselves. However, the task of activating the regional and local communities and local resources in such a manner that they could move apace with diminishing development intervention from the state would indeed be quite challenging. It is far more than simply declaring a policy of bottom-up decision making. It is reorganising the administrative structures, or more correctly 'reinventing' regional and local governments' for building entrepreneurial public organizations. In short, it would mean a paradigm shift, away from conventional thinking which equates effective government with bureaucratic service delivery, to government with dramatic new incentives and operating styles. According to Michael Calavan, 'reinventing governments' should mean establishing catalytic, community-owned, competitive, mission-driven, results-oriented, customer-driven, enterprising, anticipatory, decentralized, market-oriented entrepreneurial public organizations.

Thus given the present situation, the need for operationalising the concept of 'Development from Within' and promoting a fully decentralized management of economic affairs at the regional and local levels is crucial and imperative and the central government has to provide a conducive environment and support for the promotion of regional and local initiatives. The organisational and institutional changes that are needed for this purpose are, however, difficult to effect, because this is where one comes up against the biggest political constraints and bureaucratic impediments.

An Agenda for Spatial Equity

We may now pull the threads of our discussion so as to offer some prescriptions. The economic reforms introduced in the country is a long term process calling for various kinds of multi-level correctives, if the pains of the reforms are to be mitigated and confined within safety limits. If regional and local developments are not to be sacrificed, the government should exhibit strong political will in favour of a decentralised strategy and promote 'Development from Within' in a big way. Regional and local initiatives offer great scope for promoting self-sustaining subnational development and through it, national development. The role of the central government here is crucial in providing a suitable social, economic and political environment in which regional and local initiatives and regional and local self development could flourish. In the multilevel responsibilities that should govern development in the country in future, the following should be the role of the central government :

- Maintenance of peace, stability and law and order;
- Exercising negative controls and constraints on the growth of primate cities and industrial agglomerations;
- Provision of basic socio-economic infrastructure and management of the economy;
- Provision of a policy framework to encourage regional and local

initiatives and institutions as an integral part of the national development effort;

- Reinventing regional and local governments and institutions and empowering them;
- Provision of financial, institutional and technical support for the activities of the regional and local institutions and initiatives, and
- Decentralization of decision making and adoption of a regional and local development strategy in which regional and local resources and institutions would be the major platform.

At the receiving end (i.e. the regional and local levels), internal capabilities have to be built up for self-reliant development. In a way, the current crisis has, in itself created the preconditions for such development and prepared the regional and local communities mentally and emotionally for accepting and initiating such endogenous development. It has now to be operationalised through a tripartite cooperative approach. In which the regional and local communities, the non-governmental organisations and the central government should mutually supplement and complement their efforts and steer regional and local development in space and time in accordance with the needs, desires and capabilities of the local communities.

The above, in broad terms, constitute an 'agenda for spatial equity', which seems quite relevant when we are faced with the liberalisation and other economic reforms and their consequences.

Steering economic reforms in a big federal country like India is however, a very delicate task, as multiple decision points and multiple objectives like economic growth, poverty alleviation, balanced regional development and maintenance of macro-economic balance are all involved. In particular, the untangling of the distributional effects of the structural adjustment programme in India is very complex and requires much further research which links micro analysis with an understanding of macro economics at the national and international levels. The basic point here is not how well a particular effort is doing in the short-term, but where, over the long term, it is headed. Spatial perspectives are as important as macro-economic perspectives.

NOTES

1. Dr. Manmohan Singh in his 'Preface' to the paper by Jagdish Bhagwati and T.N. Srinivasan, "India's Economic Reforms". July, 1993.

2. Deepak Nayyar, 'Indian Economy at the cross roads-illusions and realities', EPW, April 10, 1993. Some statistics quoted by the author are quite interesting. Public investment certainly declined in real terms. The proportion of capital expenditure in total expenditure was on an average 31 per cent during 1987-88 to 1990-91, but dropped to 26 per cent in 1991-92 and to 25 per cent in 1992-93. Plan expenditure on infrastructure (energy, transport and communications) as a proportion of central plan outlay dropped from an average of 19 per cent during the period 1987-88 to 1990-91 to 14 per cent in 1991-92 and 12 per cent in 1992-93. Plan expenditure allocations for rural development and the social sectors (education, health, family welfare, water supply, sanitation, housing, urban development, labour, social welfare and nutrition) as a proportion of central plan outlay declined from an average of 16.1 per cent during the period 1987-88 to 1990-91 to 15.7 per cent in 1991-92 and 14.1 per cent in 1992-93. Rural development : Plan expenditure as a proportion of GDP on rural development and the social sectors declined from 1.2 per cent during 1987-88 to 1990-91 in both 1991-92 and 1992-93.

3. The author's analysis of these changes may be seen in his paper K.V. Sundaram: 'Territorial division of labour for optimum resource use in India', *The Indian Geographical Journal*, Vol. 59, No. 2, December 1984, pp. 196-204.

4. These have been mainly in the form of : (i) Financial assistance on concessional terms, (ii) Supply of land at concessional rates, (iii) Supply of power and water at concessional rates, (iv) Supply of scarce raw materials on priority basis, (v) Sales tax concession, (vi) Exemption from Octroi/terminal tax/entry tax, (viii) Exemption from stamp duty and registration fees, (ix) Price preferences; and (x) State transport subsidy.

5. The Aggarwal- Sondhi study has probed into this aspect of industrial dispersal. the study by Awasthi has also established through a 'behavioural model' analysis that in the early phase of industrialization, supply side factors were more important in explaining regional variations in the level of industrial development. However, over time, focus has shifted on the demand side variables.

6. The information quoted here is based on discussions with Mr. P.M. Shahul Harneed, Consultant, Indian Council for Research on International Economic Relations, New Delhi.

7

RECKONING WITH LIFE

MADHAV GADGIL

The Threshold

From the perspective of life sciences, even more than that of economics or international affairs, we stand on the threshold of a new world. For over the last decade people have learnt to move genes - units of heredity - around at will, creating new life forms like tobacco plants into which have been inserted genes from a bacterium. A host of other technological breakthroughs have ensured that biotechnologies are getting all set to revolutionize plant and animal production, food processing, waste treatment and other applications as yet only dimly perceived. With biotechnologies emerging as major players on the world economic scene, all the rules of the game as to how life should be treated are being turned on their head. Living organisms were once treated as a common heritage of human kind, accessible to all, freely exchanged around the world. Today, GATT calls for patenting of micro-organisms and protection of varieties of cultivated plants developed by plant breeders. And the now operative International Convention on Biodiversity to which India is a party asserts national sovereignty on all genetic resources (UNEP, 1992). The state of Queensland in Australia has already enacted legislation giving force to this claim of sovereignty, and other states and countries would no doubt soon follow suit.

Hope and Despair

These developments have evoked two markedly different reactions. The prophets of doom foretell the living wealth of India coming under control of avaricious multi-national corporations, who would patent, exploit, poison and finally wipe it out, leaving us worse off than ever before. Others more optimistically view the times as an opportunity to rid the nation of the stranglehold of the iron triangle of greedy politicians - corrupt bureaucrats - unscrupulous businessmen, to inject some efficiency in our economic enterprises, to create wealth based on our biological heritage, to empower our people to serve as effective custodians of our natural resources and to share in the fruits of their utilization. The purpose of this chapter is to argue that in the ambiance of the new economic policy there is much merit in accepting this counsel of hope and working towards making it a reality.

Vanishing Forests

Permit me to narrate an experience to suggest why I see signs of progress in the jolts that the old order is beginning to receive. The living wealth of the Western Ghats, now considered one of the eighteen hot spots of biodiversity the world over, has been the focus of my scientific work over the last two decades. The green mantle of these hills has fared poorly over the last forty years, the hill tracts in western Maharashtra having suffered worst. In many parts the only remnants of the pristine rain forest still to survive are tiny sacred groves, protected for generations by local communities abodes of their deities. I have therefore been involved in making inventories of such groves over many years (Gadgil and Vartak,1981) . While so engaged, I one day received a letter from villagers of Gani, a small hamlet in Shrivardhan taluk of the Raigad district of Maharashtra. The letter stated that their village had a good sacred grove of some 10 ha, which was marked for felling by foresters, and could I help them save it. So along with my teacher and collaborator, V.D. Vartak, I reached Gani, after a trek of several kilometers over hills shaved clean as a head of a monk. And there at Gani was a pristine stand of magnificent old tree growth, through which flowed the only perennial stream for the village. The villagers told us that they had witnessed the destruction of forest and drying up of the hill streams one by one over the years, and were determined that this one last forest, saved by all as the residence of the goddess Kalkai shall not be destroyed. It was not only the source of the one perennial stream, but also of many medicinal herbs. But it was slated to be cut, and the local Ranger had pleaded inability to stop the cutting unless orders for its cancellation came from the top. But he was aware of our interest in the sacred groves because of an enquiry for the inventory that had reached him, and had suggested that the villagers try approaching his Chief through our good offices.

Convinced of their case, we met the Chief Conservator of Forests, who was an old friend of my collaborator, Dr. Vartak. He said that he would agree to our request as a friend, but failed to appreciate our interest in these "stands of overmature timber" as he dubbed the sacred groves. Indeed the forest authorities all over have been taking such a narrow view of the resources at their command, thinking of forest as so much grist for the paper or plywood mills and totally ignoring their value in performing ecosystem services or as storehouses of genetic resources. And the wood on forest department's estates has been given away to the industries at throw away prices. Thus in 1958, the Government handed over bamboo resources of the district of Uttara Kannada in Karnataka Western Ghats at Rs. 1.50 per tonne, when the prevailing market rate was over Rs. 3000 per tonne. The prices have now been raised to Rs. 600 per tonne while the market rates have climbed to over Rs. 12000 per tonne. The plywood industry too has been given whole giant mango trees for as little as Rs. 100, when the annual yield of fruit of wild mangoes, prized for pickling would fetch more than that for the local villagers. Pampered by such subsidies, the forest based industry has only concentrated on making quick profits, in the process wiping out its own resource base through over exploitation. Thus 1960's and 1970's saw the destruction of plywood species of Western Ghats, 1980's that of Assam and Nagaland, 1990's is witnessing that of the last strongholds of the forest in Arunachal Pradesh and Andaman and Nicobar Islands (Gadgil, 1991 a).

The Iron Triangle

Indeed over the last four decades the process of development has degenerated into a process of the state sponsoring subsidized fluxes of resources to a narrow elite comprising organized industry and services and the more influential landholders. These have received water, power, forest and mineral resources all at large public subsidies in various forms, as well as license to pollute the commons without paying for the damage it inflicts. This has created an atmosphere in which manipulating the state machinery to get access to such favours has become the focus of all enterprise, throwing to the wind considerations of efficiency and sustainability. It has also encouraged continual borrowal of technology, without investing in innovation. So we have seen the coming into being of an iron triangle with its three vertices being made up of (1) Organized industry, services and bigger landholders who benefit from state subsidies, (2) Bureaucracy administering these subsidies, and (3) Politicians deciding on who gets what level of subsidies.

The operation of this iron triangle has led to a liquidation of the country's base of natural resources – including its heritage of biological diversity to profit a few. In the process are hurt people like villagers of Gani, rural landless and artisans, small and marginal farmers, herders, country boat fisherfolk, tribals, nomads.

International Links

The constituents of India's iron triangle have strong links with organized industry and services abroad as well. This has added to the pressure of erosion of country's biological resources, often bringing little benefit to anybody within the country. This is well illustrated by the story of Sarpagandha, *Rauwolfia serpentina*, a herb of our humid tropical forests. This herb contains an alkaloid, reserpine, of considerable utility in treatment of blood pressure disorders. This use was known to some tribal groups in Kerala, and from them to some local Ayurveda practitioners. This came to the notice of the western pharmaceutical industry who went ahead and isolated the active ingredient. That created a tremendous demand for the herb, which was exploited from our natural forests without any regulation whatsoever, while the state machinery was busy organising subsidized supply of timber to the industry. The trade was banned only after natural populations of *Rauwolfia serpentina* had been nearly exterminated.

Indians evidently got little out of this, barring subsistence wages for tribals collecting the herbs, and small profits for traders exporting them abroad. No rewards have flown to the tribals whose knowledge was the basis on which the drug was discovered, no royalties have come to India as the country of origin of this genetic resource. That is a regime about to be changed under the new Convention on Biodiversity.

Efficiency, Equity, Sustainability

Efficiency, equity and sustainability may be considered as three desirable attributes of any regime of management of natural resources. The old bureaucratic regime of state sponsored fluxes of resources at high levels of subsidies to influential segments of the society has failed on all three counts. Given that consumers are not being asked to pay a fair price, they have little concern for efficient resource use. Thus owners of irrigation pump sets paying no electricity charges have no interest in ensuring that state power corporations are running the electricity generation stations efficiently. The technocracy responsible for the power stations has a vested interest in running the operation wastefully, for that calls for less effort while enhancing the scope for misappropriation. Nor have the political masters been worried about efficient functioning of the state machinery.

The state was expected to look after the weaker sections, and subsidizing them at the cost of the rich might serve the cause of equity. But most subsidies have instead been cornered by the powerful, ensuring that landowners get cheap irrigation water and urbanites highly subsidized water in their taps, while the poorer peasants whose lands are submerged under river valley projects are inadequately compensated and pauperized. Where money is supposed to flow to the weak, as with tribal welfare schemes, much of it has been misappropriated by a corrupt bureaucratic-political machinery.

Sustainability too has fared badly in the process. The West Coast Paper Mill in Uttara Kannada district was expected to derive its raw material in perpetuity from the forests of that district. Within fifteen years it had exhausted bamboos-the most favoured raw material for paper making from the region. Our irrigation projects have been plagued by poor planning for drainage, so that as much land goes out of production through water logging as is brought under irrigation. Subsidized irrigation pump sets have driven aquifers down to hundreds of meters in areas like the Coimbatore district. There can be no doubt whatsoever that centralized, bureaucratic management of country's natural resources has been a dismal failure on every count.

What Can Markets Do ?

The recent moves in the direction of scrapping the old system can then be only welcome. But what can the central element of the new system, the market achieve. One hopes that through doing away with a monopoly of the state bureaucracy it can enhance efficiency. It is unlikely however that markets could promote either equity or sustainability. Markets may at best efficiently produce what those with purchasing power went right away. They may organize quick, efficient capture of prawn, their quick, efficient packing, their quick efficient shipping to European or Japanese tables. But markets have no mechanism for looking after poor in India's coastal tracts, for whom prawns, once a cheap, easily accessible source of protein, is now completely out of reach. Nor have markets any mechanisms to ensure that overfishing does not wipe out prawn stocks.

Indeed overfishing has been a serious problem, as much for Canadians and Italians as for anybody else. The New Economic Policy cannot therefore bring about a really desirable pattern of natural resource use, although it may still be far superior to the old bureaucratic management through bringing about improvements in efficiency.

Ecosystem and Biosphere People

The best bet for ensuring sustainability is to put the decisions on resource use regimes in hands of people who have a stake in sustainable resource use. Unfortunately this is not the case with any segment of the Indian population today. From a human ecological perspective one may recognize three categories of people; ecosystem people, biosphere people and ecological refugees (Dasmann,1988, Gadgil, 1991 b). The ecosystem people are those living close to the earth in their traditional habitats, meeting most of their needs by gathering natural resources, or producing them through subsistence agriculture or animal husbandry from their own environments. Tribals, artisanal fisherfolk, subsistence agriculturists, herders have lived in this fashion for generations, in the process evolving cultural traditions of prudent resource use. But most ecosystem people of India today have lost control over their resource base which has been overexploited and depleted to meet commercial demands. This has turned them into ecological refugees, as with basket weavers who have no more bamboo to ply their trade, or nomadic shepherds whose traditional grazing grounds have either been brought under the plough, or under forest plantations. Such ecological refugees have tended to lose their traditions of prudent resource use as fisherfolk start dynamiting river pools that were once set aside as refugia in form of sacred pools. The country's resource base is primarily devoted to meet the ever growing needs of the third segment of the population, the biosphere people. Biosphere people have been defined as those who can access the resources of much of the biosphere through market mechanisms; they are people like you and me who after a meal that has included wheat from Haryana and rice from Andhra Pradesh, coconut from Karnataka and fish from Goa, munch on an apple from Shimla while watching an American game of basketball on a Japanese television set. For us it matters little if the demand for crating apples has led to deforestation of Himachal Pradesh or overfishing in Goa has meant serious hardships for countryboat fishermen. We are far removed from where our resources come from, and have no feeling for extent of sustainability of their use. But it is the biosphere people who today govern the affairs of the country, and who would continue to have a strong say in the affairs under the new economic regime.

Protecting Forests

It is the ecosystem people and the ecological refugees who must perforce gather resources they need with their own labour from environments they are intimately familiar with who suffer from non-sustainable resource use. And they would work towards sustainable resource use if only empowered to do so and relieved from the strong pressures of having to eke out a living somehow.

That this works has been demonstrated most convincingly recently by the experience of village forest protection committees of West Bengal. These committees comprise members from all households in a given village who share the responsibility of protecting a forest area assigned to them against tree cutting. Members of the committee harvest other usufruct, such as sal seed and sal leaves which brings them substantial income, though often lower than the incomes they used to realize by marketing fuelwood. The VFPC's have also been assured of a share in the income that will be realized by harvesting timber when it has grown to an adequate size. Beginning with a small scale experiment in the predominantly tribal area of Arabari, VFPC's now cover many districts of West Bengal. They have served as a model for the joint forest management schemes which are now accepted by most of the state governments. These experiments of course, do have antecedents in systems such as ban panchayats of Kumaon, many of which have been functioning successfully since late 1920's; and more significantly have led consequences such as the spontaneous establishment of thousands of village forest committees in the state of Orissa over the last few years (Malhotra and Poffenberger, 1989).

Empowering People

Conferring a measure of control over a forested area adjoining the village is but one instance of the whole series of measures that must be promoted to ensure greater sustainability in the use of natural resources and greater equity in sharing benefits flowing from them. The present day system of a centralized bureaucratic apparatus deciding on some appropriate measures and then spending public funds without any genuine public accountability must now be replaced by a decentralized system of decision making in which local communities are given untied public funds to use for natural resource development in ways they consider most desirable, ensuring that the entire local population can participate in monitoring how the funds are being spent.

Permit me to cite a relevant personal experience. I was involved in planning a basket of eco development projects in a village in coastal Karnataka as a part of the Western Ghats Development Programme (Gadgil, 1993). On the basis of our own studies and discussions with the local people we made a series of proposals accepted at the highest level of the state government. These included a number of small check dams beginning in the upper reaches of the hill streams down to the lower levels as part of soil/water conservation measures. But when the implementation started, the soil conservation wing of agriculture department set these suggestions aside and took up creating a number of bench terraces on the hill slopes. Now if carefully executed these bench terraces may have helped in soil/water conservation and created additional cultivable land. But they were most sloppily executed, so that the slope of the bench terraces was not against the general hill slope; rather it was in line with it. The concerned land owners had no role in deciding on the location of the bench terrace, nor in supervising the quality of its execution. If they had, they would have insisted on proper slopes. As it happened, when the rains came, the loosened soil of the bench terraces actually enhanced the rate of soil erosion. The farmers could not effectively use these poorly constructed terraces for cultivation, all the more because the absence of any co-ordination between soil conservation and crop production wings of the Agriculture Department meant that they had no technical advice on an appropriate cropping pattern for the terraces. So the only parties to benefit form this whole exercise were the contractors who cut many corners to construct shoddy bench terraces.

Now if the local community had been handed the funds for soil conservation with the gramsabha authorized to decide on the appropriate measures with only technical advice coming from the agriculture department, they could have devised a more appropriate mix of programmes, executed them at greater economy with local labour, and seen to it that these genuinely benefited the concerned land holders. I am convinced that despite the inequities and political factions in India's village communities, this would be the approach which would deliver far better returns, both in terms of sustainability of use of natural resources, and taking some benefits of natural resource use to the weaker segments of the community.

The Panchayati Raj system now being organized throughout the country ought to serve the purpose of putting on ground such a system throughout the country.

Access to Knowledge

Such a programme should be linked to the "Land and Water literacy programmes" that have been initiated on a pilot scale in four districts throughout the country by the Bharatiya Gyan Vigyan Samiti as a part of the post-literacy activities following up on the Literacy Mission. This mission was one of the most progressive of the Government initiatives in recent years, and met with widespread positive response and involvement of NGO's over many parts of the country. The post-literacy programme visualizes involving people from local communities in mapping land, water, vegetation, habitation, each in their own panchayat areas on the basis of cadastral maps on 1:7000 scale. Such mapping could then be used to pinpoint problems such as gully erosion, water pollution, ground water depletion, or invasion by weeds in a highly site specific fashion to help in deciding on appropriate development interventions.

The Convention on Biological Diversity calls for giving respect to and conferring an important role on the knowledge and management practices of local communities. It would then be most appropriate to include inventorying and mapping of biological communities, and specific elements of biodiversity such as medicinal plants, varieties of cultivated plants and wild relatives of cultivated plants as an integral part of the Land-Water Literacy Programme. This would both generate an invaluable data base to help India foster indigenous biodiversity based enterprises, but would also provide us with a way to monitor the biodiversity conservation effort at a highly decentralized spatial scale.

Implementing Biodiversity Conservation

It has been forecast that biodiversity based industrial activities - pharmaceuticals, cosmetics, seeds, food processing, waste treatment - would come to account for a third or more of the world economy in the twenty-first century. India is one of the world's top twelve megadiversity countries. It is to be hoped that India would seize the opportunities that have opened up with the recognition of national sovereignty over genetic resource to nurture vigorous growth of biodiversity based enterprises in the coming years. Hopefully the new economic regime would help catalyse such growth.

But such growth would not by itself ensure conservation and sustainable use of biodiversity, nor equitable sharing of benefits arising out of utilization of biodiversity. Two measures might greatly help bring this about:

(1) Local communities must be given much more secure and meaningful rights over public lands and waters in their own localities, following the lead of joint forest management programmes.

(2) Local communities should be given substantial incentives to continue conserving biodiversity resources on private and public lands in their own localities by linking financial inputs, perhaps through the Panchayat Raj system, to the biodiversity levels. An open, transparent process of monitoring biodiversity levels, perhaps through the Post-Literacy Mission activities in collaboration with schools, colleges and research institutions could map the levels of biodiversity throughout the country. Payment from a National Biodiversity Fund could then be made in some proportion to biodiversity levels thus being maintained.

Finances flowing into such a fund could come from a cess on all biodiversity based commercial products like drugs and seeds, international grants for conservation purposes as from the Global Environment Facility, income from royalties from industry using Indian genetic resources, and Central and State Government allocations for conservation programmes.

Conclusions

The new economic regime is a welcome development, hopefully promoting greater efficiency of use of natural resources. But in itself it will not promote more sustainable and equitous use of such resources. In the more open democratic atmosphere that the new economic regime has fostered, we must now craft other people-oriented institutions to promote sustainability and equity. India's accession to the Convention on Biological Diversity could greatly help foster such initiatives. It is to be hoped that our country would in the coming years rise to this important challenge.

8

MANAGING CHANGE IN SOCIAL SECTOR: Post Script[1]

V. K. AGNIHOTRI and H. RAMACHANDRAN

Introduction

A one week modular programme was designed for a pre-identified group of senior officers representing selected areas such as social welfare, rural development, health, education and food & civil supplies and organised from 17th to 22nd October 1994 at Lal Bahadur Shastri National Academy of Administration, Mussoorie. Eleven officers participated in the programme.

The programme was structured to include five one-day modules covering: (i) Managing changes in the social sector; (ii) Structural Adjustment and anti-poverty strategy; (iii) Reforms in health care delivery; (iv) Reforms in education; and (v) Role of Food Security in the new economic climate.

The programme was designed with the following objectives:

(i) to discuss and debate implications of the New Economic Policy with reference to social sector;

(ii) to grasp the nuances of the interface among selected sectoral policy changes and administration;

(iii) to develop an agenda of follow-up changes in procedures and regulations; and

(iv) to demarcate areas, levels and nature of intervention in certain areas of social sector such as Education; Anti-poverty Strategy; Health and Food Security.

Managing Changes in the Social Sector[2]

The discussion on this overview module brought into focus three broad themes that were taken up for group deliberations: (a) Mobilisation of resources for social sector including maximisation of returns on investments; (b) Privatisation of Social Sector Services; and (c) Re-prioritisation within sectors and Targeting of Social Sector Programmes.

The group which deliberated on the issue of mobilisation of resources for the social sector made the following recommendations:

(i) Disinvestment or government withdrawing from sectors which are not relevant to the present economic scenario, is the pillar of New Economic Policy. This will throw up surplus funds which should be utilised to increase the allocations to the social sector. This will re-emphasise the importance of this sector in the new economic climate;

(ii) Private sector should be allowed to come into the social services sector fully, where they can serve by levying user charges which the people can afford to pay. This may be in higher education, superspecialisation in curative medicine etc. This will reduce the strain on government institutions which can concentrate on the poorer segments of the population. Services in the social sector should be charged to those who can afford at least at subsidised rates or token rates. Differential rates for different income groups can be tried. However, this has practical problems in implementation;

(iii) At present, there is a tendency to allocate funds first for the so called 'priority sectors' viz. agriculture, industries, power, irrigation works etc. The residual amount is allocated to the social services. This should change. Social services allocation should be made on the basis of specific goals to be attained in a particular period. Balance has to be maintained between economic and social sectors. Investment in the social sector which is for immediate benefit of the poor should not be sacrificed for the sake of achievements in priority sectors whose returns may take long time to fructify;

(iv) If the return for the rupee spent on the social services sector is to be maximised the functionaries in those sectors should be made accountable to the implementing authorities. The persons involved in delivery of social services at the cutting edge level should be appointed on contract basis to get good results. Decentralisation of decision making process will also save resources and yield good results; and

(v) Investments in certain essential social sectors in an integrated manner will yield better results in terms of PQLI. To get effective results from the investments in these sectors the resources should be spent in a concentrated manner rather than spreading them thinly.

A second group had detailed discussion on the feasibility of bringing about privatisation of social sector services. There was consensus among the members of the group that there was need for privatisation of social sector services. The group identified the main sectors where privatisation could be brought about, such as housing, education, health and sanitation and Public Distribution System. The objectives of the proposed privatisation are greater efficiency, reliability in services and cost effectiveness. The group found that the present system suffers from lack of motivation, lack of accountability, inherent leakages etc. The group confined itself to three sectors – health, sanitation and education

The group considered the extent of privatisation that could be effected in the health sector. The following areas were identified for being privatised – hospital services and public health. In respect of hospitals there are a variety of services that could be privatised immediately: security, cleaning, ambulance, catering, laundry, diagnostic services and dispensary.

It is not claimed, however, that by privatising them, these services will improve dramatically. Privatisation is bound to throw up a number of problems especially in the transitional period. For example, the group considered as to what would happen to the employees who are already engaged in these services. The affected employees should be given certain safeguards such as protection of their pension even in respect of the remaining period of service.

It was felt that out-patient treatment in Government hospitals should be considerably strengthened and made free for all, and other services should be charged on a cost-basis. This recommendation is being made taking into account the fact that out-patient facility is largely used by poor people. While charging for all other hospital services, there is need to ensure that the poor people who cannot afford to pay are not neglected. We have to evolve a system by which the poor and deserving people can be charged on the basis of income.

The group then considered the extent of privatisation that can be brought about in the area of sanitation. There are three major elements to be considered under sanitation and they are collection of garbage, transportation and disposal. The group felt that all these activities should be privatised.

The group devoted considerable time to the question as to whether any privatisation could be effected in the education sector. After detailed discussions, the group felt that it was worthwhile considering privatisation of higher education. So far as primary and secondary education is concerned, the present pattern, which is a mix of private and government enterprise, should continue.

While privatising higher education, we should not lose sight of the imperative need for protecting the interest of students who cannot afford to pay for their higher education. The suggestion is that a suitable scheme should be devised for awarding scholarships to students who come from weaker sections of society. During the transitional period, Government may have to bear the capital and maintenance cost of these educational institutions till they become self-supporting.

The group also recommended the urgent need for improving the quality of school education. It should be examined whether the private schools too could be brought under the effective control of some authority like the Zilla Parishad, to ensure that they function in a better manner.

The third group began with the assumption that resources are limited and inadequate even if we discount the possible contraction in social sector spending as a result of the restructuring and stabilisation programme. Hence optimisation of the use to which resources are put is an inescapable need. The group believed firmly that reprioritisation and targeting are both necessary in optimising resource utilisation. The major sub-sectors identified are Education, Health, Water Supply & Sanitation, PDS, Anti-Poverty Programmes and Housing.

The first three: Education, Health and Water Supply & Sanitation are in one category and the other three in the second category. Education, Health and Water Supply & Sanitation are important in that order of priority while we consider resource allocation. PDS (food subsidy), Anti-poverty Programmes and Housing should come next in that order of priority.

Within each sub-sector also, there is a need for reprioritisation. The cardinal principle should be: allocate more resources to those activities which benefit a larger majority and are more basic in nature. Thus primary education (and vocational training) and primary health care, should get a greater share of resources from the State.

Targeting is unavoidable given the size of the cake. The objective is to benefit those who cannot afford the service/facility without State subsidy. There are practical problems in devising the criteria for targeting and in implementing them. This may even lead to corruption of a new kind. But, however imperfect the system, ways can be found for organising targeting which should not be given up on account of practical problems. The poorer and disadvantaged groups to whom the benefits are targeted should not miss the opportunity. For this purpose targeting should not be defined too narrowly.

Institutions of higher education or such other institutions which are compelled to be financially independent as a result of reprioritisation, should be free to charge fees for their services both from the poor and the rich. Ways should be devised to reimburse the poor in a direct manner. If they are allowed free services, there is every possibility that they may be denied access to these services while the rich and the privileged may monopolise the facilities. No service should be given free. Everything should be paid for even if the payment is not very high. There is a strong case for revising the fees in institutions of higher learning.

Reforms and Anti-poverty Programmes

The participants recommended that (i) the delivery system must be improved. For this three alternatives can be considered: (a) active involvement of competent NGOs, (b) taking the maximum help of Panchayati Raj Institutions, and (c) consideration of contracting out some of the components of Anti-Poverty Programmes. (ii) Educating and training the officials and staff of NGOs and Panchayati Raj Institutions, so as to improve their performance and productivity. (iii) Encouragement should be given to Rural Industry. The State in this case should play the role of a facilitator. The granting of licenses, procedures for clearance, the relevant technology and a proper marketing strategy were some of the areas identified for streamlining. (iv) The rural poor should be divided into three categories, destitutes for whom dole is the only alternative. Simultaneously, efforts being made to improve their skills, for which the maximum age limit should be 40 years; poor without any skills for whom the alternative should be wage employment for which more and direct funds should be given to village Panchayats; and the last category consisting of those poor who are on the margins of poverty line, for whom self-employment should be the main vehicle for improvement. (v) A watershed should be taken as a unit for planning, as local plans are essentially agro-based. This process of planning should ensure community participation. Gram Pradhans, Block Panchayat members and Zilla Parishad members should be actively involved in preparation and implementation of these Plans. (vi) Panchayats and NGOs should be encouraged to create awareness amongst the local poor about the anti-poverty programmes. (vii) NGOs should also be involved in a big way in upliftment of urban poor. They can play a key role by giving training or helping the skilled poor to form cooperatives. Voluntary organisation can also be asked to play a key role in getting urban poor, certain jobs like house-wards, domestic helpers, gardeners, etc. (viii) The budget allotment for urban poor upliftment programmes should be enhanced. For rural poor this has increased significantly in 1993-94, but no matching increase has been there for the urban sector.

Reforms in Health Care Delivery

The Group on Intersectoral Co-ordination noted that the Central investment in Health Sector has increased after the commencement of the New Economic Policy. It was also noted that there is a perception even among the external funding agencies that health is a sector to be supported and not one for which allocations can be reduced in the context of structural adjustment. But such an increase in allocation is not noticed in the State Sector.

As far as intersectoral collaboration is concerned, Education, Water, Sanitation, Nutrition etc. are areas which need to work in unison ("Collaboration"). In this context, the group recommended to all State Governments the Nutritious Meals Programme of Tamil Nadu. This scheme brings out strongly the linkages between Nutrition and Health, as well as Health and Education. Apart from enhancing the nutrition levels of children, it has substantially increased the retention rate of children in schools, leading to higher literacy (and Education) which in turn has further enhanced health awareness. In fact, the progress achieved by Tamil Nadu in Physical Quality of Life Indicators can be largely attributed to this one scheme. Education by itself is a strong catalyst for achievements in health. Hence, mainly by increasing the retention rate, the health of the community will improve, as is evidenced by the Kerala experience. Education for All and Health for All by 2000 AD is an appropriate slogan.

Investment in Water Supply and Education should be commensurate with the goals set in the Health Sector. Potable drinking water supply should be extended to all villages at least by 2000.

It is noticed that even in the sanctions issued by Government of India under operation Black Board, there appear to be no provision for toilets to be attached to school buildings. Either Government of India should include this too in the scheme or States should construct it under JRY etc.

NCERT, while drawing up the syllabi, includes various Health messages in the lessons. This should be done by States as well. Similarly, in the literacy campaigns, health and sanitation efforts should be emphasised.

Doctors should visit schools periodically to check children's general health, nutrition, eyes, etc. Under the new Panchayati Raj Act, the Primary Health Centres may be transferred to the Panchayati Raj Institutions. States should immediately do this. It was noticed that Karnataka has already done it.

For prevention of diseases and even detection of certain diseases, the help of trained paramedical staff or even volunteers could be taken. The media (TV, Radio, Newspapers etc.) should be used more extensively for prevention and detection of diseases and spreading health messages. The Information, Education and Communication (IEC) component for all Health schemes should be enhanced and fully made use of.

The Group recommended that all Doctors should undertake compulsory rural work for say, 5 years. This could be insisted upon as a prerequisite for post-graduate admissions and Government jobs and even for getting the basic degree.

The Group on Role of the State vis-à-vis Private Sector recognised the dominant role of State uptill now in the making of Policy and implementation of programme. However, it was also felt that the Private Sector, specially on the curative side, has had a role which has now grown and physically expanded even into geographical areas hitherto untouched. The group also took into account the fact that the role of Private Sector is no more restricted to simple medical practitioners. Now hospitals and nursing homes etc. of varying sophistication have come up all over the country.

While trying to demarcate a fresh role for the State and the Private sector, the group thought that emphasis should be continued to be placed on integrated approach in the delivery of health care. This should go hand-in-hand with other sectors/sub-sectors like nutrition, water supply, sanitation, etc.

The Group then looked at the preventive, promotive, curative and rehabilitative aspects of the health policy and the role that the state and the private sector can play. On the preventive side it was recognised that in a country like India the State shall continue to have a pre-emptive and dominant role. While the state shall continue to place emphasis on and hopefully direct its revenues in larger chunks to this area, the size of task calls for a role for the private sector too, however small it may be in the beginning.

This could include responsibility to be given to private hospitals on the medical side, and to NGOs on both medical and promotional side. State funding should be made available. As the preventive side will be primarily the responsibility of the State, IEC (Information, Education and Communication) and MIES (Monitoring, Information, and Evaluation System) will also be its responsibility. However, private sector can be encouraged in this task, and voluntary efforts encouraged with or without State funding.

On the curative side the group looked at the primary/secondary and tertiary segments. While at the primary level the state shall have to continue to play the dominant role, there is room for both the state and the private sector of secondary level. The efforts of the private sector, to establish facilities should be encouraged. These facilities can also be linked to the primary level institution for referral matters. As for the tertiary level, it was felt that the State should increasingly allow and facilitate private sector entry and expansion

On medical education the consensus was that future expansions should be in the private sector. Existing facilities in the government sector can be considered for privatisation so as to reduce the burden on the State. Same will hold true for para-medical and other associated aspects of education. In medical education it was felt that while the private sector will have the main role, in future expansions, funding for weaker sections shall be the State's responsibility.

On the rehabilitative aspects, it was stated that the State has a large role to play and in fact this area is in need of greater State attention.

Finally, it was also stressed that in the context of expanding private sector it is necessary to evolve appropriate regulatory mechanism for both private and autonomous public institutions.

Reforms in Education

Four broad themes were taken up for group discussion:

(a) Resources for education and;
(b) their utilisation and improving the quality of education;
(c) Industry/private sector role in education; and
(d) vocationalisation of secondary education.

The following major recommendations emerged for reforms in education:

(1) An education cess should be levied as recommended by the Central Advisory Board on Education and the National Development Council and the modalities for its imposition and utilisation should be worked out. The cess so collected should be utilised for education sector only.
(2) More investment in education should be made by the state governments.
(3) Community participation in higher education needs to be stepped up by way of scholarship, endowments etc.
(4) Private sector participation in education should be encouraged.
(5) In utilising the available resources, greater allocation for provision of educational aids should be made as against 95% of the resources being expended at present on salaries.
(6) Student-teacher ratio should be computed in the context of attendance and not admission of students. This would provide an opportunity for cost reduction in bigger schools.
(7) Teachers' training (especially in-service training) needs to be given more attention in the context of setting up of National Council of Teacher Education (NCTE) and District Institutes of Education and Training (DIET).
(8) Nine steps for promoting efficiency in higher education outlined in para 6.15 of National Policy on Education should be expeditiously implemented, especially in the area of technical and management education.
(9) For optimum utilisation of academic faculty in colleges, adoption of UGC scales of pay should be necessarily accompanied by strict compliance to other requirements of the scheme like qualification, training etc. The existing situation should be reviewed and appropriate mechanism should be established to rectify it.
(10) There is need to ensure proper monitoring and review of academic performance of college faculty.

(11) The primary responsibility to provide school education should necessarily vest with the government till such time as the private sector is able and willing to take it over either in full or partly.

(12) The government and the community should encourage private sector in all possible ways even by providing incentive in all deserving cases, especially if they set up institutions in remote areas.

(13) Quality in government run schools has to improve in order to refurbish their image in the eyes of the public and thereby prevent proliferation of private teaching shops. The measures recommended to achieve this are : refresher training for teachers, provision of adequate laboratory facilities and other amenities in schools, proper residential accommodation for primary school teachers in difficult areas.

(14) Government should desist from setting up new institutions of higher education in view of the costs involved as well as the backlog of upgradation of existing government institutions. Wherever possible, existing government institutions may be privatised. Financial support to meritorious students may be provided by way of scholarships and loans.

(15) Suitable and efficient mechanisms to regulate the functioning of private institutions of higher learning should be put in place quickly.

(16) Funding of government institutions of higher education by industry and private bodies must be encouraged with fair amount of autonomy in the utilisation of these resources.

(17) There should be continuous and constant interactions between industry and institutions of higher education at all levels: institutional, faculty and students.

(18) Vocational courses are available only in 60 to 70 specific disciplines. The objective of making them terminal and job-fetching is, however, not being attained optimally. Apart from improving the quality of existing vocational courses by providing greater practical orientation and apprenticeship schemes, a wider range of skills needs to be promoted and disseminated through new avenues of continuing and distance education such as evening programmes in ITIs and polytechnics.

Role of Food Security in New Economic Climate

Two broad areas were identified for group deliberations: (1) What can be the alternatives to the present structure of Food Administration?; and (2) How can the PDS be effectively targeted and streamlined?

The First Group which deliberated on alternatives to the present structure of Food Administration made the following recommendations:

(i) The national objectives for Food Policy must ensure that food is available at all times at all places. For achieving this, self-reliance in food should be aimed at, and necessary efforts should be made to augment food production. Alternative instrumentality of imports of food may also be relied upon.

(ii) To take care of exigencies there should be a minimum buffer stock of foodgrain in the country. This buffer stock should be maintained by the state. A national agency like the FCI is the best possible instrumentality.

(iii) The cost involved in maintenance of the buffer stock should be sustained by the Government.

(iv) The figures as worked out show that the norms for buffer stocking are holding a one year stock for PDS. Any fluctuations will have to be taken care of by imports.

(v) Progressively there should be an active policy to bring down the need for large buffer stocking by encouraging greater production of foodgrain in non-green revolution areas.

(vi) The purchase of foodgrain should be limited to the buffer stock levels and should be done at market prices.

(vii) The disposal of the foodgrain has to be done on an annualised basis.

(viii) This foodgrain should be made available for selective intervention and targeting, at a price, which may be called the "clearing price". Any subsidies involved shall be borne by the Government.

(ix) Beyond this there were two points of view. One that the foodgrain should be made available to the states at the clearing price. Beyond this any subsidy shall be on the states' account. Any saving made on the central account thus far, may be distributed to the states according to a formula to be worked out by the centre in consultation with the states. This would provide greater autonomy and flexibility to the states in devising appropriate safety nets. The other view point was that the centre has a direct responsibility, as do the states, to serve the targeted group. Therefore the subsidy should be directly built into the system by the centre. As for flexibility, the individual states can work out details of implementation in consultation with the centre.

The Second Group deliberated on effectively targeting and streamlining the PDS and made the following recommendations:

(a) *Targeting:*

(i) Targeting should be at both the procurement and the consumption points. This should essentially be for those who need it.
(ii) Procurement should be of medium variety of grain for the PDS.
(iii) The Minimum Support Price (MSP) should be fixed on a scientific basis. Frequent increases should be avoided. It has also been noticed that increase in MSP has not resulted in any appreciable increase in production.
(iv) Procurement cannot be capped. However, the excess foodgrain procured over the optimal level should be marketed through all available channels (internally and externally). FCI should develop necessary expertise for International Marketing.
(v) The optimal level for stocks with the FCI should be 10 to 11 million metric tonnes. (This is the essential quantity required to cover the below poverty line segments)
(vi) The imbalance in the subsidy level for Rice and Wheat should be rectified.
(vii) FCI should consider procurement at staggered rates. (In this case storage will be at the farmer cost.)
(viii) Marginal differential pricing needs to be adopted. This will help increase food production in the states which presently do not produce much. In this regard freight equalisation should also be abandoned as a necessary offshoot of the above.
(ix) There is no need for uniform price in the RPDS (Revamped Public Distribution System). Once targeting is done the whole system will reshape itself into a BPL (Below Poverty Line) - PDS.
(x) The consumer targetes should only be the BPL group. (The list made by GOI in this regard will be removed from this ambit of the new reshaped BPL-PDS.)

(b) *Streamlining:*

(i) Elimination of Bogus Ration Cards. The Election Identity Card should serve a dual purpose in the case of BPL who should be listed on the EI Card. This possibility needs to be explored.

(ii) Streamlining the Input cost by eliminating leakages and all other inefficiencies in the present system to make the price attractive.

(iii) Introduce regionalisation at the distribution stage.

(iv) Quality control measures at all FCI depots should be undertaken by responsible outside agencies like the (registered) Consumer Protection Council under the Act, Mahila Mandals etc.

(v) The Andhra Pradesh and Madhya Pradesh models should be attempted all over the country.

(vi) Sanctioning of retail outlets should be on the same lines as is followed in the case of LPG dealership.

(vii) The PDS outlets should be allowed to sell all items to make the unit viable.

(viii) Partial lifting of rations through the PDS should be permitted. (The ration shops should be open on all days).

(ix) The ration dealers should resort to weekly lifting from Depots (FCI).

(x) The Essential Commodities Act and the prevention of Food Adulteration Act should be strictly implemented. The enforcement aspect is critical.

NOTES

The views expressed in this chapter are personal to the authors and the participants of the training pogramme. They do not reflect the opinion of the Government or their respective organisations.

The course was designed for senior officers and as such structured to be highly interactive. In each day's module the internal faculty and the guest speakers initiated the discussion on the theme during the first session. Subsequently, the participants were divided into groups to work intensively on various issues identified in order to prepare an agenda of action, and each group presented its agenda in the plenary session each day. The agenda was thus discussed by the participants including the internal faculty, guest speakers and the programme coordinators. The in-house faculty included Dr. V K Agnihotri, Dr. H Ramachandran, Mr. K K Sharma, and Mr. Padam Vir Singh; guest speakers on different themes included Prof. Amitabh Kundu, Prof. Anand P Gupta, Mr. Lalit Mathur, Mr. S S Meenakshisundaram, Mr. B S Lamba, Prof. K N Reddy, Prof. A Prabhakar, Dr. N V Varghese, Dr. R V Vaidyanatha Ayyar, Dr. G Sundaram and Mr. R Narayanan; and the participants were: Dr. Narendra Bihari, Dr. K S Chatarath, Mr. V Thulasi Das, Mr. R Parasuram, Mr.Dheenadhayalan, Mr. D S Mathur, Mr. C T Benjamin, Mr. C Gopala Reddy, Mr. Jose Cyriac, Mr. A K Rastogi, Mr. V K Nair; and observer participants included Mr K A Chandrasekaran, Mr. T R Maakan, Mr. J L Bajaj and Mr. R Kashyap.

REFERENCES

Acharya, S.S. (1989) 'Socio-Economic Impact of 1987 Drought in Rajasthan', Department of Agricultural Economics, Rajasthan Agricultural University, Udaipur.

Aggarwal, Pawan K. and H.K. Sondhi (1991) *Fiscal Incentives, and Balanced Regional Development: An Evaluation of Section 88 HH*. Vikas Publishing House Pvt. Ltd., New Delhi.

Antia, N.H. (1993) 'Shortage of the Existing System' in Antia, N.H. and Kavita Bhatia (ed.) *People's Health in People's Hands*, FRCH, p. 61 and 71.

Antia, N.H. and Kavita Bhatia (ed.) *People's Health in People's Hands*, FRCH, p.29.

Asian Development Bank (1993) Poverty in Developing Asia: Salient Issues and Lessons.

Awasthi, D.N. (1991) *Regional Patterns of Industrial Growth in India*, Concept Publishing Company, New Delhi.

Bajpai, N. (1993) 'Stabilisation with Structural Reforms: Can the Two be Pursued Simultaneously', *Economic and Political Weekly*, 1[illegible] May, pp. 990-994.

Bhagwati, Jagdish and T.N. Srinivasan (1993) India's Economic Reforms, July.

Bhalla, G.S. (1993) Policy for Food Security in India in the Context of New Economic Policy Framework, Institute for Studies in Industrial Development, New Delhi.

Bhalla, G.S. (1993a) 'Food Security in South and Southeast Asia Countries', *Man and Development*, March.

Bhalla, Sheila (1993) 'The Dynamics of Wage Determination and Employment Generation in Indian Agriculture', *Indian Journal of Agricultural Economics,* Vol. XLVIII, No. 3, July-September (Conference Number)

Bidwai, Praful (1992) 'Public Hospitals Turn Into Illness Factories', *Times of India,* August 3.

Binswager, P.H. and B.J. Quizon (1988) *Distributional Consequences of Alternative Food Security in Developing Countries : Costs, Benefits and Policy Options,* John Hopkins University Press, Baltimore.

Brando, A.S. and W. Marlin (1993), *Implications of Agricultural Trade Liberalisation for Developing Countries,* World Bank.

Calavan, Michael M. (1993) Local Government and Central Bureaucracy : A Crucial Nexus in Democratic Nepal, *Report to the U.S. Agency for International Development.*

Chalam, K.S. (1994) Union Budget and Decline in Educational Effort, *Economic and Political Weekly,* 16-23 April, pp. 901-907.

Chambers, R. (1988) Sustainable Rural Livelihood's in Conroy, C. and M. Lit Vinoff, (eds.), *The Greening of Aid,* Earthscan, London.

Chandramohan, C. (1992) National Rural Employment Programme: An Evaluation with Special Reference to Tamilnadu, A Ph.D. Thesis submitted to Ranchi University, Ranchi.

Chopra, R.N. (1988) *Food Policy in India : A Survey,* Intellectual Publishing House, Ansari Road, New Delhi.

Chopra, V.L. (1992) Self Sufficiency in Food Production, *Yojana,* Sept. 30.

Cornia, G.A. Jolly, R. and Steward, F. (eds) (1987) *Adjustment With a Human Face,* Vol. 1, Oxford, Clarendon Press.

Cornia, Giovanni Andrea (1990) UNICEF's views on the Experiences with Structural Adjustment Programme's in Structural Change and Poverty, CDR project paper 90.2 Centre for Development Research.

Dandekar, V.M. (1994) Budget 1994-95: Fiscal Aspects and the Real Economy, *Economic and Political Weekly*, 16-23 May, pp. 983-991.

Dasmann, R. F. (1988) Towards Biosphere Consciousness, in Worsted, D. (ed.), *The Ends of the Earth: Perspectives on Modern Environmental History*, Cambridge University Press, Cambridge.

Davies, S and M. Leach (1991a) Editorial, Food Security and the Environment, *IDS Bulletin*, Vol. 22, No. 3, July.

Davies, S and M. Leach, (1991b) Globalisim Versus Villagism : Food Security and Environment at National and International Levels, *IDS Bulletin*, Vol. 22 No. 3, Institute of Development Studies, Sussex.

Dearden, P.J. and E.M. Cassidy, (1990) Food Security : An ODA View, *IDS Bulletin*, 1990, Vol. 21, No. 3, Institute of Development Studies, Sussex.

Deshpande, Sudha and L. R. Deshpande (1992) New Economic Policy and Female Employment, *Economic and Political Weekly*, October 10.

Dev, Mahendra S. and M. H. Suryanarayana (1991) Is PDS Urban Biased and Pro-Rich? An Evaluation, *Economic and Political Weekly*, October 12.

Dhar, P. N. (1992) 'Constraints on Growth Reflections on the Indian Experience' in Uma Kapila (ed), *Indian Economy since Independence : Vol. 4. Recent Developments in Indian Economy with Special Reference to Structural Reforms*, Part one. Academic Foundations, Delhi.

Downing, T.E., K.W. Gitu and M.K. Crispin, (eds.) (1989) *Coping with Drought in Kenya: National and Local Strategies*, Lynne Rienner, London.

Dreze, J. and A. Sen, (1989) *Hunger and Public Action*, Clarendon Press, Oxford.

EPW Research Foundation (1994) 'Social Indicators of Development for India' - I, *Economic and Political Weekly*, May 14, 1227-40.

EPW Research Foundation (1994) 'Social Indicators of Development for India - II: Inter-State Disparities,' *Economic and Political Weekly*, May 21, 1300-08.

Etinne, Gilbert (1977) 'Foodgrain Production and Population in Asia : China, India and Bangladesh', *World Development*, Vol. 5, Nos 5-7, pp 425-440, Pergamon Press, Great Britain.

FAO (1983) 'Committee on World Food Security, Council and Conference'.

Gadgil, M. (1991) 'Conserving India's Biodiversity : The Societal Context', *Evolutionary Trends in Plants*, 5(1), 3-8.

Gadgil, M. (1991b) 'Conserving India's Forest Wealth', *Nature and Resources*, 27(2), 12-20.

Gadgil, M. (1993) 'Involving People', *Seminar* - Special Issue on Managing Our Natural Resources, June, pp. 14-18.

Gadgil, M. and Vartak, V.D. (1975) 'Sacred Groves: A Plea for Continued Conservation', *Journal of Bombay Natural History Society*, 72: 314-320.

Gadgil, M. and Vartak, V.D. (1981) 'Sacred Groves of Maharashtra : An Inventory' in Jain, S.K. (ed), *Glimpses of Ethnobotany*, Oxford University Press, Bombay, pp. 279-294.

Ghai, Dharam (ed) (1991) *The IMF and the South : The Social Impact of Crisis and Adjustment*, on behalf of UNRISD Geneva and ISER/ UWI Kingston, 1991.

Ghai, Dharam and Hewitt de Aclantara Cynthia (1991) 'The Crisis of the 1980s in Africa, Latin America and the Caribbean' in Ghai, Dharam (ed). *The IMF and the South: The Social Impact of Crisis and Adjustment*, on behalf of UNRISD Geneva and ISER/UWI Kingston.

Ghosh, D.N. (1993) 'Level Playing Field : A Mirage', *Economic and Political Weekly*.

Ghoshal, M.K. (1992) 'India's Food Scenario By 2000', *Yojana*, March 31.

Government of India (1992-93) Ministry of Finance, *Economic Survey 1992-93*.

Government of India (1992) *Health Information of India*, p. 26.

Government of India (1993a) 'Economic Reforms : Two Years After and the Task Ahead, Discussion Paper', Ministry of Finance, Department of Economic Affairs, Government of India, New Delhi.

Government of India (1993b) Expenditure Budget 1992-93, Vol.-1.

Government of India (1994) *Economic Survey 1993-94*.

Greeley, M. (1992) 'Environmental and Food Security Objectives in Rural Project Design, *IDS Bulletin*, Vol 22, No. 3, Institute of Development Studies, Sussex.

Gulati, A. & A.N. Sharma (1992) 'Subsidising Agriculture - A Crosscountry View', *Economic and Political Weekly*, September 26.

Gupta, S. P. (ed) (1993) *Liberalisation: Its Impact on the Indian Economy*, Indian Council for Research on International Economic Relations, Macmillan, Delhi.

Gupta, S.P. (1993) 'Planning and Liberalisation', *Economic and Political Weekly*, October 23.

Gupta, S.P., Minna Bal and Rashmi Shankar (1993) 'Cross Country Analysis of Impact of Liberalisation and Economic Reforms' in Gupta, S. P. (ed), *Liberalisation: Its Impact on the Indian Economy*, Indian Council for Research on International Economic Relations, Macmillan, Delhi.

Hindle, Robert E. (1990) The World Bank Approach to Food Security Analysis, *IDS Bulletin*, 1990, Vol. 21 No.3, Institute of Development Studies Sussex.

Hsiao, William C. (1992) 'Comparing Health Care Systems: What

Nations Can Learn from One Another', *Journal of Health Politics, Policy and Law,* Vol. 17, No. 4, Winter.

International Food Policy Research Institute (IFPRI), Research Report 81.

J.M. (1994) 'Food Exports and Food Requirement', *Economic and Political Weekly,* Vol. XXIX, No. 35. Aug. 27.

Jharwal, S.M. (1993) 'Public Distribution System in India : An Empirical Study', A Ph. D. Thesis Submitted to the University of Rajasthan, Jaipur.

Jones, P.W. (1992) *World Bank Financing of Education: Lending, Learning and Development,* New York, Routledge.

Kalra, Krishan (1994) 'Economics of Health Care Services', *Financial Express,* 19th May.

Kapila, Uma (ed) (1992) *Indian Economy Since Independence*: Vol. 4, *Recent Developments in Indian Economy with Special Reference to Structural Reforms,* Part one, Academic Foundations, Delhi.

Kumar, Arun, (1991) 'Into the Valley of IMF March the 800 Million', *Mainstream,* August 24,

Lewin, K. and Berstecher, D. (1989) 'The Costs of Recovery: Are User Fees the Answer', *IDS Bulletin,* January.

Madhur, Srinivasa (1994) 'Trade and External Sector Reforms in Developing Asia : An Overview', *Economic and Political Weekly,* Vol. XXIX, No. 6, February 5.

Malhotra, K. C. and Poffenberger, P. (eds) (1989) 'Forest Regeneration Through Community Protection : The West Bengal Experience', Proceedings of the Working Group Meeting on Forest Protection Committees, Calcutta, June 21-22 Calcutta, West Bengal Forest Department. p.47.

Michalopoulos, C. (1987) 'World Bank Lending for Structural Adjustment', *Finance and Development,* March.

Misra, V.N. (1993) 'Relative Efficiency and Technological Change in Paddy Cultivation: Indian Experiences', *Journal of Indian School of Political Economy*, Vol. V, No. 3, July-September.

Mooij, Jos. E. (1994) 'Public Distribution System as Safety Net. Who is Saved?' *Economic and Political Weekly*, Vol XXIX, No. 3, Jan 15, pp. 119-126.

Mundle, S. (1992) 'Employment Effects of Stabilisation and Related Policy Changes in India 1991-92', in *ILO Social Dimensions of Structural Adjustment*, New Delhi, ILO - ARTEP, pp. 1003.

Muley, Yeshwant P. (1993) 'Experiences of a Medical Officer in a Primary Health Centre' in Antia, N.H. and Bhatia Kavita (eds), *People's Health in People's Hands*, FRCH, p. 29.

Nayyar, Deepak (1993) 'Indian Economy at the Crossroads- Illusions and Realities', *Economic and Political Weekly*, April 10.

Nayyar, Deepak (1994) 'Fiscal Adjustment : Why and for Whom', *The Sunday Times of India*, February 27.

Oommen, M.A. (1993) 'The Bhagwati Srinivasan paper on India's Economic Reforms - A Critique' - ISS Discussion paper-3, *Institute of Social Sciences,* New Delhi, October.

Prabhu, Seeta K. and Chatterjee Somnath (1993) *Social Sector Expenditures and Human Development*. Department of Economic Analysis and Policy, Reserve Bank of India, Bombay.

Ranadive, Joy R. (1994) 'Gender Implications of Adjustment Policy Programme in India', *Economic and Political Weekly*, April 30, WS 12-18.

Rangarajan, C. (1992) 'Economic Reforms: A Step in Right Direction', *The Economic Times*, August 17.

Rao, C.H.H. (1994) 'Agricultural Growth and Rural Poverty in India : Emerging Trends and Perspectives' (Dharm Narain Memorial Lecture), Institute of Economic Growth, Delhi.

Rao, Hanumantha, C.H. (1987) 'Instability in Agricultural Performance : Lessons from the Current Drought', *Economic Journalist*, Sept, 1987, pp. 9-12.

Rao, Hanumantha. C.H.(1994) 'Agricultural Growth and Rural Poverty in India. Emerging Trends and Perspectives', *Indian Economic Review*, Vol XXVIII, No. 2. pp. 129-140.

Rao, S.L. (1994) 'Labour Adjustment as Part of Industrial Restructuring : Human Dimensions of Liberalisation', *Economic and Political Weekly*, Vol. XXIX, No. 6, February 5.

Rao, Krishna, I.Y.R. (1993) 'An Experiment in Food Security: Andhra Pradesh', *Economic and Political Weekly*, Sept. 11.

Rao, V.M. & S. Erappa (1987) 'IRDP and Rural Diversification : A Study in Karnataka', *Economic and Political Weekly* (Review of Agriculture), Vol. XXII, No. 52, December 26.

Rao, V.M. (1988) 'Interventions for the Poor : Critical Dimensions, Potentialities and Limitations', *Economic and Political Weekly*, Special Number.

Rao, V.M. (1992) 'Change Processes in Dryland Communities', *Indian Journal of Agricultural Economics*, Vol. 47, No. 1, January-March.

Rao, V.M. (1994) 'Agriculture and Liberalisation : Some Implications for Development Policies', *Economic and Political Weekly*, April 9, 1994.

Reddy, K.N. and V. Selvaraju (1992) 'Containment of Food Subsidy in the Context of Revenue Deficit', National Institute of Public Finance and Policy, New Delhi, Working Paper No. 1, January.

Reddy, K.N. (1994a) 'Alternative Sources of Financing Health Care in India With Special Reference to Cities', *PRASHASNIKA* (Forthcoming Issue).

Reddy, K.N. (1994b) 'Health Expenditure in India : Is It Low?' *Finance India*, Vol. VIII, No. 2, June.

Reddy, K.N. and S. Sudhakar (1989) Who Benefits from Government Expenditure? - A Case Study of Andhra Pradesh, *Journal of Political Economy*, Vol. 1, January-June, pp. 114-137.

Reddy, K.N. and V. Selvaraju (1994) *Health Care Expenditure by Government in India: 1974-75 to 1990-91,* National Institute of Public Finance and Policy, New Delhi.

Reinhardt, Uwe E. (1992) 'The United States : Breakthroughs and Waste', *Journal of Health Politics, Policy and Law,* Vol. 17, No. 4, p. 661.

Sau, Ranjit (1993) 'Cost of Stabilising the Economy', *Economic and Political Weekly*, April 10,.

Sen, T.K. Rao, M.G. Rao and M. Ghosh (1994) 'Implications of 1994-95 Budget for Growth and Stability', *Economic and Political Weekly,* 16-23 April, pp. 969-81.

Shenoy, B.R. PL-480 Aid and India's Food Problems.

Shiva, Vandana (1993) 'Farmer's Rights, Biodiversity and International Treaties', *Economic and Political Weekly*, April 13.

Sinha, Anup (1994) 'Economic Reforms and Macro Economic Policy', *Economic and Political Weekly*, 16-23 May, pp.945-52.

Sinha, R.P. (1994) 'Efficiency Differentials in Wheat Cultivation and Their Implications for Development Policies', *Journal of Indian School of Political Economy*, Vol. VI, No. 1, January-March.

Sklair, Testie (1990) 'Regional Consequences of Open-Door Development Strategies : Export Zones in Mexico and China,' Chapter 7 in Paul David Simon (ed) *Third World Regional Development- A Reappraisal*, Champan Publishing Ltd., London.

Smith, Steven Rathgeb and Lipsky Michael (1992) 'Privatisation in Health and Human Services: A critique', *Journal of Health Politics, Policy and Law,* Vol. 17, No.2, pp. 237-247.

Sobhan, Rehman (1993) 'Structural Maladjustment, Bangladesh's Experience with Market Reforms', *Economic and Political Weekly*, May 8.

Sricharatchanya, P. (1993) 'A Peep into the Grey Zones', *Far Eastern Economic Review*, Vol.120, No.19, May 12, pp. 60-61.

Subramanium, Manohar (1994) 'Issues Concerning Food Security', Paper presented at the In-Service Course on Policy and Planning for IAS officers, LBSNAA, Mussoorie, July 25 to Aug. 12.

Sundaram, K.V. (1992) 'Decentralization of Agricultural Sector Planning in Sub-Saharan Africa', *Food and Agriculture Organisation of the United Nations*, July (To be published).

Swaminathan, M.S. (1981) *Building National Food Security System*, Indian Environmental Society, New Delhi.

Taylor, D.R.F. and Fiona Mackenzie (Eds.), (1992) *Development from within- Survival in Rural Africa*, Routledge, London,

Tendulkar, S.D. (1993) 'Macro-Economic Policies and Poverty Reduction' (an unpublished paper).

Thomas, P. *et al.* (1994) 'Dunkel Text : Implications for Rural Sector', *Economic and Political Weekly*, Vol. XXIX, No. 13, March 26.

Tibi, C. (1989) 'The Financing of Education: Impact of the Crisis and the Adjustment Process, in Caillods' (ed.) *Prospects for Educational Planning*, Paris, IIEP, pp. 100-126.

Tilak, J.B.G. (1993a) 'Prospects of Investment in Social Development during the Phase of Internationally Funded Structural Adjustment', *Journal of Higher Education*, Vol. 16, No. 4, pp. 519-538.

Tilak, J.B.G. (1993b) 'Economic Reforms and Investment Policies in Education', *Perspectives in Education*, Vol. 9, No. 3, pp.133-46.

Tilak, J.B.G. and N.V. Varghese (1991) 'Financing Higher Education in India', *Higher Education* (Netherlands), Vol. 21, No. 1, pp. 83-101.

Tilak, J.B.G. and N.V. Varghese (1992) 'Discriminator Pricing in Education', *Journal of Education and Social Change*, Vol. 6; No. 3, pp. 69-80.

Timmer, C.P., W.P. Falcon and S.R. Pearson (1983) *Food Policy Analysis,* The World Bank, John Hopkins University Press, Baltimore, USA.

Tyagi, D.S. (1991) 'Pricing of Fertilizers : Some Reflections on Subsidy Question', *Institute of Development Studies,* Jaipur (a paper presented to the National Consultation on Fertilizer Pricing held in October, 1991).

United Nations Environment Programme (1992) 'Convention on Biological Diversity', Nairobi. pp. 52.

Varghese, N.V. (1993) 'Private Schools in India: Presumptions and Provisions' in R.P. Singh (ed). *Private Initiative and Public Policy in Education,* New Delhi, Neeta Prakashan, pp. 50-74.

Vyas, V. S. (1993) 'New Economic Policy and Vulnerable Sections Rationale for Public Intervention', *Economic and Political Weekly,* March 6.

WCED (1987) 'Our Common Future, World Commission on Environment and Development', Oxford University Press, Oxford.

Whitaker, Jannifer Seymour (1986) 'The Policy Setting : Crisis and Consensus' in Berg Robert J. and J.S. Whitaker, (eds.) *Strategies for African Development,* University of California Press, Berkeley, Los Angeles and London.

Woodhall, Maureen (1991) 'Education and Training Under Conditions of Economic Austerity and Restructuring', paper prepared for the Inter-Agency Taskforce on Austerity, Adjustment and Human Resources, Paris, UNESCO.

World Bank (1986) 'Poverty and Hunger : Issues and Options for Food Security in Developing Countries' A World Bank Policy Study, Washington.

World Bank (1988a) 'Education in Sub-Saharan Africa: Policies for Adjustment Revitalisation and Expansion', Washington D.C., The World Bank.

World Bank (1988b) 'Adjustment Lending: An Evaluation of Ten Years of Experience', Washington D.C., The Bank.

World Development Report, (1992), Development and Environment.

INDEX